GOING DEEP

JOHN PHILIP HOLLAND
AND THE INVENTION OF
THE ATTACK SUBMARINE

LAWRENCE GOLDSTONE

PEGASUS BOOKS
NEW YORK LONDON

GOING DEEP

Pegasus Books Ltd.
148 W 37th Street, 13th Floor
New York, NY 10018

First Pegasus Books edition June 2017

Interior design by Maria Fernandez

Library of Congress Cataloging-in-Publication Data is available.

ISBN: 978-1-68177-429-9

10 9 8 7 6 5 4 3 2 1

Printed in the United States of America
Distributed by W. W. Norton & Company, Inc.
www.pegasusbooks.us

To Nancy and Lee

CONTENTS

PROLOGUE
DEATH FROM BELOW

September 22, 1914, 3:00 A.M. Six weeks into a war that was to become the bloodiest in human history. A tentative calm had finally descended on the North Sea after three days of savage storms, and the British Admiralty ordered a resumption of patrols off the coast of Holland. An hour before dawn, three aging battle cruisers were sent out to take positions on the line, three miles apart. While the ships were old, the crews were not. The *Aboukir*, the *Hogue*, and the *Cressy* were part of a five-boat contingent manned mostly by young reservists and thus nicknamed the "Live Bait Squadron." They would certainly be so that day. With the seas still rough, the cruisers' usual destroyer escort was ordered to remain at anchor.

At 6:30 A.M., the three ships separated to take up their stations. Almost immediately, a huge explosion shook *Aboukir*, which "was seen to reel violently, and then settle down with a list to port." The two other ships turned at once to steam to her aid. When they had closed sufficiently to lower cutters to pick up survivors, the *Hogue* to starboard and the *Cressy* to port, the cruisers came to a halt. As the rescue boats were returning with burned and wounded sailors, two tremendous blasts devastated the *Hogue*; she "leapt up like a roweled horse and quivered all over, just as a steel spring will quiver when firmly held at one end and sharply struck at the other."[1] Soon after that, the *Cressy* exploded amidships and, like the other two, sank almost immediately.

Two Dutch vessels appeared quickly and helped rescue 60 officers and 777 men. But another 60 officers and some 1,399 sailors died in the explosions, were roasted to death, or drowned.

In this singular battle, lasting less than ninety minutes, the three British cruisers had been attacked by a vessel that, until six weeks earlier, had never been employed by the German navy, or, in a real sense, by any navy at all. It sailed not on the sea, but under it.

It was only after the *Aboukir* and the *Hogue* had been torn apart that Captain Robert W. Johnson, aboard the *Cressy*, realized what had befallen his comrades, although too late to save them or himself. According to the official report, "five minutes after Captain Johnson maneuvered the ship so as to render assistance to the crews of the *Hogue* and *Aboukir* . . . a periscope was seen on the starboard quarter, and fire was opened. The track of the torpedo she fired at a range of from 500 to 600 yards was plainly visible, and it struck on the starboard side just before the after bridge."

The periscope belonged to submarine *U-9*, commanded by dashing, thirty-two-year-old Kapitänleutnant Otto Weddigen. The boat was 188 feet long and only 19 feet across. Its crew of twenty-six officers and men lived in impossibly cramped conditions, stuffed along with provisions and armaments into a narrow cylinder that provided little room to move and even less to sleep. Fans to circulate the air were so feeble that most of the sailors were left constantly gasping for breath, even when *U-9* was running on the surface. Heat from the engines was stifling and sanitary facilities were worse than in a prison. But neither Weddigen nor his crew would ever register a single complaint. They were pioneers, entrusted with a potent new weapon they were certain would be instrumental in their nation's victory.

Postcard depicting Weddigen's triumph

Weddigen had gained his commission four years earlier, when *U-9* first put to sea, and just days before he left on patrol, he had been married to his childhood sweetheart. With the sinking of the *Aboukir*, *Hogue*, and *Cressy*, *U-9*'s captain became a national hero. "I reached the home port on the afternoon of the 23rd," he said later, "and on the 24th went to Wilhelmshaven to find that news of my effort had become public. My wife, dry-eyed when I went away, met me with tears. Then I learned that my little vessel and her brave crew had won the plaudit of the Kaiser, who conferred upon each of my co-workers the Iron Cross of the second class and upon me the Iron Crosses of the first and second classes."[2]

In Great Britain, the reaction was far different. Within days, the Admiralty issued a statement: "The sinking of the *Aboukir* was of course an ordinary hazard of patrolling duty. The *Hogue* and *Cressy*, however, were sunk because they proceeded to the assistance of their consort, and remained with engines stopped, endeavoring to save life, thus presenting an easy target to further submarine attacks. The natural promptings of humanity have in this case led to heavy losses, which would have been avoided by a strict adhesion to military consideration. Modern naval war is presenting us with so many new and strange situations that an error of judgment of this character is pardonable."

War on the high seas had changed forever.

———

On August 12, 1914, roughly six weeks before Weddigen fired his torpedoes, John Philip Holland died of pneumonia at his home at 38 Newton Street in Newark, New Jersey. Holland, a former schoolteacher and once a choirmaster at his local church, was by all accounts a gentle, modest man, and he rated only a brief obituary in local newspapers. He had been born seventy-three years earlier on the west coast of Ireland, in County Clare. Gaelic was the chosen language in the Holland home, since his mother spoke no English. John had been a sickly child, plagued with chronic respiratory problems that followed him into adulthood and would eventually kill him. Because of his delicate health, he had been sent to the Christian Brothers for his education; he stayed on to teach but left the order just before he was to take his final vows. Shortly afterward, he immigrated to the United States, where he spent the remainder of his life. While he never waned in his passion for Ireland, Holland chose to be buried in his adopted homeland rather than the one of his birth.

John Holland emerging from one of his creations.

Although he had died in near obscurity, John Holland cast a shadow over those fifteen hundred deaths in the North Sea and also the thousands of other encounters between traditional warships and this new instrument of stealth and surprise. He was then and still widely is considered the father of the modern submarine, but he would never know that he had helped create one of the defining killing machines of two world wars.

———

For millennia, the ocean depths have held as great a fascination as the heavens, and undersea travel has been a fantasy equal to the dream of flight. Just as virtually every society created fanciful machines to allow men to soar into the sky, there were similar fancies about devices that could sustain humans under the water. Leonardo, as did many of the greatest scientific thinkers, theorized about both but failed to bring either to fruition. But, like Wilbur and Orville Wright, who had also followed in many of the same footsteps, John Holland did not fail. For decades, combining insight with perseverance, and enduring frustration, trial, and much error, Holland turned imagination into reality. And, as with every journey of exploration, death waited constantly in the wings.

Frank T. Cable, an engineer who, after four decades, penned the definitive firsthand account of submarine development, wrote, "The submarine is an American invention—it is the genius of an ardent Irish-American patriot. It belongs to America—with the telephone, the telegraph, the steamship, the airplane, electricity, and the other wonders of the modern world that marked the beginnings of new epochs."[3]

John Holland was not the only man who labored for decades to design and build a successful undersea craft. Although twenty-five years his junior, a precocious inventor from New Jersey named Simon Lake would become Holland's fiercest competitor, both under the water and in the committee rooms of Congress, where each man fought to have his design accepted as the paradigm for the American navy's nascent submarine fleet.

Lake and Holland were separated by a good deal more than age and could not have come to the quest by a more different route. Where John

Holland initially had sought a means for Irish nationalists to combat the overwhelming dominance of the British navy, Lake was inspired by an adventure novel he read as a twelve-year-old boy. While Holland was an immigrant who never lost his Irish brogue, Lake was descended on his father's side from one of the founders of Atlantic City, New Jersey, and on his mother's from one of the founders of Hartford, Connecticut. Where Holland was self-taught, Lake received an engineering education at Pennsylvania's prestigious Franklin Institute. Precisely because of their differences, however, and that they approached every problem from a different perspective, the two men became responsible for nearly every feature of the modern submarine.

But theirs was a war with no winners. After decades of working to solve one of humankind's great mysteries, Holland and Lake would be shunted aside, replaced by those for whom innovation was far less important than profit.

One man in particular would be nemesis to both Holland and Lake. Isaac Leopold Rice was one of the most remarkable men of a remarkable age—a chess master, social commentator, musician, lawyer, innovator, philanthropist, and one of the most ferocious competitors of an age of breakneck innovation to rival any other. To Holland, in theory a business partner and ally, and to Lake, an avowed rival, Rice would demonstrate that an elegant design or watershed invention was no guarantee of success in either the boardroom or the marketplace. In the process, he would repeatedly confound Congress and then fashion one of the United States' most powerful and enduring engineering conglomerates.

And so today, when submarines can travel around the world and remain submerged almost indefinitely, limited only by the amount of food they carry, John Holland and Simon Lake have all but disappeared from the history books. Why these men are not known to every American and have not been accorded the same posthumous accolades as other great innovators of the period, is a tale of genius and stupidity, persistence and deceit, vision and blindness, and, ultimately, tragedy.

CHAPTER 1
BLURRED BEGINNINGS

It is fitting, perhaps, that the first accounts of a working submarine are as murky as the underwater depths its inventor claimed to have navigated. The inventor himself, in fact, has been described as "a shadowy figure, a kind of dismembered historical ghost." Now generally referred to as Cornelis Drebbel, he was at various times known to contemporaries as Drubelsius, Derbbel, Dribble, Tribble, and De Rebel.

Drebbel was born in Alkmaar, Holland, in 1572. He received a solid education, became an engraver, and married an extremely profligate woman who kept him in constant debt and bore him six children, four of whom survived. Drebbel, always casting about for ways to earn a bit of extra money, came across the works of the renegade physician, astrologer, alchemist, botanist, and natural scientist, Philippus Aureolus Theophrastus Bombastus von Hohenheim, later known as Paracelsus.

Paracelsus was half-genius, half-fabulist, a sort of combination Jonas Salk and P. T. Barnum. "Bombast" was coined from his name. He was the most prominent early proponent of the germ theory of disease;

he also initiated the notion that some ailments spring from psychological disorders and others from environmental pollution, which he discovered by studying miners with lung disease. Paracelsus has been variously credited with founding psychotherapy, toxicology, and pharmacology. But he also claimed to have transmuted base metals to gold, to have cured the sick with spiritual intervention, and that the key to good health was an enema at the time of the full moon. Despite a brilliant record as a physician, Paracelsus was so personally unpleasant that he spent a good deal of his later life moving from one city to another to avoid being murdered by his enemies. The cause of his death, at age forty-seven, and whether it was from natural or unnatural causes, remains unclear. But Paracelsus left behind a stunning legacy in a wide variety of disciplines, which spurred generations of youthful acolytes across the scientific spectrum. Drebbel's work too would cross many disciplines and be a combination of the practical, the unlikely, and the impossible.

Brimming with ideas, Drebbel crossed the Channel in 1605, shortly after the ascension of James I to the English throne. James's interest in science and innovation was well known and, with Mrs. Drebbel's pecuniary appetites undiminished, the new king seemed the perfect patron.

Drebbel had chosen well. He secured an audience with the king, who, impressed with what seemed a wondrous range of knowledge, sent him to live in Eltham Palace in Greenwich, where Drebbel would be left free to tinker as he pleased. James visited frequently to view his "wonder-worker's" creations.

James also appeared to have chosen well. Described by a visiting courtier as a "very fair and handsome man, and of very gentle manners, altogether different from such-like characters,"[1] Drebbel designed intricate gardens and fountains, introduced to the English court Paracelsus's notion of iatrochemical medicine, in which cures to disease are found in chemicals—drugs—rather than in a rebalance of the humors, and produced impressive innovations in pumps, clocks, and dyes.* He

---

*   Iatrochemical medicine would later be championed by a young physician named John Locke, who later abandoned doctoring for political theory to write *Two Treatises on Government*, which would provide significant philosophical underpinning for the American Revolution.

is said to have built improved telescopes and microscopes, although evidence for this is sketchy. Drebbel is also purported to have designed a perpetual motion machine mounted in a globe that tracked the time, date, and season. He put this device on display at Eltham and there demonstrated it to a series of notables. That a true perpetual motion machine is impossible—friction or energy loss will eventually slow it to a halt—in no way diminished the accolades. Even more dubious are Drebbel's claims to have created a means of purifying seawater, fashioning a working torpedo, and bottling a liquid "quintessence of air," this more than a century before oxygen was identified as an element by Joseph Priestley. Such were the range and mystery of Drebbel's achievements that he has been theorized to be Shakespeare's model for Prospero in *The Tempest*.

And then there was the Drebbel submarine.

The notion of underwater boats had been introduced to the English Court in 1578, when a mathematician, William Bourne, who had served as a Royal Navy gunner, published a treatise titled *Inventions or Devices*, "very necessary for all Generals and Captains, or Leaders of men, as well by Sea, as by Land." In one section, Bourne wrote, "And also it is possible to make a Ship or Boat that may go under the water unto the bottom, and so to come up again at your pleasure . . . that any thing that sinketh is heavier than the proportion of so much water, and if it be lighter than the magnitude of so much water, then it swimmeth or appeareth above the water, according unto the proportion of weight." Bourne included detailed instructions on how to construct an underwater craft. "Let there be good store of Ballast in the bottom of her, and over the Ballast, as low as may be, let there be a closed Orlop [deck] such that no water may come into it, and then in like manner at a sufficient height, to have another closed Orlop that no water may come through it, and that being done, then bore both the sides full of holes between the two closed Orlops: and that being done, then make a thing like the side of the Bark or Ship that may go unto the side of the Ship . . . and that must be made so tight and close, that no water may come through it, and that done, then take leather, such a quantity as is sufficient for to serve your purpose, and that leather must be nailed with such provision that no water may soak thorough." The vessel was to be propelled by oars, the exact placement of which was left vague.

Bourne included a diagram that showed ballast controlled by drawing water into or forcing water out of the body of the vessel by means of a capstan screw mechanism.

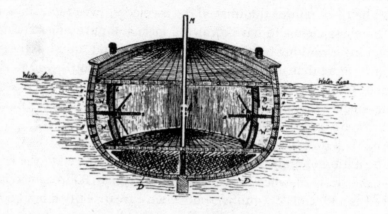

FIG. 3A.—*BOURNE'S SUBMARINE BOAT*, 1578.

A.—Air Holes.	*L.*—Leather.
B.—Bulkhead which is screwed in and out.	*O.*—Orlop.
C.—Capstan for screwing Bulkhead in and out.	*M.*—Hollow Mast for Air Supply.
D.—Ballast.	*W.*—Space occupied by Water when Craft is submerged
H.—Inlet Holes for Water.	*S.*—Screws.

Bourne's design

There is no record of Bourne ever attempting to build such an impractical craft—it would have been fatally unstable and there was virtually no room for a crew—but the idea struck the fancy of many English nobles. (Naval officers, on the other hand, thought it ridiculous.) The underwater boat remained only an alluring theory until 1620, when Drebbel announced that he had built one.

He claimed to have come to the idea "walking on the banks of the Thames [when] he noticed some fishing-boats dragging baskets of fish, and whilst a strain was on the towing-line, the boat was more immersed in water than when it was slack." He decided that there was "no reason to doubt that a boat could be kept partially under water by means of oars or poles, provided she was weighted down with ballast."

Drebbel then, the story went, built two boats. "The larger had twelve oars, and the hull was made of wood, strengthened inside with iron bands and covered over with tightly stretched hide soaked in grease in order to keep out the water when submerged. The oars passed through holes in the sides, and leather joints were used to make them water-tight."[2]

There are many reports of this vessel regularly navigating up and down the river under the water, some of the sojourns going as far as London. Other accounts had passengers aboard and "some authorities even go so far as to say that, as the savant was a personal friend of James I, he persuaded that monarch to overcome his constitutional timidity, and go for a trip under water in the Thames." (This last assertion was not taken seriously. That James, by then hugely fat, would venture into a closed vessel that would submerge in the Thames would have evoked chuckles or worse.)

The most famous account of the Drebbel submarine was published by Ben Jonson in his immensely popular play *The Staple of News*. In Act III, Scene 1, his characters have the following exchange:

THOMAS: They write here, one Cornelius-Son
Hath made the Hollanders an invisible eel
To swim the haven at Dunkirk and sink all
The shipping there.

P. JUNIOR: But how is't done?

CYMBAL: I'll show you, sir. It's an automa, runs under water,
With a smug nose, and has a nimble tail
Made like an auger, with which tail she wriggles
Betwixt the costs of a ship and sinks it straight.

P. JUNIOR: A most brave device
To murder their flat bottoms.

But Jonson had never actually seen Drebbel's boat cruise underwater, nor had any other of those who extolled the new invention.

There were, in fact, no first person accounts, except those issued by Drebbel himself. And Jonson had hardly wished to be taken seriously. *The Staple of News* was a lacerating send-up of dishonest news agents and the credulity of their customers. In the passage immediately following, for example, a character discusses a plan to launch a surprise attack on an enemy by fitting the invaders' horses with cork shoes. When asked, "Is't true?" the speaker replied, "As true as the rest." Moreover, Jonson had long since considered Drebbel a fraud and lampooned him mercilessly. As far back as 1609, in a relationship "characterized over many years by relentless public ridicule from Jonson's side," Jonson had also dismissed the perpetual motion machine as a laughable humbug.[3]

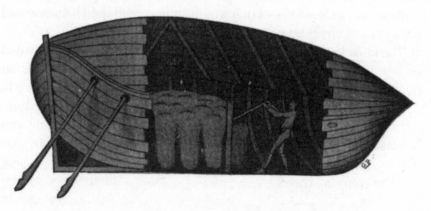

An early depiction of Drebbel's "design." Drebbel himself left no drawings.

Nonetheless, Jonson's description began to circulate as a true account, confirmation of other assertions that not only had Drebbel built an underwater boat, but that a few sprinkled drops of his "quintessence of air" had allowed the crew to breathe air "as fresh and as pure as if they were on the top of a mountain," and that he had lit the interior without candles.[4] In 1623, Francis Bacon, another non-witness, doubtless influenced by all the hoopla, decided to immortalize the Drebbel submarine in *New Atlantis*, his utopian vision of a just and prosperous society ruled according to the principles of natural science. As this society was also governed by scientists, Bacon's unfinished work became required reading for anyone of scientific bent coming of age in the seventeenth century.

As the decades passed, others, including the polymath Robert Boyle, who was not born until 1627, the year *New Atlantis* was published, made specific scientific reference to Drebbel's invention, stating categorically that the vessel "went under water perfectly, and was rowed at a depth of twelve or fifteen feet for several hours." In fact, Boyle undertook his landmark "Experiments On Air," largely as a result of his belief in Drebbel's achievement. Boyle would become so obsessed with the Drebbel submarine that he sought out the Hollander's daughter and son-in-law, who, even as late as 1662, were trying to find ways to make money from the elder Drebbel's "terrible destroying invention."

That Drebbel's legend thrived, and that it would captivate as brilliant a scientific mind as Robert Boyle, is largely due to the mass of propaganda that was thrown up around him. In a nineteenth-century publication by the British Museum with the alluring title, *England as Seen by Foreigners in the Days of Elizabeth and James the First, Comprising Translations of the Journals of the Two Dukes of Württemberg in 1592 and 1610; Both Illustrative of Shakespeare*, the editor did admit, "The accounts we have of that 'deservedly famous mechanician and chymist,' as the Hon. Robert Boyle calls Cornelius Drebbel, are confused and inexact." But that did not prevent chroniclers from waxing rapturously of Drebbel's alleged achievements. This extraordinary testament made its way across Europe and deserves to be read in full:

> Other epithets have been bestowed upon Drebbel, as alchemist, empiric, magician, and professor of the black art. But, however extravagant and improbable some of the following descriptions may appear . . . Cornelius Drebbel is entitled, we think, to hold a respectable position among the ingenious inventors and mechanicians of the early part of the seventeenth century. . . . *He built a ship, in which one could row and navigate under water, from Westminster to Greenwich, the distance of two Dutch miles; even five or six miles, or as far as one pleased. In this boat a person could see under the surface of the water and without candlelight, as much as he needed to read in the Bible or any other book. Not long ago this*

remarkable ship was yet to be seen lying in the Thames or London river. Aided by some instruments of his own manufacture, Drebbel could make it rain, lighten, and thunder, at every time of the year, so that you would have sworn it came in a natural way from heaven. By means of other instruments he could, in the midst of summer, so much refrigerate the atmosphere of certain places, that you would have thought yourself in the very midst of winter. This experiment he did once at his Majesty's request, in the great Hall of Westminster; and although a hot summer day had been chosen by the King, it became so cold in the Hall that James and his followers took to their heels in hasty flight. With a certain instrument he could draw an incredible quantity of water out of a well or river. By his peculiar ingenuity he could at all times of the year, even in the midst of winter, hatch chickens and ducklings without the aid of hens or ducks.*

So comprehensive was Drebbellian lore that whether the Drebbel submarine was ever launched, or even if it existed, the details of its construction, disseminated almost certainly by Drebbel and his friends at Court, have inspired replicas to be built for numerous museums, one, not surprisingly in Alkmaar, and even for a television documentary.

One description, by BBC History, had the craft "based on a rowing boat with raised and meeting sides, covered in greased leather, with a watertight hatch in the middle, a rudder and four oars. Under the rowers' seats were large pigskin bladders, connected by pipes to the outside. Rope was used to tie off the empty bladders. In order to dive, the rope was untied and the bladders filled. To surface the crew squashed the bladders flat, squeezing out the water."[5] There is no direct evidence that any of this is true.

An article in *Scientific American* in 1909 added flourishes that even Drebbel had not considered. "It was provided with boring tools, working in stuffing boxes in the side of the vessel, by which the enemy's ships could be perforated, and with long poles carrying torpedoes at their ends."[6]

---

*   Italics added.

The most curious aspect of the Drebbel submarine, however, is not whether it was simply an elaborate hoax perpetrated on a guileless king by an ambitious mountebank, but that, real or not, it helped spark genuine innovation by a series of inventors that resulted in vessels that could do everything Drebbel claimed to do and more.

The progression began in 1648, when Bishop John Wilkins published his most famous work, *Mathematical Magick*, a two-volume treatise on physics and mechanical devices, meant to explain how existing machines operate and expound on the feasibility of those considered futuristic. A dozen years later, inspired by Bacon's *New Atlantis*, Wilkins would help found the Royal Society, an organization that, with members such as Boyle, Robert Hooke, and Edmond Halley, might have been the most impressive array of scientific brilliance the world has ever known.

In the sections of *Mathematical Magick* that were devoted to predictions of technological advances, Wilkins described at length Drebbel's vessel, which he called the "Ark," and for the first time discussed the potential uses of an undersea craft, in peace and in war:

> A man may go to any part of the world invisibly without being discovered or prevented in his journey. Man will be safe from the violence of tempests which never move the Sea more than five or six Paces deep; they are safe from Pirates and Robbers, from Ice and great Frosts which are such deadly foes to us in our passages towards the Poles. One is also free from the uncertainty of the tides. It may be of a very great Advantage against a Navy of Enemies, who by these means may be undermined in the Water and blown up.[7]

Interest in perfecting the science of underwater travel increased through the remainder of the seventeenth century, everyone using Drebbel as his model. In the 1650s, Charles, Landgrave of Hesse-Kassel, ordered a submarine built based on the Drebbel design, but the man who received the assignment discovered to his chagrin that Drebbel had died in 1633, leaving no records or accounts of his most famous invention. No drawing, model, or even description of the vessel seemed to exist. The project was soon abandoned. Others across Europe drew up plans for undersea craft, boasting of their prowess, but none of these were constructed either. Principles of submarine travel, these inventors discovered, were a good deal more arcane than would allow a simple closed vessel to be slapped together and successfully launched.

Some returned to more basic undertakings with better results. Edmond Halley joined the Royal Society in 1672, when, thanks to Boyle, undersea travel had become one of the more alluring scientific conundrums of the age. Although best known for the comet that bears his name, Halley's experiments were vital to solving the formative problems of underwater navigation. Halley dropped into the water a primitive diving bell, something of a giant inverted barrel, weighted with lead along the bottom. As long as it dropped straight—thus the lead weights—air would remain trapped inside and sustain the man stationed there. Another man could even venture outside with a primitive helmet, air fed to him from the supply under the bell. To raise the device, the operator would simply remove weights on either side.

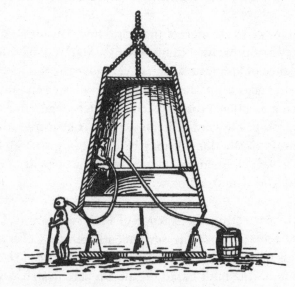

Halley's diving bell

In 1690, Halley demonstrated his device in the Thames. It was useful for little more than staring at the river's bottom or picking up curiosities—when light permitted—but Halley had demonstrated a relationship between air and water pressure. In some senses, Halley did not advance underwater technology any more than Christiaan Huygens's gunpowder-filled cylinder provided a blueprint for the internal combustion engine—theoretical knowledge of air and water pressure was not new—but his design established a paradigm for more complicated vessels in which the taking on and expelling of ballast would be crucial to stability.*

Also in 1690, a more serious effort to build a submarine boat was undertaken by Huygens's former assistant, French mathematician, Denis Papin, again financed by the Landgrave of Hesse-Kassel, son of the man who had financed the 1640 attempt, and again based on the Drebbel model. Papin had been one of the first foreigners invited to join the Royal Society and was an original member of the French Académie des Sciences. At the Royal Society he had spent a good deal of time with Boyle, Hooke, and Wilkins, all of whom were actively considering the viability of submarine navigation. Still, Papin's primary interest was steam power. He had experimented widely with devices that would convert steam pressure to thrust, in the course of which he invented the pressure cooker. He had done no work with underwater vessels, however, beyond talking about them, but the landgrave was wealthy and eager, so Papin took on the project. In 1691, he described the plan for his underwater vessel in a letter to his mentor, Huygens.

It was neither a submarine nor even a boat. Essentially a submersible cube, the design featured a leather tube that extended to the surface to supply air, the upper end of which was attached to a wooden float.

---

* Huygens believed that power could be generated in a cylinder, closed at one end, by an explosion that pushed a fitted tool—a piston—outward. When he tried his device, he made an odd discovery. After the explosion, the piston was sucked *inward*. Unaware of oxygen as an element—Drebbel's quintessence of air notwithstanding—Huygens's could not have realized that the explosion would burn off the gas and create a partial vacuum that would suck the piston in. Engines of that sort were later described as "atmospheric," and dominated piston power until the discovery that compressing the fuel—by then hydrocarbon—before ignition, would result in an explosion that drove the piston outward.

An entrance turret was placed at the top, and other openings were configured through which explosives could be attached to an enemy's ship without admitting water into the interior. This device was never tested, undergoing serious damage when the crane lowering it into the water snapped.

The landgrave then was said to have financed construction of a second apparatus, this one cylindrical, which Papin took beneath the surface of the river Fulda in 1692. Although the experiment was said to have been a success, "land-locked Hesse had little use for submarine boats," and so the effort was abandoned. Never explained is why the landgrave, having undertaken expenditures for two vessels, would refuse to continue to fund the project only *after* it had proven successful.

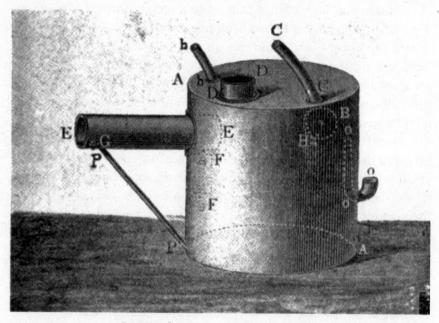

Papin's submarine . . . or pressure cooker

Whatever the reason for the termination of his contract, Papin produced a monograph detailing his findings and then never experimented with underwater boats again. His work was forgotten until 1747, when an article on the Papin submarine, complete with a drawing, appeared in *The Gentleman's Magazine*, a popular English monthly. The drawing seems scant, unlike anything that could move underwater, or even on land. In addition to lacking any means of propulsion, the entryway on the top appears far too small to admit a person. Speculation exists that, instead of a submarine, Papin had thrown the monograph together and simply inserted one of the first renderings of his pressure cooker.

CHAPTER 2
MADE IN AMERICA

More important, however, than the devices that may or may not have been fabricated—each of them even if completed a technological dead end—was the literature suggested by those putative researches that speculated on both the uses and construction of a vessel that could travel underwater and surreptitiously deliver a weapon to the hull of an enemy ship.

In Bacon's *New Atlantis*, for example, the Father of the House of Solomon informs his guests that the halls contained "ordnance and instruments of war, and engines of all kinds: and likewise new mixtures and compositions of gunpowder, wildfires burning in water, and unquenchable." Just after this passage, suggesting underwater mines, the Father continued, "We have ships and boats for going under water, and brooking of seas." Robert Hooke discussed the nature of explosions in *Posthumous Works*; Bishop Thomas Sprat penned a dissertation on the development of saltpeter and gunpowder in *History of the Royal Society*; and Robert Boyle described burning and explosions in a vacuum and underwater in *New Experiments Physico-Mechanicall: Touching the Spring of the Air and Its Effects and Tracts about the Cosmical Qualities of Things, the Temperature of the Subterraneal and Submarine Regions, the Bottom of the Sea, &tc. with an Introduction to the History of Particular Qualities.* Boyle also discussed in *New Experiments* the theory of buoyancy and displacement, which he labeled "the grand rule of Hydrostaticks," as well as going on at some length on great achievements of Cornelis Drebbel.

As it turned out, all of these works, as well as *Mathematical Magick* and other source materials on underwater warfare were on the shelves of the Yale library when thirty-one year old David Bushnell enrolled in 1771.

Bushnell was born in Saybrook, Connecticut, on Long Island Sound, at the mouth of the Connecticut River, a town where ships were built and sailed. Saybrook had also been the home of the Collegiate School, which had migrated west in 1718 to become Yale College. The school's departure, and especially its thirteen-hundred-book library, had not sat well with many local residents and after a good deal of wrangling, including a "battle of the books," joined on occasion with closed fists, only one thousand of the volumes managed to make their way to New Haven. So David Bushnell, though from a farming family, grew up in an environment where scholarship was valued and had been fought for.

Although he managed the family farm with his brother, Bushnell was more attracted to the sea and read what he could on shipbuilding. At twenty-nine, the soil could no longer hold him. He sold his share of the farm to his brother and began to study with the beneficently named Reverend John Devotion. Reverend Devotion was a Yale graduate and so, two years later, Bushnell left Saybrook to enroll in his tutor's alma mater.

With Reverend Devotion, and at Yale, Bushnell studied religion—as did just about everyone else—but discovered his real interests were in mathematics, geometry, and the sciences. He spent a good deal of time in the Yale library, which had grown fourfold from the one thousand volumes spirited away from Saybrook, part of which was the most comprehensive collection of scientific texts in the colonies.

Although Bushnell had not previously exhibited any particular flair for invention, as relations with England deteriorated, he began to focus on underwater explosions, an interest that moved quickly from the theoretical to the practical. Tales of students and teachers frightened by loud reports in the night followed Bushnell during his stay. He learned quickly that keeping the charge dry was not difficult; the principle problem was detonation. Bushnell solved the problem by removing the flintlock from a musket and, using a spring mechanism, converting it to a time fuse. After Lexington and Concord, David Bushnell resolved to design a vessel to deliver his underwater charge; his ambition was no less than to cripple the British fleet. In late 1775, he demonstrated his newly designed mine for a group of dignitaries, including Connecticut Governor Jonathan Trumbull, and was given financing to build a boat to deliver it.

While Bushnell must have been thinking of an underwater craft for a while—if not, why go to so much trouble to ignite gunpowder underwater—just when he got the idea is not certain. But the where is almost certainly the Yale library. While there is no record of the specific volumes Bushnell pored over, it seems unlikely that a man who boasted of the long hours he spent studying there would not have received both inspiration and practical suggestions from the very texts that bore most on his interest and later work. And, although *The Gentleman's Magazine* was not part of the Yale collection, it was the most popular magazine in colonial America, especially in New England, and back issues would have been readily available to anyone who took a bit of time to seek them out.

Whatever Papin's illustration depicted, Bushnell's design shared a number of features with it: approximate dimensions, top opening, and outboard weaponry, in this case an auger that could drill into an enemy hull, allowing a mine—which Bushnell dubbed a "torpedo"— also mounted outside the hull, to then be attached.* Bushnell eschewed Papin's square and cylindrical design, however. He called his craft the *Turtle*, and in a 1787 letter to Thomas Jefferson, he described how he came up with the name. "The external shape of the submarine vessel bore some resemblance to two upper tortoise shells of equal size,

---

* Bushnell named his explosive device after a fish of the same name, *Torpedo nobiliana,* an electric ray common to Atlantic waters.

joined together; the place of entrance into the vessel being represented by the opening made by the swell of the shells, as at the head of the animal." For that opening, Bushnell wrote, "Above the upper edge of this iron band there was a brass crown or cover, resembling a hat with its crown and brim, which shut watertight up on the iron band."[1] Each half shell was to be crafted from a single hollowed-out oak log, bound at the waist with a copper band, and tarred along the seam. Three small windows were cut into the brass conning tower but vision would be clouded at best underneath the surface.

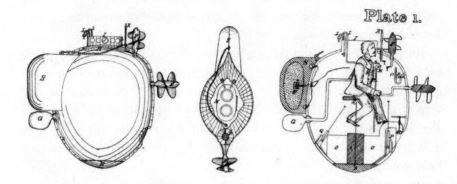

Plate 1.

Bushnell's Turtle. *All depictions of the craft came decades later.*
Bushnell also left no drawings.

Although the *Turtle* was designed to travel awash—only the conning tower visible—and with its hatch and windows open, it could also run partially and even fully submerged, at least for short distances. When the vessel was just under the surface, fresh air could be taken in by two snorkels that snapped shut when it moved deeper. Below snorkel depth, breathable air for the *Turtle*'s single operator would be exhausted after thirty minutes. Bushnell's plan, therefore, was to have the *Turtle* submerge only to avoid detection while maneuvering to and then underneath a British warship to plant the mine.

For lateral power, the *Turtle* was propelled by a hand crank connected to an Archimedes screw with a supplemental vertical screw to aid in submerging and surfacing. A rudder with a long tiller extension was positioned behind the operator. "At the bottom opposite to the entrance," Bushnell wrote, "was a fixed quantity of lead ballast. An aperture at the bottom, with its valve, was designed to admit water for the purpose of descending; and two brass forcing pumps served to eject the water within, when necessary for ascending."

The man charged with operating the *Turtle*, "sat on an oaken brace that kept the two sides of the boat from being crushed in by the water pressure, and did things with his hands and feet." One commentator noted, "He must have been as busy as a cathedral organist on Easter morning."[2]

As crude as the device appeared, it contained many innovations, such as a barometric device to measure depth, that would be carried forward to more sophisticated craft.

In September 1776, after months of experimenting and testing in Connecticut, Bushnell was ready. But the mission did not get off to an auspicious start. As the moment arrived to launch the new secret weapon, Bushnell's brother, who had trained to pilot the *Turtle*, developed a high fever. An infantry sergeant, Ezra Lee, volunteered, as he later put it, "to learn the ways and mystery of this new machine."

In complete secrecy, the *Turtle* was transported from Long Island Sound to the southwest edge of New York Harbor to prepare for its first assault. There would be no small measures. Bushnell intended no less than to have Lee attack and sink the sixty-four-gun HMS *Eagle*, flagship of Admiral Richard Howe.

Lee described his mission: "The Whale boats towed me as nigh the ships as they dare go, and then they cast me off. I soon found that I was too early in the tide, as it carried me down to the transports. I, however, hove about, and rowed for 5 glasses [2.5 hours], by the ship's bells, before the tide slackened so that I could get alongside the man of war, which lay above the transports."[*3]

It was near dawn before Lee managed to maneuver his vessel to the *Eagle*. "When I rowed under the stern of the ship, I could see the

---

* Although Lee refers to "rowing," there is no indication that the *Turtle* had oars. Likely he was using the term generically. In addition, since the rudder had to be operated by hand, it is unlikely Bushnell would have designed a craft in which the operator could not propel it forward and steer at the same time.

men on deck and hear them talk. I then shut down all the doors, sunk down and came under the bottom."

It was time to plant the charge. The auger on the top was not meant to bore a hole through the keel but rather to be screwed in and left as an anchor for Bushnell's "torpedo." Attached to the shaft by a rope were two other hollowed-out, tarred sections of oak, inside of which was 150 pounds of gunpowder and the flintlock fuse, which would begin to run as soon as the auger was set and Lee cast it off.

Lee tried to breach the hull with the drill "but found that it would not enter." Bushnell thought he would be boring into wood, but the keel was copper-sheathed, although Lee later said he struck an iron bar holding the rudder. He tried another spot, but with no more success.

With daylight a potentially lethal enemy, Lee decided to abort the mission and make for shore before he was discovered. But soon after he surfaced, the *Turtle* was spotted by a guard boat, which began to sail ominously in Lee's direction. Lee jettisoned the mine and cranked furiously. He managed to elude his pursuers—aided when the mine exploded under the water—and, exhausted, he returned to safety several hours later.

Many might have been discouraged by such an unpromising initiation, a few days later Ezra Lee insisted on trying again. He chose a different warship as his target, but this time his barometric depth gauge failed and he sailed completely underneath the hull. While the *Turtle* was being conveyed on the Hudson River to position it for a third attempt, a British frigate sank both transport and its cargo. Although Bushnell eventually retrieved his invention, he dismissed any thought of bringing it again into action. "I found it impossible at that time to prosecute the design any further," he wrote later to Jefferson. "I had been in a bad state of health from the beginning of my undertaking, and was now very unwell; the situation of public affairs was such that I despaired of obtaining the public attention and the assistance necessary. I was unable to support myself and the persons I must have employed had I proceeded."[4] His resentment for not being paid for his time and effort would fester, but he left behind a brilliant design and a unique episode in America's struggle for freedom. "I thought and still think that it was an effort of genius," wrote George Washington, characterizing Bushnell as "a man of great mechanical powers, fertile in invention, and master of execution." He added, however, "too many things were necessary to be combined to expect much against an enemy who are always on guard."[5]

After the war ended, Bushnell did not fare a good deal better than his submarine; in the postwar euphoria both he and his weapon were ignored. By the early 1790s, he was barely a footnote in the new nation's lore. Embittered at receiving neither the acclaim nor the remuneration that he thought were his due, he sailed for Europe, intending to sell his invention to what he was certain were more scientifically enlightened governments on the Continent. His first stop was England, but he could not even gain an audience in the Admiralty. Bushnell's lack of success in attacking the British fleet did little to dispel the prevailing feeling in Whitehall that the submarine was a gimmick rather than a warship. He then headed across the Channel. When he arrived in France, Bushnell looked up Joel Barlow, an old Yale chum and Francophile, who was a passionate advocate of free trade and freedom of the seas. Barlow thought his houseguest's submarine a brilliant idea, a foolproof means of keeping sea lanes open, especially for a nation with a weak navy, such as France. But though he had many well-placed friends, Barlow could not get anyone interested in Bushnell's idea.

A dispirited Bushnell soon sailed for home, but he refused to return to New England. With Barlow's reference, he contacted Abraham Baldwin, a congressman from Georgia and Barlow's cousin. Georgia was then a thinly populated wilderness and Baldwin found Bushnell a post as a teacher and physician, although there is no record of Bushnell having any formal medical training. Most important, Baldwin agreed to keep Bushnell's identity a secret, identifying him as "Dr. Bush."

David Bushnell died in Georgia in 1826. Only then, when his will was read, was his true identity revealed. He never knew that his visit to Joel Barlow would spark interest in what would become the next great advance in submarine research, undertaken by a man known for pioneering a very different type of marine technology.

CHAPTER 3

AN AMERICAN IN PARIS

Robert Fulton was born into a Scotch-Irish immigrant family of modest means in Lancaster, Pennsylvania, in November 1765. His father, also Robert, was active in both church and community affairs, and signed the charter for only the third town library established in the Colonies. The family purchased a farm just before young Robert was born, and the boy was sent to Quaker school when he was nine, soon after his father died.

From the first, he had been fascinated with drawing and, at seventeen, Fulton left home for Philadelphia, to try to earn his living as an artist. The war was drawing to a close and Philadelphia was vibrant with the sense of possibility. He enrolled in art school and took commissions where he could. At various times, he painted signs, produced mechanical drawings, copied sketches, and designed carriages. By age twenty, he graduated to painting miniatures, portraits, and landscapes, and was registered in the city directory.

In 1787, the year the United States would draft its Constitution, Fulton got his big break. Benjamin Franklin, who had admired the young painter's work, commissioned a portrait. That commission led to many others, including a miniature for Mary West, whose father had been a close friend of the elder Robert Fulton. Mary's cousin Benjamin, an expatriate living in London, was one of the most celebrated artists in England, his patron none other than King George III. (Although the war had caused ongoing political tensions between the United States and Britain, their mutual roots ran too deep for estrangement to totally sour social relations.)

After a debilitating pulmonary illness, which might have been a mild case of tuberculosis, Fulton accepted the prescription of a sea voyage and decided to sail to England to study painting. Benjamin West, perhaps because of the family connection, perhaps based on Fulton's talent, took on the young visitor as a protégé. West would mentor other promising American painters, among others, Samuel Morse, Gilbert Stuart, and Rembrandt Peale. Fulton moved into his patron's sumptuous home and set up an easel in his studio. With the eminent Benjamin West providing introductions, Fulton's career blossomed. He received many prestigious commissions and in 1791 even succeeded in placing two paintings at the Royal Academy of Arts, of which West was about to be named president.

West was providing social introductions as well, and Fulton became a familiar figure in British society. At one point, he met the aptly named Duke of Bridgewater, who owned a series of coal mines and had recently supplanted the standard pack horse means of transporting his product to market by digging a canal. So successful was the venture that Bridgewater had interested investors in a plan to create a network of canals across the English countryside. But terrain was an impediment; Bridgewater's canal did not vary a great deal in elevation, but where topography was uneven, prohibitively expensive locks would be required. If a simpler and less expensive means to equalize water levels could be developed, Bridgewater's venture could be immensely profitable.

Fulton found himself fascinated with the problem and began devouring everything he could find on canal building. The more he read, the more enthralled with engineering he became. From that point on, painting would never be more than an avocation. In 1794, Fulton had patented a system of inclined planes to replace locks and published the definitive *Treatise on the Improvement of Canal Navigation*. In September 1796, he sent copies of the book to George Washington, Napoleon Bonaparte, then an army general, and the governor of Pennsylvania.

To President Washington, he wrote that he was sending the book "to Exhibit the Certain mode of Giving Agriculture to every Acre of the immense Continent of America By Means of a Creative System of Canals." Fulton added, "When this Subject first entered my thoughts, I had no Idea of its Consequences: But the Scene gradually opened and at length exhibited the most extensive and pleasing prospect of Improvements; hence I now Consider it of much national Importance." Washington politely acknowledged the letter in December but, to Fulton's disappointment, expressed no interest in actively pursuing the project. Nor did the publication of a series of articles on canal building in the London *Morning Star* arouse the interest in England Fulton had expected.

Also in 1796, Fulton became a partner with the utopian socialist, Robert Owen, in the Inclined Planes and Canal Excavations Company. But Fulton chafed at the requirements of day-to-day business and the partnership lasted only one year.

Although Napoleon did not reply to Fulton's letter, he must have passed it along, because Fulton received word from Paris that his method would be employed in a planned canal from that city to Dieppe, on the Channel coast. In 1797, during a rare pause in the ongoing hostilities between Britain and France, Fulton traveled to Paris and there was taken in as a houseguest by Joel Barlow. He would remain at the Barlows' for seven years, developing a relationship so filial that Barlow and his wife, who were childless, came to call Fulton "Toot."

Whether Bushnell's and Fulton's stays at Barlow's overlapped is not certain, although they well may have. Even if they did not, Bushnell would have only very recently departed when Fulton arrived at Barlow's door. And while Fulton never acknowledged Bushnell as the source for his idea, he began talking of building a "plunging boat" soon after his arrival in Paris, having not uttered a word about it previously.

The Paris to Dieppe canal was never undertaken, but Fulton quickly moved on to other ventures.* In addition to aggressively pursuing submarine design, he took on another major engineering project, this of a far different sort. While there were no moving pictures in the 1790s, approximately a decade earlier, an enterprising painter named Robert Barker had devised a primitive facsimile that he called a "panorama." First exhibited in Edinburgh in 1791, the panorama was an enormously long painting, eight to ten feet high, mounted on spools, similar to camera film. The spools were offstage, left and right, and the canvas would be steadily advanced, again like film, depicting to a theater audience a series of episodes painted on the backdrop. To the audience, it would seem as if they were peering at the tableau out the window of a moving train. A narrator dramatically described events as the tale unfolded, or more accurately, unspooled. Panoramas were an immediate rage—exhibitors could feature any theme, from the classics, to romance, to melodrama, to war—and remained so until the second half of the nineteenth century.

Fulton's panorama was huge, almost twice the size of Barker's, who by that time had moved to London and grown extremely rich. In April 1799, Fulton was granted a French patent on the machinery he had designed to advance the spool. He then purchased land on the right bank, built a circular loft, and, to great fanfare, presented his first panorama, "The Destruction of Moscow," a tableau of "pillage and devastation," complete with the city being set ablaze. Tickets were 1½ francs, pricey by the standards of the day, but Fulton rarely did not sell out. So popular was Fulton's extravaganza that the street outside his theater was dubbed "Passage des Panoramas."** A dozen years later, life would imitate panorama, and Moscow would indeed be beset by pillage, devastation, and fire, this

---

*   Funding was not approved until more than a century later, in 1919, but the canal was not built then either.
** Passage des Panoramas, in the 2nd arrondissement, still exists, now the oldest surviving covered passage in Paris.

time marking the beginning of the destruction of Napoleon's Grand Armée.

Fulton followed his Moscow depiction with others, but once again, despite making quite a bit of money, he found that he had no taste for running a business day-to-day. With what he hoped was a favorable change in the French government, he licensed the company and devoted himself fully to his submarine.

As early as 1797, Fulton had written to the Directory, which was running France at the time, "having in view the great importance of lessening the power of the English fleet, that he had a project for the construction of a mechanical Nautilus." This letter came only months after Bushnell had proposed an underwater boat to the Directory and been rebuffed. In January 1798, Fulton submitted a formal proposal to the marine minister. Among his requests was a commission in the French navy lest he be deemed a pirate if captured by the British. But Fulton had no better luck than Bushnell. The following year, Fulton's proposal was declined.

But unlike Bushnell, Fulton did not give up. He waited four months, until a new marine minister had been appointed, and tried again. This time, he included detailed plans and a drawing of his *Nautilus*. It was by far the most advanced and sophisticated vision of an undersea boat ever devised.

Twenty feet long and cylindrical, the *Nautilus* bore a much greater resemblance to a modern submarine than Bushnell's ovoid. It was also powered by a crank, but the propeller it turned, four blades mounted on the same axis, was far more efficient than the screw. The conning tower was a small, raised, windowed bubble in the front that replaced the *Turtle*'s cylinder. Like the *Turtle*, however, there was neither an internal mechanism to supplement the ambient air inside nor a source of artificial light except oxygen-eating candles, so the *Nautilus* was also built to spend the majority of its time on the surface. To add speed, Fulton included a sail on a collapsible mast. Once again, the weapon was a powder charge that would be fastened to the hull of an enemy ship, this time by means of a detachable spike, designed to be more effective than Bushnell's augur against copper sheathing, but still not guaranteed to pierce metal.

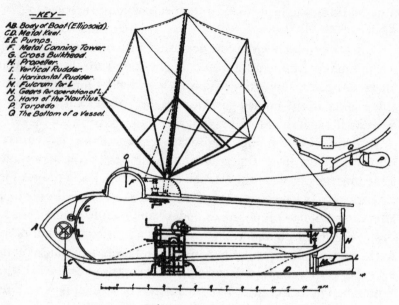

—KEY—

AB. Body of Boat (Ellipsoid).
CD. Metal Keel.
EE. Pumps.
F. Metal Conning Tower.
G. Cross Bulkhead.
H. Propeller.
I. Vertical Rudder.
L. Horizontal Rudder.
M. Fulcrum for L.
N. Gears for operation of L.
O. Horn of the Nautilus.
P. Torpedo
Q. The Bottom of a Vessel.

Fulton's Nautilus

But it was in navigation that the *Nautilus* was most advanced. The quantity of lead ballast she held in her keel was such that the difference between the vessel's flotation weight and that of the water displaced was only four to five kilograms. That meant in order to submerge, only that much weight in water needed to be taken on and to surface only that much expelled. For depth control, Fulton turned to the inclined planes that had served him so well in canal design. Mounted at the rear, attached to the sides of the steering rudder, were "horizontal rudders," which could be manipulated up or down from inside the boat to either bring it closer to the surface or deeper. In some form, those diving planes, either at the bow or the stern, have been a feature of submarine design ever since.

Along with his specifications, Fulton included a cover letter in which he promised to send English ships to the bottom. He proposed to be paid a rather hefty commission, "by the cannon"—the more a destroyed English vessel carried, the greater the bounty.

Initial French objections to Fulton's proposal were, oddly, not in the money he was asking but rather in the use of a weapon of stealth.

The French naval minister and many in government considered such a device "dishonorable." But pragmatism won out and a commission was impaneled to study Fulton's design. The commissioners, all scientists or engineers, did a creditable job of evaluating both the strengths and shortcomings of Fulton's submarine. In the end, though they thought the sail arrangement flawed, they recommended, "Citizen Fulton be given the authorization and necessary means to construct the machine of which he has submitted a model." The commission was in part persuaded because the French navy could not hope to defeat the British fleet by conventional means.

Despite the committee's recommendation, however, the French ministry refused to move forward. In October 1798, Fulton tried again. He based payment strictly on performance. If he sank an English ship of the line, he would immediately receive five hundred thousand francs, with which he would build a squadron of ten more *Nautilus* boats. He would then be paid one hundred francs for each pound of caliber of the guns of English ships subsequently destroyed or put out of action, in other words, five hundred francs for a five-pounder, one thousand francs for a ten-pounder, and so on. By this time, England had established a blockade off the French coast, and Fulton insisted that not only could his submarines destroy the British fleet, but they could also allow the French to set up their own blockade at the mouth of the Thames. Still, his proposal was again rejected.

Fulton had yet to attempt to construct an actual *Nautilus*, although he had built a small wooden model, which had been insufficient to persuade the French ministers. After he licensed the panorama, he traveled to Holland but could not interest the Dutch in the idea either. While there, however, he learned that Napoleon had been named first consul. He immediately returned to Paris and submitted his proposal once more, this time accompanied by a detailed strategic plan of how to use the *Nautilus* against the English, and why undersea craft would change the face of naval combat. As to the immediate conflict, once the *Nautilus* wreaked its havoc, "The result would be that deprived of Pitt's guineas, the coalition would vanish and France thus delivered from its numerous enemies, would be able to work without obstacle for the strengthening of its liberty and for peace."[1]

Fulton even insisted that with the destruction of its fleet, "England would become a republic. Soon Ireland would throw off the yoke and the English monarchy would be wiped out. A rich and industrious nation would then increase the number of republics of Europe."

It was a brilliantly conceived document, combining science, tactics, and hyperbole and, at least from a strategic standpoint, would form the basis of submarine warfare a century later. The proposal came to Napoleon's attention and, soon afterward, Fulton was building his plunging boat at Rouen.

In July 1800, the *Nautilus* had its first test. Fulton piloted the boat, and two crewmen operated the crank. It submerged for seventeen minutes in twenty-five feet of water, but when the test was completed, Fulton announced that he wanted to make improvements. In November, he conducted a more extensive test at Le Havre, in which the *Nautilus* remained submerged for six hours. This time, he kept a candle lit and replenished the air supply by means of a tube that extended to the surface. The float that supported the tube could be seen only at a quarter mile away or less. But some observers pointed out that speed and maneuverability of the vessel were not such that it would be capable of engaging a British warship and escaping unscathed.

Nonetheless, the launch of a craft that had the potential to attack the British fleet undetected stoked Napoleon's interest. He sent a curt note to the marine minister: *Je prie le Ministre de la Marine de me faire connaitre cequ'il sait sur les projets du capitaine Fulton. Bonaparte.* (I ask that the minister inform me of what he knows of Captain Fulton's projects.)[2]

But even the first consul's interest did not convince French naval officials to make a commitment to undersea warfare. Fulton continued to refine the design, and on July 1801, he launched the *Nautilus* at Brest. He sent a glowing report of the results to the ministry, in which he also included the testimony of witnesses. The minister sent a reply to Fulton that, although it has not survived, must have infuriated the American inventor.

Fulton's response to the minister was both evasive and antagonistic. It included regrets that he had not known of the first consul's interest—Napoleon had apparently asked to see the boat—with the explanation that "she leaked very much and being but an imperfect engine I did not think her further useful hence I took her to Pieces, Sold her iron work, lead, and Cylenders and was necessitated to break the greater part of her movements in taking them to Pieces, So that nothing now remains which can give an idea of her Combination."[3]

He also respectfully declined to submit his drawings—Napoleon had apparently asked to see those as well—on the grounds that, since the French government had not contributed to the effort, the plans remained the private property of the inventor. Lest he be misunderstood, Fulton added, "I have now labored 3 years and at considerable expense to Prove my experiments. And I find that a man who wishes to Cultivate the useful Arts cannot make rapid Progress without Sufficient funds to put his Succession of Ideas to immediate Proof." When a favorable reply was not forthcoming, Fulton attempted to bypass the bureaucracy and sent a personal letter to Napoleon, whom he had always judged to be the man most receptive to new ideas. Napoleon did not respond. Disgusted at the failure of his submarine to sell, Fulton terminated negotiations with the government and began dabbling with another idea that had piqued his curiosity—the use of steam power for surface vessels.

Fulton's *Nautilus* had not faded from everyone's interest, however. In 1803, a member of the British Secret Service reported to his superiors that he "was informed that a plan has been concerted by Mr. Fulton, an American resident at Paris, under the influence of the First Consul of the French Republic for destroying the Maritime force of this country."[4]

British officials decided that, despite any immediate lack of interest from the French, leaving Fulton with their enemy was not a good idea. Through Fulton's friends, they let it be known that he would be welcome in England. In May 1804, Fulton accepted the invitation. He packed up and left Paris for London, where he promptly offered his submarine to the British navy.

It appeared for a while that Fulton's invention would finally get the attention he was convinced it deserved. Fulton undertook a series of communications—using the alias "Robert Francis"—with Lord Hawkesbury—who adopted the alias "Mr. Hammond"—describing what was needed to make the British navy the first to add undersea boats to its fleet. Hawkesbury recommended to Prime Minister William Pitt that the £100,000 Fulton had requested be set aside to see him through his researches. To help things along, Fulton submitted a series of scrupulously detailed plans for his new *Nautilus*, which contained many improvements, and the same sort of strategic précis that he had given to the French. Lest his motives be deemed pecuniary, Fulton explained his reasons for leaving France in a letter to Lord Melville:

> I feel no enmity to the people of France, or any other people; on the contrary, I wish their happiness; for my principle is that every nation profits by the prosperity of its neighbours, provided the governments of its neighbours be humane and just. What is here said is directed against the tyrannic principles of Bonaparte, a man who has set himself above all law; he is, therefore in that state which Lord Somers compares to that of a wild beast unrestrained by any rule, and he should be hunted down as the enemy of mankind. This, however, is the business of Frenchmen. With regard to the nations of Europe, they can only hold him in governable limits, by fencing him round with bayonets.[5]

But the Lords of the Admiralty were unmoved. Employing dubious logic, they declined to approve production of a revolutionary and potentially superior new technology on the grounds that only a weak navy should pursue such a course. As Britain had a strong navy, there was no need to do anything but continue to produce traditional sailing ships. This thinking would predominate among naval strategists on both sides of the Atlantic for another century. (The English did have the foresight, however, to pay Fulton not to build any submarines for their enemies.)

With Lord Nelson's victory at Trafalgar in 1805, any chance of British expenditure on submarines ended. The following year, with no market for his *Nautilus*, Fulton, like Bushnell before him, returned to America. But Fulton did not slink off into the wilderness and oblivion. He set his energies to surface vessels and in 1809 launched his steamship, the *Clermont*, for its historic voyage on the Hudson. Robert Fulton would not usher in the age of the submarine, but he would fashion the means by which surface vessels were powered for the better part of a century.

CHAPTER 4
STARS AND BARS

While Fulton's *Nautilus* could hardly be considered the first modern submarine, the advances in his design—cylindrical shape, the addition of horizontal planes—moved the technology far closer to the issues that would need to be resolved before a true undersea vessel could be designed and built.

The first lesson drawn from the *Nautilus* was that simply finding a way to keep a boat submerged and powered would not be sufficient. As with the airplane, stability, not buoyancy (as opposed to lift), or power, would prove to be the key to successful submarine navigation.

There were five fundamental engineering problems inherent to creating a functional submarine, with an added sixth, weapons delivery, to turn the craft into a warship. The boat had to be able to successfully get under water from surface running (and rise to the surface afterward), called controlled buoyancy; be able to run on an even keel while submerged, longitudinal stability; not roll from side to side, latitudinal stability; have a means of motive power to both generate forward momentum and to help keep the vessel submerged; and, of course, if the submarine was going to spend any significant time underwater, there needed to be a means to supplement the air the crew breathed when the hatch was closed.

The degree to which a vessel could control its environment placed it in one of three classes. A submersible could spend time completely under the water but lacked the means to move about to any significant degree; a semisubmersible could move about but not run completely submerged—some portion of its frame had to remain on the surface, usually to provide air and vent the engine; and a true submarine, which could run effectively while completely submerged.

Drebbel's notion that negative buoyancy—the tendency to sink—could be created by forward motion might have been his only insight that survived. Even here, however, in the absence of planes to steer his craft downward, it is unclear how his rowers could have sent him deeper under the Thames, no matter how hard they pulled on the oars. The only way to achieve negative buoyancy without planes is by weight. Until Fulton, then, the only way to keep a vessel submerged was to carry sufficient ballast. As ballast was a necessity even on sur-face vessels—to allow them to ride low enough in the water to keep them stable—every early designer from Bourne on knew to supplement lead or iron with water-filled tanks that could be emptied or filled by operator intervention to adjust buoyancy. Pumps and later compressed air were the means generally employed.

But ballasting presented its own difficulties. An undersea vessel would not retain stability as a surface ship would—by riding with its hull partially submerged in the water. Water, denser than air, would tend to right a ballasted surface ship if it began to roll side to side, or even if it pitched forward. A submarine, however, was surrounded by a medium of equal density, so that there would be no tendency to "pop up" if stability was disrupted. If water flowed into the bow, for example, and the submarine began to head to the bottom, it would simply continue downward unless the water could be removed. Even under normal running conditions, if a ballast tank were only partially filled, which would be most of the time, the water would tend to slosh about and disrupt undersea stability along both axes. The tanks therefore would need to be of a particular size and construction, and placed either along the hull or within the body of the vessel so that longitudinal and latitudinal stability could be maintained.

These lessons took some learning, and so for the next fifty years submarine technology proceeded in fits and starts. Most of the efforts were total failures, some silly, some fatal, but occasionally a feature would find its way into a design that would come into play later in more serious craft.*

The most noteworthy of this group was a Bavarian, Wilhelm Bauer, who journeyed from country to country in Europe, trying to find a home for his design. His first effort, *Le Plongeur-Marin* (the Sea Diver), built in 1850 for the army of the German state Schleswig-Holstein, was treadle-powered, and contain a lead weight mounted on a threaded rod along the keel, which could be moved forward or backward to aid in diving, surfacing, and sailing on an even keel underwater. The vessel performed well on the surface, but when Bauer attempted to submerge, both his lead weight and the water ballast he had taken on, placed in the bow, caused the boat to dive directly to the bottom. It settled in sixty feet of water, with Bauer and his crew helpless to lighten its weight. Five hours later, with air running out, Bauer convinced the crew to take in enough water to equalize the pressure so that a hatch could be opened and they could swim to the surface.

Bauer tried Austria next, but could only interest a wealthy dowager in providing funding. He may or may not have produced a boat, but in any event it was never put in the water. The English were next, but that effort also fizzled when his boat sank during trials. This time his crew was not so lucky and half of them drowned. Neither the United States nor Germany would allow even a test, but Bauer, ever perseverant, finally found support in czarist Russia. He traveled to St. Petersburg and built his most advanced boat, *Le Diable-Marin* (the Devil Diver).

---

* One of the later failures, designed by two Americans, was the whimsically named *Intelligent Whale*. Its acumen turned out to be suspect when it flooded and sank during testing, but the crew managed to escape.

Bauer's Russian boat was constructed of sheet iron, fifty-two feet long, thirteen across, and eleven high. Its propeller was powered by four man-driven treadmills. It held forty-seven tons of iron ballast, with three ten-foot cylindrical ballast tanks to control buoyancy. A small supplementary tank was used to trim the boat—control its longitudinal stability. Bauer had installed two air locks to allow crew members to leave the boat, presumably with explosive charges that they would attach to an enemy hull with a suction device.

In May 1856, *Le Diable-Marin* was ready for testing. Bauer had submitted a list of experiments he wished to carry out, including how a compass would work at various depths, how sound would carry, how temperature would vary, how long a man could remain in a sealed chamber without ill effects, and whether compressed air was a practical means of maintaining the atmosphere.

Bauer's craft proved satisfactory in diving and remaining under the surface, but less so in maneuverability. How Bauer steered the vessel is a mystery, as a rudder is conspicuously absent from prints of the period. A larger problem was that Russian naval officials, all drawn from the aristocracy, loathed Bauer for his middle-class origins—they called him the "Austrian corporal"—and attempted to derail the project at every turn.* Eventually they made his life so miserable that Bauer left Russia. As a result, after more than one hundred successful dives, the Bauer submarine was abandoned and left to rust. Bauer, who might well have perfected his vessel with a bit more support, abandoned his research and returned to Bavaria, where he lived the remainder of his life in obscurity.

Wilhelm Bauer was not alone in his inability to pierce the military bureaucracy. Almost universally accepted among military men was that pursuing an innovative weapons system, such as a submarine, announced that a nation's traditional forces were substandard. The irony was that, in most cases, none more than Russia, traditional forces *were* substandard, made so in no small part by senior officers' refusal to admit it.

---

* The same epithet would be used sixty years later by German generals in describing Adolf Hitler.

To move submarine technology forward, therefore, would take a combatant so outmatched as to render the weak-navy-strong-navy argument moot. Improbable in some ways, obvious in others, that combatant would be the Confederate States of America, fighting for what seemed an increasingly hopeless cause in the American Civil War.

By early 1863, although holding its own on the battlefield, the Confederacy was feeling the impact of fighting an enemy vastly superior in manpower and industrial output. With each battle, the Confederate army, unable to fully replace its losses, grew weaker, while the Union simply drew from its immense reserves to return to full strength. In addition, the South's two most important seaports had been rendered useless. New Orleans had fallen early in the war and the Union had successfully blockaded Charleston, South Carolina. In July, Lee would be turned back at Gettysburg and, of greater strategic significance, Grant would choke off the Mississippi by taking Vicksburg. Outmanned and outgunned on land and sea, its trade routes throttled, the Confederacy found itself willing to try just about anything to even the odds.

The Confederates chose as a first priority an attempt to break the blockade of Charleston Harbor, which would open Atlantic trade routes and allow sympathetic European nations, especially Great Britain, to supplement the South's dwindling supplies. A frontal assault would have been futile, so Confederate engineers decided to attack by stealth. They cut a thirty-five-foot, steam-powered gunboat down to the waterline and covered the top with iron plating. A fifteen-foot spar protruded from the bow and held a sixty-pound gunpowder charge. The boat would hold a crew of four. A night attack was planned, of course, and while the boat could never fully submerge, it ran very low in the water, "awash," with only a low conning tower and exhaust stack exposed. The low profile would give Union sentries little to spot and their gunners not much to shoot at. To make the craft even more difficult to detect, the exhaust stack was hinged and could be lowered during an attack. Either because of the respective sizes of the gunboat and the Union ship it was to assault, or just the state of the war in general, the builders christened their boat the David, as in *David* and Goliath.

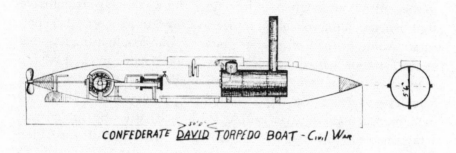

CONFEDERATE DAVID TORPEDO BOAT - Civil War

A "David"

On October 5, 1863, at about 8:00 P.M., Lieutenant William T. Glassell maneuvered the *David* toward the new Union battleship USS *Ironsides*, which was lying off Morris Island in Charleston Harbor. It was history's first attack by a motorized "torpedo boat" on a surface vessel.

Lacking the ability to fully submerge, however, would prove a major impediment. Despite its low profile in the water, the *David* was spotted fifty yards away and hailed by the *Ironsides*'s officer of the deck. Glassell, standing in the open hatch, responded with a blast from a double-barreled shotgun, killing the Union sailor. With both sides firing, the charge at the end of the spar exploded prematurely, sending a torrent into the hull. On the *Ironsides*, thinking the explosion would sink their ship, panicked sailors began jumping overboard on the far side until the captain, who had quickly surveyed the damage, convinced them that there was no danger.

On the *David*, there was panic as well. The crew thought that the water that had flooded into the hull had put out the engine's boiler and that the boat was about to sink. Glassell and the fireman jumped overboard, taking the only two life preservers with them. The other two crewmen, however, restarted the fires and, with chaos reigning aboard the *Ironsides*, were able to steer the *David* once more through the Union fleet back to the pier at Charleston.

The *Ironsides* was damaged sufficiently that it had to be taken out of service and returned to Philadelphia for repairs. Word leaked out that the Confederates had employed "some kind of an infernal machine," as the *New York Times* phrased it, although with the *David* avoiding capture, no one was quite certain of the vessel's capabilities. But the result was clear enough. In his report to Secretary of the Navy Gideon Welles, a Union admiral wrote, "The secrecy, rapidity of movement, control of direction, and precise explosion indicate, I think, the introduction of the torpedo element as a means of warfare. It can be ignored no longer."[1]

To prepare for the next attack—Union spies reported that two-dozen *David*s were under construction—the blockading ships altered their positions in the harbor and some dropped shot-weighted nets off their hulls. But a *David*-type vessel was not used again in combat. Running on the surface with the Union ships by then on their guard seemed suicidal. In addition, the Confederates had another design almost ready to go, one that would leave the Union gunners nothing at all to shoot at.

It was called the *American Diver*, and the Confederates believed it could change the course of the war.

In early 1862, in New Orleans, with Union admiral David Farragut's fleet closing in, Confederate captain James McClintock approached Captain Horace Hunley and Baxter Watson, a local businessman, and asked for money to use in building an underwater craft he had designed. The craft had the virtue of sailing fully submerged, but as a result needed to be powered manually. But McClintock, who had likely read up on Fulton's efforts, had included bow planes, which would help keep his boat stable underneath the waves. Hunley and Watson agreed to provide funding—without some new weapon, New Orleans was certain to fall. Even that early in the war, the South was short on supplies, so McClintock had to scrounge about to obtain enough scrap iron plate to forge into a hull. He named his invention the *Pioneer*. The boat required only one crewman to crank the screw propeller, and would carry an explosive charge that would be attached to an enemy hull and be detonated by a timing device.

But during tests, the *Pioneer* could not maintain either longitudinal or lateral stability. McClintock scuttled the craft rather than let it fall into Farragut's hands, and he, Hunley, and Watson fled the city for Mobile, Alabama. There they built a second submarine, once more from discarded boilerplates. The boat, now called the *American Diver*, successfully completed practice dives, but when it was sent out to attack a Union frigate, a squall blew water into its open hatch and the crew was lucky to escape with their lives as it headed toward the bottom. When the Confederate government refused to participate to fund a third attempt, Watson and McClintock dropped out. But Hunley was determined to see the project through and financed the enterprise on his own. He would name the new machine after himself.

Once again, scrap metal was used for construction, this time a twenty-five-foot boiler, four feet in diameter, which was sliced lengthwise with a foot of iron plating riveted between the cut halves. Wedge-shaped, rounded bulkheads were attached fore and aft to serve as ballast tanks, which could be flooded by a valve in the main section. Hand pumps connected to iron pipes were used to empty the tanks.

As with all early boats, the *Hunley* was to run mostly awash with the hatch open, but to refresh the air when submerged, an "air box" was placed on top of the hull between forward and rear eight-inch-high conning towers. Hunley at first hoped to use steam or electricity, but neither of these could be made to work with the boat submerged, so he was forced to settle for a crank. Eight sailors would sit lengthwise, providing power to a stubby, four-bladed propeller. Like the *David*, an explosive-tipped spar protruded from the front end.

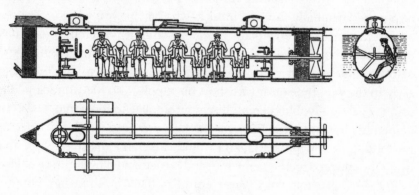

CSS Hunley

Hunley's creation had any number of obvious flaws. The boat was extremely slow, capable of only four knots at full crank. The air box turned out to be ineffective, so the sole way to refresh the air was to surface and open the hatches. Ballasting at the ends created extreme difficulty maintaining longitudinal stability. Weapons delivery was also problematic—the original plan, to drag a ninety-pound explosive on a two-hundred-foot towline under a target and allow the charge to explode on impact with an enemy's hull proved unworkable in the shallow water. Also, the boat moved so lethargically that a strong current might well bring the explosives back to the submarine.

Tests were almost uniformly disastrous. During the first run, after cruising acceptably on the surface, the boat submerged and immediately sank to the bottom. The nine crewmen failed to get out, and drowned. Undaunted, Hunley had the boat raised and transported from Mobile to Charleston. To entice sailors to volunteer for what could well be a suicide mission, a South Carolina businessman announced a $100,000 reward—greenbacks, not Confederate—for the destruction of a Union battleship.

Dollar incentive proved effective. Lieutenant John Payne offered to the pilot the craft, and eight other sailors agreed to work the crank. The *Hunley* was fitted with a spar torpedo, the towline plan discarded. Just as the boat left the dock, however, a wave created by a passing steamer sent water pouring over the tiny conning towers and into the hull. Payne, who was standing in the conning tower, escaped, but the other eight did not. Penned in by the onrushing water, they drowned as the *Hunley* settled at the bottom of Charleston Harbor.

Once more, the boat was raised and refitted; once more, Payne took the boat out for an attack; once more, it flooded; and once more Payne escaped while most of his crew was trapped inside. Although the boat was again raised, Payne was done. He never again ventured into a submarine.

With Payne gone, Hunley himself took charge. He hired a crew, trained them, and on October 15, 1863, took the boat out for a test.

Just after the *Hunley* left its moorings, Hunley ordered a test dive. As soon as it disappeared under the surface, bubbles were seen rising to the top. The boat sank, nose down, in nine fathoms of water. No one got out. Horace Hunley died in the boat that bore his name. When the boat was located three days later, the forward ballast tank was full and the aft tank empty.

But the Confederacy was sufficiently desperate to keep trying. Engineers raised the boat yet again and manned it with another volunteer crew of seven. Lieutenant George Dixon assumed command and proved quite able. He drilled his sailors for months, first on the surface, and then with shallow dives. He pored over the *Hunley*, demanding alterations where needed—tighter gaskets on the hatch covers and a more effective sealing off of the ballast tanks. The line on the spar torpedo was lengthened to 150 yards to prevent the explosive from damaging the boat as it reversed away from its target. Only when he deemed his crew expert, would Dixon venture out for an attack.

On February 17, 1864, conditions finally seemed right. A mist hung over the harbor, which would make the boat difficult to spot, and the winds, and therefore the waves, were light. Shortly after sundown, the *Hunley* cruised awash toward the newly commissioned USS *Housatonic*.

As the *Hunley* approached its target, Dixon, peering out of the forward conning tower, prepared to dive. But before he could, the officer of the deck on the *Housatonic* spotted a school of fish and, with his attention drawn to the waters over the side, noticed the Confederate submarine and raised the alarm.

But it was too late. Before the *Housatonic* could make steam and cruise out of danger, Dixon struck with his torpedo. The explosion detonated ordnance in the *Housatonic*'s stern magazine and blew away the entire rear of the ship. The *Housatonic* sank almost immediately. But the torpedo had exploded prematurely, before Dixon could get safely away. Either the *Hunley* was sucked into the breach in the *Housatonic*'s hull or was swamped by the resulting wave. In any case, the boat sank, following its quarry to the bottom of Charleston Harbor, taking Dixon and his crew to their deaths.*

---

* Finding the *Hunley*'s wreckage defied explorers and treasure seekers for more than a century. P. T. Barnum offered a reward of $100,000 early in the twentieth century and bestselling author Clive Cussler funded a fifteen-year search, all in vain. Finally, in 1995, three archaeologists working for Cussler's group located a metal object off the coast of Sullivan's Island with a magnetometer. Under three feet of sediment in thirty feet of water, divers discovered one of the *Hunley*'s conning towers, and soon the entire boat. It was raised in 2000 and is now on display in a Charleston museum.

CHAPTER 5
ENTR'ACTE: A FICTIONAL INTERLUDE

While to the *Hunley* goes the honor of the first sinking of a surface ship by a submarine, it was still a submarine propelled in roughly the same fashion as a Roman galley. No one had figured out how to power a boat underwater, nor how to make one sufficiently stable to be navigated effectively. Steam was the prevailing technology for motive power, but steam involved fires and fires made smoke, which need to be vented. It was theoretically possible to vent smoke into the water, but no one had figured out how to do it. Venting it above the surface involved either running awash or piping the exhaust through an extremely long tube extended to the surface, which would always be prone to flooding in rough seas. The same was true of any tube to allow the crew of a closed vessel to breathe.

For a time, two French inventors seemed to have found the solution by abandoning steam for a promising new power source. In 1859, Siméon Bourgeois, a navy caption, and an engineer, Charles Brun, began construction of a 150-foot-long, 12-foot-wide cylindrical vessel they called *Plongeur* (Diver), which would be powered by an eighty horsepower motor that ran on compressed air. The notion of compressing air for mechanical tasks had been around since the bellows in 3000 BC, but the ability to harness the substance for industrial uses had only been introduced in the 1780s. And it was not until 1857 that French engineers developed a way to effectively "cool" compressed air so that it could be safely stored for use on demand, in this case to power pneumatic drills that were cutting into mountains to excavate for railroad tunnels. Bourgeois and Brun almost immediately recognized that here might be a power source for the world's first true submarine.

In 1863, before either the *David* or the *Hunley* was launched, they began testing their design. The *Plongeur* was structurally quite advanced, built with iron plates riveted to a supporting frame and a heavy iron keel that extended ten feet out from the bow to hold a spar torpedo. Brun, who drew up the plans, was at least aware of the need for stability, as he installed "bilge keels" on either side to prevent rolling, but these would only function effectively when the submarine was running awash. Watertight bulkheads were installed both lengthwise and across to prevent flooding, and planes were fitted at the stern.

Plongeur

But the great departure was the twenty-three compressed air reservoirs, each of which could be charged to 180 pounds per square inch. Even at such a relatively puny compression—all that could be attained in an era before true high-pressure cylinders—leakage was a constant problem, so much so that when the hatch was opened upon surfacing a cloud of fog emerged before the crew.*

During tests in shallow water, the boat functioned well. It could remain submerged and invisible, with the crew drawing on the same

---

* The fog was as a result of air expanding to normal pressure.

air supply that would power the motor and blow the ballast tanks. But when used so liberally, the air reservoirs, which took up most of the space in the boat, discharged very quickly. It would, then, be impossible for the boat to undertake anything but a very short journey unless a surface vessel carrying stores of compressed air accompanied it. In addition to the problem of depletion, loss of air also altered the weight distribution and therefore the longitudinal stability of the boat. In shallow water, the loss of stability appeared manageable, but when the *Plongeur* was taken out for deep-sea trials in autumn 1863, severe shortcomings became apparent.

According to one observer, the boat could not maintain either constant depth or stability and "kept bouncing up and down like a rubber ball." In addition, "the horizontal rudders were not powerful enough, [and] consequently the boat, on more than one occasion, touched bottom, as she was always either up or down."[1] Although Bourgeois and Brun kept tinkering with the design, nothing seemed to work. The boat was simply uncontrollable and eventually the two gave up. The *Plongeur* was converted into "a common water-tank."

But the *Plongeur*'s demise was not quite complete. During the International Exposition in Paris, in 1867, two models of Brun's boat were exhibited and drew quite a bit of attention. One of the exposition's visitors was particularly fascinated. He was not a trained scientist but had a keen eye for mechanics and an even keener sense of innovation. He was already famous in France for applying these skills to a series of novels that combined adventure with an enticing vision of the future. After his visit to the exhibition, Jules Verne would begin his most famous work, *Vingt mille lieues sous les mers: Tour du monde sous-marin*, which was translated, loosely, into English as *Twenty Thousand Leagues Under the Sea*.

Verne's novel, first published in France in 1869, was an instant sensation and did more to bring submarines into the public consciousness than any event prior to Weddigen's three-destroyer sinking in 1914.

Twenty Thousand Leagues Under the Sea is known largely in the United States as a futuristic adventure novel, most popular with adolescents. It is anything but. Verne's narrative is an examination of man's interaction with technology, how scientific advances are too often used primarily as weapons of war, and also a herald of the environmental movement. It is a highly sophisticated work, which aroused a good deal of philosophical controversy in France. The reason for the difference in the book's reception is that, when it came time to render *Vingt mille lieues* into English, its translator, Reverend Lewis Mercier, not only made countless translation errors and altered substantial sections of the work, but he also eliminated almost one-quarter of the original text.

The most drastic changes were to the novel's protagonist, Captain Nemo. Verne's original idea was to make him a Polish nobleman, but that was soon abandoned for a more controversial rendering. In the French editions, Nemo was in no way the cultured Western European depicted by Lewis in translation. He was not even white or Christian, but rather Prince Dakkar, an Indian, Hindu, or Muslim, "son of a rajah of the then independent territory of Bundelkund." Dakkar was sent to Europe for his education, where he remained until age thirty, acquiring both a love and knowledge of science, and the ambition to "become a great and powerful ruler of a free and enlightened people." After returning to India, he got married, had two children, but then he helped lead the anti-British Sepoy Rebellion in 1857. His cause was hopeless and, after the inevitable defeat, Dakkar returned to the mountains of Bundelkund. As Verne described him in the sequel, *The Mysterious Island*, "There, alone in the world, overcome by disappointment at the destruction of all his vain hopes, a prey to profound disgust for all human beings, filled with hatred of the civilized world, he realized the wreck of his fortune, assembled some score of his most faithful companions, and one day disappeared, leaving no trace behind. Where, then, did he seek that liberty denied him upon the inhabited earth? Under the waves, in the depths of the ocean, where none could follow. Upon a deserted island of the Pacific he established his dockyard, and there a submarine vessel was constructed from his designs. He named his submarine vessel the *Nautilus*, called himself simply Captain Nemo ['No Man' in Latin], and disappeared beneath the seas."

Nemo is, therefore, a fierce anti-imperialist who loathes the British over all others. Lewis removed all traces of those sentiments. The ship Nemo sinks in revenge is conspicuously British in the original, unidentified in the English translation. Lewis also made certain that American sensibilities were not trifled with. In Verne's original, on the walls of Nemo's cabin was a series of portraits of "great men of history who had devoted their lives to a great human ideal." Washington and Lincoln were there, but also "that martyr to the emancipation of the black race, John Brown, hanging on the gallows, just as Victor Hugo had drawn him." The first two remained in Lewis's version, but Brown was expunged.*

In addition to its scathing treatment of racism—as prevalent then as now in both Europe and the United States—Verne was prescient in some surprising ways. Nemo says in an exchange with one of his captives, "'I know that [killing for killing's sake] is a privilege reserved for man, but I do not approve of such a murderous pastime. In destroying the southern whale (like the Greenland whale, an inoffensive creature), your traders do a culpable action, Master Land. They have already depopulated the whole of Baffin's Bay, and are annihilating a class of useful animals. Leave the unfortunate cetacea alone.' The Captain was right. The barbarous and inconsiderate greed of these fishermen will one day cause the disappearance of the last whale in the ocean."

With Nemo essentially neutered in translation, American readers were left to marvel over the *Nautilus*, Verne intentionally giving the same name as Fulton's submarine. As always, Verne had made a careful study of the science and prevailing technology before beginning, and so his model was remarkably detailed, although vague where technological problems remained to be solved. The vessel was powered by electricity, for example, although how the energy was generated was barely hinted at.** Verne's *Nautilus* was cylindrical, as was Brun's design—Nemo described it as "cigar shaped"—but was seventy meters long, much

---

*   Although a slightly better English translation was produced in the 1890s, and others were published in the 1960s, it was not until 1993 that a "fully restored" English edition by Walter James Miller and Frederick Paul Walter was put out by Tom Clancy's original publisher, the Naval Institute Press.

**   Verne can be excused for this lapse. Commercial electricity, which would be restricted initially to direct current, mostly in small factories, would not come into use until the next decade.

larger than the *Plongeur*. Inside, the ship was marvelous, spacious, and fanciful. Not until nuclear-powered submarines would sailors enjoy such amenities.

Verne included a double hull, eventually standard in submarine construction, but in 1869 present in only one or two otherwise abortive designs. A four-bladed propeller drove the craft, a single-blade rudder steered it, and diving planes were placed amidships, which seemed a logical location but would prove unwieldy in practice. A large air reservoir was in the bow, but with the *Nautilus* spending so much time submerged, Verne did not indicate how or if the air regenerated.

Most significantly, although the *Nautilus* could and did sink surface ships by ramming them, its main purposes were peaceful—exploration and salvage. Large glass windows were built into the hull to allow the submariners to view the wonders outside and a hatch was built so that divers could exit the vessel underwater and patrol the sea bottom. A bright light would be shone outward to facilitate the task. Perhaps never before had an author portrayed the undersea world with such wonder. These sections escaped Lewis Mercier's red pen and as a result, thousands upon thousands of American children experienced the fascination of exploring beneath the waves.

Even unutterably bad translations may have their virtues, it seemed, for one of those children was a New Jersey boy named Simon Lake. Within a decade of reading about Nemo and the *Nautilus* as a boy of twelve, he would be planning and then building a practical version of Verne's fanciful craft.

CHAPTER 6
FOR AN INDEPENDENT IRELAND

John Holland joined the underwater ranks inspired not by an adventure story or any nautical deed but rather by that most land-based of activities: farming, specifically potato farming, and the failure of Ireland's potato farmers to defeat the insects that ravaged a crop on which was based both their economy and their diet.

The result was the Great Famine, in which at least one million people in Ireland—one resident in eight—died of starvation or disease between 1845 and 1852, causing another million to flee the country, many if not most of them sailing across the Atlantic to America.

The incredible devastation aroused both deep resentment and fervent nationalism. Conviction was widespread that the English had at best sat on their hands and at worst engaged in a calculated policy of genocide. (To this day, debate over whether the anemic English response would qualify as genocide continues.) An uprising against the English had failed in 1796, and for almost six decades Irish nationalists had attempted to gain freedoms through peaceful negotiations. But the famine had ended all that. By the end of the 1850s, a number of new Irish nationalist groups had sprung up, all of which were either willing or eager to engage in armed struggle. Because the expatriate community was so large and vibrant, the push for Irish independence was equally fervent among those who had settled in the United States.

On March 17, 1858—St. Patrick's Day—James Stephens, still in Dublin, and John O'Mahony in New York City, members of a group called Young Irelanders, founded the Irish Republican Brotherhood, called the Fenian Brotherhood in the United States, taking the name from a band of legendary third century Gaelic warriors. The group, soon referred to as Fenians on both sides of the Atlantic, was a precursor of the twentieth-century Irish Republican Army. They wanted an Ireland totally free from English rule and, like just about every other of the nationalist groups, were convinced only violent overthrow could achieve their aims. At the Fenian Congress in Chicago in November 1863, the group swore "intense and undying hatred towards the monarchy and oligarchy of Great Britain." The English had "ground their country to the dust, hanging her patriots, starving out her people, and sweeping myriads of Irishmen, women, and children off their paternal fields, to find refuge in foreign lands."[1]

While the Fenians possessed no shortage of fervor, their execution could be lacking. A planned invasion of Canada in 1866 went awry when their chief-appointed strategist, a sympathetic Frenchman named Henri Le Caron, turned out actually to be Thomas Beach, an agent of the British Secret Service.* In fact, the Fenians were so rife with informants and so prone to infighting that the British were sometimes aware of their plots only hours after they had been hatched. Not surprisingly, many of their number were arrested and sentenced to long prison terms, some of the more prominent members shipped off to Australia.

---

* With so many Irish immigrants drafted to fight for the Union in the Civil War, the Fenians had a wealth of army veterans on whom to call. They sought to draw on the animosity toward Canada that had festered since Confederate raiders had openly used Quebec as a staging ground for attacks in Vermont in 1864. Fenians also believed that they had received veiled assurances that President Andrew Johnson would recognize an Irish republic north of the American border, although no formal commitment was ever forthcoming.

But a series of conspicuous failures in no way dulled Fenian ardor. In 1875, John Devoy, one of their more adept operatives, and John Boyle O'Reilly, approached the sympathetic captain of the whaling ship *Catalpa* and proposed a round-trip voyage to the west coast of Australia.* Western Australia was isolated and desolate, and Fremantle, Devoy's destination, was notable only for being home to one of the continent's more notorious penal colonies. O'Reilly had, in fact, escaped from Fremantle in 1869 when he broke away from a work detail and, after a harrowing trek through the jungle, had been able to secure a place on a departing freighter. Letters from other prisoners spoke of the horrible conditions, and Devoy and O'Reilly intended to free six Fenian leaders who had been sent to Australia in chains ten years earlier to begin life sentences.

Devoy told the captain of the plan and offered him enough money to quell any potential objections. No other member of the crew was aware of the true nature of the voyage when the *Catalpa* set sail from New Bedford, Massachusetts.

The scheme was audacious and complex, involving expert coordination and a good bit of guile. Soon after the *Catalpa* weighed anchor, a second ship, carrying the remainder of the rescue party, led by John J. Breslin, was to sail from San Francisco. When it arrived at Fremantle, Breslin, traveling as "James Collins," would convince the superintendent that he and his fellows were British officials, there for a surprise inspection. The flustered superintendent would then, it was hoped, arrange for an escort to conduct these "officials" on a tour of the prison. During the inspection, the Fenians would pass notes to the six prisoners, giving details of the escape. A seventh Fenian, whom the others suspected of being an informer, would be told nothing of the plan.

Although this was the very type of adventure for which the Fenians had previously exhibited striking ineptitude, Devoy, Breslin, and their comrades pulled it off. They overcame every obstacle they had anticipated and a number that they hadn't.

---

*   Devoy was one of a number of Fenians imprisoned in England who had been granted amnesty if he agreed to leave Great Britain. Almost all of the amnestied prisoners settled in America. Devoy had secured employment at the *New York Herald*, while O'Reilly was working for a newspaper in Boston.

The false inspection went off without a hitch. The superintendent was so credulous that he led the tour himself. So determined was he to demonstrate his fitness for the post that one of the Fenians had no trouble drifting away from the group and arranging details of the escape.

On April 17, 1876, Easter morning, two groups of prisoners set out from the prison, in theory for work details in the town. The imprisoned Fenians had become trustees and, with escape over land thought impossible, they were allowed to make the short journey unguarded.

The prisoners did not report for work, but rather, after trekking miles through underbrush, met the rescue party at a waiting whale-boat. As they rowed out to the *Catalpa*, which, for security reasons, had been forced to anchor far out in the bay, they saw police ride to the shore. They rowed for seven hours in heavy seas but still could not reach the ship. The six waited until morning when the seas had calmed before once again taking up the oars. As they began, they saw that a British frigate, the *Georgette*, was also steaming toward the *Catalpa*. The prisoners reached the ship just before the *Georgette*, but were seen getting on board. As the *Catalpa* was getting under way, the *Georgette* ordered it to halt or be fired upon. The captain of the *Catalpa* raised the colors and shouted, "If you fire on this ship, you fire on the American flag." After a brief standoff, the *Georgette* steamed off.[2]

By all accounts, the return voyage was a raucous affair, featuring copious bouts of drinking, roistering, and vomiting over the side. The captain was unable to quell the celebrations and found himself more or less captive on his own ship. With great relief, he discharged his passengers—now known as the "Fremantle Six"—in New York on August 19, 1876. They were greeted by a horde of well-wishers and the "*Catalpa* Rescue" made news around the world. So wondrous was the freeing of the six revolutionaries that the warring factions of the Fenian movement called a truce to celebrate as one.

Emboldened and united, the Fenians decided to plan their next spectacular demonstration of revolutionary zeal. At a celebration for their freed comrades, Devoy and Breslin sought out just the man who might help them provide it.

For about a year, John Holland had been trying unsuccessfully to persuade members of various factions within the Fenian movement that he could build a small, undetectable craft that could travel underwater and place an explosive charge to sink even the most intimidating British battleship. He even claimed to have completed a design for a one-man vessel that could carry four torpedoes. Holland was an amiable enough chap, and everyone was impressed by his obvious technical knowledge, so he wasn't rebuffed as much as humored. He had not been able to find a single person who would take him seriously.

But in the Fremantle Six euphoria, two men finally did.

How John Holland came to submarine research is not clear. There was no nautical background in his family—his father had patrolled the Irish coastline on horseback for the British Coastguard Service—and there is no record of him spending any time in a boat as a child. His mechanical aptitude had come to the fore at a Christian Brothers school, where, as the novitiate Brother Philip, he was under the tutelage of two outstanding science teachers, Brother Bernard O'Brien and Brother James Burke.

By his early twenties, Holland was teaching at a monastery in Cork. Although he showed great interest in drawing and "was constantly engaged in devising mechanical contrivances and in beautifying the grounds around the Monastery"—he designed and built a windmill to pump water—Holland most distinguished himself as a choirmaster.

In 1872, Holland's term of triennial vows ended and he had to decide whether to take perpetual vows and commit himself to the Christian Brothers for life. His mother and one of his brothers had immigrated to the United States earlier in the year and Holland decided to join them. Just before Christmas 1872, he informed the order of his decision and five months later, he boarded a ship at Liverpool bound for New York. Holland lived for a time in Boston—where he was bedridden for weeks after slipping on an ice-glazed street—but moved away and eventually found work as a schoolteacher in Paterson, New Jersey. Soon afterward, his younger brother Michael, active in the cause, introduced him to the Fenians.

Holland must have been tinkering with submarines for some time, because shortly after those introductions, he began to tout his invention to his Fenian acquaintances. His one-man craft, powered by a foot-treadle, showed great ingenuity—the operator would wear a diving helmet and breathe through tubes attached to a compressed air reservoir. But the notion that a volunteer would squeeze himself into a boat the size of a coffin and launch weapons with his feet seemed harebrained, to say nothing of suicidal. In late 1875, absent any encouragement from his countrymen, Holland approached the United States Navy, but with no better result.

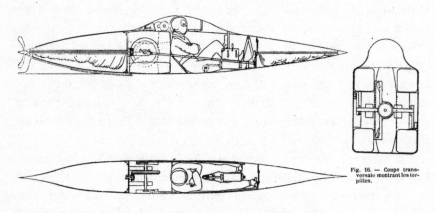

Fig. 16. — Coupe transversale montrant les torpilles.

Fig. 14 et 15. — Coupes verticale et horizontale du torpilleur sous-marin système Holland (1875).

Holland's one-man design

Before the *Catalpa* rescue, even had the Fenians wanted to employ Holland's invention, they could not have. Infighting and unwise expenditures had left the various competing factions virtually bankrupt. But after *Catalpa* docked in New York, money poured into Fenian coffers from Irish immigrants across America.

Suddenly the "Skirmishing Fund," as it was called—a pool from which each of the factions could draw—was bulging. Monies were allocated for any number of crackpot schemes. Delegations were sent to Russia, Mexico, and even to what is now Belize to determine if any of these locations could be a site to foment mischief against Great Britain. (For reasons never disclosed, Belize had been identified as a possible site for an independent Irish government in exile.)

At the reception for the newly freed prisoners, Devoy and Breslin approached Holland, who had come with his brother Michael, and queried him at great length about his potential super-weapon. Holland told them that he had already moved past the treadle to a mechanized design, which was much more sophisticated and powerful. The more Breslin and Devoy heard, they more they were convinced that the idea should be pursued. Devoy later wrote, "Holland was well-informed of Irish affairs and was anti-English and with clear and definite ideas of the proper method of fighting England. He was cool, good-tempered, and talked to us as a schoolmaster would to his children."[3] Although they refused to commit any monies, Devoy and Breslin told Holland that if he could create a working prototype, they would tap the Skirmishing Fund to create the actual submarine.

Inspiration for Holland's new design emanated from his visit to the 1876 International Exhibition of Arts, Manufactures, and Products of the Soil and Mine in Philadelphia, the first official World's Fair ever hosted within the United States. Among the exhibits celebrating the nation's centennial were such mechanical, agricultural, scientific, and cultural marvels as the bicycle, the typewriter, Heinz Ketchup, and Hires Root Beer. On display as well were the giant Corliss steam engine and the steam locomotive *John Bull*. There was also a new sort of engine, called the "Ready Motor" by its creator, an English inventor living in Boston named George Brayton. As reported in *Scientific American*, "The distinguishing features of this engine are that it can be started in a very short time, that it is economical in its consumption of fuel, and that, owing to the constant maintenance of carburetion, it is claimed, the danger of explosion of the hydrocarbon vapor is as greatly reduced as to be practically obviated."[4]

The operative word in that description was "hydrocarbon." The Brayton Ready Motor was an internal combustion engine, and it ran on a muscular new fuel—petroleum.* The motor that Brayton brought Philadelphia was huge—more than eight feet high and floor-mounted—but the principles seemed applicable to smaller versions, such as would be required to power a submarine. (Another interested spectator had been George Selden, who would create the first internal combustion engine to power a motorcar and later would become embroiled in a bitter and ultimately fruitless patent suit against Henry Ford.) Freeing up the operator and any sailors from supplying power to the propeller would allow the entire crew to focus on navigation, engine maintenance, and weapons delivery. And the weapon that a submarine could deliver had suddenly become more sophisticated as well.

Previously, a torpedo attack required a vessel to come virtually alongside its target and then make its escape before the explosion killed predator as well as prey, as it had with the *Hunley*. But two years after the *Hunley* sank, in 1866, Robert Whitehead, a British engineer, developed a torpedo that could power itself through the water and thus be delivered from a safe distance.

Born in 1823 to a cotton bleacher, Whitehead trained as an engineer and then moved to Europe to ply his trade. Eventually, he was hired by an Italian firm in Fiume, northeast of Venice, which built steam boilers and engines for sailing ships. Fiume was not far from the Austrian border and that nation's navy was one of Whitehead's customers. On a stay in Austria, he met Giovanni Luppis, a recently retired naval officer who had been attempting to perfect a self-propelled torpedo using compressed air as a power source. The two formed a partnership to continue the work.

Luppis's conception of a "torpedo boat" built to fire his projectile was unwieldy and impractical, so Whitehead substituted a design of

---

* Petroleum had been used as a crude lighting fuel for centuries, but the vast industrial potential of oil and its distillates was only then coming to be understood. The first modern refinery had been built less than twenty years earlier and America's first oil well had not been sunk until 1859. As petroleum and its by-products became adapted to commercial uses, it eventually became clear that pushing a piston by exploding a compressed mixture of, say, atomized gasoline and air was more efficient than steam power. In the early 1900s, with automobiles as the primary spur, internal combustion would replace steam.

his own, which included launching tubes mounted in the bow and the stern. He, as everyone, viewed the torpedo only as a surface weapon. An officer of the Austrian navy got wind of Whitehead's experiments and obtained authorization to purchase both the torpedoes and launching tubes and to then mount them in gunboats. The Austrians tried to keep tests of the new weapon secret, but word leaked out and naval officers across Europe became convinced that the "Whitehead torpedo," as it was soon known, must be part of their arsenal. A number of other nations purchased Whitehead's invention, each with the understanding that the specifications remain proprietary.

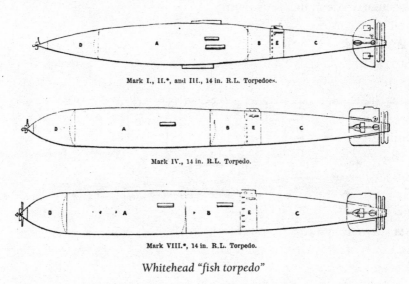

Mark I., II.*, and III., 14 in. R.L. Torpedoes.

Mark IV., 14 in. R.L. Torpedo.

Mark VIII.*, 14 in. R.L. Torpedo.

Whitehead "fish torpedo"

The United States, however, whose senior naval officials were notoriously conservative, resisted all entreaties by junior officers to purchase the new weapon. In 1875, Lieutenant Francis Barber, the navy's foremost expert on shipboard ordnance—and submarines, as it would turn out—gave a lecture to a group of admirals and senior commanders extolling Whitehead's device. "This remarkable invention, as at present furnished to the different European powers which have purchased the secret, is a vessel of very nearly the shape of a 'spindle of revolution,' of a length of nearly 14 feet, and a diameter of 14 inches. It is constructed of iron and steel, and carries an exploding charge of

20 lbs. of dynamite. It is driven by a propeller, the motive power being compressed air. Behind the propeller is a rudder capable of regulating the depth at which the torpedo shall go, and also keeping it straight or sending it on any curve which may be desired. The propeller is surrounded by a ring, and the bow compartment which contains the explosive, can be separated from the body of the torpedo for storage aboard ship in a suitable magazine, and this compartment is provided at its point with an arrow head to stick into the side of a wooden ship."[5] Since, as Barber noted, "Mr. Whitehead has so far succeeded in keeping the vital portions of his inventions perfectly secret," he included some speculative designs of his own.

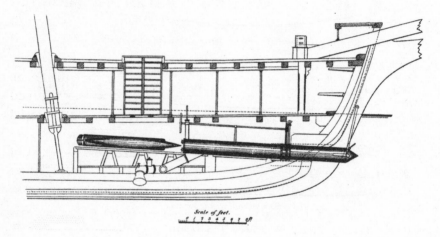

Scale of feet.

Torpedo boat

Barber's exhaustive research was for naught; he remained unsuccessful in softening the prejudices of his superiors. Still, despite a lack of specifics as to how to replicate Whitehead's invention, just the fact of its existence began to impact the design of surface ships. Once John Holland began to experiment, it was applied to submarines as well. In fact, he based the shape of what would be called the *Holland 1* on Whitehead's design.

But Holland did not include the torpedo itself. For his prototype, he was unconcerned with armaments. He was interested only in making navigation practicable and for that, stability was the key. Although his improved design was also a one-man affair, it would be much larger—fourteen feet long, although only three feet across. To keep weight distribution equal, the Brayton motor would be mounted in a center compartment, just forward of the conning tower. Compressed air tanks would be used to blow ballast, to surface, and to allow the operator to breathe if the vessel remained submerged for any length of time.

Even in this first model, two of Holland's great contributions to submarine technology were manifest. For the first, just as flight pioneers often studied birds to derive their designs, Holland took the porpoise as his model. To dive, rather than establish negative buoyancy, which would make handling more cumbersome, he used diving planes mounted just forward of center that could be swiveled downward. With the motor providing sufficient power, the boat could be forced under by the water flowing over the planes. In addition, if for any reason the engine were disabled, the vessel would float to the surface instead of sinking to the bottom, a feature that submarine crews would find appealing. Demonstrating that a craft that retained a store of positive buoyancy could submerge and run effectively proved key to the development of more advanced submarines.

His second insight was that a submarine needed a fixed center of gravity to maintain stability. If weight inside the craft shifted, either from movement within ballast tanks or the firing of a weapon, the center of gravity would shift as well. To counteract such changes, Holland installed a series of "trimming tanks," which would take on or discharge small amounts of ballast as needed to keep the boat on an even keel under the water. For general ballast and to help withstand water pressure, Holland employed a "double hull" a cylindrical chamber inside the outside skin. Water could be taken into or expelled from the gap between the two shells as needed.

He engaged the Albany City Iron Works in New York City to fashion his prototype and then moved it near his home in Paterson, New Jersey, for testing. In May 1878, Holland's machine was dragged by ropes from the back of a wagon into the Upper Passaic River. Although the Brayton motor proved balky at best—Holland was forced to run a steam line from a surface ship to get the engine to fire—the *Holland 1* actually performed like a submarine. In three different tests, for which John Breslin and two other Skirmishing Fund trustees were among the witnesses, Holland successfully submerged, cruised under the water at a depth of twelve feet, and then surfaced. William Dunkerly, an engineer Holland had hired to assist in the construction, patrolled along the surface in a launch, and described the event.

> Mr. Holland climbed into the submarine, closed the hatch, and started the engine. The bow went down first, and before we realized the fact, the boat was under twelve feet of water. The ropes were a safeguard in case the compressed air should not prove sufficient to expel the water from the ballast tanks. Holland was also given a hammer with which to rap upon the shell of the boat should he find himself in difficulties. After being submerged one hour, Holland brought the boat to the surface, to the great relief of all who were witnessing the test. As soon as the boat came up, the turret opened and Holland bobbed up smiling. He repeated his dive several times, and then he invited us to try it, but we preferred to "stick to the ropes." About the third trip we made up the river, a stranger was seen hiding behind the rocks on the river road. He had a powerful field glass, and it was said that he was an agent of the British Government.[6]

Even if the successful tests had not provided sufficient incentive, the rumor that the British might be interested surely did. The Skirmishing Fund trustees immediately offered to finance a larger Holland boat.

But the tests had also exposed flaws in Holland's design that would need to be corrected. "The vertical rudders, those that controlled horizontal motion, proved to be very effective," he noted, "but the horizontal rudders, placed on the level of the centre of buoyancy, proved to be useless. The boat should move three or four times more rapidly before they could produce a useful effect. This experiment showed the folly of attempting to control the degree of submergence of the boat by the employment of central horizontal rudders, a method on which so much importance was placed by some of my predecessors and successors."[7] From that point forward, Holland would not place diving planes amidships, but rather forward or aft, near the propellers, as all modern submarines are configured.

With no need to retain a model already obsolete, Holland removed all the equipment from his prototype and scuttled the *Holland 1* near the Spruce Street Bridge. Some local men retrieved the turret to sell as scrap and it was not until more than fifty years later that the remains of the hull of the first true submarine were raised and presented to the Paterson Museum, where they have been on exhibit ever since.

CHAPTER 7
THE *FENIAN RAM*

By 1879, the good fellowship engendered by the *Catalpa* rescue had faded—Fenian factions were again more bickering internally than fighting for an independent Ireland.

The most serious dispute was between Clan na Gael, among whose leaders were Devoy and Breslin, and an even more extreme and violent offshoot, which had retained the name Fenian Brotherhood. This latter sect was led by a fire-breathing, exiled former prisoner, Jeremiah O'Donovan Rossa. In 1864, Rossa had been given a life sentence for treason, but so harsh were his years in various British jails—at one point his hands were manacled behind his back for thirty-five straight days—that his treatment was widely seen as the impetus for William Gladstone to initiate the commutation for exile arrangement. (In 1874, Rossa published a detailed record of his captivity, *Prison Life: Six Years in Six English Prisons*, which scandalized the British and brought sympathy, particularly in America, to the Fenian cause.)

Rossa and Devoy, who had been serving a fifteen-year sentence, were released together, on the condition that they both leave Ireland forever. Those two, plus three other exiles, were placed on the SS *Cuba*—they became known as the "Cuba Five"—and shipped to the United States. On his arrival in America, Rossa and Devoy were greeted with an immense celebration, which included a torchlight parade. As did a number of other exiles, both took to journalism. Devoy got a job with the *New York Herald*, and Rossa started a nationalist newspaper, *The United Irishman*.

The two, each strong-willed and fervent, almost immediately came into conflict over tactics. Where Devoy thought in practical terms and favored "honorable warfare," Rossa was determined to initiate a bombing campaign—he would later be called "O'Dynamite Rossa"—to bring England to heel through terror. It was Rossa, and another radical, Patrick Ford—editor of another newspaper, *The Irish World*—who had first suggested the Skirmishing Fund, with whose proceeds they intended to fund their dynamite campaign against British interests in Europe and North America.

His enemies in Clan na Gael attempted to paint him as an unstable madman who drank too much and might sink them all, but Rossa was in reality more theatric than crazed. He favored guerilla warfare because he believed conventional military tactics would be useless against the British. (Even today, there is debate in Ireland over whether Rossa should be thought of as "the first terrorist.") He was also a charismatic showman who would have three wives and eighteen children, and had little patience for skulking about in secret. In his newspaper, Rossa took credit for any mishap that befell prominent Englishmen. When Queen Victoria slipped on a flight of stairs, Rossa insisted his followers had treated them with oil. He did not shy from American politics either—he railed against Tammany Hall corruption and Boss Tweed, and then ran for local office as a Republican (and lost). What infuriated Devoy and his fellow conspirators the most, however, was that Rossa had succeeded in making himself the face of the Irish rebellion in America.

Rossa had been against funding the submarine from the start. For him, every dollar not used to buy and plant dynamite was a dollar wasted. But Devoy was not without political skills of his own.

He maneuvered to deny access to the Skirmishing Fund to Rossa and Ford—although Rossa remained a trustee—and in 1878 had it renamed the "National Fund," to make clear that the money would be allocated as Clan na Gael saw fit. Devoy had become enamored with Holland's submarine and so Holland was given the go-ahead to set to work in May 1879. While it would be two years before it was ready for even preliminary testing, the *Holland 2*, as it was initially called, would represent a stunning leap forward in submarine technology.

Perhaps too stunning. Although sworn to the strictest secrecy, the Fenians once again proved completely inept in maintaining even a semblance of internal discipline. Whether it was Devoy's allies unable to keep quiet or Rossa's trying to sabotage the project, so public was the awareness of what Holland was up to that it could not even rise to the status of open secret. At least a half-dozen foreign navies heard about the project and pronounced themselves eager for a demonstration, and a seventh, Britain's, monitored Holland's progress as closely as if the boat were being built on the Thames. Moreover, progress reports appeared regularly in New York newspapers, along with the inconvenient snippet that the new craft had been financed by Irish nationalists. Because of the design, Blakely Hall, a reporter at the *New York Sun* dubbed the boat the *Fenian Ram*, and that was what it was called from then on, even by Holland.

With secrecy by then out of the question, and "public curiosity aroused," Hall pressed Holland to allow a series of feature articles to announce his invention publicly. "The same Mr. Blakely Hall seldom missed reporting every run or experiment we made while at Bay Ridge," Holland reported. "He explained to me that I was foolish in not wishing to advertise my invention, because the Government would certainly wish to acquire boats of the same type, as he could see by the newspaper reports that they were already preparing to build them in France."[1] But Holland was aware that the French experiments were not nearly as advanced as his own and also that if he drew further attention to himself, his access to Fenian funds might cease.

By June 1881, Holland was ready to put his boat in the water. Although it seemed clear that his creation would eventually work, refining the design would take almost two years, delays that only inflamed the volatile Rossa. "Fifty fires like that," he would write in the *United Irishman*, referring to dynamite blasts, "would frighten England more than fifty rams lying dead in Jersey mud."[2] Had Rossa know that Holland's experiments would cost nearly $60,000 of the $90,000 the Skirmishing—now National—Fund had taken in between 1877 and 1880, he might have been moved to violence against his former brethren, but Devoy made certain to keep itemized expenditures secret.

Whether or not he would create the means to cripple the British navy, what the Fenians did get for their money was an extraordinary machine, by far the most advanced undersea vessel ever conceived. Holland's boat was thirty-one feet long, six in diameter, and sharply tapered at either end. It had a shallow conning turret, and was powered by a two-cylinder, seventeen-horsepower Brayton-cycle engine that Holland had reworked to improve its performance. Compressed air compartments in the bow and stern kept the *Ram* positively buoyant, while also providing breathable air to the crew. Compartments for water ballast were placed fore and aft, both capable of being minutely adjusted to maintain an even keel. The design was ingenious—the *Fenian Ram* was the first submarine able to maintain a fixed center of gravity and therefore longitudinal stability. Holland had solved the exhaust problem by installing a "check valve," a one-way door that would close when no exhaust was emitting from the motor, with a compressed air barrier serving to prevent leakage.

Fenian Ram

The boat carried a crew of three. The operator was positioned amidships, and sat "in a kind of bucket seat perched over the engine." He controlled two levers, one for the rudder and the other for the diving planes. While surfaced, if he stood on the seat, his head and shoulders would protrude from the conning tower. The engineer ran the motor, monitored the flow of fuel and air, maintained constant pressure inside the hull, and controlled the water ballast, which could be blown in an emergency to send the boat quickly to the surface. The third crewman would fill a role not heretofore assigned in any vessel built to cruise underwater—weapons control.

Holland had built into his design a pneumatic gun—a nine-inch tube, eleven feet long, which ran through the center of the forward air compartment—which, using compressed air, could fire an underwater missile designed by John Ericsson, who had also designed the Civil War ironclad USS *Monitor*. Ericsson's torpedo was, according to its inventor, superior to the Whitehead fish, which had yet to be proven capable of being launched from a submerged vessel.

Since the *Fenian Ram* was already to carry a store of compressed air, the gun's placement and mechanics were typical of Holland's clever, efficient designs. "Its breech of heavy iron casting was centered in the forward water-ballast tank, opening by means of a hinged door into the control compartment. With the pointed bow cap screwed down into a watertight position, the gunner's task was to undo the inner door, load a six-foot projectile into the tube, shut the inner door, turn a crank which opened the bow cap, reach down and unscrew the balance valve sending a four-hundred-pound air charge into the breech, and thus fire the projectile. Water rushed in to fill the tube. The gunner cranked the bow cap closed. Then he blew the tube forcing the water into the ballast tank that surrounded it, and restoring the fixed center of gravity."[3]

When the *Fenian Ram* was finally launched for operational testing, the results were spectacular. Even during the shakeout cruises, which began in June 1881, Holland was able to remain submerged for hours. On one occasion, the men at the dock became so frightened when the boat did not surface "that they began to grapple for the hull in an effort to raise her."[4]

By mid-1883, Holland was cruising to the Narrows in New York Harbor and along the Brooklyn shore at depths up to fifty feet. The vessel could make nine knots on the surface and nearly that submerged. Young boys took to loitering about in rowboats where Holland was testing the *Ram*, hoping to get a tour inside. Holland, "the schoolteacher," was always happy to oblige. But not everyone was so taken with Holland's craft. During one trial run in the Narrows, "the captain of the ferryboat *St. Johns* observed a strange metal monster spouting a mass of water as it reared up in a steep, porpoise-like dive. He brought the ferryboat to a sudden stop; whereupon the monster disappeared below the surface of the harbor. Shaken by the apparition, the captain suddenly turned his vessel in a hasty retreat for shore." Witnesses watching from shore broke out in laughter, "jumping around and acting as if demented." When Holland reached the dock, one of the men guffawed, "You frightened the devil out of the *St. Johns*."[5]

"There is scarcely anything required of a good submarine boat that this one did not do well enough, or fairly well," Holland wrote later. "It could remain quite a long time submerged, probably three days; it could shoot a torpedo containing a 100 pound charge to 50 or 60 yards in a straight line underwater and to some uncertain range, probably 300 yards over water."[6] Lighting the boat, however, remained a nagging problem; at fifty feet, there was insufficient light for the engineer to read the pressure gauges. Holland eventually carried a lantern that he used for only brief periods so as not to deplete the air supply. Those were the only times he could check the compass he used to maintain course.

As successful as he was, Holland had ideas on how to improve maneuverability, speed, range, and navigation. He not only tinkered with his design, but also built a sixteen-foot, one-ton model on which he intended to experiment. By this time, even the United States Navy began to express some tentative interest in Holland's handiwork.

But the *Ram* was not destined to be the navy's prototype submarine, the Fenians', nor anyone else's.

While the course of the events that doomed Holland's boat is not in dispute, what sparked the drama is unclear. The bitter factional disputes in the Fenian ranks had escalated, so much so that a Clan na Gael member, one Denis Mulcahy, actually sued the Skirmishing Fund's trustees—National Fund had not stuck—for his unreimbursed expenses in returning a dead Fenian's body to Ireland. (The suit was eventually thrown out.) The reason Mulcahy was left to foot his own bills was that funds were getting tight. Although the exact amount spent on the submarine was known to only a few, the sum was obviously quite large and there seemed no date in the foreseeable future when it would be employed as a weapon against the British navy. Rumblings began that perhaps the boat should be sold to recoup expenses and the proceeds applied to more practical pursuits. (Rossa knew precisely what those should be.) When Holland learned of these sentiments, he voiced his concerns to John Breslin, his official liaison to the nationalists. Breslin, fearing to be the focal point of growing suspicion of financial mismanagement, publicly attacked Holland for profligacy. Holland appealed to another of the fund's trustees, a more sympathetic ear, who then tried to persuade Breslin to allocate an additional $15,000 to build a fleet of submarines. At that point, however, the fund no longer had $15,000 in its account.

Distrust and recrimination remained unabated when, after midnight one night in late November 1883, a tugboat pulled up to the dock where the *Fenian Ram* was moored. When the night watchman inquired, a group of men stepped forward, one of whom handed the watchman a pass signed by John P. Holland, with instructions that the submarine be towed away to an undisclosed location for safekeeping. The watchman, seeing nothing out of the ordinary about such an order, given that everything surrounding the building, testing, and possession of the boat seemed bizarre, gave the tugboat crew leave to haul it away. The sixteen-foot prototype seemed to fall under the same aegis, so that was secured by a towline to the larger vessel. As the tugboat with the two vessels in tow steamed off, the watchman was doubtless quite pleased to be relieved of them both.

So pleased that he had made only a cursory examination of Holland's signature on the pass, which was in fact a clumsy forgery. Holland would not hear of the boat's departure until the following morning, when he arrived at the shipyard. And the man who handed the note to the watchman was John Breslin. Why Breslin chose to steal the product of at least two-thirds of the precious Skirmishing Fund dollars was never ascertained. Perhaps it was to keep it away from Rossa, or even from Holland, each of whom might sell the vessel and pocket the proceeds. But for whatever reason Breslin committed the act, he did so with stunning ineptitude. Half of his haul never made it out of the East River. He had neglected to secure the hatch of the sixteen-foot model, and it was swamped in the choppy water. The weight of the water snapped the towrope and it sank, never to be seen again.

The full-size *Fenian Ram* was taken to New Haven, where it was secreted in the harbor. There, Breslin and his mates decided to use the new weapon on their own, although it was unclear against who or what, but they discovered only then that it was a bit more complicated to operate than they'd thought.

"I am told," Holland wrote later, "that they attempted to make dives, but handled the boat so awkwardly that the harbor master decided that she constituted a 'menace to navigation,' and demanded a bond if any further trials were to be made. As a result she was hauled out of the water on the property of [James] Reynolds, another member of the committee, and there she still is. There is also a rumor that they have tried to sell her to the Russian Government, but failed, as on investigation the prospective buyers found that title to her was not clear."[7]At that point, Clan na Gael contacted Holland and asked for his help in sailing the boat they'd stolen from him. Holland refused. "I received no notice of the contemplated then, nor was I notified after. I'll let her rot on their hands," he said. From there, the trustees of the Skirmishing Fund announced they would no longer finance submarine research, which was moot because Holland was through with the lot of them.*

---

*   Rossa finally got his dynamite campaign. He began a "dynamite school" in New York and then shipped his trainees across the Atlantic and orchestrated the bombings in key English sites, including Whitehall, Victoria Station, the House of Commons, and the Tower of London. He became a reviled figure in England and a revered one in Ireland. Rossa and Devoy remained estranged until 1915, when Rossa was on his deathbed. His funeral in Dublin was attended by thousands and served as a rallying call for the Easter Rising, which took place ten months later.

Having no further use for it, Clan na Gael abandoned the boat in New Haven and left the most advanced submarine ever built to the mercy of the elements. Eventually, they had the boat hauled ashore and deposited in a lumber shed. They gave the Brayton engine to a foundry owner to operate a forge. There it sat until 1916, when the *Fenian Ram* was brought to Madison Square Garden and exhibited to raise money for victims of the Easter Rising. In 1927, Edward Browne purchased the boat and moved it to Paterson, where it joined its predecessor at the Paterson Museum.

CHAPTER 8
COMPETITION FROM THE CLERGY

F ew innovators work in a vacuum. Ideas, as they near practical application, will spawn a variety of approaches. As a result, whether or
not inventors are even aware of the existence of their competitors,
the process is generally more a race than a solo journey. Gutenberg had
challengers, as did Newton, the Wright brothers, Alexander Graham
Bell, and Henry Ford. One of those with whom Holland had to compete
was an eccentric English clergyman, George William Littler Garrett,
and his creation *Resurgam* ("I will rise again" in Latin), which may—
or may not—have been at the finish line with the *Fenian Ram* as the
world's first successful motorized submarine.

Garrett was born a decade after Holland, on July 4, 1852, in London,
son of an Anglican curate. Soon afterward, the family moved to Moss
Side, in central Manchester, where Garrett received his early education. Industrialization was raging in the city, with new inventions and
manufacturing processes introduced seemingly by the day. By the time
Garrett left for Trinity University in Dublin, at age seventeen—where

a fellow student would be Oscar Wilde—he had studied chemistry and mechanics, and been thoroughly inculcated with the miracles of applied science. He was a brilliant student, reported to have passed all his first-year undergraduate examinations in one week. While at Trinity, he accepted a headmaster's post at a local school, and then was made a master at the Manchester Mechanics' Institute, where he also passed examinations in chemistry, geology, geography, general science, and art.

Still in his teens, Garrett left Dublin for London to take instruction in the science department of the South Kensington Museum (now the Victoria and Albert.) He squeezed some theological training into his studies as well, because when he returned to Manchester to teach mechanics, he was appointed by the local bishop as a deacon at Christchurch, his father's curacy.

After Garrett received his bachelor's degree in 1875, he left almost immediately to spend a year traveling around the world. His itinerary included such exotic stops as New Zealand and Fiji, by which time he had become sufficiently versed in marine navigation to be allowed to teach the subject. When he returned to Manchester, he was ordained, took up his position in the church, got married, and had a child. George Garrett was not yet twenty-five years old.

Garrett never said specifically why he turned his attention to submarines, although some members of his family claimed that, ironically, the Fenian riots of the mid-1870s led him to attempt to build a weapon that could effectively protect British ports and harbors from unfriendly incursion. But Garrett's father and son also cited two incidents in 1877 during the Russo-Turkish War as spurring him to build a tool of attack and not just defense. In both, Russian torpedo boats were unable to penetrate anti-torpedo defenses—chains stretched across the water's surface—to attack Turkish warships anchored in the Black Sea. Garrett supposedly decided that surface defenses could be penetrated by a submarine cruising under the surface, which could then attach explosive charges to an enemy's hull.

At about the time John Holland launched the *Holland 1*, George Garrett took on two projects simultaneously. The first was to build an undersea vessel and the second was to create a diving suit that would allow a man to breathe inside that vessel. Such a suit could be used on its own, of course, and could also be employed in coal mines in case of a cave-in, of which there were many in the British midlands.

Garrett seemed to have had some success with the breathing apparatus, which he called a "pneumatophore," although details of its design and construction remain vague. There are no surviving drawings, but it almost certainly did not resemble modern scuba equipment. His brother described it as a "sort of diving helmet with a knapsack attachment," but his son (who was too young at the time to give a first-person account), wrote that it was "a chemical device contained in a case attached to a regulation diving suit doing away with the air tubes which are a source of discomfort and danger." Garrett's brother added that Garrett, "was always dabbling with chemistry and scientific subjects" and his "starting point was his discovery that caustic potash will absorb carbonic acid given off in a man's breath . . . The pneumatophore provided for the absorption of carbonic gas by means of sticks of caustic potash, and then he had an attachment for supplying oxygen."[1]

Unfortunately, there is no record of what this "attachment" was and whether it was internal or external to the device. But whatever the configuration, two journal accounts of a demonstration in Paris, each purportedly by an expert eyewitness assigned by the French marine ministry, were translated and published in the *Manchester Courier* in May 1880. They described Garrett descending into the Seine and remaining underwater for thirty-seven minutes and then emerging "in perfect health and spirits." It is possible that the reports were fabrications, since, despite its success, neither the French nor any other government or industrial concern sought to purchase Garrett's invention, nor even to fund further research.

The issue would be largely moot, however. Garrett had not designed his breathing apparatus for underwater sojourns but to overcome one of the two primary obstacles he saw in creating an effective submarine. So, in addition to developing "some handy and effective method for purifying human breath," he needed to find "some motive power . . . which would not betray the position of such a vessel by giving off smoke or other evidence of her whereabouts."

While Garrett certainly intended to employ some form of mechanical propulsion, he began his submarine research much as had Holland, with a one-man, manually powered craft, only theoretically capable of carrying a weapon. And like Holland, his first design never made it past the drawings. But Garrett soon designed a more sophisticated one-man vessel that was built and tested, although once more how effectively is uncertain. However it performed, Garrett sought a patent for his design in spring 1878.

This craft, which marine historians have dubbed "the Egg," for its ovoid shape, did not employ Garrett's breathing device—no man or machine ever would—but required the operator to sit in the center with his head protruding from the conning tower except for the short distances the vessel could travel underwater. Two gloves made of oil-soaked leather were attached to the outside of the conning tower, which would, in theory, be used to attach a mine to the hull of an enemy ship. Power was supplied by a handwheel, and another wheel operated a piston that would take in or expel water to fine-tune buoyancy. Ballast was adjusted by means of a third hand control, and the rudder and horizontal planes by a fourth.[2]

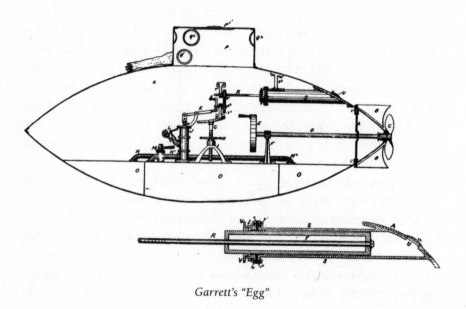

Garrett's "Egg"

Although he was "extremely secretive" about his work and gave no specific details, Garrett implied that this design, of which there were at least two more sophisticated redrafts, performed creditably in tests. It is difficult, however, to imagine a one-man-band layout so unwieldy as to require the manipulation of four different wheels or levers at roughly the same time achieving anything more than frustrating anyone who took on the task. At one point, Garrett's brother reported that one of the gauntlets split, sending a torrent of water into the hull, which Garrett, after furious bailing, finally managed to clear.

Garrett paid great attention to the state of research and potential competitors. When news reached England of the *Holland 1*—and that it was powered mechanically—Garrett abandoned the egg design and set to work finding a propulsion system. What he settled on was clever and creative, a power source that would seem to allow his boat to run both on and below the surface while maintaining the stealth that an attacking submarine required. It was called the "fireless steam engine," and at the time was most notably used to power French streetcars.

The motor had originally been fabricated by Émile Lamm, a dentist and inventor who, in 1848, at age fourteen, had emigrated with his parents from Paris to New Orleans. In the late 1860s, after service in the Confederate army, Lamm took out a patent for "sponge gold," a more effective gold filling. During the same period, he also decided he could improve the quality of New Orleans life by limiting the sooty, gag-inducing exhaust fumes that were spewed from the city's steam-powered streetcars. In 1869, he introduced an ingenious engine where a piston was driven by boiling off pressurized ammonia housed in a series of holding tubes, which would reduce the pressure in the tubes, resulting in more ammonia boiling off. All that was required to initiate the process was to heat water in a tank surrounding the tubes, which were kept closed to allow the pressure to build. This might take up to three days, but once the proper temperatures and pressures were reached, the engine would run for some distance emission-free.

New Orleans officials were enthralled and installed Lamm's motors on the St. Charles Avenue streetcar. Two years later, Lamm came up with a way to use steam power instead of the more-difficult-to-handle ammonia, a design he patented in 1872. He was on the verge of selling the new engine for widespread use when, on July 15, 1873, he drowned after he fell out of his boat while fishing on Lake Pontchartrain.

After Dr. Lamm's death, interest in fireless steam engines waned until a Frenchman, Léon Francq, happened on the technology in 1878 and proposed using it on Paris trams. Garrett read of Francq's tramcars and realized that here was a steam motor that, in a submarine, could run in the conventional manner on the surface, with boiler smoke vented through an exhaust pipe, then shut down and run on stored steam when submerged. As with ammonia, as water boiled in the reservoir and the resulting steam was channeled to drive a piston, the decreased pressure would cause more water to boil, creating more steam.[3]

In 1879, Garrett mounted his engine in his design, which he named *Resurgam*.

This new model, forty feet long, was a huge improvement over the Egg, and for more than its innovative power source. The gloves were gone and four ports in the conning tower allowed for much better vision. It took a crew of three, two of whom would man the boiler and the motor.

But as sophisticated as the design appeared, it was riddled with flaws. The center section was cylindrical, but the front and rear sections were cones, creating inefficient hydrodynamics where they were all joined. Buoyancy and longitudinal stability would be problematic at best. *Resurgam* carried no ballast tanks, no means of adjusting buoyancy while at sea. Even worse, buoyancy was set to be near neutral when the *Resurgam* set sail, but would become more positive as the coal store was burned. Controlling the boat would thus be progressively more difficult and the engine would need to work harder and harder to dive. Horizontal planes, placed amidships, were Garrett's only means of keeping his boat submerged. Holland also relied on his motor for downward momentum but had learned the diving planes needed to be placed fore and aft. Placing them in the center of craft would only exacerbate the instability.

Even without the control issues, sailing *Resurgam* would be a nightmare for the crew. The boiler and engine took up most of the space, so the engineer and fireman would be impossibly cramped. And the heat within the hull would be stifling, even running with the hatch open. When it was closed and the boat ran submerged, it would be near to unbearable.

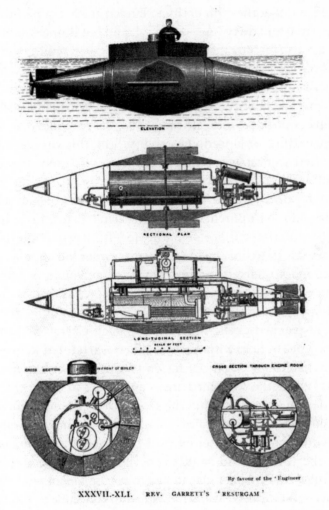

XXXVII.-XLI.   REV.   GARRETT'S   'RESURGAM'

Resurgam

Garrett claims to have conducted any number of positive tests at Liverpool, and then, on December 10, 1879, sailed from Birkenhead, across the River Mersey, to Rhyl, down the coast, a distance of approximately twenty miles. Although there were no published reports of this voyage, Garrett kept a detailed log, which was published in Liverpool newspapers the following week. In it, he claimed that *Resurgam* sailed for thirty-six hours without incident, both on the surface and submerged and that the crew of three "landed at Rhyl in perfect health but rather tired and dirty." A "good wash and hot dinner" was all that was needed to "restore their comfort," and "we could congratulate ourselves on having passed successfully through as novel and interesting a trip as any sailor could wish to experience."[4] Garrett did not, however, provide details on how long the boat ran submerged and at what depth. Nor did he indicate how *Resurgam* responded to shifts in either longitudinal or latitudinal stability. Still, this voyage—if it had been reported accurately—would be the first time a submarine sailed successfully fully under mechanical power.

Garrett decided the time had come to unveil *Resurgam* to potential purchasers, and so he purchased a yacht, *Elphin*, to tow his submarine to naval headquarters at Portsmouth. He left Liverpool on the night of February 24, 1880, just before high tide, under fair weather and an almost full moon. Garrett and his crew remained on *Resurgam*, while the yacht's captain maneuvered west along the Welsh coast. But only about forty miles into the voyage, *Elphin* developed engine trouble. A skiff was dispatched to the submarine to fetch Garrett and the crew so that they might help with repairs. When Garrett left *Resurgam*, he closed the hatch but could not fasten it shut as it only sealed from the inside. While the combined crews attempted to repair the yacht's engine, the wind picked up and the seas with it. Water began to pour into the submarine, which quickly settled deeper into the water. The lower it sank, the more water entered the hatch and *Resurgam* soon snapped the towline and sank to the bottom. Compounding the disaster, the steam tugboat dispatched to rescue *Elphin* pitched in the heavy seas and rammed the yacht instead. It too sank to the bottom.

Neither vessel was insured. In one night, John Garrett went from the verge of a seemingly great triumph to having neither a submarine nor the funds to build another. The Admiralty, which had overcome a century of resistance and finally showed some interest in undersea navigation, promptly lost it. Garrett, his resources exhausted, took a job as an engineer, helping design the docks at a minor British seaport.

In 1881, as part of this assignment, he traveled to London to investigate arc lighting, where he met a Swedish arms manufacturer, Thorsten Nordenfelt. After a brief stint in banking, Nordenfelt had turned to steelmaking and then weaponry. He had bankrolled a Swedish engineer who had designed a multibarreled gun, one of the stipulations that the weapon be called the Nordenfelt gun. He made the same proposal to Garrett. He would supply the financing, lease the shipyard facilities, and handle logistics, for which Garrett would receive a percentage of the profits for the Nordenfelt submarine. Garrett accepted.

They would build four boats together, *Nordenfelt I* to *IV*.

The first boat, begun in 1882, was sixty feet long, nine wide, and cigar-shaped, an improvement over *Resurgam*. Garrett had built in an extremely clever set of features. The hull was fitted with a retractable glass dome conning tower in the center to allow the operator a full field of vision when the vessel ran awash. When submerged, an iron cover kept water out. There were three engines, all of which ran on steam and the Lamm reserve principle: one for the main screw, and one for each of two vertical side propellers that Garrett had installed to help the boat remain submerged. These motors were vented through a stack that was also retractable, fitted with a similar iron cover. The side propeller motors were designed to be controlled automatically, with a mechanism that would sense depth through pressure and engage or disengage as appropriate.

According to Garrett, the boat ran well both on the surface and submerged, and so, in the summer of 1885, Nordenfelt considered it time to stoke demand for his product. In September 1885, he scheduled a three-day test off the coast of Sweden, where the *Nordenfelt I* had been built—Nordenfelt was a partner in a shipyard there—and to make the event as much a social event as a technical one.

Nordenfelt's talent as a marketer proved every bit the match for his skill as an engineer. To make certain the boat's triumph received the international coverage it deserved, he persuaded an impressive group of luminaries to attend, including the king and queen of Denmark, the empress of Russia, and the prince and princess of Wales. The assembled nobility, accompanied by an entourage of military officers and retainers, were to observe the new miracle boat from the deck of a luxury yacht, which Nordenfelt had stocked with an imposing array of accoutrements to help persuade his guests to speak well of the experience. The press would be well represented as well; the *London*

Times, among other newspapers, sent a reporter specifically to cover the festivities. All that was needed was for the *Nordenfelt I* to perform as George Garrett had assured his benefactor it would.

It did not.

The first day was plagued by mechanical problems, and on the second, Nordenfelt was very cautious in running underwater, and even on the surface. Only on the third day, "in a very calm sea," did the submarine "exhibit her power of moving under water, disappearing for periods never exceeding 4½ minutes, and moving for distances apparently of about 300 yards." In running with stealth, the boat was largely a success. "There was no smoke or escaping steam to proclaim her presence at a distance of many miles, and up to 1,500 yards range at least she could probably advance with absolute impunity."

But in approaching awash, as the Nordenfelt would have to do, risk of discovery was manifest, especially if sailors on a surface ship knew what to look for. "Riding light on a grey, and almost motionless sea, the hull of the torpedo boat was scarcely visible at 1,000 yards. In spite of her light grey color, however, the vertical combings supporting the cupola showed out dark on account of the abrupt change in the angle of reflection. Thus, viewed broadside on, the appearance was that of a short dark log lying on the surface of the water. In this position, and in a calm sea, the wash of the screw was visible, and in broad daylight could hardly fail to attract attention. It was generally felt, however, that such a boat advancing end on at speed would offer a particularly unsatisfactory mark to fire at, even with machine guns; while in a bad light it would be almost impossible to shoot with any chance of effect."[5]

Still, early accounts in scientific journals were largely positive. "Mr. Nordenfelt's invention appears to fulfill the numerous requirements necessary for overcoming the difficulties and dangers of maintaining, driving and directing a boat beneath the water," wrote *Science* magazine. (An almost verbatim account also appeared in *Scientific American.*) "When it is wished to sink the boat, enough seawater is taken in to reduce the buoyancy till the tower is just above the surface. The side propellers being then set in motion, the vessel can be sunk to any required depth, there being an automatic arrangement by which the engines are stopped directly that depth is exceeded. An automatic horizontal steering gear also prevents the boat from going down or up headforemost, an even keel being preserved throughout all the maneuvers. Should a breakdown of the engine occur, the boat from its own buoyancy at once rises to the surface."[6]

But for all the improvements and creative touches, the *Nordenfelt I* contained fatal design flaws. One was the inability to vent the intense heat in the cabin, especially when submerged. Simon Lake later reported, "A former chief engineer of Mr. Nordenfelt informed me that the heat from the large amount of hot water stored up in the reservoirs—for submerged power—made the interior of the vessels almost unbearable for the crew when the hatches were shut down, and that he did not believe the submarines ever made any submerged runs after being delivered." Lake added, "I also judge from his description of his experiences with the vessels, that they lacked longitudinal stability and were difficult to hold in the horizontal position, which Mr. Nordenfelt claimed was a sine qua non for a submarine boat."[7]

According to another expert, the vertical propellers, necessary to keep the boat submerged, were a major contributor to the stability problem. "However accurately a mechanical contrivance might be made for the regulation of this machinery," he wrote, "there is little doubt but that a boat fitted in this way would steer a very erratic course, the depth of the deviations in the vertical sense being regulated by the amount of reserve buoyancy. The course of these submarines was found on experiment to be 'jagged,' since the action of the propellers prevented the deviations being made in the long smooth swoops that characterizes the 'errors of route' of the submarines fitted with horizontal planes or rudders."[8] In other words, the submarine would not run at a constant depth but rather in a sawtooth manner, and need constant ballast or speed adjustments to keep it on course.

American Engineer, a respected trade journal, had many good things to say about the concept of submarines for both attack and defense, but said of the *Nordenfelt I*, "Certain defects are obvious. The speed is insufficient; the period of twelve hours required to get up pressure is too long; there is no means of getting in or out of the boat when it is submerged; the perfecting of the vertical steering arrangements is perhaps doubtful."[9]

But flaws or no, Nordenfelt's demonstration turned out to be a success—he found a buyer for his submarine. Greece, then under threat from its traditional enemy, the Ottoman Empire, purchased the *Nordenfelt I* for £9,000. Just why the Greek admirals thought to purchase what even George Garrett's biographer called a "white elephant," is not known. "The *Nordenfelt I* was never used operationally by the Hellenic Navy, and probably never fired its main armament."[10] The only explanation seems to be psychological. "Greece had acquired a hidden asset, a secret weapon which they knew did not pose a real threat (except to the boat's crew), but which was of real concern to their traditional enemy."[11]

If that was the ploy, the Greeks were unsuccessful. As soon as the Turks got wind of the purchase, they contacted Nordenfelt and ordered two submarines for their own navy. Nordenfelt rushed the Turkish boats into production. Garrett made a number of changes to attempt to improve performance but lacked the time to properly reengineer his design. Both boats were delivered by May 1887, only five months after the order had been placed. The sultan renamed the boats the *Abdul Hamid* and *Abdul Mecid*, the first for himself and the second for his brother. The *Abdul Hamid* was demonstrated with great fanfare in 1887, and, like the Greek boat, it cut a sleek figure on the surface but performed poorly under it. It did succeed in firing a Whitehead torpedo while submerged, the first submarine to do so successfully, although it was for demonstration purposes only, not at a target, and seems to have veered sharply off course. Nonetheless, the sultan was sufficiently impressed to take delivery and pay Nordenfelt an undisclosed sum, which might have been substantially less than the Greeks had paid for an inferior boat.[12] But also like the Greek boat, neither Turkish vessel was ever put into service, either in combat or for coastal defense. All three were ultimately left to languish and eventually cut up for scrap.

Nordenfelt's continued lack of success did not deter him. Even before the Turkish boats were delivered, he laid the keel for the *Nordenfelt IV*, his most ambitious effort. One hundred twenty feet long, and twelve across, it carried a crew of nine and was fitted with two torpedo tubes and a more powerful engine, which could make fifteen knots on the surface and five submerged. The shape was odd—cylindrical in the center, but tapering into flat vertical edges fore and aft. One-inch steel armor plate protected the deck and dual conning towers from gunfire from surface vessels. The diving propellers remained but operated in recesses cut into the top of the hull instead of in the open.

But bigger and more powerful did not necessarily mean better performing. The new vessel "suffered from the same want of horizontal stability as her elder sisters, and her trials were not at all encouraging. Despite the unsatisfactory nature of her performance she was dispatched to St. Petersburg. But she never got there, as she was wrecked on the coast of Jutland on September 18, 1888."[13] After the wreck, which had been caused solely by inherent instability, the Russian government canceled the contract, leaving the boat as a total loss. With that, Thorsten Nordenfelt was finished with both submarines and with George Garrett.

The saga of the Nordenfelt submarine was not quite done, however. It turned out that the positive reports of the four submarines' performances—many of which emanated from George Garrett—had also been influenced by Nordenfelt and his high-placed friends. It was not until more than a decade later that the full truth came out. In February 1901, the British journal *Engineer* published a full account. These reports are useful not only as a testament to Nordenfelt's willingness to end-run performance requirements but also as an indication of just how difficult designing a practical submarine was.

Of the *Nordenfelt IV*, *Engineer* wrote, "To all intents and purposes the Nordenfelt was a total failure as a submarine boat." The magazine found more than one fatal flaw. "As soon as she was launched from the stocks at Barrow, it was seen that a mistake had been made in calculating weight, as she was down by the stern, drawing 9 feet aft and about 4 feet 6 inches forward. This would have been partially rectified by her torpedoes, but she never had one on board. Extra ballast had to be put in forward, and it was always held, rightly or wrongly, that this made it all the more difficult to keep her on an even keel when submerged. The extra weight carried mitigated greatly against her speed as a surface boat."

The boat's ballasting was no better. "Another mistake was that the water-ballast tanks were too large, or perhaps it would be more correct to say that they were not sufficiently subdivided. When she was in just the proper condition to be manoeuvred by her horizontal propellers, the ballast tanks were only about three quarters full, and the water being left free surges backwards and forwards in them." Any surge of ballast water, of course, would have upset the boat's stability. "If, for example . . . water surged forward in the tank, she would proceed to plunge, unless checked, and in shallow water would touch the bottom, or if in deep water she would run down until the pressure of water collapsed her hull. No one who has not been down in a submarine can realise their extraordinary crankiness. The Nordenfelt was always rising or falling, and required the greatest care in handling.[14]

With all this, however, the Garrett/Nordenfelt boats occupy a singular place in the history of technology. While they may have not been successful in navigating as submarines, they did succeed in sparking the first undersea arms race. And in doing so, Nordenfelt and Garrett piqued what had been moribund interest in a number of admiralties for whom submarines had previously evoked only sneers or snickers, and thereby set the stage for the next wave of innovation.

———

As do many who brush against fame and glory only to watch it evaporate, after Nordenfelt terminated their partnership, George Garrett's plunge into degeneracy was precipitous and tragic. In 1890, he packed up his family, sailed across the Atlantic, and bought a 150-acre farm on the shores of Lake Tohopekaliga, in central Florida. There is no record of why Garrett chose such an unlikely location in which to settle, or even why he immigrated to the United States. But the decision in any event seemed ill considered. The farm failed in two years and Garrett was left with neither an income nor an occupation.

Then in a move even more bizarre, George Garrett, then forty years old, moved his family to New York, where he joined the United States Revenue Service, signing on as ordinary seaman aboard one of the service's steamships, which sailed out of Galveston, Texas. He was promoted to seaman first class, than promptly busted back to ordinary seaman for "incompetency."[15] The following year he was discharged, after a stay in the ship's hospital with an undisclosed ailment.

Garrett rejoined his family in New York, but soon afterward, apparently desperate, traveled to Europe to solicit aid from Thorsten Nordenfelt. None was forthcoming. He returned to New York and enlisted in the army, to join the war against Spain. He was assigned to an engineering company in Puerto Rico, promoted to corporal, busted to private for drunkenness and ultimately discharged, likely for the same reason. Back in New York, Garrett worked at a variety of jobs for the next three years. On February 26, 1902, afflicted with chronic respiratory problems likely exacerbated by alcohol, George Garrett died at Metropolitan Hospital in New York City. He was forty-nine years old.

CHAPTER 9
TREADING WATER

In December 1883, John Holland was facing financing problems of his own. The Fenians might have been bumbling and self-immolating, but they were also his only source of income. Holland hadn't taught in years and was not anxious to abandon his dream and return to the classroom. To make ends meet while he sought a means to get back to submarine design, he found a job as a draftsman—working with George Brayton to improve the Ready Motor.

But Holland found out he had not been working without notice. Just after the *Fenian Ram* was towed to New Haven, he received an invitation to a shipboard dinner at the Brooklyn Navy Yard from a United States naval lieutenant, William W. Kimball. Kimball told Holland that he had become interested in submarines after seeing the first plan Holland submitted to the navy, the design for the one-man craft that Holland had assumed no one had ever looked at. "After dinner," Kimball wrote, "we went over the main principles of his methods for the control and maneuvering of a submerged craft."[1]

The conversation was long, detailed, and technical, covering for example, "how to get the requisite low but safe meta-centric fore-and-aft height, so as to make the craft handy on her vertical helm and be at the same time stable enough to be safe." What most impressed Kimball were the principles around which Holland insisted any successful undersea vessel be built. Kimball wrote later, "These three requirements—normal buoyancy, immovable center of gravity, and control in the vertical plane . . . are today very simple, very apparent. They were not so in 1883."[2] Before Holland left the ship, Kimball made him an offer. "If I could arrange it, he would work on a draftsman's pay in the Bureau of Ordnance on his designs. He was to make a cast-iron contract with the Department to receive, if his designs proved practical and were adopted, such compensation as a board of officers, appointed by the Department, should find fair and just." Further, if the designs remained proprietary to the navy and not marketed to outside buyers, Holland's compensation would increase. Holland was "delighted with such a prospect," and Kimball told him a few days later that the head of the Bureau of Ordnance was also keen to finalize a contract.

Had such an arrangement been entered into by Holland and the navy, the course of submarine development would have been radically altered, to say nothing of the course of John Holland's life. But it was not. "Congress had adjourned. There was absolutely no money available to pay Holland as a draftsman. Had there been, Uncle Sam would have saved many millions and would have had the Holland type of submarine as his private property for many years."[3] While Holland waited for his promised contract to slog its way through the government bureaucracy, Kimball was ordered to ship out on an extended tour of duty in the Atlantic. Before he left, however, Kimball introduced Holland to an army lieutenant, Edmund Zalinski, who was doing weapons research that might have application in submarines. Kimball told Zalinski hands off, that Holland was going to work for the navy. But after waiting in vain for three months, with Kimball still at sea, Holland, by then almost broke, agreed to sign on with Zalinski instead.

Zalinski seemed to be someone with whom Holland shared a great deal, an outsider working to achieve a vision. He had been born in Poland but immigrated to the United States when he was four. When the Civil War began, he joined up and was assigned to an artillery battalion, eventually promoted to lieutenant. After the war ended, most volunteers mustered out, but Zalinski stayed on. It was a risky choice. Senior officers were virtually all West Point graduates, and a lieutenant working his way up through the ranks would be looked on like a caddy applying for membership at a country club.

But Zalinski had a talent through which he thought he might gain membership—invention. By the 1880s, he had fashioned an advanced telescopic sight for large bore artillery, a ramrod bayonet, and a range and position finder for coastal guns. At the time he was introduced to Holland, Zalinski was engaged in perfecting the design for a surface ship-mounted pneumatic gun, much as Holland had created to launch a torpedo in the *Fenian Ram*.

The weapon, which Zalinski called a "dynamite gun," has been described as "one of the most curious pieces of military hardware ever adopted by the United States armed forces."[4] Dynamite, which had only been patented in 1867, was nitroglycerin based and had much greater explosive power than traditional gunpowder. But dynamite could not be fired out of an ordinary cannon. Nitroglycerin is highly unstable and, even with the buffering in the dynamite formula, the heat and pressure within the gun barrel and the shock of kinetic energy as the shell was launched might explode the mixture before it cleared the breach. Zalinski was experimenting with a steam-powered compressor to force air into an elongated cannon barrel with sufficient force to drive out a dynamite shell and send it traveling for up to two miles. If successful, the compressed air would expel the shell at a lower muzzle velocity than standard artillery and produce "no heat, almost no shock, and pressures that were extremely low."[5]

Zalinski had gotten the idea in 1883, shortly after he was assigned to Fort Hamilton, on the Brooklyn side of the Narrows, which helped guard the entrance to New York harbor. (At the time, John Holland was testing the *Fenian Ram* less than a mile away.) An Ohio schoolteacher named Mefford brought a pneumatic device he had invented to the fort for trials. Mefford's invention appeared to be more science project than weapon—a long brass tube attached to a compressed air reservoir by a rubber hose. The army thanked him for his time and sent him home. But Zalinski grasped the potential of the concept and began experimenting with different configurations. His notion was to mount pneumatic guns on warships, whose heavy armor plating had made them impervious to gunpowder charges but remained vulnerable to dynamite. In addition to ensuring that the gun crews were not the only casualties of dynamite shells, the decreased pressure in the barrel meant that lighter gauge metal could be used—although the gun would be a good deal longer—and would thus be easier to manufacture. It did not take long for Zalinski to attract investors, and they established the Pneumatic Dynamite Gun Company to fund his efforts.[6]

Zalinski's pneumatic gun

In early 1884, shortly after the company's inception, Zalinski and Holland met in Brooklyn. Despite news reports of Holland's activities, to which an inventor like Zalinski would ordinarily have been drawn, until Kimball made the introduction, the lieutenant did not seem to have known that a pneumatic gun had been cruising back and forth under the water near where he was standing.

Most subsequent accounts indicate Zalinski solicited Holland because he thought a submarine would be the perfect vehicle in which to mount one of his guns, but this is unlikely. Zalinski, an army officer, had never before been interested in submarines and after he and Holland parted ways, never would be again. In addition, a submarine, with its potentially radical changes in pressure and jarring ride, would have been a less than ideal storage facility for dynamite. More likely is that the partnership was symbiotic. Zalinski offered to help Holland finance continuation of his experiments, and Holland offered to help Zalinski develop his dynamite gun for ship and land-based applications. With Zalinski soliciting investment capital from Pneumatic Dynamite Gun shareholders, they jointly founded the *Nautilus* Submarine Boat Company in 1884.

Holland began work on the parade grounds in the ruins of Fort Lafayette, which had last been in use as a Union army prison. The fort was on a small island, actually a reef, in the Narrows, just north of Fort Hamilton.* Zalinski had raised enough money for Holland to build a prototype, but not enough for a true oceangoing vessel. One of the first causalities of the shoestring financing was a metal hull—the "Zalinski Boat," as it would come to be known, was constructed of wood on iron framing. It would, however, incorporate a number of improvements spawned from Holland's previous efforts.

During the *Fenian Ram* trials, Holland had written, "It was proved that guiding the boat by direct vision while submerged was impracticable, that steering a straight course under water, although not regarded as a difficulty by anyone up to that date, was a problem that must be solved before submarine warfare could be made practical under modern conditions."[7] Zalinski's plan was that the boat's captain would spot a target through a camera lucida, a primitive periscope, and then partially surface so that the bow was exposed at an up-angle from which a projectile could be shot through the air.** After the gun was fired, the boat would quickly submerge, leaving no target for accompanying vessels. Zalinski claimed his gun could carry a high-explosive projectile of several hundred pounds almost half a mile. Only Holland,

---

* The island was demolished in 1960 to make way for the Verrazano-Narrows Bridge.

** A camera lucida—Latin for "light chamber"—is a device that uses an arrangement of mirrors to project an image of an object onto a surface. Because the object is not viewed directly, the person at the eyepiece has no sense of depth—distance—or the actual size of what he is looking at. In a submarine, it would provide the direction in which a surface ship was sailing, but little else. In modern applications, the projections are generally to a piece of paper and are used to trace a copy of a drawing or graphic.

whose submarines would dive and surface at an angle and not on an even keel, could design a craft to pull off such a precise maneuver.

Holland was skeptical that this arrangement would work at all and, even if it did, that the missile could actually hit anything, shot as it would be from a boat halfway out of the water, needing to hold a precise position while being buffeted about by waves. But if he wanted to build a submarine, he had no choice but to go along, so he drew plans for a fifty-foot vessel with a dynamite gun mounted horizontally in the bow. Other features of the new boat were less whimsical. Holland installed a platform under the conning tower to allow the captain to position head and shoulders in the turret with access to the viewing tube, a precursor to more advanced designs. A simplified and recrafted main cabin put controls for diving planes, steering, ballast, and throttle all within easy reach of the engineer. Many of the improvements that first appeared in this wooden boat would become standard as submarines moved closer to becoming a wartime weapon.

By late August 1885, the boat was nearing completion and anticipation was running high. "A New Marine Monster," a *New York Times* headline proclaimed on August 31. "Busy laborers have been hard at work for several months in the ruins of Fort Lafayette constructing a boat which, if a success, will prove a submarine wonder that will startle the world." The article fawned on Zalinski, who by that time, was rarely present, and it did not mention Holland at all. Zalinski, according to the *Times*, "has made marine vessels an especial study and no more capable person could have been given charge of the construction of the important boat than he." The newspaper went on to assert that the lieutenant, who had examined every piece of material in the "hoped-for wonder," and directed its proper position, would give the boat "a thorough test in all respects," when it was launched the following week.[8] Four days later, the *Times* reported that the huge flow of visitors engendered by its previous article had prevented the boat from being launched. Once again, Zalinski was said to be "personally in charge," although there was also mention of an unnamed "inventor." The day after that, an article reported that the planned launching had to be postponed for twenty-four hours due to high winds and rough seas, a decision made jointly by Lieutenant Zalinski and the "leading spirit of the Torpedo Boat Company," a "Dr. Cyrus Edson," who was in fact only an investor.[9] On September 4, 1885, the Zalinski Boat was launched for its first test run. The *Times* covered this event as well. In its article, for the first time, perhaps ominously, the very first name it listed as those present at the event was "the inventor, J. T. Holland [*sic*]." The piece had also been pushed back to page eight from the previous page-one coverage. Nonetheless, optimism was said to be the prevailing sentiment; "everybody was sanguine of complete success."

Except Holland. To get the twenty-eight-ton boat into the water, ways had been laid from Fort Lafayette's parade ground, over a high sea wall, then down to the bay, which was later described as "an almost impossible launching site." To make the process even more precarious, Zalinski had assigned a young, inexperienced naval engineer to supervise, of whom Holland later said "had either insufficient knowledge of the subject or lacked the ability to put his knowledge to practical use."[10] The result was predictable. Holland tried to shore up what he saw as insufficient bracing, but at three thirty, Zalinski, by now impatient to conclude the proceedings, wanted to give the order to begin sliding the boat down the ways. Holland "begged for a few minutes more time," but at 3:38 Zalinski yelled, "Let her go, boys." From there, the *Times* report differs from other accounts. The newspaper had the stern first launch go smoothly, with Holland pleased, until four minutes later, when the vessel unaccountably began to sink.[11]

Holland remembered things differently. When the stays were knocked from under the submarine, it moved far too quickly down the steep incline and could not be slowed by the rope attached to the bow. "The result was that . . . the launching ways suddenly collapsed and [the boat] crashed into some piling near the water's edge, tearing out the greater part of her side and bottom."[12]

What happened next is also in question. According to some newspaper accounts, the craft did not totally sink. It was raised to make repairs, and Holland eventually made some test runs in the Narrows, determining that his design was sound. Holland's account is more final. "On investigation it was found that the cost of repairs would exceed the amount of money still on hand in the company's treasury. Accordingly the wrecked boat was broken up where she lay, the engine and fittings removed and sold, and the proceeds used to partly reimburse the stockholders for the money they had invested."[13]

Whichever version is correct, it was clear to all concerned that this was a venture that had no future. Holland in particular had experienced too many frustrations to engage in self-delusion. "This accident discouraged my company from any further attempts at submarine construction," he said. "Had this boat been successful, submarines would have become an accepted success years before they did." When Kimball returned from sea duty, Holland told him that the partnership and the company were doomed, and by the end of 1886, both were just that.

There is no evidence that the *New York Times* accounts, which remained unstinting in praising Zalinski, had been influenced to Holland's detriment by either the lieutenant or the army. Still, the tone of the articles and the failure to mention Holland's name until the boat sank seem unlikely to be pure coincidence. Moreover, Holland lacked the inclination—and likely the skill—to properly court the press or ensure that his reputation would not suffer the slights of others. In the years to come, that failing would cost him dearly.

What Holland never said publicly, and what was not reported in the press, was that in the months before the boat went into the water, Zalinski's oversight of the project, and even his participation, had been almost nonexistent. Weeks would go by during the construction phase without him setting foot in Fort Lafayette. When he finally showed up to be the public face of the launch, his decisions—both in the setup of the ways and the naval officer to be in command—were disastrous, but not a word of criticism ever came his way.

By that time, in fact, Zalinski had lost interest in submarines entirely. He began testing basic gun designs in spring 1884 and soon turned his focus totally to his shipboard cannon. In March 1885, he produced an operational prototype, with an 8-inch smoothbore cast-iron barrel, sixty feet long, which could fire a one-hundred-pound dynamite charge two miles. In tests, the long barrel proved to be more accurate than the standard gunpowder cannon and could hold a larger explosive charge. Even at two miles, however, the gun's range was inferior.

But Zalinski had added a wrinkle that might make his invention irresistible to the navy. His shells detonated electrically, by means of a battery embedded in the tail. Depending on the sensitivity of the battery, the charge could detonate on contact or at any depth underwater that was desired. This latter feature could obviously be used to blow out the hull of an enemy ship.

Interest in Zalinski's gun increased with each firing and eventually, in October 1885, the Navy Department sent a three-man delegation to observe the army officer's invention firsthand. A twelve-foot by five-foot target was placed in the bay, one mile from the gun, surrounded by a circle of barrels thirty feet across. Ten empty shells were fired and each fell within the circle. Zalinski then loaded a live shell, which was shot more than two miles across the bay before it exploded on contact with the water.

There was exultation at such spectacular results, of course, but also relief. No one knew whether to trust Zalinski's arrangement—there was no shortage of experts who insisted that the gun would blow up with the dynamite inside. When the live shell was loaded into the gun, the naval officers took flight and observed the proceedings from behind a tree, taking "surreptitious peeps from time to time at the arrangements."[14]

Foreign governments also showed up to observe, including representatives from China, Turkey, Prussia, Brazil, Spain, and Britain. But at home, despite a string of successes, Zalinski encountered resistance. His guns' lack of comparable range, critics insisted, would make them ineffective for coastal defense, as an enemy fleet could simply station itself too far out to sea for the dynamite shells to travel and pummel targets on the shore. Zalinski countered that because his gun was lighter, it could be mounted on a fleet of torpedo boats that would be faster and more maneuverable than enemy ships weighed down by traditional cannon. Finally, in 1886, the navy agreed to build a "dynamite cruiser," and sent a proposal to Congress. Lieutenant Zalinski was called as a witness when hearings were held to debate whether to approve the appropriation. He was billed as "the inventor of the dynamite gun and submarine torpedo boat."[15] The congressmen were suitably impressed and construction was begun the following month.

When the cruiser *Vesuvius* was completed in 1888, Zalinski's star seemed in full ascent. In addition, over the next few years, enormous dynamite guns were employed to guard the harbors of New York and San Francisco. Every time a gun was test-fired, observers were amazed at its accuracy.

But the same bureaucratic intransigence that would frustrate John Holland did in the pneumatic gun as well. Some of the issues that bedeviled Zalinski were real—the gun's lack of range would surely make it vulnerable to long-range pounding, either on land or at sea, and on the *Vesuvius*, the breach of the gun needed to be below deck, meaning that its position was fixed and the ship had to change course to fire in a different direction. Also, the velocity of shells shot pneumatically was not sufficient to pierce the thick armor found on large warships. But Zalinski's most intractable problem was opposition from his fellow army officers. His lack of West Point lineage finally caught up with him. When he was promoted to captain in 1889, after more than two decades as a lieutenant, and then assigned as military attaché to St. Petersburg, Russia, resentment among his peers boiled over. Impediments, delays, and negative reports trailed after every new dynamite gun installation. Zalinski, then in Russia, was helpless to defend his invention.

Eventually enthusiasm for Zalinski's weapon evaporated. The dynamite guns installed for shore defense were replaced and, after a brief, inconsequential appearance in the Spanish-American War, the *Vesuvius*, the only dynamite cruiser ever built, was scrapped. After two bouts of illness, Edmund Zalinski, over his vehement protests, was forced to retire from the army in 1894. He lived for another fifteen years before dying of pneumonia in 1909. He chose to be buried in Rochester, New York, rather than Arlington National Cemetery.

CHAPTER 10
CHASING THE CARROT

John Holland was once again out of work. Although William Kimball had called him "the best submarine man in the United States, if not the world," the Navy Department had been unable to secure an appropriation to pay him a draftsman's salary. But the environment for innovation appeared to be improving. After nearly two decades of almost total atrophy, the navy finally seemed committed to a program of modernization.

The change had begun in early 1881, when James A. Garfield replaced Rutherford B. Hayes in the White House and appointed William H. Hunt to be secretary of the navy. In November 1881, Hunt, appalled at the condition of the service he was to oversee, began his annual report to Congress with a dire warning:

> The condition of the Navy imperatively demands the prompt and earnest attention of Congress. Unless some action be taken in its behalf, it must soon dwindle into insignificance. From

such a state it would be difficult to revive it into efficiency without dangerous delay and enormous expense. Emergencies may at any moment arise which would render its aid indispensable to the protection of the lives and property of our citizens abroad and at home, and even to our existence as a nation. We have been unable to make such an appropriate display of our naval power abroad as will cause us to be respected. The exhibition of our weakness in this important arm of defense is calculated to detract from our occupying in the eyes of foreign nations that rank to which we know ourselves to be justly entitled. It is a source of mortification to our officers and fellow-countrymen generally, that our vessels of war should stand in such mean contrast alongside of those of other and inferior powers.[1]

Until that point, few questioned the army's first call on the Treasury. For more than a decade after the Civil War ended in 1865, the army had been required to staff an occupation force in the old Confederacy to enforce the Reconstruction Acts and ensure that newly freed slaves were not murdered wholesale by resentful whites. After the army was pulled from the South in 1877, attention had turned west, where the bluecoats were overrunning various Native American tribes to secure expansion of the nation's boundaries. In addition, the previous presidents, Hayes and Grant, had been decorated army generals.

Still, a nation whose east and west borders were oceans needed a navy, at least for defense, and the United States essentially didn't have one. "The year 1881, when Garfield succeeded to the Presidency, marks the lowest mark to which the navy has ever sunk since the days when the United States had to pay ransom to Algiers. Out of 140 vessels on the navy list in 1881, 25 were tugs and only a few of the rest were in condition to make a cruise. Not a single ship was fit for [military] service. An engraving published in 1881 pictured the fleet being reviewed by the President, a pathetic attempt to put the best face possible on our miserable ships. This group represented the best dozen vessels in the navy at that time; they were all built of wood, and included not only the side-wheel steamer *Powhatan*, but the ancient Frigate, *Constitution*! And the batteries mounted by these ships were chiefly smooth-bores left over from the Civil War."[2]

Secretary Hunt appointed an advisory panel of senior naval officers—who had little else to do—to make recommendations for improving the fleet. That act caused sufficient resentment among army brass and Congressmen that Hunt was shunted from office by new president Chester Arthur only six months later and shipped off to Russia as the new ambassador.* The panel's recommendations, of course, included sweeping changes in procurement, and building essentially a new navy from the ground up. They called specifically for building two first-rate steel unarmored cruisers; six first-rate steel double-decked, unarmored cruisers; ten second-rate steel cruisers; twenty fourth-rate wooden cruisers; five steel rams; five torpedo gunboats; ten cruising torpedo boats; and ten harbor torpedo boats.** The total cost would be $29,607,000.***

Congress initially balked at doing anything—the same posture they had taken for years—on the grounds that the American people did not care to spend money on a more modern navy and, besides, there was no need to improve the fleet until a war actually began. A New York congressman observed, "I believe if there were any deep-seated and well-founded sentiment among the people that we ought to increase and build up our navy, the present Congress as well as past Congresses would have received demonstrations upon this subject which would have demanded an affirmative answer."[3]

But Congress had misread public sentiment—the state of America's fleet had become so scandalous that inaction was becoming untenable. Admiral George Dewey, later to become "the hero of Manila Bay," wrote that "In October 1882, I was ordered to the command of the *Juniata*, which was to proceed to China. She was a relic of a past epoch of naval warfare, which you would have expected to see flying the flag of some third-rate power. She was as out of date as the stagecoach. One reason, perhaps why so little was seen of our ships in home ports for twenty

---

* President Garfield had been assassinated in September 1881.
** Rating was determined by how many guns and men a ship carried.
*** About $750,000,000 today.

years after the Civil War was that the sight of them might arouse the people's demand for a naval policy which did not represent a mere waste of money in keeping relics in commission."[4]

Reluctantly and with a good deal of grumbling, in March 1883, Congress allocated funds for the construction of three modern, armored cruisers, and one dispatch boat. Prophetically, given the building frenzy to come, these became known as the "ABCD ships"—*Atlantic*, *Boston*, *Chicago*, and *Dolphin*. Construction on those vessels was begun almost immediately. In 1885, Congress authorized two more heavy cruisers and two gunboats. Sentiment about a modern navy had changed to the point that the *Chicago Tribune* in July 1886, wrote in an editorial, "There never was a time when the call for a navy and adequate coastal defense was more pressing. There never was a time when the people were more unanimous in demanding them. There never was a time when the country was in better financial condition to afford it."[5]

Such was the popularity of the new naval program that each party in the 1884 presidential election tried to outdo the other in its commitment to America's naval might. Republicans, under Maine senator James G. Blaine, claimed a commitment to restoring the navy to past strength, although the party was unclear as to just what that meant. Democrats, whose standard bearer was New York's Grover Cleveland, proclaimed that government had a sacred duty to protect the rights of all its citizens at home and abroad, and this could only be achieved if the nation had modern warships to enforce its edicts. When Cleveland was elected, he declared that, in addition, a nation with as extended a seacoast as the United States needed a powerful navy, and to give it one, Cleveland appointed as his secretary of the navy, William Collins Whitney.

Patriarch of the great family fortune, Whitney would enter the submarine saga twice, from essentially opposite directions, which was fitting. Whitney's life was replete with opposites: he was at once a political reformer and a political hack; a man whose sound management saved New York City millions and one whose stock manipulations bilked both private and public interests out of just as much; a generous patron of the arts and the epitome of Gilded Age greed. Whitney was described by a muckraking journalist as "having wonderful mental gifts . . . brilliant, polished and suave . . . physically handsome, loved by most men and all women . . . displaying those talents for diplomacy that made him the mastermind of presidential cabinets and the maker of American presidents."[6]

Whitney was born in 1841 into a distinguished family—his father was an army general and his mother was descended from William Bradford, a signer of the Mayflower Compact and governor of the Plymouth Colony. At the outbreak of the Civil War, many men of Whitney's background entered the officer corps of the Union army, but Whitney chose to remain at Yale. After he graduated, in 1863, Whitney moved on to Harvard to study law, and then joined a prominent New York firm after one year in Cambridge. At the same time, he married the daughter of future Ohio senator Henry Payne.

Whitney began his professional life as a progressive reformer. He helped found the Young Men's Democratic Club, and then was hired by Samuel Tilden to help build the case that brought down Boss Tweed. He failed to gain elective office on his own, when he was defeated in a run for district attorney in 1872. But when Tilden was elected governor in 1875, Whitney was appointed as New York City's corporation counsel. In addition to gaining an insider's knowledge of city politics, Whitney oversaw agreements with private contractors and holders of city franchises, experience that he would later put to extremely profitable use. In his seven years as the city's top lawyer, Whitney also burrowed into records and files and helped recover as much as $20 million that Tweed had stolen from city accounts.

When he left city government in 1882 to help Grover Cleveland get elected president, Whitney's credentials as an honest, brilliant administrator were unquestioned. He proved to be one of Cleveland's most successful fund-raisers and was rewarded with his pick of jobs in the new administration. He chose the Navy Department.

Whitney built on the progress that had begun in the previous administration, so much so that he would ultimately receive the lion's share of credit for creating a modern American navy. By 1890, although it was in his successor's administration, Congress had become so caught up in the spending frenzy that it appropriated funds for the construction of three state-of-the-art battleships. More would follow.

When naval modernization began, basic needs were such that appropriating funds to add submarines to the fleet was not a possibility. But Whitney aggressively pursued every option. Submarine experiments were sufficiently in the news that it seemed undersea warfare, at the least, deserved study. William Kimball urged the head of the Ordnance Bureau, Commander (later Admiral) Montgomery Sicard, to urge Whitney to move forward with a submarine program.

The problem was that no one in the navy or anywhere else in government knew how to go about it. In 1887, Kimball suggested the navy "ask for bids for furnishing a submarine just as bids were asked for furnishing shoes or canvas." Although the idea was at first "considered revolutionary and impractical," with no better ideas forthcoming, Kimball was asked to draw up specifications for the competition.[7] The winner, a skeptical Whitney agreed, would be awarded a sizable government contract (up to $2 million) to produce the vessel.

Kimball's requirements, published in August 1888, were quite sophisticated. To be awarded a contract, a "Steel Submarine Torpedo Boat" must cruise at fifteen knots on the surface and eight submerged; retain positive buoyancy at all times; be able to remain submerged for two hours at a time; carry provisions for ninety hours at sea; be able to withstand water pressure to 150 feet; complete a turn in an area no more than four times its length; and deliver a torpedo with a one-hundred-pound charge. The boat would need to displace at least forty tons but no more than two hundred tons submerged, and it was "suggested," although not required, that the motor generate one thousand horsepower.

While subsequently there would be accusations that these requirements were drawn to guarantee Holland won the contract, Kimball had little to draw on but his knowledge of Holland's designs. By this time, as many as a dozen others were experimenting with undersea craft in various parts of the United States and Europe, but no one had succeeded in creating a working boat and Kimball had, correctly as it turned out, accepted Holland's basic principles as the basis to create a working submarine.

Designs had to be submitted through a builder recognized by the Navy Department, and Holland chose Cramp & Sons Shipbuilding of Philadelphia, an experienced shipyard, well thought of in Washington. He was surprised to find out that another competitor, Thorsten Nordenfelt, had submitted a bid through Cramps as well. Nordenfelt had evidently submitted the same design as for the boat that sank on its way to Russia. Although a full postmortem on the sinking had yet to be published, a boat that had come to such an accursed end was unlikely to garner much support.

In addition to Nordenfelt, two others submitted designs. One, George Baker of Chicago, seemed to be a serious inventor, but he had yet to go beyond preliminary planning. But lack of specific construction costs would not prevent his winning the contract, and his plans were conceptually quite refined. His manner of driving the boat was particularly advanced and would eventually be adopted by other designers, including Holland. "He combined two independent sources of power, steam for surface propulsion and an electric motor for running submerged. A clutch connection with the steam engine enabled it to drive the electric motor as a dynamo to charge the accumulators while running awash."[8] Baker's means of maintaining stability, however, two propellers on beveled gears that could rotate 180 degrees, would prove impractical.

The other entrant epitomized the sort of experimentation that is inevitably undertaken before any great technological breakthrough, when designs get closer and closer to the ultimate solution but fall short of the right combination for success—they tend to be inventive, quirky, with certain features that are quite clever, all on a machine that doesn't work.

Josiah Tuck of San Francisco fell into this category with a submarine he called the *Peacemaker*. Thirty feet long, with a crew of three, his first design required the captain, dressed in a diver's suit and helmet, to stand outside the hull, "in a kind of well amidships up to his waist," from where he would steer the vessel and release a set of mines with cork floats that would rise through the water and attach themselves with electromagnets to either side of the hull of an enemy ship. The *Peacemaker* would then cruise a safe distance away and the mines would detonate electrically. Unmanned, the *New York Times* described the boat as looking like "a shark with a hole in its back."[9] Depth was controlled solely by taking on or expelling ballast. The most salient feature of the *Peacemaker* was a "fireless engine," in which a solution of caustic soda was used to generate steam. Representatives of both France and China expressed interest in purchasing the vessel, but a deal was never consummated. Tuck eventually abandoned the notion of the captain standing outside the boat, and he installed a clear dome over the well.

Tuck's Peacemaker

In August 1886, "in the broiling sun," the *Peacemaker* made a test run in the Hudson River, in front of "300 persons, 50 of whom were ladies in charming Summer costumes." While those spectators were in awe of a boat that disappeared under the surface and remained hidden for thirty minutes, the submarine had actually performed poorly. Once submerged, it was unable to maintain either constant depth or longitudinal stability. In a demonstration in November, before a number of senior military officers, including William Tecumseh Sherman, the *Peacemaker* would not submerge at all and "obstinately remained on the surface of the water."[10] As a result, Tuck's invention "went to join the long list of non-successful submarines."[11]

With a choice of one design whose prototype sank, another that could not stay submerged, a third whose architect had yet to build anything, and John Holland, the Bureau of Ordnance did not have a great deal of difficulty coming to a decision. Holland was overjoyed.

But not for long. Either because Cramps shipbuilding refused to guarantee all six specifications or because Secretary Whitney found the costs to high, or possibly because pressure was brought to bear not to waste precious funds on the silly and fanciful, the contract offer was withdrawn. Shortly afterward, however, the competition was reopened, in theory to new designs although none were submitted. Holland was again declared the winner.

This time, before a dollar was disbursed, Grover Cleveland was out and Benjamin Harrison was in. Harrison's navy secretary was an army man, Benjamin F. Tracy, who saw the lack of a credible surface fleet as a much more pressing need than Holland's undersea phantasm. Tracy diverted the funds to traditional warships and Holland was once again without working capital. John Holland, after fifteen years of work and despite being widely considered the most accomplished and knowledgeable submarine designer in the world, found himself broke, jobless, and without prospects.

For the first time, it seemed that Holland might give in to frustration and despair, as had Bushnell, Garrett, Bauer, and others before him. But William Kimball urged him not to give up, that submarines were the future and Holland would eventually have a hand in shaping it. Another man, Charles Morris, owner of a dredging company, who had briefly employed Holland during the *Fenian Ram* days, also encouraged him not to lose hope.

In addition, Holland had been tinkering with an idea for a better motor to power a submarine. The Brayton motor appeared inadaptable to underwater travel and, although only steam seemed capable of generating the horsepower the navy specifications had required, Holland sensed that the Otto-type internal combustion engine, which had begun to be employed in another recent invention, the automobile, would work for submarines as well. Morris wanted Holland to at least design the new motor until interest in submarines was rekindled.*

But Holland was no longer prepared to continue to work on designs that no one wanted. Instead, he began to tinker with a different project that had become all the rage—flying machines. Although his supporters later claimed his designs were well thought out, they were actually amateurish, showing little or no understanding of the principles of flight. While engaged in this quixote-esque pursuit, in May 1890, Holland accepted a job at Morris's dredging company at $4.00 per day.

But John Holland's life was marked by that most cruel of fates—perpetual, unrealized hope. Just when it seemed that he would pass anonymously into history, promise once more intervened. As Harrison had defeated Cleveland in 1888, Cleveland defeated Harrison in 1892, and with Cleveland's return came a return of interest in the submarine.

William Whitney did not return to the administration—he had left to seek the literally greener pastures of Wall Street, from which he would later play an incidental but key role in submarine development. In March 1893, however, Cleveland's new navy secretary, Hilary Herbert, reinstated the submarine contract. Congress appropriated $200,000 for the new venture, with the specifications the same as for the aborted 1888 bidding.

John Holland was back in the submarine business. This time, he would have help.

---

* "Otto" type engines remain standard in piston-driven automobiles. They use four strokes to complete a full cycle. During the first stroke, downward, a mixture of gas and air is sucked into a cylinder; the second stroke is up, sometimes generated by a flywheel, where the mixture is compressed; a flame is introduced into the cylinder to detonate the fuel, causing a downstroke, the power stroke; the piston is then sent back upward by the spinning flywheel, which forces the burned gasses out an exhaust valve. With multiple cylinder engines, the flywheel becomes unnecessary as the cylinders are arranged to fire at different times, which provides momentum for cylinders not experiencing a power stroke. Brayton engines also compress the fuel, but not in the cylinder. Brayton pressurized the air in its own chamber, passed it through vaporized fuel, and then into a chamber where it was ignited by a steady flame, as opposed to the spark used as ignition in the Otto. The "injected" fuel burned rather than exploded to drive a piston. The engine was reciprocal, meaning that the piston was driven back and forth by alternating expansions on either side. Each thrust allowed the spent fuel from the previous thrust to be expelled. The "constant pressure" principle was later called the "Brayton cycle" and found application in gas turbines, which are now employed to power jet engines.

CHAPTER 11
CHALLENGERS

Well before the November 1892 election, a clever, young, well-connected attorney named Elihu B. Frost, "E. B.," decided that Holland's "torpedo boat" might be an idea worth investing in. He spoke with Charles Morris and tried to get a sense of what was needed to get Holland restarted. He was pleased to learn that Holland had obtained a string of patents for his designs and had even more pending; less pleased to know that Holland—and Morris—had no investment capital of their own. Frost asked his father, Calvin, also his law partner, to ask around in Washington and find out if submarines might be in the navy's future plans. (Their law offices were at 120 Broadway in New York City, but Calvin in particular did a good deal of business in the capital.)

Frost did nothing further for some months, likely because he had heard from his father that Secretary Tracy had no interest in reinstating the submarine contract. But as soon as the election was over, Frost either learned of or strongly suspected that the submarine competition would be revived. He began laying the groundwork for a partnership with Holland. On February 28, 1893, in advance of Cleveland's inauguration, Frost told Morris he was prepared to form a company with Holland and would provide whatever funds were necessary to get the inventor back to the shipyard.[1] A few days later, on March 3, 1893, Congress approved an appropriation of $200,000 to fund the construction of a working submarine. The navy's ordnance bureau appointed three serving officers to form the Board on Submarine Torpedo Boats, which would evaluate the competing designs and construction cost estimates, and then submit recommendations to Commander Sicard and incoming Secretary Herbert. Just weeks after that, the John P. Holland Torpedo Boat Company was incorporated in New York State—John P. Holland, manager, and Elihu B. Frost, secretary-treasurer.

By June, Holland had completed plans for his board submission, a significantly improved design from the one that had won the previous two competitions. The unreliable Brayton was scrapped. On the surface or running awash, the boat would be powered by twin one-thousand-horsepower steam engines, each of which would turn a rear propeller. Once submerged, the exhaust stack would be retracted, and the boat would be powered by a battery array. Storage batteries, called "chloride accumulators," were a nascent technology and performance and life of the charge were ongoing problems. Still, electricity was silent, did not generate excessive heat inside the hull, and required no venting. To recharge the batteries, Holland, like Baker, would install a dynamo that would turn when the steam engines were engaged.

The vessel would carry sufficient compressed air to run submerged for up to twelve hours, and compressed air would also be used to launch Whitehead torpedoes from the dual tubes mounted in the bow. The air reservoirs could be refilled with retractable tubes thirty feet long that would be extended above the surface while the boat remained submerged.

As with all Holland designs, the boat, eighty feet long and eleven across, had a fixed center of gravity, was always positively buoyant, and could dive at however steep an angle was required. Diving planes were at the rear. A pressure gauge would automatically halt the dive before the boat reached its crush depth of 180 feet.

As in Tuck's *Peacemaker*, the captain would stand on a platform in the center of the boat, allowing him to peer out of a domed conning tower fitted with plate-glass windows. From there, he could pilot the boat and fire the torpedoes. The turret was armored to protect the conning tower and the smokestack. An engineer was stationed immediately below.

Holland and Frost submitted the $7,500 deposit and $90,000 surety bond required with each bid, and then, at the end of June, traveled to Washington to officially present their plans at the office of the secretary of the navy.

Although the board had expected as many as eight designs to be submitted, it turned out that there were only three. Nordenfelt and Tuck had dropped out. George Baker, however, was still in the hunt. He had come a long way since the previous competition four years before. Not only had he built a submarine, he had sailed it.

Baker, who had made his money inventing a machine to fabricate barbed wire, had been fascinated with undersea navigation for years, although for most of his life, he lived and worked in Iowa. He set up a Chicago office in 1887, mostly to have access to Lake Michigan, and then moved to Detroit, also to be on the water.

Completely self-taught, his 1893 boat was an odd combination of primitive and predictive. In an era of ever-heavier armored construction, he had fashioned his submarine of wood—oak, six inches thick, with one-inch wood sheathing. He had installed a dual propulsion system, steam on the surface and a battery array when submerged. Baker's exhaust stack would also be retracted, but he had no armor protection for it or the conning tower. His captain was stationed on a center platform as well, peering out of a windowed dome. The first prototype was a disaster. It leaked through the wooden seams at a twenty-foot depth, his steam motor was balky, and at one point during surface running, the batteries exploded. If he had been submerged, he could not have gotten out alive. By July 1892, however, he had built a functional vessel and was making test runs in the Detroit River.[2]

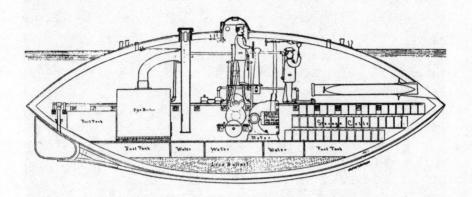

Baker boat

His working boat was cigar-shaped, forty feet long and nine across—much stubbier and less hydrodynamic than Holland's—and could be operated by a crew of two, although there was room inside for five, if necessary.[3] It seemed to retain a store of positive buoyancy but some reports indicate that it became negatively buoyant to submerge.

The vessel was propelled by twin four-bladed propellers, mounted amidships rather than at the rear. It could make eight knots on the surface, but only four or five submerged. The propellers were mounted on a bevel that would turn on an angle to submerge the boat or bring it to the surface, and then return to the horizontal to propel it forward. "By placing the propellers also at the point of the boat's centre of gravity," an engineering journal observed, "Mr. Baker has sought to secure greater stability and to maintain the craft, under all circumstances, with its keel parallel to the surface of the water."[4] But mounting the propellers as Baker had done created difficulties in maintaining stability and constant depth, and the only report of its underwater performance indicated that he had been unable to solve either problem.[5] Baker's craft would also descend on an even keel, a method Holland had disparaged as slow and unwieldy.

Interior of the Baker boat

But George Baker knew that coming up with a design was only one part of the requirements—as important, likely more so, was gaining the influence to get it approved. This Baker had done superbly. By the time the contract was to be awarded, Baker had cultivated an impressive array of supporters for his wooden boat in Congress and the Navy Department.[6] Among his most important converts was the new head of the ordnance bureau, Captain William T. Sampson, a highly touted line officer who had captained an ironclad in the Civil War and would command the blockade of Havana in the coming war with Spain. As soon as Sampson took up his duties, replacing Montgomery Sicard, Baker traveled to Washington to meet him. The two spent a good deal of time together, and also with Iowa senator William Allison. In addition, while in the capital, Baker had the foresight to hire a retired army general as his lawyer.

By the time the board was to officially accept plans and specifications, June 30, 1893, Baker was confident he had outmaneuvered John Holland, at least sufficiently to prevent Holland from grabbing an outright victory. Still, there was a third entrant, a newcomer to submarine design, someone who neither Baker nor Holland had ever before encountered. His name was Simon Lake and, astoundingly, he was only twenty-seven years old.

Lake had been raised in Toms River, New Jersey, on the Atlantic Ocean, sixty miles east of Philadelphia. He had a lengthy pedigree—his father's family had settled in America in the 1700s and his mother's ancestors had landed in Massachusetts in1632. The elder Lake was a successful businessman, the owner of a foundry and machine shop, and *his* father, also named Simon, had built the first bridge to Atlantic City, a city he had helped found.

The younger Simon had become fascinated with submarines as a boy, when he read *Twenty Thousand Leagues Under the Sea*. "Shortly afterward, I took up the study of natural physics and became interested in the use of the diving bell. Being an excellent swimmer and fond of boats, I spent most of my vacation times on or about the water." In 1880, at age fourteen, as John Holland was testing the *Holland 1*, Lake drew up a design for an undersea vessel that contained many of the elements he would use in later craft, such as diving planes and an air lock so that divers could enter and exit the craft underwater, as they had in Verne's *Nautilus*. "These plans were shown to my father, who rather discouraged me in the matter on the ground that submarine navigation was something that great engineers had given a lot of attention to, and that I had better give more attention to my regular school studies than to fooling around with experiments of that nature."[7]

He followed his father's advice to a point. Although he stayed in school, he left a year later to study mechanical engineering at the Franklin Institute in Philadelphia. He returned home at seventeen to work in his father's foundry, where he showed sufficient flair to be made a partner just after his twentieth birthday. It soon became apparent that Lake's real talent was invention. He designed and built a number devices used in local fishing boats, including a dredge and steering gear, but he never stopped tinkering with the idea of a vessel that could navigate under water.

Simon Lake

Unlike virtually everyone else who was involved in the same quest, Lake was not thinking of developing an undersea craft as a weapon of war, but rather for commercial use, primarily salvage. His idea was to build a boat with a wheeled bottom that he could literally drive along the seabed. Divers would be able to gather whatever had sunk there, entering and exiting the boat by means of the air lock.

He applied for a patent for a basic design in 1893. Like Holland and Baker, he would employ dual propulsion—a steam engine on the surface or shallowly submerged, but compressed air rather than electricity if the boat went deeper. Also like Baker—but unlike Holland—his boat would not dive and surface on an angle, but rather on an even keel, always parallel to the sea floor. A "viewing tube" would allow the captain to peer above the surface when submerged, and other, longer tubes would extend to the surface to refresh the air for the crew and vent exhaust if the boat was running on steam.

When he heard of the 1893 competition, Lake drew up his plans and traveled to Washington full of optimism, with visions of leaving as the United States Navy's anointed submarine builder. As soon as he arrived at the office where the bids would be opened, however, he realized that water was not the only medium in which he needed to learn to navigate.

> I was still a youngster and knew nothing about the difficulties met by outsiders in getting hearings before government officials in Washington. On the appointed day, in June 1893, on which the bids were to be opened, I appeared in Washington with my plans and specifications under my arm, and was directed to the room adjoining the Secretary's office, where a large number of people were assembled. At this time I knew nothing of anyone else's experiments in submarines, and thought that I was the first and only one. I was consequently much disturbed to see so many people present. I sat down on a lounge, and a young man a little older than myself sat down on the lounge alongside of me and said, "Well, I suppose you are here on the same errand as the rest of us; I see you have some plans, and I suppose you have designs of a submarine boat which you are going to submit." I said, "Yes, and I guess there are going to be a good many plans submitted, judging by the number of people who are here." The gentleman then said, "No, I only know of two others who are going to submit plans: there is Mr. J. P. Holland, the gentleman standing over there, and my father, Mr. George C. Baker, of Chicago."[8]

Lake then inquired as to the identity of the others in the room. Young Baker, as it turned out, knew just about all of them. "There is Senator So-and-so, and Congressman So-and-so, and Mr. So-and-so, the great lawyer." When Lake realized that all the notables were there to lobby for his opponents, he said to himself, "Well, Lakey, it looks as though you were not going to have much of a show here."

Lake's account from there differs from others. According to Lake, he returned to Baltimore after the submission "to tend to other business," but "was much surprised, therefore, to receive, some time afterward, a telegram from the editor of the *New York Tribune*, a Mr. Hall, stating that he had received information from Washington that my plans were looked upon most favorably by the majority of the Naval Board and that they were going to adopt my type of boat." Lake claimed that Hall asked for a description of his submarine and an interview, but neither appeared in the *Tribune* until October 1894, more than one year later.* [9] Further, Lake said he did not bother returning to Washington, because he assumed he would be informed by the navy secretary's office when the contract was official, "which is proof positive," he added, "that I was still young and ignorant." [10]

But no summons to the capital was forthcoming. "Nothing further was heard of the matter until I saw a notice in the paper that it had been decided not to build any submarines at that time, and that the matter had been postponed indefinitely." Lake never backed away from the assertion that his design had been chosen. "Some years afterward I met the late Admiral Mathews, and he informed me then that he had been a member of the board, and that four of the five members of that board were in favor of adopting my type of boat and of having the government start the development of a submarine on those lines, but that the constructor of the board opposed it on the grounds that when the boat was running on the bottom on wheels she might run off from a precipice and go down head first, and reach so great a depth as to be crushed, evidently not realizing that her great static stability and the use of her hydroplanes would prevent this from happening."

---

*   In addition to being one of the submarine's most notable pioneers, Lake was also its most prolific chronicler. He produced at least three books and more than a dozen articles or monographs on submarine technology and development. While his insights are often invaluable, he devoted a substantial portion of his writings to his frustrations over injustices that were seemingly foisted on him consistently throughout his career. He had a wide range of antagonists, which included naval officers, financiers, government officials both elected and appointed, and sundry bureaucrats and opportunists. In many cases, fortunately, Lake's recollections can be either verified or refuted independently, and while his immense contribution to submarine development is beyond question, the unique position he claims for himself does not always hold up under scrutiny.

Despite the detail in which Lake recounted this exchange, there is no independent confirmation that his design was ever seriously considered. In fact, the evidence strongly indicates that his was the only entry eliminated. For one thing, there was no "Mathews" on the review board, which consisted of three, not five, men. In addition, two weeks after the competition closed, the *New York Times* ran an article whose headline read, "Plans for Submarine Boats: A New York Inventor Likely to Build the First Vessel," referring to Holland, and that the other boat that had been under consideration was Baker's. But the *Times* indicated that the review board had ultimately rejected Baker's design because his sole means of undersea propulsion was battery power, a system that at the time was "considered insufficient," which is odd since Holland's boat was powered similarly.[11] But in every account except Lake's, the Holland boat, larger, faster, and more sturdily built, was considered the superior design.

But despite the board's finding no flaw in Holland's design, expressing no hesitation as to whether the boat would function as described, agreeing that Holland's "porpoise" method of diving was more speedy and efficient than either Baker's or Lake's, and submitting in its report that the Holland boat "meets every requirement of the service 'fairly well'" and that "the inventor's experience with submarines also counts in his favor," Holland was not quickly declared the winner.

From the "ominous silence," Holland and Frost knew problems were afoot. When word did finally arrive from the board, it was not what the Holland forces had hoped to hear. It was rather "a request from [board member] Lieutenant Commander C. S. Sperry for further descriptions and calculations to support Holland's drawings." Holland and Frost knew that "such an inquiry could only mean that pressure was being placed on the Board to postpone a final decision."[12]

Baker had indeed pulled the right strings. It was revealed later that the board had recommended that Holland be awarded the contract but had been overruled by Commodore Sampson. E. B. Frost had tried to pull some strings of his own, of course—Baker's supporters were not the only lobbyists Simon Lake saw in the anteroom—but Baker had simply done a better job.

Once Sampson had deferred the contract, Baker claimed that he was "fully prepared to demonstrate [his boat] on Lake Michigan for the benefit of the Navy. Senator William B. Allison of Iowa and General C. M. Shelley, Baker's lawyer, persuaded the Secretary of the Navy that the Board on Submarine Torpedo Boats should put Baker's little vessel through her paces. The Board, in fairness to Holland, Baker's major competitor, offered him the opportunity to present a boat of his own."[13]

At that point, of course, Holland didn't have a boat of his own. He hadn't thought he needed one. Frost then "set out to counteract the Baker lobby. He requested Holland to find a shipbuilder for the submarine should he, Frost, be able to negotiate a contract with the Navy."

In the meantime, Holland responded to the board's offer. He wrote to them noting that "The *Fenian Ram* still existed, but vandals had stripped her of gauges and other machinery; and she lay in a state of neglect in the yard of James Reynolds in New Haven. The cost of refitting her would be considerable; and his company, already financially embarrassed as a result of the design competition, should not have to bear the expense." He then pointed out that the official circular advertised for designs only and that a July 28 editorial in the *New York Times* stated categorically that the Holland design had been accepted by the board without need of further testing. "Did the Board now intend to change the tenor of its report?" he asked.[14] Having heard that the board members were to be inside Baker's boat during its test run, Holland could not resist an acerbic jab at his wooden competitor and its creator. "If the newspaper description of Mr. Baker's boat is anywhere near accurate, I entreat you to examine the structure carefully before you submerge below 20 to 25 feet. My motive for this request is, I admit, a very selfish one—of objecting to the risk of having to wait for a decision until a new Board can be appointed."[15]

Captain Sampson was none too thrilled with suggestions of chicanery or favoritism in the awards process, likely even more so because he was guilty of one or both. He replied through the board that "the *New York Times*, or any newspaper in the country for that matter, was not the official organ of the Navy Department. The Board also asserted that, when a boat such as Baker's existed, it was quite proper to desire to test her. The case rested there as far as the Navy was concerned."[16]

The three board members traveled to Chicago and the Baker boat was tested on September 6, 1893, with all the members aboard. Although they did emerge alive, the submarine's performance was apparently inauspicious. The board members returned immediately to Washington, and three days later, newspapers reported that they had again recommended that Secretary Herbert award the contract to Holland rather than George Baker. This time, Sampson did not object. Five weeks later, the *New York Times* reported that the "Holland Submarine Boat, practically indestructible" had been "unanimously approved," awaiting only Secretary Herbert's approval to disburse the funds.[17]

But despite the poor performance of his boat, Baker refused to give up. If Sampson could no longer be relied on, he would move up the line to Sampson's boss. Through Senator Allison and other surrogates, Baker lodged another protest, this time to Hilary Herbert. And so, "in spite of the optimism among the officials of the John P. Holland Torpedo Boat Company over the decision," when the board's report reached Secretary Herbert's desk, he refused to approve it, claiming for the moment that "the appropriation should be diverted to other naval construction."[18]

With no money coming in and the possibility looming of having to actually build a boat before the contract was awarded, Frost cast about for a solution. His father had witnessed the test in Chicago, so E. B. knew that Baker wasn't close to building anything that would satisfy the navy's specifications. To try to break the stalemate, hoping it was simply a matter of money, Frost offered Baker $200,000 in Holland company stock to sign over his patents and allow the process to go forward, but Baker turned him down. With Secretary Herbert at the least vacillating and at the most trying to steer the contract his way, Baker saw no need to accept $200,000 when a contract with the navy, already upped to $250,000, could ultimately be worth millions.

Herbert did not disappoint him. Purely of his own volition, "In November, he ordered the Navy Department to conduct tests to determine if the crew of a submarine could survive an underwater explosion. The tests were conducted in December at the Naval Torpedo Station in Newport, Rhode Island. The tests consisted of submerging a tank containing a cat, a rabbit, a rooster and a dove, then setting off a series of explosions progressively closer to the tank. The cat and the rooster survived, but the rabbit and dove did not. The decision to award a contract for the construction of a submarine boat was further delayed as the Secretary mulled over the results of these tests."[19]

Secretary Herbert continued to mull for three months. Even Baker grew frustrated with the wait—total recalcitrance was not what he had had in mind. In March 1894, he traveled to Washington to meet with Herbert in the hopes of prodding him to a favorable decision, although how he could assert that wood construction would protect a crew more than iron is a mystery. Before he could even meet with the secretary, however, he was rushed to the hospital with appendicitis, a far from routine ailment in the 1890s. The surgery to save him was unsuccessful and on March 23, 1894, George Baker died. He was fifty years old. Any chance of a government contract for the Baker submarine died with him.

Unfortunately, the absence of a competitor did mean a good result for Frost and Holland. Hilary Herbert, it seemed, despite congressional authorization and numerous recommendations from naval officers, had no intention of spending any money on submarines. He gave no reason for his obstinacy, which many found puzzling. "Secretary Herbert's disinclination to build a submarine torpedo boat has been a matter of wonderment. The experts have generally agreed that sub-aquatic navigation is feasible and, applied to naval warfare, advisable," wrote the *New York Times*.[20]

But, freed from the Baker threat, E. B. Frost found some creative ways to motivate the navy secretary. Hilary Herbert might not have seen the promise of submarines as both a means of coastal defense and of surprise attack, but others most surely did. The *Times* had also noted, "The foreigners who have pretended to a progression in the art have readily experimented with submarine boats, and some of the European navies, notably that of France, have adopted the idea." And so the company took out patent applications everywhere from Italy to Germany to Japan to Chile, and appointed agents—one of whom was Edmund Zalinski, another the now-retired Francis Barber—to represent its interests in foreign capitals. Frost made it known that no arrangement with another nation would be finalized until one year after a contract had been signed with the United States Navy, but of course if no such contract were signed, he and Holland would have no choice but to seek another buyer for their invention.

Herbert protracted the process as much as he could—for one thing, the economy was deeply in recession and spending money on an untried invention that turned out to be a frivolity would be an enormous embarrassment—but allowing an effective and deadly new weapon of naval warfare to fall into the hands of other nations while the United States dithered was equally unpalatable. In August 1894, Herbert moved the process forward by passing the buck. As reported in the newspapers, "The Secretary of the Navy has referred to the Construction Board of Bureau Chiefs the submarine boat project for their opinion as to whether it would be advisable to build a vessel of that type during the present depressed condition of the Treasury, when the necessity for economy is so urgent." Herbert also asked their opinion on whether the Holland boat should be accepted if they agreed to move ahead. Within weeks, the construction board issued an enthusiastic approval of both the project and Holland's design.

Still, the process dragged on. Other bureaus were required to sign off on the design, each meeting taking place weeks after the one before. All the while John Holland, now married with two children, had no income save the $100 per month salary the company could afford to pay him. At the end of November, newspapers reported the Holland submarine had finally been given the go-ahead to be built, and at the end of December that Secretary Herbert had given his official sanction to the project, but those reports turned out to be premature as well. It was not until March 1895 that Hilary Herbert finally agreed to add submarines to the United States naval fleet and awarded a construction contract for $200,000 to the Holland Torpedo Boat Company.

CHAPTER 12
UNEASY NEIGHBORS

George Baker may no longer have been around to bedevil Holland and Frost, nor Tuck nor Nordenfelt, but in their place was an adversary more talented, more committed, and more sensitive to perceived injustice than any of them.

Whether or not Simon Lake had actually been told that his design had been looked on favorably by the review board, he was certain that any submarine based on Holland's "porpoise diving" principles would fail and that only he, Lake, had designed a workable boat. As the months dragged on, Lake's resentment grew, as did his conviction that he had lost not on merit, but only because of politics.

Lake did realize that, not yet thirty, with no capital, no track record, no investors, and no friends in Washington, he faced challenges that his competitors did not. Also, he had submitted only a design, without a construction bid. Rather than continue to try to penetrate the armor-plated government bureaucracy, Lake decided to instead simply build his own boat.

He lacked the money to build a full-size submarine, which was to be called *Argonaut*, so as an interim step, he chose to build a small, crude prototype he would dub *Argonaut Junior*. The experimental craft would "demonstrate the two principal features over which almost every one seemed to be skeptical. These were the ability to navigate over the bottom of the ocean and the ability to enter and leave the boat while submerged without any water coming in and foundering her."[1] After successfully sailing his model, Lake was certain that he would have no difficulty attracting private investors.

Argonaut, Jr.

To describe the *Argonaut Junior* as built on a shoestring would be an understatement. Only fourteen feet long, four wide, five high, and displacing a mere seven tons, it was essentially a large wooden box shaped like a flatiron, with ballast chambers that could be blown with compressed air. Compressed air would also pressurize the inside of the craft so that water did not flood in when a trapdoor was opened at the bottom. A set of wooden wheels was attached to the underside, powered by a foot treadle. As Lake described, "She was built of yellow pine planking, double thick, lined with canvas laid between the double layers of planking, the outer seams caulked. She was a flat-sided affair and would not stand great external pressure. She was propelled when on the bottom by a man turning a crank on the inside. Our compressed-air reservoir was a soda-water fountain tank. The compressed-air pump was a plumber's hand-pump, by which means we were able to compress the air in the tanks to a pressure of about one hundred pounds per square inch."[2]

Lake designed a means to exit and enter the submerged vessel as well. "My diving suit I built myself by shaping iron in the form of an open helmet, which extended down as far as my breast; this I covered with painted canvas. I used the dead-light from a yacht's cabin as my eyeglass in front of the helmet. I tied sash weights to my legs to hold me down on the bottom when walking in the vicinity of the boat."

Lake began tests of his vessel in December 1894, with the help of his cousin, Bart Champion. Their first test voyage turned out not to be what Lake, and especially Champion, were expecting. "The first time we went under water a stream of water came through a bolt-hole which had not been plugged and struck Bart on the back of the neck. He said, 'Ugh!' and made a dive. The *Argonaut* had a little port-hole in one end about six inches in diameter, and Bart said afterward, 'I made a dive for that port-hole, but came to the conclusion that I could not get through, so I stopped.'" Lake quickly plugged the hole and he and a shaken but relieved Champion navigated the wooden boat across the Shrewsbury River and back.

From there, Lake and Champion became regular fixtures along the riverfront and their voyages almost always included trips outside. At one point, "we took the boat up to Atlantic Highlands and had a lot of fun running around on the bottom of New York Bay picking up clams and oysters, etc."[3]

Lake reported that his little wooden boat was receiving "no little newspaper notoriety," although he could not help but notice "a vein of skepticism and sarcasm running through most of these early accounts." In early January 1895, for example, the *Argonaut Junior* received a glowing, albeit somewhat tongue-in-cheek write-up in the *New York Herald*. "This Boat Crawls Along the Bottom," read the lead to the piece. "At Least That's What It Was To Do, but It Escapes and

Astonishes Folks in Oceanic, N. J." Just underneath, it read, "It Will Crawl Five Miles Without Coming Up to Breathe When Inventor Lake Completes It. Fun for Merry Mermen."[4]

The body of the piece maintained the tone. "Strange things come in with the tide in the ungodly hours of the night, and in the stillness of the night strange things follow them, but the strange thing which came up the North Shrewsbury a day or two ago, and which lies high and dry on Barley Point, is a new one on the good folk of Oceanic. Now that they have fairly discovered it, they are sorry that it didn't wobble ashore in the summer, when Normandie-by-the-Sea below the Point is crowded with curious persons from the city. Any enterprising Oceanic man might have fenced in the queer thing and charged every one a quarter to see it."

For serious followers of submarine research, of course, the reaction was far different. Any success in navigating underwater served to at least prod the skeptics. Still, Lake's *Argonaut Junior* did not change anyone's mind in Washington, DC. It did, however, allow him to attract sufficient investment capital to undertake construct of a full-size version of his submarine. Although he wanted to build the boat to correspond to the plans he had drawn up for the navy competition, to control costs he was forced to scale down some of his more ambitious accessories.

Financial challenges would prove greater than Lake anticipated. Although he was fortunate that one of his investors was William Malster, president of the Columbia Dry Dock and Iron Works in Baltimore, where the *Argonaut* would be built, he was not so lucky when another investor turned out to be a swindler.

Lake, by his own admission, still callow, was approached by a man he later called only "Mr. H-" who purported to be friends with the Vanderbilts, the Astors, and the Goulds. He was living in a mansion in Baltimore and was introduced to Lake by an officer of the bank in which Lake intended to keep his new company's accounts. After a lengthy and elaborate series of feints and dodges, Mr. H- succeeded in being named general manager of the new firm and was on the verge of obtaining Lake's signature on blank stock certificates and $2,000 in company funds, as well as the rights to the patents Lake had applied for, when Malster intervened and saved the young inventor. It cost Lake and Malster a bit of money to untangle the company's affairs, but Lake had learned a lesson that would stay with him his entire career.

"The raising of capital to most inventors is a serious problem," he wrote later. "It has been so with me. I have always been interested in mechanical accomplishments, but dreaded the necessity of trying to raise capital to carry on those experiments. I have never valued money for itself or felt the need of it except when I did not have it. I think this is the case with most inventors, which is the reason why so many of them go to unscrupulous promoters who rob them of their inventions, or else often tie them up so that they themselves are incapable of continuing their development work."[5]

Free of Mr. H-, Lake began to oversee construction of the *Argonaut* in autumn 1895 at Columbia Dry Dock, and he soon acquired an interesting neighbor. Holland too chose to build his submarine at Columbia, issuing a deposit with funds he had obtained from the United States Treasury. E. B. Frost was uncomfortable with Holland being in such proximity to a former competitor, especially since William Malster was a principal in Lake's new venture.

But Holland did not share Frost's concern. Lewis Nixon, who supervised construction at the Cramps' shipyard, had become someone with whom Holland worked very well. But Cramps had mishandled the first bid, which might well have been the cause of the two-year delay, so Holland solved the problem by hiring Nixon as a consulting engineer, where he could supervise construction of the Holland boat at Columbia, and also make sure that both Malster or Lake behaved aboveboard.

But despite the advantage of an assured sale to the navy, and for once not having to put up any money, it became apparent early in the process that Holland's contract would not mark the end of his frustrations. The naval experts assigned to oversee production of the boat, to be called the *Plunger*, and ensure adherence to the agreed specifications, were notably inexpert—like most naval officers, they had no practical experience with submarine design—and, as is often the case with those who lack knowledge, were that much more inflexible for their ignorance.

As a further complication, Holland was forced to deal with multiple panels of experts. While the Bureau of Ordnance was responsible for overseeing most of the construction, the Bureau of Steam Engineering was responsible for determining propulsion specifications. Holland had initially wanted to use a gasoline engine, but the navy had no "Bureau of Gasoline Engineering," so steam it would be—as it turned out, quite a lot of steam.

When Holland asked "what propulsion would be approved for the *Plunger*, he was told that twin screws must be installed, whatever else." The twin screws, which would need be powered by a massive engine generating fifteen-hundred-horsepower, was the only means the steam engineers could divine to achieve the required horsepower and fifteen-knot cruising speed on the surface or awash. Holland tried to explain that "he had to have a propeller in the axis of the spindle-of-revolution shaped boat [along the keel] to push her under and to push her up, and if compelled to install twin screws in addition to their engines, there would be great and unnecessary complications." For one thing, the navy did not shield steam engines in those days, and the temperature the motors would generate inside the hull, especially when the vessel was submerged, would be sufficient to "roast the crew." But the steam engineers were having none of it. "Holland was told that was a matter for him to meet, but that she must have twin propellers."[6]

To power the boat when submerged, Holland feared that he would be forced to used stored steam, but he was allowed to switch to far more efficient battery power. Thus in addition to three steam engines, the *Plunger* would also carry a battery array capable of powering an electric motor at seventy horsepower. To accommodate all this equipment, much of which Holland considered unnecessary and detrimental to performance, the *Plunger* was designed to be eighty-five feet long, as opposed to thirty-six for Lake's *Argonaut*.

Size and weight would not be the only detriments to performance. Holland wanted to control the depth as he always did, with horizontal planes, but the navy decided that the submarine must essentially hover underwater, maintain depth without moving forward, so vertical propellers were added.

How the *Plunger* was armed also became contentious. The Bureau of Ordnance insisted on two torpedo tubes. Holland had designed the craft for one and explained that "in view of the shape of the bow, two eighteen inch tubes would destroy her bow lines," thus making the vessel more difficult to maneuver. But "twin torpedo tubes were declared to be absolutely necessary, so Holland sorrowfully got to work to get those requirements into his working plans."[7] Holland became so frustrated at dealing with "boards" that when asked to define one, he referred to a dictionary entry that read, "long, narrow, and wooden."[8]

William Kimball was appalled, but he had once again been assigned to extended sea duty, so the navy's most knowledgeable officer would be unavailable until construction was under way. Before he left, however, he met with Frost and said, "In my opinion, the *Plunger* had been made an utter failure. I expressed the opinion that the only practical thing to do, provided the company had the necessary pluck and the more necessary money, was to build a boat of their own and demonstrate what she could do."[9] It was a course that Holland would have been thrilled to follow, but the "necessary money" was not there to do it. There was no choice but to move forward with the navy's specifications and hope a workable boat could be salvaged.

That task was made even more complicated when Holland was taken ill with respiratory problems. That summer, he also welcomed into the world his third child. Holland did his best to remain engaged on a project on which his reputation and posterity depended, but it is difficult not to conclude that he felt the fates had once more aligned against him.

E. B. Frost faced the same issues but from a different perspective. He was far too wily a lawyer and a businessman not to see that a future so problematic must be somehow prepared for. Regardless of the impediments, the success or failure of the company, at least for the immediate future, was totally dependent on John Holland. Only he could salvage the *Plunger* and, if he could not, only he could develop an alternative. As any positive outcome was dependent on chronically fragile lungs, Frost took out a hefty life insurance policy on Holland, which would not, however, cover fatality during an underwater voyage.

But to Frost, the risk of a dead inventor was potentially no greater than the risk of an unhappy live one. Nothing prevented Holland, who Frost had come to see as a "mechanical genius, who, properly handled, was worth millions of dollars," from simply leaving his company and starting over if he became sufficiently disgusted with the navy's bastardization of his design. So to bind Holland to him, Frost, with great fanfare, granted him a large, although less than controlling, block of stock in the company.[10] In return, Frost convinced Holland that, as an owner, it was only fair that anything he developed remain property of the company, rather than pass to Holland as an individual. Holland, thus approached in a spirit of honor and fairness, agreed and signed over his patents. There are indications that Frost tried also to obtain patents Holland held not related to submarine design, but it does not appear that he was successful. Holland's short-sightedness in signing over patents potentially worth a fortune to a company he did not own has been explained away as naïveté, idealism, or simply a lack of alternatives, but a man who had spent two decades dealing with the Fenians, Edmund Zalinski, naval bureaucrats, and a variety of other self-interested characters should have known better.

As 1895 drew to a close, Holland had become more and more frustrated with the navy's intransigence. He was now certain, as Kimball had been certain, that the submarine he had been forced to design would not work. Nonetheless, if he spoke publically of his convictions or stopped work, the company's financing would disappear. Holland wasn't alone in being discouraged. Lewis Nixon, the consulting engineer he had hired, threw up his hands in despair and refused to even visit the Baltimore shipyard. Holland was unsuccessful in luring a replacement, and William Malster was not going to help, since, if Holland's company failed, Lake's—and Malster's—would rush in to fill the void.

Oddly, the closer the *Plunger* came to becoming an immense boondoggle, the more fawning the coverage became in the press. By early 1896, "Holland's name appeared almost daily in the great metropolitan newspapers, and magazines sent feature writers to Baltimore to report on the progress of the *Plunger*." In February 1896, for example, an article in the *Washington Morning Times* extolled Holland's craft, which it compared to the "the mystic ships of the Arabian Nights," one that "will do away with the necessity of warships for defense or fighting."[11] *Harper's Round Table* added, "It may make as great a revolution in naval warfare as the famous *Monitor*, built by Mr. Ericsson, did in the war of 1861. For what battle-ship would be proof against it? The biggest of all battle-ships would only sink quicker than smaller ones, and huge warships of all kinds would be nothing more than death-traps for all those aboard them."[12] An engineering trade magazine was less flamboyant but equally enthusiastic. "The Holland submarine boat, invented by Mr. John P. Holland, has awakened wonderful interest in this country [and] shows the tremendous advantage possessed by a vessel of this description over one floating on the surface of the water. It proves that the construction of submarine vessels which can be perfectly controlled is no longer a matter of experiment, and in addition shows that warfare in the future, when carried on at sea, may be like the battles of great cetaceans."[13]

The accolades stoked public—and congressional—anticipation for a vessel that most Americans considered only as science fiction. In May 1896, as Holland was beginning to consider that he might have no choice but to abandon the project, the House held hearings on the *Plunger*. One of those called before the naval affairs committee was Captain (later Admiral) Alfred Thayer Mahan, a past president of the Naval War College, whose books, *The Influence of Sea Power upon History, 1660–1783* and *The Influence of Sea Power upon the French Revolution and Empire, 1793–1812*, would have perhaps more influence on American foreign policy than any volumes in United States history.[14] "In our present unprotected position," Mahan testified, "the risk of losing money by the government by reason of the boat's being a failure is more than counterbalanced by the protection the boat would be if a substantial success."[15] Lieutenant Commander Kimball was another witness. "Give me six Holland submarine boats, the officers and crew to be selected by me, and I will pledge my life to stand off the entire British squadron ten miles off Sandy Hook [New Jersey] without any aid from our fleet."[16] The following month, Congress voted to appropriate

$350,000 for the construction of two additional submarines "of the Holland type."[17]

That none of the senators and representatives even considered any other type of undersea craft further inflamed the man building a very different sort of vessel just yards from the *Plunger*, who was absolutely convinced that they should have. Simon Lake rarely needed a spur to righteous indignation, but $350,000 made him even more determined to make his enemies, real and imagined, regret their lack of foresight.

CHAPTER 13
ARGONAUT

Lake had a good platform from which to do so. Unfettered by navy requirements and working with private funds, he was free to build the *Argonaut* to any specifications he pleased. As a result, rather than build a warship, Lake chose to return to his original vision of building a vessel that could patrol the bottom for exploration and salvage. This design would not be immediately adaptable as a warship, but Lake, never perturbed by the opinions of others, was convinced that it was what the navy wanted nonetheless.

Building his *Argonaut* within hailing distance of the Holland boat had the obvious potential of causing friction between the two camps, but, although the two sides did not fraternize a great deal, there were no reports of hostility. Lake, even at this early stage of his career, seemed to have understood that the eighty-foot behemoth being thrown together next to him would never sail successfully; and Holland, forced to build such a contraption, was embarrassed to be doing so next to a competitor who he knew would appreciate just how poor a design it was.

In any event, while construction of the *Plunger* limped along, progress on the *Argonaut* proceeded apace. Although he would adhere to the same principles as with the *Argonaut Junior*, the full-size boat was built of steel plates, three-eighths of an inch thick, and displaced fifty-nine tons when submerged. Lake would submerge the *Argonaut* more like a submersible than an attack vessel, essentially dropping it like a stone to the sea bottom. He would first release half-ton anchor weights, then take on water ballast until the vessel was negatively buoyant. The *Argonaut*, like all boats he designed, would then descend on an even keel, parallel with the sea floor, rather than diving at an angle. In this first model, Lake did not install diving planes, the only serious submarine designer who failed to do so. (Subsequent models would have them.)

At a depth of fifty feet, which was as deep as the *Argonaut* was designed on most occasions to operate, a crew might succeed in escaping if the negatively buoyant vessel was disabled; at greater depths they were almost certainly doomed. The fifty-foot limit was set by a ventilation pipe of that length carried on the outside of the hull, which could be raised to the surface, supported by a float. The air taken into the hull would supply the crew by means of an internal blower, and, more important, feed the submarine's motor. Another pipe of equal length extended from the stern to carry exhaust gases.

The *Argonaut* employed a gasoline-powered internal combustion engine; Lake later claimed he was the first to do this. In fact, since Holland had tried the ill-fated Brayton engine previously, Lake was merely the first to employ an Otto-style engine, the sort of internal combustion engine that would become commonplace in automobiles and surface ships. Holland had tried to install an Otto-style engine in the *Plunger* but had been refused by the navy's steam engineers.

Lake initially designed his boat to carry a crew of five. As with his wooden model, three corrugated wheels were fitted to the bottom of the hull, the rear wheel smaller than the two seven-footers in front. The thirty-horsepower engine would drive both the single propeller and the wheels, which, once the *Argonaut* had settled on the bottom, would, in effect, simply drive about looking for available salvage. A powerful electric searchlight was mounted in the bow, and the boat also had a system of internal lighting, all run off storage batteries charged by a dynamo, again driven by the gasoline engine. (Lake would later admit that the searchlight had little utility, except for patrolling the sea bottom at night, which he had scant intention to do.) Compressed air tanks were installed to create sufficient pressure inside the boat to allow a diver to enter and exit through a compartment built in the bow. In case of a mishap, the compressed air would also provide a reserve of breathable air for the crew that could last up to twenty-four hours. While the air reserve would seem to mitigate the risks from negative buoyancy, in practice, locating and then safely removing a crew from a disabled vessel resting on the bottom in seventy-five or one hundred feet of water in one day presented enormous challenges with the technology available in 1896. It would likely require a second *Argonaut*-style submarine standing by to effect the rescue.

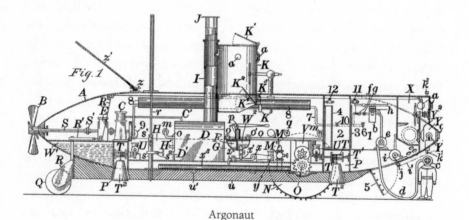

Argonaut

By early 1897, the *Argonaut* was near completion. *Scientific American*, the nation's most prestigious science magazine, sent a reporter to examine Lake's boat and he came back with a glowing report, describing the vessel as "capable of rising to the surface and submerging at will, and propelled in any desired direction when on the bottom. A door may be opened, through which the occupants, by donning a diving suit, may pass from the interior to the outside and back again. The boat will be used principally for searching the bed of the ocean adjacent to coastlines, and in locating and recovering sunken vessels and their cargoes."[1] Engineering journals were equally enthusiastic.

Accolades notwithstanding, use of an internal combustion while submerged necessitated a series of modifications. Although "special care" had been given to seal the fuel tanks, with the tanks internal, it proved impossible to prevent gasoline fumes from filling the cabin. "The tanks were tested under hydraulic pressure and found to be tight, but the fumes from gasolene (petrol) are very searching, and, after filling the fuel tanks and keeping them filled overnight, gasolene fumes were found to exist in the boat the next morning to such an extent that I would not venture to make a start until a fuel tank had been built outside of the vessel, where any escape of fumes would not form an explosive mixture."[2]

Carbon monoxide was another problem. "On our first submarine run, after we had been down about two hours some of us commenced to experience a dull pain at the base of the brain and a decided feeling of lassitude. On coming to the surface a couple of our men collapsed completely, and one was very sick all night. I could not understand the cause of this, as nothing of the kind had occurred in my previous hand-propelled vessel, so we made another submerged run the following day, and after about the same period of time the pain in the head and weariness came on again."[3] Lake discovered that when the engine backfired, carbon monoxide was escaping past the piston rings and seeping into the base of the engine and from there into the boat.

To prevent the crew from being overcome, he designed an ingenious device he called an "induction tank." The tank was connected to the air intake, the engine base, and the exhaust. A slight vacuum in the tank would draw in air to be fed to the engine, but also spent gases to be vented through the exhaust. A valve was designed to remain open while the engine ran normally, but to snap shut in case of a backfire. From there, "the gases from the backfire were caught in the induction tank, from which they were drawn out on the next stroke of the engine. This solved the difficulty, and thereafter the air was always fresh and pure when running submerged even after a submergence of several hours' duration."[4]

Although the *Argonaut* was being built for commercial rather than military use—it had no weapons capability at all—Lake's bitterness at being denied the navy contract in favor of John Holland continued to build. He would insist for years afterward that, as war was nearing with Spain, the then assistant secretary of navy, Theodore Roosevelt, had been sufficiently interested in his design that he promised to empanel an advisory board to study the feasibility of using Lake submarines to clear minefields. The board failed to materialize, Lake asserted, because Secretary Roosevelt resigned his post to lead the Rough Riders.[5] But there is no mention of any such intention in naval records, nor in Roosevelt's. Lake further claimed that to prove its worth, he took the submerged *Argonaut* to the mouth of Chesapeake Bay, charted the mines and cables, and then presented a detailed map to the local commanding officer. Rather than congratulate him and recommend a feasibility study, the commander told Lake that if he entered the bay again, he would be arrested. The reason the navy was steadfast in rejecting his overtures, Lake contended, was because it had already contracted for the *Plunger* and was unwilling to admit any possible error in the award of the contract.[6] Once again, there are no other accounts to corroborate these assertions.

But there is extensive corroboration that, in the *Argonaut*, Simon Lake was building an exceptional and unique machine. From its first trials, the vessel demonstrated that not only was it capable of successfully discharging the tasks for which it had been designed, but that it could do so with extraordinary efficiency. In October 1897, for example, "A successful trial of the submarine wrecking-boat 'Argonaut' was made at the Columbian Iron Works, Baltimore, Md. The inventor, Simon Lake, accompanied by six men, remained for two hours in the vessel without discomfort while submerged in twenty-one feet of water. There was an abundance of light and air, and cigars were smoked in the cabin."[7]

Lake saved his most impressive demonstration for the press and the public on December 16. "In the presence of 1000 persons the *Argonaut*, built by Simon Lake of [Baltimore], was submerged in twenty feet of water, and remained at the bottom of the Patapsco for four hours. After cruising on the surface, the little craft took up a position a short distance from shore, and in two minutes after coming to a standstill went to the bottom and cruised around at the will of those inside. Those who accompanied the inventor say they experienced no unpleasant sensation." But the onboard guests, which included some reporters, were in for an additional treat. "When at full stop, a diver entered an airtight compartment and made his way out of the vessel. Those within were able to watch him as he moved about at the bottom of the river. A dinner was served underwater and the guests experienced no difficulty while eating."[8] The dinner, oyster stew and coffee, was cooked on the submerged boat.

Although in some other early newspaper accounts the boat was described as one of "the queerest craft ever constructed," by January 1898, the *Argonaut* had attracted sufficient renown to be featured in a full-page Sunday magazine feature article in the *New York Times*. Titled "A Submarine Search Boat," the piece opened, "Jules Verne in his wildest imaginings, which were the foundation of the stories so dear to the schoolboy's heart, 'Twenty Thousand Leagues Under the Sea' and 'Around the World in Eighty Days,' entertained but visionary ideas of what Simon Lake, a Baltimore inventor, has put into practical shape by the completion and successful trial of his submarine wrecking steamer *Argonaut*." From there, the reporter recounted, with some accuracy, the ventures of Bushnell, Fulton, and Hunley, but made no mention of John Holland, the *Fenian Ram*, or the contract with the navy. That he was taking Lake's version without further investigation was made clear when Lake was described as having worked fifteen years to perfect his design. At the time, Simon Lake was only thirty-one years old.

He spared no accolades, exclaiming, "The *Argonaut* has undoubtedly accomplished results never before achieved by submarine vessels." Although noting that because the river bottom was covered with mud "several feet deep" that rendered the wheels on the craft "of no practical use," the reporter proclaimed that, "The Argonaut has undoubtedly accomplished results never before achieved by submarine vessels." The descent was described as causing "no vibration whatever." The reporter noted that *Argonaut*'s prime purpose would be for salvage, where the estimate value of cargos at the bottom of the sea was $100,000,000.*

Finally, the boat's interior was described as nothing short of commodious. "The living room," one of the *Argonaut*'s four compartments, was described as having "comfortable seats on one side," and "the entire boat is lighted by electricity, and a telephone system connects each of the smaller apartments with the main room."[9]

The telephone connection would prove an especially attractive publicity feature. Lake announced his intention "to establish connections with the Baltimore Exchange and also the Long Distance Telephone, and proposes talking to New York, Chicago, and other distant cities from the bottom of the Patapsco."[10] The communication could not be wireless, of course, but Lake found a way to communicate effectively while in the vicinity of any port. "The arrangements are unique. The wire, which is on a reel, is enclosed in water-tight tubes and can be extended for several miles if necessary."[11] Lake placed his first telephone calls to his company offices, the owner of the telephone company in Washington, DC, and to the mayor of Baltimore. "A new telephone number, 3,041, was inscribed in the local directory today," newspapers reported on January 7, 1898. Shortly afterward, Lake could not resist placing a call to the Holland Submarine Boat Company in New York City. Neither John Holland nor E. B. Frost was in at the time.

To Lake's annoyance, neither the *Times* feature not the spate of other glowing reports piqued the interest of the navy. It did, however, attract the attention of two visiting naval officers from Japan. In late January, they toured the *Argonaut* and, while they expressed some interest in that boat, they were far more keen when Lake reportedly showed them the plans for a "torpedo boat he was perfecting." Lake had made no public mention of designing a boat to directly compete with Holland's nor was there any record that he had informed American naval officials of such an intention.

The following month, however, Lake tried once more to interest the admirals in the boat he had already built. After the battleship *Maine* exploded and sank in Havana Harbor on February 15, 1898,

---

* $2.5 billion in current value.

killing three-quarters of its crew, Hearst and Pulitzer newspapers began to beat the drums for war. The cause of the explosion aboard the antiquated relic was unknown, and remains so today, but that did not prevent widespread speculation that the sinking was an act of terrorism precipitated by Spain.

Seeing a unique opportunity to prove the *Argonaut's* mettle, less than seventy-two hours after the *Maine* went down, Lake sent a special delivery telegram to the secretary of the navy promising to lend invaluable assistance to both the inquiry and the recovery efforts.

Dear Sir: We hereby offer our services and the use of our submarine boat *Argonaut* for recovering the bodies of the crew, the armament, supplies and hull (if same is not too badly injured) of the United States battle ship *Maine*, sunk in Havana harbor. The *Argonaut* will be of great service in investigating the cause of the explosion and the condition of the ship. If it had been caused by the explosion of a submarine mine, with shore connections, there are, undoubtedly, other mines or some underwater evidence in the vicinity, and the *Argonaut* could be used in locating them, and also to see where their connections terminate. We can take your board of inquiry down alongside the *Maine*, and allow them to view or inspect the hull and photograph same, if the water is reasonably clear. Telephone connections could be kept up with the submarine boat while at work on the bottom. The boat is provided with powerful electric lights for lighting up the locality over which she is traveling or while at work. The divers are not discommoded by surface conditions or currents; they have their tools right at hand and machinery for their assistance. The *Argonaut* is capable of carrying a crew of seven or eight persons and remaining on the bottom for several days at a time. We have special tools and apparatus, which will greatly facilitate the raising of vessels.[12]

All these claims seemed within the boat's capabilities, although Lake had never before asked the *Argonaut* to perform under such conditions. He did admit that the *Argonaut* lacked the speed to sail to Havana under her own power, but he proposed either having the boat towed or hoisted to the deck of a steamer ship and transported piggyback to Havana Harbor.

Although accounts began to appear in newspapers that the *Argonaut* had indeed been towed to Florida, in preparation for the final leg, this seems never to have happened. Lake was furious at being turned down on what he saw as a free offer to demonstrate in a practical setting what his invention could do. Almost certainly, he blamed E. B. Frost for closing him out with the military. Almost four decades later, in his autobiography, his antipathy had not cooled.

> I was bitterly angry at the Army and the Navy at this time. Of course I was. I had developed a submarine which . . . was able to deliver the goods I promised and no other submarines could or did. I was thirty-two years old, full of strength as a barracuda, red-headed and, as I believed, a deeply injured man. I saw other men with other submarines get sympathetic hearings from congressional committees and naval authorities, and money and contracts. I was the only man who could do anything under water and I was not even permitted to show what I could do. Because what I was doing every day was so far ahead of what any one else had done, I was looked on as a nut. The joint attitude of the Army and Navy was: "Lake is a crank and a liar. He cannot do what he says he does. If we catch him doing it we'll knock down his ears."[13]

His plan to make worldwide headlines with the salvage of a celebrated battleship thus thwarted, Lake returned to his initial plan of recovering sunken material less glamorous but a good deal more lucrative. In July 1898, he took the *Argonaut* for an exploratory salvage voyage off Cape Henry, Virginia. He sighted a number of wrecks but realized that he lacked the necessary equipment to actually extract material in any volume, load it onto his boat, and then convey it to the surface. (Lake only admitted this later. To do so at the time would have blunted his claims about what he could achieve with the wreck of the *Maine*.)

A larger problem, he decided, particularly with the navy, was that the *Argonaut* was almost universally seen as a vessel whose main use would be in shallow water, close to shore, whereas Holland's craft, using his porpoise diving and surfacing techniques, was assumed to be effective in deeper water. To debunk those characterizations, Lake decided to take the *Argonaut* into the open ocean and travel from Norfolk, Virginia, to Sandy Hook, New Jersey, an unthinkable one thousand miles. Most of the voyage would be spent on the surface, but Lake would make certain to submerge often. While doing so, he could also check for salvage opportunities which he could map and return to when he had refitted his boat. During a storm, he simply remained on the bottom until it passed. He later claimed two hundred vessels were lost in stormy conditions during his voyage, such a blatant exaggeration that even his most sympathetic biographer admitted that to reach that number, Lake would have had to include rowboats.[14]

During the voyage Lake did encounter several wrecks, especially in the Chesapeake Bay, "principally coal-laden," one of which contained two hundred tons of material. Coal, which would not be affected be lying on the bottom, was potentially of enormous value if Lake could build a vessel to extract it. He would undertake that task the moment he completed this voyage, planning a boat three times the length of the *Argonaut*.

When Lake docked in New Jersey at the end of September, he had become a sensation. Reporters wanted to hear about the longest undersea journey ever attempted, or at least the longest journey by an undersea boat. One article observed, "The little ship made seven knots running on the surface and eight knots when submerged. She is painted white, so that she may be readily distinguished by the diver who walks out of her on to the sea bottom and happens to get far away. The crew of the *Argonaut* always have plenty of fresh sea food when they are working under the surface. Whenever they run over an oyster bed the diver simply goes out and rakes in a few bushels. If crabs are wanted he takes a net and gathers them in much as a picker in a berry patch gathers berries."[15]

But still, Lake's protests to the navy notwithstanding, there was no question of the boat being considered suitable for battle, but rather only for "wrecking work"—salvage. "Her purpose is not one of war," the *New York Times* wrote, "but from the victories of peace and in their trophies she expects to find her renown."[16]

Lake's journey was written up around the world, and among the telegrams of congratulations he received was one of particular import. The cable read:

> While my book "Twenty Thousand Leagues Under the Sea" is entirely a work of imagination, my conviction is that all I said in it will come to pass. A thousand mile voyage in the Baltimore submarine boat (The *Argonaut*) is evidence of this. This conspicuous success of submarine navigation in the United States will push on under-water navigation all over the world . . . The next great war may be largely a contest between submarine boats. I think that electricity rather than compressed air will be the motive power in such vessels for the sea is full of this element. It is waiting to be harnessed as steam has been. It will then not be necessary to go to the land for fuel any more than for provisions. The sea will supply food for man and power without limit.
>
> Submarine navigation is now ahead of aerial navigation and will advance much faster from now on. Before the United States gains her full development, she is likely to have mighty navies not only on the bosom of the Atlantic and Pacific, but in the upper air and beneath the water's surface.
>
> Jules Verne

Lake later wrote that the cable from Jules Verne "whose *Nautilus* had been responsible for my descent into the sea in a submersible . . . was one of the finest moments of my life."[17]

CHAPTER 14

THE PLUNGE

While Simon Lake was designing, building, and then launching the most sophisticated undersea craft the world had ever known, John Holland, as far as Lake knew, was forced to plod along, trying to salvage something from the government contract that it had taken him a decade to secure. Even the enthusiastic support of Alfred Thayer Mahan and William Kimball, by then the navy's foremost submarine expert, had not been sufficient to allow his adversary to escape the mediocrity of the *Plunger*. Lake's conclusion was quite reasonable—any observer at the Columbia Iron Works shipyard in Baltimore would have thought the same. Work on the *Plunger* proceeded laboriously, its inventor seeming to have little or no interest in its construction or testing.

Observers at the newly established Crescent Shipyard in Elizabethport, New Jersey, however, would have judged events quite differently. They would have seen a fully engaged John Holland building the world's first true attack submarine, a design that would change the face of undersea warfare and be the model of everything that has come since.

By mid-1896, John Holland had realized he was out of alternatives. With Simon Lake clearly capable of producing a boat superior to his, one that would undoubtedly at some point pose a challenge to his contract with the navy, Holland decided that, no matter what it took, he would follow Kimball's advice. He would scrap the *Plunger* and build a new submarine from the keel up, following his own designs and, like Lake, finance it privately.

For once, Holland's timing seemed to be excellent. Lewis Nixon, who Holland respected for both ability and honesty, had left Cramps' shipyard in Philadelphia to strike out on his own. Nixon was an obvious talent. He had graduated in 1882 from the Naval Academy first in his class and had then been sent by the navy to England to the Royal Naval College in Greenwich. He graduated first in his class there as well. On his return, Nixon had been chosen as one of the chief architects of the ABC cruisers, the first to be built after the navy began to modernize. In 1895, he had partnered with another talented Cramps engineer, Arthur Busch, and leased a vacant shipyard. In Nixon and Busch, Holland had two men perfect to bring his vision to fruition and at the same time keep costs to a minimum.

The problem was that any costs were beyond the means of Holland's company at that time. Every penny had been thrown into the *Plunger*. But then, either a benefactor or investor identified only as a "wealthy New York woman," put $25,000 into the company and the new boat was begun.[1] For most of 1897, while Simon Lake was building his *Argonaut* next to the boat he thought was his principal competition, his actual competition was being constructed at an entirely different location.

Lewis Nixon was everything Holland had hoped for. By May 1897, the new vessel had not only been designed, but was ready to be put into the water. Although Holland and Nixon had tried to keep the boat's construction a secret, word had leaked to the press and several reporters showed up for the christening. Descriptions of the event appeared in New York newspapers the following day. "Without any fuss or celebration, the submarine boat *Holland* was launched from Lewis Nixon's shipyard this morning. Mrs. Nixon broke a bottle of wine on the craft's bows just as the last timber was sawed away, and the boat began to slide down the ways. As the saw went through the last block, the *Holland* began to move and Mrs. Nixon broke the bottle on the boat's bows, exclaiming: 'I christen thee *Holland*.'"[2] The launch was preliminary to sea tests as Holland insisted that "no submarine work will be attempted until he has satisfied himself that everything runs smoothly, and that the curious craft answers every motion of the powers that control her." No matter how preliminary, however, once the *Holland* had become public knowledge, Simon Lake realized that his competition was not the mess being cobbled together next door, but rather a boat far more formidable.

Holland

The *Holland* was indeed an immense advance from the *Plunger*, or from any other attack boat ever put into the water. Propulsion was with a single screw, powered on the surface by a forty-five-horsepower Otto-type gasoline engine—precisely the sort that Holland had not been allowed to install on the *Plunger*—and a seventy-five-horsepower electric motor powered by an Exide battery array that could run for eight hours underwater.[3] Exide batteries, also called "chloride accumulators," were fabricated by a recently developed lead-acid process someone had dubbed "excellent oxide." They were not only far more powerful than any batteries previously available but also longer lasting and rechargeable. The process had been patented and the product was sold exclusively by the Electric Storage Battery Company, a corporation that had recently been acquired up by a New York financier named Isaac Rice.

With the Otto engine and Exide batteries, dual propulsion had become practical. In a rendition quite likely overdramatized, Holland was later said to have come upon the arrangement serendipitously. After encountering "the usual difficulty in obtaining the right engine," he had "almost despaired of finding one." But then, "Chance took the inventor to an electrical exhibition at Madison Square Garden, where he noticed the exhibit of an electric-light plant designed for a country home. The generator was driven by a 50 horsepower Otto gasoline engine . . . the internal-combustion gasoline engine giving large power with small space and weight had just been developed . . . 'That is what I want for my boat!' he exclaimed. He promptly bought the engine and installed it on the Holland."[4]

In his new boat, Holland found a simple means to ensure a fixed center of gravity, thus solving the longitudinal stability problem that had bedeviled designers since the *Hunley*. Because the *Holland* dove and surfaced at an angle, no significant volume of water could be allowed to slosh around in ballast tanks that were only partially filled, which could lead to a fatal uncontrolled plunge. Other designers had tried pendulums, some, like Bauer, lead weights that would ride forward or back along the keel, and still others had installed pumps that would be activated automatically to return the vessel to proper attitude.[*]

---

[*] For Simon Lake, whose *Argonaut* more or less settled in the water much as had Edmond Halley's diving bell, a fixed longitudinal center of gravity was less important. For a boat rising or submerging on an even keel, there were many methods to compensate for the sloshing water problem, corrections that could be made before the orientation of the boat shifted too far from the horizontal.

Each of those methods, however, was slow and cumbersome. Holland correctly assumed that an attack submarine would need the enhanced speed and maneuverability angle diving would create, and so boats would be driven downward by rear diving planes, not gravity. The *Holland*, according to its designer, would be able to submerge in sixty seconds, three or four times faster than an even-keel descent. Skeptics, of which there were many, including Simon Lake, considered "porpoise diving" inefficient and dangerous in that it might provoke fatal instability—excess water in the bow could not be compensated for quickly enough.

Holland's epiphany was that in order to create a fixed center of gravity, ballast must remain fixed as well. He therefore designed his main ballast tank to fit around the center of the vessel like a belt and to always be completely full. A smaller, rear tank was kept full as well. Holland then installed a forward trim tank that was only two feet long, not enough to affect the boat's attitude when only partially full. He could take on and expel water from this tank to compensate for used fuel, a fired torpedo, or any other incident that would alter the distribution of weight inside the boat. (He would soon install dedicated compensation tanks that would hold the same weight in water of a fired torpedo.) With stability thus maintained, the stern planes could angle the boat up or down with little difficulty.

The hull of the *Holland* was extremely hydrodynamic—Nixon and Busch contributed a great deal to its design—and for armaments, the *Holland* had one eighteen-inch torpedo tube in the bow, as well as an eight-inch pneumatic gun mounted above it. An additional pneumatic gun was mounted at the rear. The boat carried three torpedoes, which were pressure sensitive to control their depth.

Holland had devised an ingenious additional wrinkle to aid in underwater navigation. Previously he had discovered that, contrary to his initial belief, steering a straight course underwater by compass alone was nearly impossible. After he leveled off from a fifteen-degree down-angle dive, the compass needle "swung around to a complete circle and vibrated a good deal before coming to rest."[5] The craft was then found to be approximately ninety degrees off course. Additional tests determined that error was constant, but the degree and direction were not. With no other means of determining direction while submerged—looking through the conning tower ports achieved nothing—a submarine commander would have either to surface often or run awash to know where he was going and thus could hardly approach an enemy with stealth.

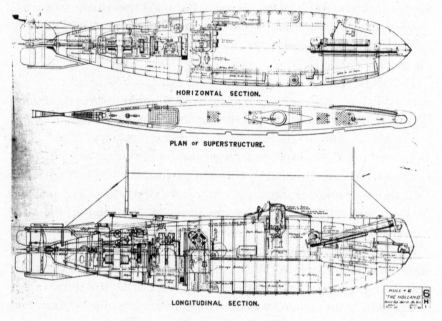

HORIZONTAL SECTION.

PLAN OF SUPERSTRUCTURE.

LONGITUDINAL SECTION.

Holland *cross-section*

Holland discovered that the compass error was caused by a variety of iron fittings and machine parts that changed position during and after a dive, altering the orientation of the compass's compensating magnets, installed to correct false readings caused by that very iron machinery. To solve the problem, he created (and patented) a mechanism he called a "triangular drag," which he positioned just above the diving planes, and which would serve as a primitive autopilot for ensuring straight-line travel while submerged. Like many Holland innovations, the triangular drag was deceptive in its simplicity. "It is necessary, when the boat is running on the surface, to put it on the exact course it is to follow just before the dive is made. The [planes] are tipped, and then this drag comes into play. If the boat veers to the right or left this drag sways to the opposite side. It is so arranged that it works a lever that at once swings the steering-rudder of the ship to the side that will bring the boat straight on its course again."[6] Holland also created a water-pressure-sensitive control device to automatically maintain the submarine's depth, both at the end of a dive and when cruising underwater. Also lever-based, the mechanism connected directly to the diving planes, which would then be angled in either direction to compensate for any deviation from the depth set by the operator. A third device, similarly constructed, would allow the boat to be steered automatically.

These innovations were all built into the *Holland*, and although the May 1897 launch of the new boat did not lead to immediate sea trials, Holland, or more likely Frost, used the occasion to exert pressure on the navy. The press, willing to print any story that was fed to them about the glamorous new technological wonder, would be employed regularly in the coming years as a surrogate publicity agent. "Requests were made by the United States and other Governments for permission to have engineers on board on the trial trips," one story revealed. "Mr. Holland will not grant the requests. After the success of the boat is shown he will accommodate all representatives of the Governments, but not before. It is said that several Governments have already bid for the boat, untried as she is. The plans upon which she was built were unofficially approved by naval officers, and are patented in this country and abroad by Mr. Holland."[7] There were at that time no bids for the boat, but for what Holland and Frost had in mind, the appearance of foreign demand would be crucial.

The idea was to swap out the *Plunger* for the *Holland*, to demonstrate to Congress that they could have the superior vessel at no additional cost. But since the navy was committed to the *Plunger* design, until the new boat was built, Holland had to at least give the appearance of progress on the old or risk cancellation. With Simon Lake waiting eagerly in the wings, cancellation was an untenable risk. But as long as work on the *Plunger* appeared to be moving forward, the navy could be kept at arm's length until Holland and Frost could try to persuade the congressmen to amend the contract in favor of the new boat.

So, on August 7, 1897, Holland announced that the *Plunger* had reached a stage of completion sufficient to be given a trial at the shipyard, albeit to an audience that included no senior naval officers or members of Congress. Friendly journalists were invited, however, and from the news reports, a casual observer would have thought the test run a staggering success.

As reported in the *New York Sun*:

> Amid a din of cheers and the shrieking of steam whistles, the Holland submarine torpedo boat *Plunger* slid down the ways of the Columbia Iron Works at noon today. As she struck the water she rolled violently from side to side, and the men on her superstructure, who had volunteered to go with her on her first plunge clung to the masts, which bore the Stars and Stripes and Navy Jack. Several ladies screamed in fright but after a second or two the steel fish slowly righted and rested with about a third of her body above the water line. On a platform erected beside the port bow of the boat stood Miss Ernestine Wardwell and her father, Col. Wardwell. In her right hand Miss Wardwell held a bottle of champagne decorated with ribbons of the national and Maryland colors. The moment the vessel moved she shattered the bottle against the bow and said: "I christen thee *Plunger*." A cheer arose from the assemblage, which for an hour previous had been pouring through the gateway of the iron works, and then everything inshore and afloat in the neighborhood that possessed a steam whistle blew it in salute to the strange new craft.[8]

But Holland most wanted to use the occasion to provoke interest in the boat he was building up the coast. Reporters obliged. "The *Plunger* is not regarded as so efficient a boat as the *Holland*, launched at Nixon's ship yard in Elizabeth, N. J., last spring. She can only use torpedoes from two tubes in her bow in her warfare. The *Holland* not only has a torpedo tube in her bow, but an aerial gun in the bow and a submarine gun in her stern. The *Plunger* is simply a submarine torpedo boat. The *Holland* can fight most destructively, probably, when running on the surface, being capable of hurling dynamite cartridges through the air for a distance of a mile or more."

Holland also did not resist the temptation to take shots at the navy. "The *Plunger*, being the first vessel of the kind authorized by the Government, was loaded down with requirements by the experts, which, it is known, were supplied by the Holland Company simply because the Government insisted upon them, and against the better judgment of the Holland Company's naval experts. One of these requirements was the downhaul screws, to enable the vessel to remain stationary in the water when submerged. Another was the use of two torpedo tubes in the bow. It is said that only one could be used at one time and therefore an extra tube is superfluous. The use of steam for surface running and the consequent necessity of coal bunkers is also regarded as a drawback."

The original Plunger *with its unworkable three-screw design.*

What the article failed to report was the performance of the *Plunger*, which was because the boat did not perform. It neither submerged nor cruised for any significant distance. Unlike the *Holland*, which had slid off the ways without fanfare in order to be fine-tuned, the *Plunger* did not venture out of port because there were doubts it could return. In fact, the *Plunger* would *never* cruise successfully out of Baltimore harbor.

The stage thus set, E. B. Frost made his move—he proposed to the navy that they be willing to write off the *Plunger* experiment if the Holland Torpedo Boat Company, which had used its own money, demonstrated that *Holland* was a superior craft. The company would do so in a series of official tests undertaken solely at its expense. As a further display of good faith, work on the *Plunger* would continue as well. If those conditions were met, Frost offered, the contract would remain in force and no one else would be allowed to submit an alternative design.

Although the navy did not immediately agree, nor did they reject the notion out of hand. Lake was livid. His opinion of the officers charged with military procurement had remained deeply negative, although his denunciations seem more appropriate to Holland's experiences than his own. He wrote later:

> It has been said that Americans invent and the Europeans develop. This statement seems to be borne out in fact, so far as our military inventions at least are concerned. From the time the Wrights first introduced the flying machine in Europe all the important countries over there have been consistently assisting inventors in improving the construction of the planes and machinery for driving them, while our own country has stood almost at a standstill. Our government gave no aid to foster this American invention so that it could be gradually developed, but rather our authorities made the first requirements so difficult to fulfill that there was no incentive to work; which is a mistake often made by men with a theoretical rather than a practical education. A practical man may evolve something radically new in the arts or sciences, but to get it introduced into the government service it must first be passed upon and approved by men who at the country's expense have received, for the most part, a purely theoretical education; and nine times out of ten these men get some additional

theories of their own which they insist must be incorporated in the machine or apparatus, and thus make it impossible of operation or delay its accomplishment. It is probably due to this cause that we are now forced to go to France for plans of our aeroplanes and their driving machinery to enable us to compete with the Germans' machines.[9]

Lake accused the naval officers charged with evaluating inventions as being "too busy with the routine of their professions to give the necessary time to a through investigation of devices other than those with which they are . . . familiar," a clear reference to Holland's design. He further insisted that "not a single fundamental invention . . . has emanated from an army or navy officer during his service," a statement that was blatantly false, as Lake, familiar with Zalinski's pneumatic gun, was clearly aware. Over the course of the next decade, in fact, Lake would consistently decry the rigidity and the lack of support for inventors by Congress and military brass, while at the same time accusing Holland's company—although not Holland himself—of using all means possible, both immoral and illegal, to obtain special treatment for its submarines and bilk the Treasury out of hundreds of thousands, if not millions of dollars.

But Holland was having difficulties of his own. On October 13, 1897, with his boat nearing completion, after a day of fine-tuning inside, a "careless workman," neglected to close a small valve before he left work. The boat took on water throughout the night and when Holland arrived the next morning, he found that his boat had sunk to the bottom of the slip. It was raised eighteen hours later, but all the electrical equipment—motors, generator, wiring, and insulation—the most costly machinery in the vessel, had been damaged by the salt water and was no longer functional. Replacing the electrical system was out of the question—as it was, the company had spent its every last dollar building the *Holland* on speculation. Dismantling the equipment to clean each part individually was equally out of the question, as it would involve removing most of the steel plates on the upper half of the hull. In desperation, Holland and his engineers tried "every known method of drying out the motors by applying heat externally," even keeping oil stoves burning inside the hull day and night and applying "superheaters" to the motors, but nothing worked.

In early November 1897, Holland contacted the Electro-Dynamic Company of Philadelphia, which had built the dynamos, and asked that they send "their best technician" to Elizabethport. They sent thirty-four-year-old Frank Cable.

It was a fortuitous choice. Cable was bright, clever, and inventive. After studying the equipment, he decided that "there was only one way of remedying the trouble, and if this course was adopted there was a chance of restoring the boat." He proposed to reverse the current in the armatures of the dynamo, which, he said, would generate heat internally, within the mechanism itself. Of course, it might also burn up the equipment, removing any remaining faint hope of repair. At that point, Holland felt there was nothing to lose and he gave Cable the go-ahead. Four days later, the electrical system was again in working order. Workmen then removed battery acid from the bilges, and replaced dead battery cells, and by mid-December, Holland could resume work on completing the boat. Not surprisingly, he requested that Cable remain at Elizabethport, which Cable very much wanted to do as well. But the Electro-Dynamic Company refused to part with him, so Cable returned to Philadelphia. He would be back.

CHAPTER 15

SHEDDING BALLAST

Two months later, the *Holland*'s construction was complete. On February 25, 1898, ten days after the *Maine* had been sunk in Havana Harbor and at the precise time that Simon Lake claims to have been rebuffed in his offer of service, John Holland took his boat out for the first time, into the Arthur Kill, the channel that runs between Staten Island, New York, and New Jersey. Observers watching from shore later declared, "The submarine disappeared before our very eyes." When Frank Cable heard the news, he sent a telegram of congratulations, thrilled that the dynamo had not failed "in time of need."[1]

The following month, Holland ran a series of short test voyages off Perth Amboy, New Jersey. In some cases, the boat ran only on the surface, in others awash, and only occasionally fully submerged. After each test, Holland made minor adjustments, most frequently to the fixed ballast. On March 12, during the first serious underwater test, when the boat was to remain submerged for thirty minutes, Holland and his two crew members took diving helmets with them as a precaution, but the *Holland* ran perfectly, and was ready for more extensive and challenging maneuvers.

On March 17, 1898, St. Patrick's Day, precisely forty years after the founding of the Fenian Brotherhood, Holland took his boat into Staten Island Sound for an extensive sea trial. The *Holland* ran successfully both on the surface and submerged, and after its return to dry dock, Holland decided he was ready to schedule a demonstration for the navy.

Argonaut II

The test would take place on March 26, but Holland decided to conduct one more full-blown sea test on March 21, to which the press would officially be invited. The day before, Holland and "a score of assistants" checked every inch of the boat and determined that "all the machinery and other appliances to sink the boat and bring her to the surface again have worked satisfactorily." The crew was also said to have been drilled in working the torpedo and the dynamite gun, both of which were also to be included in the next day's test, and that they had "perfect control" of each.[2]

But newspaper editors did not wait for the test to be successful. Across a nation preparing for war, articles hailed the new weapon in vivid page-one stories, complete with artists' renderings that bore only a vague resemblance to the actual boat. On March 20, for example, a syndicated feature, titled "FIFTY HOLLAND SUBMARINE TORPEDO-BOATS MAY GUARD OUR COAST," ran in newspapers from Virginia to California. The text under a drawing of what could have been a swollen pig bladder read, "This is an accurate picture of the Holland submarine boat." (It wasn't.) "The government has been considering building fifty of these submarine terrors to scatter along our coasts. It has been demonstrated that one of these boats could easily take care of three battleships of the *Vizcaya* style.* Upon sighting the enemy, the boats at the different stations along the coast would be sent out and could annihilate the enemy before any damage could be done or a landing secured. A successful trial of the boat was made on Thursday."[3] That cruising at eight knots, to protect thousands of miles of coast, would require some significant multiple of the fifty Holland-style submarines was omitted from the piece. Also omitted was the fact that the weapons' system on the *Holland* had yet to be successfully engaged.

A similar feature article, this one with a more accurate, cross-section depiction of the submarine, read, "That latest invention in naval warfare, the Holland submarine boat is practically finished and will be ready far use against Spain if necessary. Joseph P. Holland [sic] the inventor is sanguine that his submarine destroyer will be a match for any battleship afloat. He asserts that the boat will be under absolute control and may be operated below the surface, rising only at intervals to admit a fresh supply of air." That piece went on to describe how the submarine could approach by stealth and destroy a vessel many times its size, using either torpedo or pneumatic gun. In this case, no mention was made that true stealth would be impossible since the operator of a submarine had no effect means of locating an enemy craft while submerged and therefore would need to run awash with a crewman in the conning tower, visible to sharp-eyed lookouts.

---

* The Spanish battleship *Vizcaya* had steamed to New York Harbor under the command of a Spanish admiral as a show of strength after the *Maine* exploded.

But hyperbole, not accuracy, was precisely what press-savvy E. B. Frost had aimed at. After the press event, it was undiminished. In an article headlined "The Holland Dives Again: The Submarine Boat Shows that She Will Fulfill Her Inventor's Claims; A Most Successful Trial," the *New York Times* stated, "That the Holland submarine boat will do all that has been claimed for it by John P. Holland, its inventor, was demonstrated at yesterday's trial, which was the most successful one since the vessel was launched." The article went on to praise the boat for sailing both on the surface and submerged in "inclement weather and [in] treacherous channels."[4] Only toward the end of the piece was it noted that neither the dynamite gun nor the torpedo was tested since both tubes were found to contain small leaks, nor could the boat "steer accurately" or determine depth since there was no light on the compass or depth gauge. While most of the flaws were easily correctable, this was not a boat that was "practically finished and ready for use against Spain."[5]

After this test, Lake once more petitioned for his boat to be tested by the navy, if not before Holland's March 27 event, then at least soon after. He made no secret that he expected the *Argonaut* to perform so brilliantly in contrast with Holland's boat that Holland's contract would be canceled in favor of one for him.

But the navy would not budge. The *Holland*, after all, was designed to be a warship, which is what the admirals wanted, and despite its shortcomings, it had demonstrated speed and maneuverability far superior to what Lake could offer. And Holland had promised, no matter what the result of the March 26 trial, to conduct an additional series of test runs quickly and bring the boat to a state where it would replace the *Plunger*.

For this crucial test, Holland would have a new crew member. Frank Cable had finally persuaded his bosses in Philadelphia to lend him temporarily to the submarine builders, to ensure that the electrical systems functioned properly. If they failed, he told them, Electro-Dynamic might easily be seen as ruining one of the American navy's most important new weapons. Temporary, however, would become permanent. Frank Cable would work with and in submarines for the rest of his life.

March 27 dawned cold and rainy. For the previous weeks, New York newspapers had been running feature articles highlighting the vulnerabilities of the local coastline to Spanish warships, which coupled with tales of the *Holland*'s prowess, invested the public in the success of the trial. Naval officers, however, remained skeptical. Rather than exhibit the eagerness for Holland's machine that Lake had complained about, the notion of investing money in a vessel most of them still thought of as crackpot when the needs of surface fleet remained acute was somewhere between irresponsible and idiotic. In order to have any chance at all to change their minds, the *Holland* would have to perform brilliantly. Frost counted on his friends in the press to make certain that, short of catastrophe, that was at least what the public would believe.

They did not let him down. The *Brooklyn Daily Eagle*'s headline was "The Holland Boat A Diving Wonder," with an opening line that read, "The submarine boat *Holland* gave a remarkable exhibition of her powers in the Staten Island Sound." The piece went on to describe how Holland and his crew of five—one of whom was an army lieutenant—made four distinct dives, all "under perfect control," while an army colonel, company officials, and newspapermen observed from a nearby tugboat. The boat was on the surface until, "Suddenly the bow of the *Holland* disappeared at an angle of 15 degrees and her stern rose in the air until part of the propeller was visible. In less than a minute, she was completely out of sight. Her flag staffs, which are about sixteen feet high, could not be seen." A few minutes later, four-hundred yards away, the *Holland* surfaced. It did so on an even keel, "which naval experts declared was impossible, holding that in rising the boat would stick her bow above the surface and then her turret, which would expose her to the fire of rapid fire guns."[6] In fact, there was nothing in Holland's design that prevented even-keel diving or surfacing; he simply believed that such maneuvers were generally inefficient. *The New York Times* added, "It was shown beyond any doubt that the boat can do all that has been claimed for it."[7]

Although no torpedoes were fired, Holland's biographer, Richard Morris, son of Holland associate Charles Morris, claims that the dynamite gun was engaged before the official test began, successfully hurling a "three-foot, fifty-pound, wooden dummy-projectile [in] a graceful trajectory three hundred yards out into the channel."[8]

A main question, however, was the *Holland*'s ability to navigate with sufficient accuracy and stealth to be effective as a warship. When submerged, the boat steered by compass alone, which, after some trial-and-error experimentation with compensating magnets, was reasonably effective when merely cruising from place to place. But to locate, track, and attack an enemy, compass steering was useless. Periscopes had been around since the 1430s, when Johann Gutenberg had mounted two parallel mirrors in a tube with opposite right-angle extensions at the ends, so that spectators might view the visiting pope from the rear of a huge crowd, but no one had quite figured out how to attach an effective viewing tube to a submarine. There had been a number of attempts to employ a camera lucida, and French submarine designers had experimented with a lens and prism device in 1889. But an effective mechanism for viewing surface objects from the inside of a submarine proved surprisingly thorny, with issues such as resolution, field of vision, distortion, range, and storage thwarting each inventor who had made the attempt.

Lacking a means of tracking an enemy while submerged, in order to mount a torpedo or dynamite gun attack, the *Holland* would engage in a maneuver Cable described as "porpoising," in which "the boat ran a short distance submerged and then came to the surface far enough to expose the conning tower, thus getting a chance to look around, and then diving." As awkward as this seemed, Cable thought it was an effective means of attack. "This bobbing up and disappearing was swiftly effected; the boat would rise to the surface from a depth, say, of thirty feet, focus on an imaginary target, if such was the occasion for the maneuver, fire its torpedo, and be quickly under water again."[9]

Since the viewing windows were placed at the top of the conning tower, it was in theory possible for the *Holland* to porpoise its way into a position to attack an enemy while keeping its profile low enough in the water to avoid detection. But on the open sea, where the water was rarely calm, far more likely was that the boat would either rise out of the water enough to be spotted, or that waves would break across the surface of the viewing windows, rendering clear vision impossible.

Still, Holland's boat was able to do what no other had ever done, and its virtues for forward thinking naval officers and government officials outstripped its shortcomings. Holland continued to test-run the boat for two weeks, with a steady improvement in performance. On April 10, even before a torpedo had been successfully fired—although one soon would be—Theodore Roosevelt, still assistant secretary of the navy, wrote to navy secretary John D. Long: "I think the Holland submarine boat should be purchased. Evidently she has great possibilities in her for harbor defense. Sometimes she doesn't work perfectly, but often she does, and I don't think in the present emergency we can afford to let her slip. I recommend that you authorize me to enter into negotiations for her, or you authorize the bureau of construction to do so, which would be just as well."[10] In addition to casting further doubt on Simon Lake's assertion that Roosevelt favored his design, this letter offers corroboration that Holland's boat had indeed satisfied the requirements that the navy had stipulated in its initial contract.

But either because of Lake's furious lobbying or simply because of intransigence, the navy refused to purchase the new boat. Their objections, ironically, were not centered on the *Holland*'s flaws—inability to approach an enemy submerged and an untested weapons system—but rather on quibbles about navigation and instrumentation. Nor did they reject the *Holland* in favor of the one on which they had imposed a design—the *Plunger* did not seem to be a part of the conversation. Most likely, the admirals' reluctance to make a decision stemmed from an inherent prejudice against undersea vessels coupled with a fear of making a mistake and looking foolish in overcoming it.

Unable to pierce the naval bureaucracy, Frost escalated the publicity war. "Reporters were invited to inspect the boat. *Harper's Weekly*, *Leslie's Weekly*, and the leading metropolitan newspapers published fanciful accounts of the strange craft, often in nothing short of the most sensational journalism."[11] For example, on the day before the war with Spain would officially begin, newspapers across the nation ran a syndicated feature on "Inventor Holland's New Sea Fighting Monsters," complete with half-page cutaway drawings and descriptions of performance that had yet to be attained. Failure to see the virtue of the new technology was condemned. "Naval experts of course are divided on the question, they always are whenever any new instrument of destruction is introduced. The more conservative shake their heads gravely and dwell on the many limitations which natural law imposes on submarine navigation; the younger and more enthusiastic members of the profession make light of these difficulties and claim that we have here a weapon which, in deadly effect, will outrival even the torpedo."[12]

Adding to the confusion, someone in the Navy Department decided "the *Holland* had designs on the *Vizcaya*," the Spanish battleship that had been sent to New York Harbor. In March, the commander of the New York Navy Yard had received an order to keep the *Holland* under observation and seize the vessel if he thought it was preparing to open fire on the Spanish ship.[13] Navy tugboats shadowed the *Holland* to and from its mooring at Perth Amboy, New Jersey. At one point, Holland submerged his boat and surfaced behind an old canal boat while the tugboats searched vainly to locate it.

On April 20, the same day William McKinley asked Congress to declare war on Spain, Holland's frustration boiled over. An official board of inspection had been sent from Washington to observe a sea test, possibly in response to Roosevelt's letter, but the board members seemed not especially interested in seeing the *Holland* perform. All they requested was that Holland demonstrate his boat could actually dive and surface, making it clear they were impatient to return to the capital and deal with *genuine* naval business. Holland decided to give them a demonstration they would not soon forget.

At the accompanying tugboat's signal to begin, Holland took his boat under the surface "in seconds." He had removed the usual ten-foot flagstaffs, so the inspection board members were left to scan the surface, but there was no indication of where the boat might be. In previous tests, the Holland had remained submerged for perhaps ten minutes, but forty-five minutes later it had not yet come to the surface. Another tugboat was dispatched to search as board members and crew frantically looked for some sign of the boat most thought had flooded and sunk.

Finally, just short of an hour from when it had submerged, the *Holland* broke the surface, just a few feet away from its tugboat escort.

Holland himself "must have taken particular delight in revealing that he and his crew had traveled several miles in a sweeping circle while submerged in the bay. He had disobeyed the prearranged orders, but he had given the Board a show it had not expected."[14] With this voyage, Holland exceeded every performance standard the navy had established for the *Plunger* and, in addition, demonstrated that the *Holland* could quite effectively steer by compass alone—although its conning tower would still need to break the surface in order to mount an attack.

The board members may have been impressed, but they were not amused. Rather than recommend the navy move forward with what could have been a devastating new weapon, they "quibbled over details," such as pointing out that they had no confirmation of the depth at which the boat had traveled since the flagstaffs had been removed. (In any case, they would have disappeared at a depth greater than ten feet.) When he heard of the board's decision, Holland, as had Lake, insisted his boat would be a potent addition to the fleet and, also similar to Lake, issued a public offer to sink the Spanish fleet in Santiago de Cuba Harbor where it had been trapped if the navy would transport his boat to the Caribbean.

The offer was leaked, of course, to the press, which immediately leaped on the idea. "When the news that [Admiral Pascual] Cervera and his fleet were bottled up in the harbor of Santiago became pretty well confirmed, it was suggested to John P. Holland, the submarine boatman, that he could submit the practical value of his invention to no better test than to take her to Cuban waters, enter the harbor of Santiago, destroy the mines and sink the Spanish fleet with a neat hole in each of them, just enough to sink her, not enough to spoil her, because we want those ships ourselves. When the suggestion was made, Mr. Holland said that under certain conditions he was quite willing to undertake the job."[15]

Holland's conditions were much the same as Lake had proposed in the wake of the *Maine* sinking. "If the government will transport the boat from the Erie Basin, where it now is, to some point near the entrance to the harbor of Santiago, and a crew can be secured to man the boat, Mr. Holland will undertake the job of sinking the Spanish fleet, commanding the boat in person. If his offer be accepted, and he is successful in his undertaking, he will expect the government to buy the boat."

As with Lake, the navy refused. Holland then granted an interview that was printed in newspapers across America under the headline, "Why His Boat Was Ignored." "It has taken me 23 years to educate the United States government up to the idea of the submarine boat, and the education is still incomplete apparently. Twenty-three years ago I submitted my first plans for a submarine boat to the government. They were returned with the criticism that my invention was impractical, as the men could not be found who would be willing to operate such a craft as I designed to build. You see, the idea back of this objection was that a submarine boat would be a death trap for her crew. I have made simply hundreds of tests to overcome this and similar objections. Each new administration has brought a new set of officials into power, and these I would find entrenched behind the very same prejudices I had had to meet and overcome in the case of their predecessors. That is why it has been such a labor to even partially educate the government." Holland added, "There are still men in the navy who are bitterly hostile to the torpedo, the ram, and who see only cause for alarm in each step that tends toward the final perfecting of the fighting machine. Innovation of any sort acts on these timid souls just as a sudden plunge in ice water would. Fortunately, they form a hopeless minority."[16]

Whether Frost had approved the interview is doubtful. Public rebuke of reluctant customers was hardly likely to soften their opposition. Nor was Holland's unstinting praise of some younger officers, such as William Kimball, going to have much impact. Hopeless minority or not, opposition to submarine technology was centered at the top of the officer pyramid, not the middle. And so, while over the next weeks, Holland ran many successful test voyages and newspapers continued to publish laudatory feature articles, the navy continued to refuse to conclude a purchase.

Even worse for Holland—and for Lake as well—it soon became apparent that the United States would not need to rely on a new secret weapon to defeat its opponent. Spain would prove to be an adversary a good deal less intimidating than Hearst's and Pulitzer's newspapers had made it out to be. With war no longer a goad, both companies attempted to use the prospect of overseas sales—both Lake and Holland had been contacted by representatives of a number of foreign navies—to prod the admirals into action.

Once again, the battle was joined in the press. In October 1898, news services reported,

> The agents of the Holland submarine boat have abandoned their efforts to get the United States to purchase their craft, and have turned to foreign governments. It is more than probable that an announcement will be made shortly to the effect that France has secured the exclusive right to build the Holland vessel, for that country has been after this privilege for some time. At any rate, the United States has lost the opportunity to control the Holland submarine boat. 'We are handicapped,' said one of the agents, 'by the narrow minded prejudice of naval officers who are unable to see any good in a ship that is not constructed entirely by men in the service. They condemned our boat before even seeing it, and we were unable to get a fair test of it. It is lost to this government, and France or some European power will get it. I firmly believe that the craft will turn out to be a most potent factor in future marine fights.[17]

There was in fact no serious interest from France, but the bluff worked. The following month, the navy granted the *Holland* an additional test, and in this one a dummy Whitehead torpedo would be fired at a target. Moreover, the boat would be piloted not by its inventor, but by a naval officer. Another naval officer would serve as engineer. Although both had been aboard the *Holland* during earlier test runs, neither man had any experience at the controls. It took them a full twenty minutes just to load the ballast correctly, something Holland would have achieved in less than half that time. In addition, the cold had caused the grease inside the torpedo tube to congeal, and so loading the weapon also took a good deal longer than it should have.

Nonetheless, the test seemed to go well. The torpedo was fired while the *Holland* ran on the surface and struck its target four hundred yards away. The boat also performed nineteen dives, cruised underwater, and completed a series of navigational maneuvers both on the surface and submerged. The naval officers on board reported favorably on the *Holland*'s performance, despite having some difficulty with the steering and diving gear, which the officers attributed to their own inexperience with the controls.

But the navy was still not ready to recommend purchase. The board members decided that an additional test be made under war conditions. A hulk was to be anchored in a test course, "and to make the test a success the *Holland* must rise to the surface, discharge a torpedo effectively at the hulk and then disappear beneath the surface. Whether the boat will be accepted by the government will depend on the successful accomplishment of this program."[18]

But with winter closing in, the requirement for an additional test meant a delay of at least three months, quite possibly more. Rather than sit idly, Holland decided to dry-dock his boat and make some major modifications. Most significantly, he would remove the rear dynamite gun and use the space for a better exhaust system, and correct what seemed to be a design flaw. In the *Holland*, as in all of the *Holland*'s previous designs, the rudders had been placed forward of the propeller. Although Holland, who had to this point always "navigated the boats himself and claimed their steering qualities were good," Frank Cable discovered that was not the case. "My first attempt at navigating the Holland was during a run several weeks before the official trials, and I found steering her was the most unsatisfactory task I had ever undertaken. The criticism annoyed Holland, but he encountered worse from a group of spectators who had been watching our maneuvers from the deck of a small tug. One of them compared the course of the Holland to that of a drunken washerwoman."[19]

While the comparison was likely an overstatement—other reports have the *Holland* steering satisfactorily—Holland was ultimately forced to agree that reorienting the propeller and the rudder would improve performance. But dry-docking and rebuilding had its costs, in this case an estimated $30,000. After building two submarines, neither of which had yet been purchased, the Holland Torpedo Boat Company was out of money.

With the war with Spain over and the navy bloated with triumph over what had proved to be an inept and under-armed foe, Simon Lake had also decided to suspend his short-term sales effort and instead greatly modify and improve his boat. Lake's refitted vessel, which he would christen *Argonaut II*, would be "20 feet longer and carried above a buoyant superstructure with a swan bow and overhanging stern, so that at the surface her hull looked very like that of an ordinary yacht. Her engines were by the same makers but were twice as powerful, and she carried a 4-h.p. auxiliary engine in addition. Her internal arrangements were very similar to those she had before alteration, and she proved as great a success as before, with the advantage of greater stability, seaworthiness and accommodation, for she could now carry a crew of eight men and had a cruising radius of 3,000 miles."[20] Unlike Holland, Lake's boat would give him the means to self-finance its improvements—he intended to use it to scoop up the riches he had located on the sea bottom and become a wealthy and influential man. Although once again, Lake would install neither torpedoes nor guns, he still intended to pursue his crusade against the navy.

Facing a competitor with superior resources and having few of their own, Holland and Frost found themselves in increasing desperate straits. Late in 1898, however, a savior appeared. He was smart, savvy, and was just about to garner windfall profits from the sale of another company he had built from nothing. He offered not only to fund the refitting but also all future construction, and he promised to use his considerable expertise to ensure that John Holland and not Simon Lake, nor anyone else, would supply the navy's submarine fleet.

He was the chairman of the Electric Storage Battery Company, Isaac Rice.

CHAPTER 16

KING'S GAMBIT ACCEPTED

Isaac Leopold Rice was a combination visionary, scholar, and bare-knuckles prizefighter, an amalgam that made him one of the most unusual and fascinating figures of the Gilded Age. He made fortunes, occasionally lost them, founded both one of the United States' most important defense contractors and one of its most prestigious intellectual journals, endowed a variety of progressive causes, and designed and built one of the most unique and enduring mansions in New York City.

Rice—probably originally "Reiss" or "Reich"—was born in Bavaria in 1850, but his family immigrated to Milwaukee when he was six, then moved to Philadelphia four years later. Even at ten, it was clear Isaac was a chess prodigy, and he also showed preternatural talent in music. After six years in the Philadelphia public schools, Rice, by then fluent in English, German, and French, was sent to Paris for advanced studies in music, literature, and philosophy. He supported himself there and later in London by teaching piano and languages, vocations he continued when he returned to America in 1869. Rice settled in New York and, in addition to teaching, wrote for local newspapers. At twenty-five, he published a technical book on musical theory, *What Is Music?* (republished for lay readers as part of the *Humboldt Library of Science*) and a few years later, *How the Geometrical Lines Have Their Counterparts in Music.* Each was critically praised but hardly a boon financially.

Isaac Rice

Deciding that he'd rather be rich than poor, at age twenty-eight Rice enrolled in Columbia College of Law, from which he graduated cum laude two years later, earning prizes in Constitutional and international law. While he cast about for the appropriate venue in which to ply his new trade, Rice became a fixture at chess clubs, was appointed as a lecturer and librarian at Columbia's new School of Political Science, and wrote scholarly pieces for respected intellectual journals, especially *Harper's* and *North American Review*. In one, "Has Land a Value?", Rice offered a critique of the theories of the economist David Ricardo, who had coined the term "comparative advantage," and in another he launched a scathing attack on Herbert Spencer's theories of Social Darwinism.* In a third, "A Definition of Liberty," he wrote, "Civil liberty is the result of the restraint exercised by the sovereign people on the more powerful individuals and classes of the community, preventing them from availing themselves of the excess of their power to the detriment of the other classes."[1] With increased wealth, he would come to alter that perspective.

A story made the rounds in chess circles, quite possibly apocryphal, that Rice's first job as a lawyer came in 1882 as a result of the client's friend watching Rice play chess. Although Rice had never tried a case, the man insisted that such a mind as Rice's could not lose in court. And, as the tale goes, Rice did not.[2]

However he began, in 1883, Rice turned his attention to railroads, a booming industry where millions were being made and, less frequently, lost. His first clients were bondholders of Brooklyn Elevated Railroad Company, dissatisfied that the company seemed to be languishing while others thrived, and fearing it might soon fail altogether. Rice saw opportunity, not in fee generation, but on the balance sheet. He persuaded the company to engage him as its attorney, grant him a large block of stock, and eventually to appoint him a director. Then, although he had no training in finance, he supervised a creative restructuring that allowed the company to appear healthy enough to solicit public funds, providing the capital the railroad needed to improve its performance—and also providing the existing stockholders a windfall. All the while, he was teaching at Columbia Law School, where he had accepted an instructor's appointment in 1884.

The following year, Rice married Julia Hyneman Barnett, daughter of a prosperous and socially prominent New Orleans merchant. She had been classically educated in music, art, and philosophy, but chose to enroll in the Woman's Medical College of the New York Infirmary, from which she had graduated with a medical degree 1885. Rather

---

* Spencer, not Darwin, coined the phrase "survival of the fittest," which Rice ridiculed as encouraging the very sort of behavior that would doom the human species rather than advance it.

than enter private practice, she devoted herself to her husband, whom she called her "intellectual partner." That same year, in addition to beginning a marriage, Rice, with Julia's assistance, founded *Forum*, a magazine that published scholarly articles on politics and finance, theater reviews, and political and literary commentary. Thomas Hardy, Jules Verne, and Henry Cabot Lodge would be among the magazine's contributors. Rice continued to publish *Forum* until 1910. Adding magazine publishing to his other activities was too much even for a man of Rice's formidable talents. The following year, he resigned his teaching position at Columbia.

The creative machinations he had brought to Brooklyn Elevated had made Rice something of a celebrity in financial circles, and he found himself solicited to provide similar services elsewhere. For sizable remuneration, he oversaw reorganizations of the St. Louis & Southwestern Railway and the Texas and Pacific Railroad. In 1886, he was appointed counsel and director for the Richmond Terminal Railroad and also as a director for the Richmond, Danville and East Tennessee System, and the Central Railroad and Banking Company of Georgia. He consolidated these companies as the Southern Railway System.

While financial legerdemain certainly played a part in each of these transactions, Rice was no mere speculator. "Rice's corporate approach was honest. He invited investors to join him in his ventures but insisted that they risk their own capital. He admitted to a 'holy horror of debts, loans, bonds.' He did not want the money of widows or orphans, nor would he manipulate shares of stock. Rice encouraged investors to consider him an inventor, and he was."[3] He also had a keen eye for mismanagement and inefficiency, and not much patience for either, so any company in which he took an interest was soon operating more effectively.

By 1889, Rice had made millions, and he announced that he was retiring from the law to play chess full-time and become a patron of the game. He was elected the president of the Manhattan Chess Club—the most important in the United States—after he helped pay to move the club to new quarters. There he played a long series of practice games with world champion Wilhelm Steinitz, who had won the title in a tournament at the club three years earlier.

But the genteel world of rank and file was not sufficient to sate Rice's outsized intellectual energy. He was inexorably drawn to the rough and tumble of the business world.* Within months, he became the head of a syndicate that intended to buy up controlling interest in the Philadelphia and Reading Railroad Company.

The Philadelphia and Reading owned only four hundred miles of track but had become a sprawling concern after a period of aggressive, perhaps even reckless expansion under its president, Archibald McLeod. Pierpont Morgan was a major stockholder. That the banking titan was his adversary did not dissuade Rice one bit; it might, in fact, have encouraged him.

While Rice's syndicate succeeded in amassing the largest single bloc of stock, they lacked a majority and were unable to wrest control of the board of directors. Rice developed a blueprint to reorganize the company, dividing it into stand-alone divisions under a holding-company umbrella, which would vastly decrease its exposure in an economic downturn. The plan was brilliant and innovative—and went nowhere. Faced with no alternative but to bide his time, Rice announced that he did not favor a major management shake-up and issued a lukewarm endorsement of McLeod. In 1892, Rice and Julia decided to sail across the Atlantic, where the railroad agreed to allow him to act as its European agent.

Soon after the Rices returned, stocks crashed as the Panic of 1893 set in. During the next three years, fifteen thousand businesses would close and the unemployment rate would approach 25 percent. The first indication of the severity of the crisis came in February, when the Philadelphia and Reading Railroad, by then hopelessly overextended, confirmed Rice's every fear and declared bankruptcy. Pierpont Morgan had McLeod fired, and persuaded a sober, highly regarded, civil engineer turned railroad executive named Joseph Smith Harris to take his place. Harris was also appointed to head the board of receivers assigned to supervise the bankruptcy. Harris was at the time running a competing company, Lehigh Coal and Navigation, but Morgan would not be denied.

---

* He was inexorably drawn to Julia as well. Within ten years, she had borne them six children.

Neither would Isaac Rice. He accused Harris of being a stooge for the old guard, in place to facilitate the continued looting of corporate assets at the expense of the stockholders. When Harris proposed a restructuring that would leave Rice's group largely without power to influence policy, Rice opposed it, and then filed suit to stop it. The problem was mismanagement, he insisted, not a lack of financial wherewithal. For two years, Rice and Harris would fight it out in the courts and the newspapers.

Late in 1893, Rice mounted a proxy fight and announced his intention to replace Harris as president. The receivers fought back. They refused to give Rice access to its complete shareholder list until ordered to by the courts. They attempted to portray Rice as an unscrupulous financial manipulator, trying to loot the company as he had done with many others. Rice countered by petitioning that the receivers be removed, that they had refused to terminate leases that were shams to funnel money into the former officers' pockets, especially McLeod's, and that they had entered into leveraged transactions that would further enrich some but would break the company down the road. (Morgan's name was always conspicuously left out of the discussion.)

Sentiment was most definitely with Rice. The *Economist* wrote, "Disinterested and careful critics of Reading [meaning the editors] have expressed the opinion that the first of Mr. Rice's charges—that of speculating in securities of other roads with Reading's funds—is sustained by the facts." But the magazine was unwilling to condemn Harris and his colleagues. "But [the editors again] deprecate the attack on the receivers of the company, inasmuch, so they say, they cannot be held responsible for what has happened in the past, and cannot be criticised as lacking either honesty, ability or experience, so far as dealing with the present is concerned."[4]

The New York Times was far less forgiving. In a scathing editorial, they stated, "That the Reading receivership was a scheme, either to perpetuate Mr. McLeod and his friends in the control of the property or to further a prodigious speculation on the short side in Reading's securities, or both, no one doubts to-day. Investors stood aghast at the possibilities of profit in railroad wrecking offered by this outrageous proceeding, and America saw added the worst item to its list of railroad swindles, which it had hoped was closed forever years ago." The receivers this time were not spared, "Mr. Harris and his new companions have done less than nothing. They have carefully covered up every detail of Mr. McLeod's course, and have resented every attempt to uncover his acts." As to reorganization, the *Times* accused Harris of "the effrontery to present to the security holders a so-called plan for the rehabilitation of their property, whose price was the surrender of Reading to their absolute control." Terms such as "iniquity," "corruption," "ruin," and "disaster," were sprinkled throughout the piece. Isaac Rice and his consortium received better treatment. The *Times* described them as the criminals' "nemesis," and that he was "undeterred by the difficulty of the task."[5] It must have amused the cold and clinical Rice to be described in such heroic terms.

But in the end, Morgan's shadow proved insurmountable. Rice did not succeed in ousting Harris and was forced to "watch from the sidelines as a new syndicate headed by J. P. Morgan stole Rice's own reorganization plan by forming the Reading Company."[6]

But Rice, as he often did on the chessboard, turned sacrifice into victory. With "energetic watchfulness," he succeeded in blocking Harris's plan to place a charge of $3,000,000 for a proposed subway ahead of "general income and mortgages," ensuring that stockholders of the reorganized Reading Company, of which he was one, would be paid before money was doled out to the receivers' cronies.[7] In addition to making a good deal of money for himself, Isaac Rice acquired the reputation of honesty, probity, and a watchdog of investors' interests, not at all a detriment for a man who intended to attract still more investors to speculative ventures.

Even as the Reading fiasco was winding down, Rice decided he was done both with railroads and with restructurings that involved a large pool of stockholders and its unwieldy path to power. Rice, who saw himself, not without justification, as something of a prophet, decided to focus on coming technologies rather than past ones. Injecting himself into an entrepreneurial enterprise would also enable him to more easily seize control.

While attending the Columbian Exposition in Chicago in 1893, Rice noticed that a disproportion of innovations and gadgets were electrical. It was no secret that electric power was a burgeoning technology, but Rice had not been aware of to just what extent. After some cursory research, he discovered that so many entrepreneurs and inventors were rushing into the field that the United States patent office was swamped with more than three thousand applications per year. Many of the most sophisticated devices, it seemed, including Otis elevators and Edison's Kinetoscope, were powered by a new, robust, quickly rechargeable lead-acid battery called a "chloride accumulator." Combining the ideas of a French inventor, Clement Payen, and an American, Charles F. Brush, the chloride accumulator, which used a series of lead plates to store electricity, was a big advance over what were disparagingly called "pickled amperes."* The sole manufacturer of the device, which used a patented process called Exide, was the Electric Storage Battery Company of Philadelphia. The stock price for the company, however, did not seem to reflect the uniqueness of the product. Rice decided to find out why.

The first thing he learned was that, for this venture, there would be no Pierpont Morgan to outwit. Electric Storage Battery was owned by a fast-talking, wildcat speculator named William Warren Gibbs. Gibbs founded the company in 1888, after convincing a group of investors whom he had previously persuaded to invest in a gas company that they had bought into a failing technology. They should switch to storage batteries instead. He located some obscure patents for lead-acid rechargeable batteries—one of them Payen's—which in theory generated more energy for a longer period, although no one had thought to produce them commercially. The investors were called on once more to fund a small factory, and Gibbs then began to build batteries, initially simply to store power for electric lighting.

---

* The first true battery had been fabricated by Alessandro Volta in 1800, but it had little power and an extremely short life span. Volta had found that certain fluids could conduct a continuous stream of electricity when in contact with a set of two specific metals, such as copper and zinc. A number of experimenters tried to compensate for the shortcomings of Volta's invention—a film of hydrogen bubbles formed on the copper, and tiny short circuits degraded the zinc—but none of them found a way to extend battery life to make the device practical for industry. In 1859, however, a French physics professor, Gaston Planté, discovered the lead-acid process, which could be used to create a battery that could be recharged. Other developers, such as Payen and Brush, attempted to adapt this process for commercial application, and the chloride accumulator was the eventual result.

While early sales were not brisk, Gibbs soon realized that his batteries could be adapted to a wide variety of industrial processes. In 1891, in a major coup, he sold 13,000 Exide cells to the Lehigh Avenue Railway Company to power six of their streetcars. The horseless vehicles were immediately popular and sales boomed. By 1893, when Isaac Rice saw them in Chicago, revenue from the sale of Exide batteries was in the hundreds of thousands. But while cash poured in, expenses were sucked out. Rather than build up the company's reserves, Gibbs was buying up other companies to expand his reach, but the purchases were questionable, so Gibbs had gotten little return while diluting the stock price with each acquisition. In addition, there seemed to be a number of competing patents, although Rice determined that none of these represented a genuine threat.

So Rice began to buy. Within months, he purchased sufficient shares to become a director—and also the company's lawyer—and soon after that he gained control. Gibbs retained much of his stock and seemed relieved to turn over operating responsibility to his new partner. Rice's first act was to buy up every patent that held even a whisper of danger—more than five hundred of them—and he spent $250,000 to do it, almost the equivalent of the company's 1894 revenue.

He also divested the company of some of Gibbs's more questionable acquisitions while overseeing the purchase of a number of companies that used batteries, and thus provided a guaranteed market for his product. One of the companies that he acquired was the Electric Launch and Navigation Company, which was building pleasure boats for the wealthy, a choice customer base that was drawn to a power source that hummed instead of roared while belching black smoke. Electric Launch had been another of the featured attractions at the 1893 fair, and the company was planning to build ferries, which would also be powered by an array of Exide batteries.

The one business Rice had been unable to acquire was William Woodnut Griscom's Electro-Dynamic Company. Griscom, who had taken out almost forty patents for devices to further the use of electricity, had founded Electro-Dynamic in 1880. Its main product was an efficient electric motor that could be built in multiple sizes, sometimes as small as a fist, and that could be used in a variety of light industries, or mounted on commercial items. By the early 1890s, the only drawback to Griscom's motor was that it needed to be powered by Gibbs's Exide batteries, which, for all their virtues, were far too heavy and far too inefficient for widespread commercial application.

Rice set out to change that. Although he had no engineering training, he saw that functional improvements could be obtained just from patents the company already owned. Rice then designed and developed a hybrid Exide product, which soon was the most advanced battery in the world. He also drew up plans for containers, connections, frames, and switches, thus giving his battery more practical utility. With improved Exide technology, which would remain state-of-the-art for the better part of a century, Rice quadrupled the company's revenues, taking in more than one million dollars. Rice's batteries were eventually used in machine tools, telegraph offices, home appliances, and even player pianos, many powered by Electro-Dynamic motors. Rice once again sought to purchase Griscom's master patent, offering him one million dollars in cash, but Griscom refused to sell.[8]

Even without Electro-Dynamic, Rice's ambitions were almost limitless. He envisioned a world hurled forward by electricity—huge arrays of Exide batteries powering ships, locomotives, massive telephone exchanges, and office buildings. In early 1895, he learned of a newly patented device that might be a key beginning step in realizing that vision. Two Philadelphia engineers, Henry Morris and Pedro Salom, had publicly test-driven an electric vehicle down Broad Street. They called their invention an "electrobat," and their journey required both a special permit and a policeman to precede them for the protection of horses. Morris and Salom's vehicle was slow and immensely heavy—more than two tons, sixteen hundred pounds of which were primitive "pickled ampere" batteries. The wheels were steel to support the weight, and the front set was larger than the rear.

Isaac Rice offered to supply the two with Exide batteries, as well to provide investment capital so Morris and Salom could improve on their design. Soon they had produced a lighter and faster model, only sixteen hundred pounds, of which only a third was Exide battery. With the lighter weight came pneumatic tires and front and rear wheels of equal size. They soon had an even more efficient version, eight hundred pounds, with two seventy-five-pound Electro-Dynamic motors that could run at fifteen miles per hour for twenty to twenty-five miles on a charge from 350 pounds of batteries.

Morris and Salom entered their new "Electrobat II" in America's first automobile race, scheduled for November 2, 1895, to be run from Chicago to Waukegan and back, a distance of one hundred miles. The race had to be pushed back until Thanksgiving Day because so few of the primitive automobiles could be made ready. The delay was disastrous. The night before the race, a storm deposited six inches of "wet, sticky snow" on the streets—drifts running to two feet—and temperatures dipped well below freezing. Although the day of the race dawned "bright and clear," and "a large snow plow drawn by four horses was hard at work to make a place for the start," the previous day's weather and treacherous roads took their toll as only six vehicles made it to the starting line.[9] Although the racecourse was shortened to a round trip to Evanston, only two automobiles finished. Nonetheless, the race was an enormous success, the first chance Americans had to experience the auto-racing craze that had been sweeping across Europe. It also demonstrated to many for the first time the practicability of the automobile. Newspapers across the nation reported on the race with gusto, one offering a page one headline that read, "Horse Is Doomed."[10]

The Electrobat II did not fare well in the frigid conditions. Batteries drained quickly in the cold, so Morris crept along, often not faster than walking speed. He and Salom had placed relays of charged batteries every few miles, but Morris never made it even to the first station. He turned around halfway and barely made it back to their home base before the battery gave out. Nonetheless, the Electrobat won a gold medal for "design," and once they returned to Philadelphia, Morris and Salom set about seeking commercial outlets for their invention. In January 1896, they incorporated as Morris and Salom Electric Carriage and Wagon Company, convinced they had established beyond doubt both the technical and commercial feasibility of the electric car.

Isaac Rice agreed. He bought stock in the new company, and by early 1897, he had bought out Morris and Salom entirely. The two never said why they sold their patent but it was a terrible decision. Once Rice owned their company, Morris and Salom discovered that they had not, as they thought, taken on a partner but rather a new owner who saw little need for their continued services. After Rice made it clear that they were no longer welcome in the company they had started, they departed, bitter and disillusioned. Although they attempted other ventures—they formed the Electrical Lead Reduction Company in 1899, to sell battery components—neither Morris nor Salom was ever involved in a successful enterprise again. Isaac Rice, on the other hand, had come across a business that was the ideal match for his skills.*

His timing seemed uncanny. Batteries were coming into use for everything, from Singer's new sewing machine to player pianos, and Rice had achieved a virtual monopoly on the device. Electric Storage Battery's revenues went from $646,000 in 1896 to $842,000 in 1897, to $1,163,000 in 1898, and to $3,500,000 in 1899. But Rice saw the most important—and most lucrative—application in transportation.

In a stroke of luck for Rice—but not William Griscom—on September 27, 1897, Griscom, only forty-six years old, accidently shot himself in the head while hunting at his summer home in Canada. He died on the spot. Griscom, Rice wrote later, "had been the soul of enterprise." After his death, the company "languished and came on the market."[11] Given his opening, Rice approached Griscom's brother Clement, a prominent New York financier—and Pierpont Morgan associate—and began a business relationship that would result in a Rice buyout of Electro-Dynamic about eighteen months later. (Rice and Clement Griscom would also from time to time invest together in other ventures.) But even without yet owning Electro-Dynamic, Rice had established both unfettered access to its products and the ability to either prevent access by his competitors or charge them an exorbitant price to obtain it.

---

* Cornering the market on storage batteries did not keep Rice from the chessboard. In 1895, while experimenting with a series of moves called the Kieseritzky Gambit, Rice discovered a variation in which a knight is sacrificed. To tout the Rice Gambit, as he modestly dubbed it, Rice paid some of world's most eminent players, including José Raúl Capablanca, Emanuel Lasker, and Mikhail Chigorin, to analyze his discovery—favorably, of course. He also sponsored chess tournaments with the Rice Gambit required in the opening. He ultimately spent some $50,000 in promotion.

In terms of an electric automobile, what was immediately clear was that the limited range of a single battery charge—no more than twenty-five miles—made the machine appropriate only in cities and not on country roads. But electric-powered vehicles would not be new to urban streets. By then, in many of America's major cities, overhead trolley cables had been supplanted by huge rows of Exide cells percolating under the feet of a burgeoning number of commuters. This, the most successful experiment in mass transit yet undertaken in America, had poured money into Rice's coffers.

Wasting no time, Rice announced the introduction of a "public electric cab service," for New York City beginning with "twelve vehicles of the coupé surrey, and hansom patterns, operated with electric storage batteries." The cabs would be "handsomely constructed and finished, and equipped with pneumatic tires." Side running lights and a reading light inside would provide additional touches of modernity. The idea was so novel that Rice would need the New York City council to grant a "special license . . . as there is no provision for public cabs without horses."[12]

Rice's hansom fleet would be the first use of automobiles for public transportation in the United States. The linchpin of the system was the power and endurance of the Exide cell, of course, and thanks to Rice's continued improvements Electric Storage Battery was producing batteries that had no equal. With a range that had been improved to up to forty miles, a cab could do quite a bit of business on a single charge in the tight confines of New York City. Still, cabs obviously could not waste precious battery charge cruising the streets for fares or even waiting, as did horse-drawn hansoms, at taxi stands. Instead, they were dispatched on call from a central charging station that was constructed at 1964 Broadway in a converted warehouse. As a result, most fares originated at restaurants, clubs, hotels, theaters, or from the homes of well-to-do individuals, all of which were also the most steady and reliable sources of revenue. "Charging station" was a bit misleading as well. Batteries were not charged while sitting in the beds of the cabs. One of the key elements of Rice's plan was the quick removal and exchange for a fresh battery in the vehicle. Thus, when a battery was discharged, the driver swapped it out at the charging station and returned to work while the first battery was again brought up to snuff.[13]

Rice's taxi fleet became a fad and, after a New York blizzard in February 1899 during which only the electric vehicles could negotiate the ice covered streets, it seemed electric vehicles would soon be competing with horses for dominance among the city's well-to-do.

An electric taxi navigating New York streets.

But Isaac Rice did not wait around for that. The following month, he sold out at a huge markup to a group of speculators headed by William Collins Whitney.[14] With two associates, stockbroker Thomas Fortune Ryan, and Philadelphia speculator Peter Widener, Whitney had been buying stock for a year in the Electric Vehicle Company, the umbrella under which all of Rice's acquisitions had been consolidated. But Whitney was in a similar position that Rice had found himself with

Reading Railroad—large holdings but no control. After Rice's taxis had gained notoriety plowing through slush and snow, the company became a Wall Street darling and the Whitney syndicate felt it had no choice but to pay up if they wanted the ripe plum that was Electric Vehicle.

When they sat down to negotiate with Rice, the stock price had appreciated from about $20 per share to as much as $150 per share. In March 1899, they settled on a price of $141 per share, an enormous profit to Rice, and also for Gibbs, who had been slipstreaming along. Rice would officially remain on as president until he resigned the office in August 1899, and would keep his seat on the board for some months after that, but with the March sale, his activities at the company had effectively ended.

With a portion of the proceeds from the stock, Isaac Rice decided to build a home worthy of the success he had attained. He would call it Villa Julia, in honor of his wife. And rather than old, stodgy Fifth Avenue, he would choose the newest location for New York's elite, Riverside Drive, across from the newly completed Riverside Park. He purchased a parcel at the southeast corner of Eighty-Eighth Street, and then, in October, after he was fully paid out by Electric Vehicle and decided he needed something grander, purchased a much larger parcel one block north instead, across from the site of the planned Soldiers' and Sailors' Monument. He paid $225,000 for the new location, part of which was his Eighty-Eighth Street purchase, and agreed to have written into the contract that whatever was built there must "be a high class private dwelling house, not less than four stories, and designed for the use of one family only." Across Eighty-Ninth Street to the north and occupying the entire block to Ninetieth Street, was an immense mansion built by Cyrus Clark, a silk merchant-turned developer, whose earlier vision for what had been a sparsely inhabited backwater earned him the sobriquet, "Father of the West Side." It was Clark's lobbying that had resulted in the hiring of Frederick Law Olmsted to design Riverside Park, and Clark was also responsible for bringing to the area electric street lighting, rapid transit, and modern paved streets. To do so, he had to fight back a proposal to use part of the area for a city dump.

In his choice of architects, Rice was typically idiosyncratic. Rather than selecting a firm known for creating New York mansions, he instead hired Herts & Tallant, whose renown would come from designing theaters, such as the New Amsterdam, the Lyceum, and the Brooklyn Academy of Music. When the plans were filed in August 1900, with an estimated cost of $200,000, the *New York Times* wrote, "Isaac L. Rice will build one of the finest mansions in the city. . . . The French villa style of architecture will be followed. The house will be four and five stories in height and will stand on a plot 111 by 148 feet. The exterior will be of brick and granite, with marble trimmings. In the centre of the structure an observatory tower will rise to a height of ninety-six feet above the curb."[15] Although Herts & Tallant drew up the basic plans, Rice designed much of the interior himself, and he included a soundproof chess room in the basement, cut out of solid rock.

Villa Julia would take three years to complete and feature a drive-through entrance on Riverside Drive under a three-floors-high stone arch, on which a bas-relief was carved of six children with symbols of the liberal arts.*

But home building would hardly be Isaac Rice's sole focus. He investigated a multitude of innovative devices that used electricity, and invested in any of them that seemed to hold promise of growth and profit. One of these was a revolutionary form of communication that had been developed in Europe and which Rice believed, once again correctly, would change the world. Through the summer and fall of 1899, he recruited investors and made arrangements for trained technicians to sail across the Atlantic to set up operations in the United States.

In November, Rice was ready to announce his new venture. Articles of incorporation were filed in New Jersey for a corporation capitalized $10,000,000, to be known as the Marconi Wireless Telegraph Company of America. Rice had licensed the Marconi patents, and also acquired the exclusive rights to operate in all American possessions and Cuba.

---

*   Villa Julia was to be torn down in 1980, but it was saved by Jacqueline Onassis as a historical site. It has since become the decaying home of Yeshiva Ketana, an ultraorthodox Jewish boys' school.

"The incorporators are Guglielmo Marconi, London; Isaac L. Rice, August Belmont, and Clement A. Griscom, New York; and Robert Goodbody, Paterson, N. J."

Rice also announced factories and headquarters would be established in New York. "We shall be in active operation just as soon as it is possible to find suitable quarters and build the machinery. Special attention will be given to the manufacture of wireless instruments with which to equip ships that they may communicate at sea. There will be large orders for establishing communication between points where it is not practicable to maintain cables. We expect to equip the signal and life-saving stations along the coast with the wireless system, that they may warn approaching vessels in time of fog or storm. The uses to which the wireless system may be put are almost unlimited. There is an immense field before us, and the system is as yet in its infancy."[16]

Rice seemed prescient yet again. On December 12, 1899, for the first time, a wireless signal was sent across the Atlantic, from Cornwall, England, to St. John's, Newfoundland, and Marconi could not wait to proclaim the feat to every reporter he could find. The resulting spate of front-page stories hailing the event could have been anticipated, but there were a surprising number of in the business community who did not greet the news favorably. One of the most distressed was Edward Moeran, the Marconi Company's senior counsel. When he heard of Marconi's announcement, he exclaimed, "I wish the fellow had been hanged first. What an ass that man Marconi is. He talks too—much."[17] Moeran's problem was not the impact on the company's stock, which promised to soar, but on everyone else's. "Of course, it goes without saying that this is one of the most important things that has ever happened in the history of mankind. [But] stocks will drop like a stone on Monday. It means doom of everything except wireless telegraphy and signaling. I wouldn't be surprised if there is a drop of 100 points in Western Union Cable stock."

Although Moeran's pessimistic scenario did not play out, Marconi's invention encountered surprising resistance when plans to build relay stations were introduced. In early 1903, a consortium tendered an offer for the company, which was accepted. Many of the original investors stayed on as stockholders in the new company. Belmont and Rice did not. Although terms of the buyout were not disclosed, it is reasonable to believe that both men made a good bit of money on the deal. In any event, by 1903, Rice had fully divested his interests and moved on.

But he was hardly idle. In addition to the Marconi Company, he was also president of a concern to install street lighting, another to manufacture automobile tires, and was a prominent stockholder in as many as a dozen other firms. Rice spent a good deal of time promoting chess as well, as an officer of chess associations, a referee in international matches, and a promoter of a "cable tournament," begun in 1896, in which an American team competed against a team from Great Britain, ten players each, not face-to-face, but rather with moves transmitted by telegraph. (Wireless communication was not considered feasible to transmit the moves accurately.) Rice was particularly pleased in March 1899—the same month he sold out to the Whitney group—when the American team, which had lost in the previous two years, bested the British six points to four.

All his myriad interests notwithstanding, however, beginning in mid-1899, Isaac Rice's primary focus became submarines.

CHAPTER 17
A NEW SKIPPER

Rice's practical introduction to undersea travel had occurred in mid-1898, likely on July 4, when he had been a passenger on one of the *Holland*'s test runs. His interest, however, had been piqued some months earlier when both Holland and Lake had purchased Exide batteries; Holland to power his boat when submerged and Lake to power internal electrical systems.

To that point, Rice had not seemed especially interested in waterborne vessels. Electric Launch was a solid business, but he had done little to promote luxury pleasure boats, perhaps because for surface craft, despite the noise and smoke, both steam and hydrocarbon power held decided advantages over batteries—they had a greater range and added less weight. After his run in the *Holland*, however, Rice appeared to realize that for boats traveling under the surface rather than on it, battery power would be indispensible. In addition, submarines, precisely because they had to that point experienced so much difficulty in gaining official acceptance, were precisely the sort of undervalued asset for which Rice was always on the look-out.

The first decision he needed to make was choosing which of the submarine applications he thought would make him the most money. At that point, both Lake and especially Holland were short of capital and faced with significant expenditures to upgrade their boats. Although salvage seemed to have obvious profit opportunities, Rice must have decided warships held the greater long-term potential because he made no attempt to invest in Simon Lake's company, but instead turned his sole focus to the *Holland*.

He began in late 1898. Rice had kept abreast of the company's activities, and knew that Holland and E. B. Frost, frustrated by the navy's intransigence, had decided to use the winter to upgrade the boat, although the cost was beyond the company's resources. He contacted Frost and offered to fund the modifications planned for the boat in dry-dock. These were extensive, involving the removal of much of the stern section. Whether this initial investment was structured as a loan or in return for partial ownership is not clear, but within months the question would be rendered moot. Rice's choice of Frost for his entrée into the company was not arbitrary—for what Rice had in mind, it was better to work exclusively through the businessman and not through the inventor.

On February 7, with repairs on the *Holland* still under way, and even before the sale of Electric Vehicle to the Whitney group had been finalized, Rice created the Electric Boat Company, incorporated in New Jersey and capitalized at $10,000,000. Rice had also solidified his holdings in the Electro-Dynamic Company, Frank Cable's employer, although the degree of his participation was not yet a matter of public record.

With Electric Boat as an umbrella corporation, Rice proposed acquiring the John P. Holland Torpedo Boat Company as its major subsidiary. Part of the deal was that, in return for a large but noncontrolling block of preferred stock, John Holland would assign all of his submarine patent rights, including any patents he held in his own name, to the new venture, with Isaac Rice as president of both the parent and the Holland subsidiary. Holland would be named general manager of the subsidiary, with E. B. Frost again as secretary-treasurer.

Holland consulted with Frost, who he still viewed as a partner and friend, and with Frost's enthusiastic recommendation, took the deal. For agreeing to part with his patents, Holland has been ridiculed by historians, one of the kinder characterizations describing him as "an innocent in an era of carnivorous capitalism."[1] But it is easy to see why Holland felt he had no choice. He had been toiling with his invention for more than two decades, had been acknowledged as one of the two most knowledgeable submarine men in the world, was acutely aware that no navy would be able to successfully compete in future wars without his product, and had still been unable to make any significant dent in the naval bureaucracy. In Isaac Rice, he saw a man who was willing to invest whatever amount of money was necessary to see the project through to a successful conclusion, but, even more, had demonstrated that he could go head-to-head with the most rapacious speculators on Wall Street and emerge victorious. Holland, in agreeing to give up rights to his invention for stock was, then, no different from any modern day entrepreneur who is forced to sign away most of his company to obtain venture capital. Still, if Holland had researched Isaac Rice a bit, he might have learned that Henry Morris and Pedro Salom had felt precisely the same way before the electric automobile had almost literally been yanked out from under them.

The following month, at virtually the same moment Isaac Rice was selling Electric Vehicle to the Whitney group, John Holland embarked on a pivotal sea voyage, but this time on the surface rather than under it, and the vessel was a passenger ship, the *St. Paul*, not a submarine. His destination was Ireland, his first visit home in a quarter century. Although newspapers noted that "it is reported the British government is desirous of securing a submarine boat," and that "Holland may sell his boat to England," the actual purpose of the trip, why Holland would agree to leave the United States at this crucial moment for himself and his company, when it had just been acquired by the sort of wealthy, committed investor he had been seeking for decades, has two quite distinct versions.[2]

In one account, the trip was not prompted by business at all. After the November 1898 test, Holland was described as "a tired and discouraged man," that "the buoyant enthusiasm of earlier months had waned with each new setback." Facing bankruptcy, "E. B. Frost, concerned about the health of his friend, urged Holland to plan a voyage to England and to visit his native Ireland." Only after he was rested and once again fit, "if his energies permitted," should Holland even consider a side trip to continental Europe "to assess the foreign market for his submarine boats."[3]

It would be early May before Holland returned. As he stepped off the boat, he was met by reporters who clamored for the details of his dealings with the British and the identities of the other foreign powers that had decided to create submarine fleets. Holland's response to their badgering was testy. "There is not the slightest foundation for such a statement," he grumbled, "because the British Government was not asked to buy the boat, and could not get it if it wanted to do so. The truth of the matter is my health was run down, and I thought if I took a vacation at my birthplace, in Cork, Ireland, it might do me good. I went abroad two months ago with my family, but I seemed to get worse there, and therefore I returned."

Holland did admit to some professional activities, albeit with unsatisfactory results. "While on the other side I went to London, and of course met marine engineers. They all appear to be opposed to submarine boats, because they know nothing about submarine navigation. They have never been below the surface of the water. Still, they undertake to condemn a mode of travel which is perfectly feasible . . . their ignorance on such matters is simply ridiculous."[4]

He did not expand on those comments, which could have been instigated either by frustration at finding no interest by foreign governments or simply because he could not abide what he saw as the stupidity and shortsightedness of others. He certainly was firm in the belief that he was the only man capable of building an attack submarine. Holland knew that Simon Lake was building a more sophisticated craft, but not one to challenge his own as a warship. "The *Argonaut* is, I think, a little ahead of its time," he allowed. "It will prove of great service in submarine engineering work, and the locating of wrecks."

The other explanation of Holland's two-month hiatus is darker, and given both the identity of the players and what transpired during Holland's absence, it seems closer to the truth.

In this narrative, Isaac Rice and E. B. Frost had been in contact with each other and perhaps were even negotiating, ever since Rice's trip aboard the *Holland*. Rice had waited to make a move for the company because Holland, the headstrong and stubborn perfectionist, would rebuff any effort to shift toward a more commercial footing. Only when the Holland Torpedo Boat Company seemed certain to run out of money did Rice, with Frost's support, step in and offer to fund the refit. At the same time, Frost suggested Holland take a sojourn abroad, to get him out of the way. After the deal was consummated and Holland's patents had been safely transferred to Electric Boat, Frost's entreaties became more urgent and he did finally convince the inventor to go abroad for a rest so that he may return prepared for a major effort to perfect the boat under the new ownership. After the *St. Paul* sailed, with Holland out of the way, Frost and Rice moved quickly to shunt him aside.

According to Frank Cable, as early as October 1898, he had attempted to make changes in both Holland's method of ballasting and piloting the craft when submerged, changes Holland doggedly resisted until finally Cable succeed in demonstrating that they worked. But the biggest disagreement was in how to orient the propellers and rudder, the very repair that Rice's $30,000 would go to fund. Although Holland eventually agreed to move the rudders to the rear of the propeller, if Cable is to be believed, Holland had likely established himself to Rice as headstrong and potentially difficult to work with.

Although Cable's assertions must be taken with some skepticism, by the time Holland returned from Europe, some significant changes had taken place. For one thing, Rice had the boat removed from New York Harbor and towed to a more private facility ninety miles away in New Suffolk, at the east end of Long Island, on Little Peconic Bay. The new location provided a good deal more privacy from reporters and also a less congested waterway in which to conduct tests. (The Marconi Company, in which Rice would invest later in 1899, would shortly thereafter build a receiving station in nearby Sagaponack, on Long Island's south shore.) In New Suffolk, Electric Boat rented a dedicated storage and maintenance facility, and also leased accommodations for draftsmen, engineers, and crew.

When Holland returned to the United States, he was instructed to relocate east and to work on the boat through summer and fall. Frost lost little time in letting Holland know that his role in the company had changed. For one thing, Frank Cable would be the new captain of the *Holland*. Holland would no longer be allowed to pilot the boat because, Frost insisted, Electric Boat could not obtain insurance on his life that would cover underwater mishaps. While there is no specific evidence to refute this assertion, there is some question as to its veracity, as Simon Lake was able to obtain that very coverage for himself. Frost also informed Holland that as their focus had shifted increasingly to sales, he was not to be the general manager of the Holland Torpedo Boat Company, but rather its chief engineer, a position for which he was given a five-year contract.

The demotion and reassignment of John Holland marked the beginning of a process that would see him demeaned, marginalized, and eventually forced from the company he had dedicated much of his adult life to create. "It would be a dirty campaign of slights, demotions, petty insults, and dubious legalities exploited to the hilt . . . with scant regard for appearances or sentiment."[5]

The first salvo had been fired while Holland was in Europe. Although Holland had signed over his American patents to Electric Boat, through either an oversight or the unwillingness of Frost and Rice to risk inciting him enough that he backed out of the deal, Holland still held the rights to patents he had taken out in Great Britain, Germany, Sweden, and Belgium. Holland, however, was unaware that he retained so much leverage. It is not impossible that keeping him from finding out had figured prominently into Frost's urging Holland to leave the country.

Marketing the submarine to European navies was a key to Electric Boat's ultimate success, and unless the company could gain control of the foreign patents from their unwitting owner, sales in these nations could be blocked. But although Holland held patents, Frost wrote the checks. The company's financial straits had precluded paying taxes in these nations, and five years' arrears had accrued. With Rice's money in the bank, Frost paid off all the back taxes and he did so with Electric Boat funds, and thus established at the very least a lien on those patents. If Holland learned the true state of things and decided to dig in his heels, Electric Boat could simply bring suit and Holland, who lacked the funds to reimburse the company, would lose title in court.

Frost, however, attempted to maintain at least the veneer of cooperation so rather than threaten, he decided on subterfuge. Holland described the May meeting in a letter to a friend. "I have not transferred my European patents to my present Co. Until last Friday I was under the impression that I had done so. On that day, Mr. Frost handed me a bundle of papers requesting me to sign them. Instead of doing so there and then, as requested, I took them home to find what they were. You may guess how surprised I was to find that they were assignments of my rights in Europe. I shall take the whole bundle . . . to my lawyer for his advice and I strongly suspect that within a day or two, Mr. Frost will find that I am not such a damned fool as he thought."[6]

But whether he was a fool or merely credulous in trusting men he thought were his friends, Holland soon learned that the patents were for all intents and purposes already lost. He had closed the letter, "Europe is a free field for me so far as patents are concerned for the plain reason that the most important and vital devices are still in my head and nowhere else." Even his ideas, he would find, were not necessarily his own property.

With Holland ousted from the company's management, Isaac Rice set himself to the task of making the company commercially viable. First order of business was to amend the 1896 authorization act so the *Holland* and not the *Plunger* was officially the boat that the navy would evaluate. Work had continued on the *Plunger*, at least in appearance, although at that point it must have been obvious even to navy bureaucrats that the design they had foisted on the Holland Company was not being taken seriously.

Only weeks after he had concluded the purchase, Rice succeeded and even had the deal sweetened. Through the good offices of Nevada Senator William M. Stewart, an amendment was secured to the naval appropriation act of June 10, 1896, providing that the monies allocation for submarines should be for "two boats similar to the submarine boat *Holland*." With that change, the navy could purchase the newer boat if it so chose, potentially taking the *Plunger* off the table. Just why a senator from Nevada had become such a passionate advocate for undersea navigation engendered some raised eyebrows, but patronage directed at members of Congress whose interest in a particular measure might previously have been nil was hardly uncommon.

Within ninety days of incorporating Electric Boat, Rice had thus succeeded in obtaining a highly favorable revision of the terms of his contract with the navy, restructuring the company's management, and moving operations to a venue much more suitable to developing the product. Frost, Cable, the company's investors, and of course, Rice himself, were all beneficiaries of this whirlwind activity. John Holland was not.

But the machinations within Holland's company had no impact on Holland's celebrity. When he journeyed to Greenport at the end of June, where he had booked his family into a modest hotel, reporters were gathered to greet him. Each wanted an exclusive with the man credited with turning science fiction into reality. "John P. Holland, the inventor of the sub-marine torpedo boat *Holland*, accompanied by his family, has arrived here to prepare for the official trial of his wonderful creation," the *Brooklyn Daily Eagle* reported. When the reporter was allowed an interview in Holland's hotel room, Holland asserted, "I am satisfied with the working of the boat, but I prefer to thoroughly test her powers before proceeding with the official trial. She is a great improvement over all the others I have yet perfected, and the sixth submarine boat I have invented."[7]

Although Holland remained an effective and invaluable public face of Electric Boat, and even seem to relish the role, he soon discovered it was in fact the only role he was still allowed to play. "Chief engineer" turned out to be a euphemism since others involved in preparing the Holland for its official trials—engineers, draftsmen, and Cable and his crew—had been instructed to pay him no mind. E. B. Frost had begun a whispering campaign indicating that Holland might be showing signs of senility. "No one seemed to consult Holland any more, not even on technical matters. Soon he was to learn of Frost's order to

Morris, the inventor's oldest associate in the submarine enterprise, that henceforth Morris was not to report to Holland, because 'Holland forgets.'"[8] While Morris knew better than to take such an obvious canard seriously, others working on the project, each of whom was now staking out his own turf, were all too happy to ignore the man whose vision had presented them with such opportunity.

World's first submarine base in New Suffolk, New York

In July, to oversee the preparations for the navy trials, Rice, along with Julia and their children—five at that time—journeyed from New York to take up residence on Shelter Island, a few miles east of New Suffolk. They arrived with a full complement of servants on the Electric Boat Company yacht, *Gleam*, which was itself not an electric boat, but rather powered by steam. When they arrived, the Rices took a cottage at the exclusive Manhanset House. Among its unique amenities was a golf course, completed just three years earlier, only the third in the United States.

Shelter Island, which lies between the north and south forks of eastern Long Island, had, in the previous two decades begun to attract New York's elite, who would generally arrive by yacht and, like the Rices, bring with them all the necessities, both material and human, to allow them to summer in comfort. The New York Yacht Club had opened a wharf in 1896 a short distance from the hotel. For its guests, the Manhanset House featured an immense dining room, bathing and beach facilities, a variety of amusements, tennis courts, and miles of bicycle paths.

While Rice did not make the journey from Manhattan simply to enjoy the scenic pleasures or to play a leisurely eighteen holes, nor did he insert himself into the daily activities in New Suffolk. There are, in fact, no reports of him personally inspecting the facilities, and his name does not appear in any of a plethora of newspaper articles reporting on the boat's every movement. (Frost, who was regularly mentioned, was also reported to be the owner of the yacht.) But that he was keeping close watch through surrogates is certain, and *Gleam* was used regularly to escort naval officers, both American and foreign, and other visiting dignitaries.

And visitors of all sorts came in a steady stream. In addition to its operational advantages, relocating to eastern Long Island turned out to be a quite clever marketing tactic. The ninety-mile distance was sufficient to deter idle gossipers, but not so much to dull newspaper editors' thirst for a story. Reporters were regularly dispatched to interview the principals, usually Holland, and to cover the submarine's tests of its navigation systems and its torpedoes.

Rice and Frost cultivated the press every bit as much as they wooed congressmen. Reporters were fed, housed, entertained, and given private tours of the *Holland*. The acclamation they had hoped for duly followed. Within months, virtually every person in the United States who picked up a newspaper knew of the undersea miracle being fashioned in eastern Long Island.

CHAPTER 18
JOINING THE NAVY

Fortunately for Rice and Frost, the *Holland*'s performance gave the reporters the fodder they needed. There were many tests and trial runs to cover and the news was overwhelmingly positive. On July 28, for example, a headline in the *Brooklyn Daily Eagle* read, "The Holland's Speed Test: A Naval Examining Board Has a Two Days' Trial of the Submarine Wonder."[1] The "examining board" was actually two junior officers and a construction engineer, sent simply to watch how the *Holland* reacted to waves and currents while cruising on the surface. But that did little to suppress the hyperbole. "The test was a great surprise to the board," the article went on, "inasmuch as the *Holland* astonished them by its wonderful performance." The boat did handle well, especially with the dynamo engaged. It accelerated quickly and stopped quickly, and was able to move backward when the dynamo was reversed. It made nine knots on the surface, which was more than adequate and ran without vibration or noise.

The piece closed with some irony from the naval engineer. Referring to the *Plunger*, still under construction in Baltimore, he noted, "We had intended fitting the submarine torpedo boat with steam power to be used in propelling her while sailing on the surface, which takes from fifteen to twenty minutes to generate. Whereas we find with the gasoline engines the *Holland* can be started almost instantly when she reaches the surface. Holland, the inventor recommended the change."

It would take another five months, but the head of the navy's Bureau of Steam Engineering would finally admit the error of installing a steam engine on the *Plunger*, although he did not admit the error was his. "The generating system of this vessel has not been successful," he wrote in his 1900 annual report, "and on January 31, 1900, the Department granted the contractors permission to remove the steam machinery and substitute reversible internal combustion engines of sufficient power to give the vessel the speed required by the contract."[2]

The Whitehead torpedoes were also testing well. The first firing came on August 20, where the *Holland* was also reported to have made "remarkable speed" under the water. "The torpedo was fired when the boat was moving and about four feet below the surface. It was blown from the tube by air pressure and was taken in a straight line about seventy-five feet. There was scarcely any disturbance in the water from the discharge, only a few bubbles showing on the surface near the bow of the boat."[3] Although seventy-five feet was not a particularly long distance, the missile was not fired at a target, and held no explosives in the nose, this may well have been the first launch of a self-propelled torpedo from a submerged vessel in which the projectile ran straight, true, and maintained constant depth. Nordenfelt's exhibition in Turkey had simply launched the weapon and not tracked it.

Torpedoes were a necessity if submarines were to be a weapon, but integrating a torpedo weapons system into undersea warfare presented complex engineering problems. Robert Whitehead had created the device to be fired from a surface ship, and the many variations that had been created in the ensuing decades were built to be launched similarly. The three main components in torpedo design were power, accuracy, and strength of explosive charge. For the first, which would determine how far the torpedo could travel and how quickly it could reach the target, compressed air turning a propeller, which Whitehead had used, was effective but considered dangerous. More than one Whitehead creation had exploded, taking the ship it was housed in along with it. In the enclosed shell of a submarine, even on the surface, such a mishap would kill everyone on board. Superheated carbonic acid was tried as a substitute, but required tubes and a reservoir; some attempted "rocket" power, essentially a single explosion to send the torpedo on its way, but it lost momentum quickly beyond a couple of hundred yards; others proposed a "float-supported torpedo, electrically driven from a shore generator through a cable;" and still others transferring energy to a flywheel through a steam turbine, essentially winding a spring.[4] None of these alternatives proved suitable for submarine warfare, so compressed air was reluctantly retained.

For accuracy, the torpedo had to maintain both constant depth and a straight course. The means to ensure the first had been created by Whitehead and employed in his first prototypes. Called a "pendulum and hydrostat control," Whitehead fashioned an ingenious system in which a small chamber in the body of the torpedo was built with openings to allow it "free communication" with the water outside. Inside the chamber was a piston set so as only to remain stable at a certain water pressure, corresponding to the desired depth of the torpedo. If the torpedo was too deep, the increased pressure moved the piston backward, and the shaft attached to it lifted the horizontal diving planes causing the torpedo to rise on an even keel; too shallow and the piston moved forward, causing the diving planes to force the torpedo lower. If the torpedo moved out of a horizontal attitude, a pendulum set inside another small chamber would swing, causing the shaft to again move the diving planes up or down. In this way, the diving planes would only remain in a neutral position if the torpedo ran at the proper depth parallel to the surface of the water.[5]

Making the torpedo run straight was a greater challenge, and the problem was not solved until an Austrian engineer named Ludwig Obry employed a gyroscope to build what was later called the "Obry Gear." The gyroscope, now an invaluable navigation aid in everything from ships to spacecraft, had been developed by Léon Foucault in 1851, but was considered more of a curiosity than a tool and was not used industrially for almost a half century. Obry realized the Foucault's device had a unique ability to maintain stability, and so he employed a jet of compressed air to spin a wheel on a gyroscope that, like the pendulum and hydrostat, was linked to a shaft, this time attached to the vertical rudders. When the torpedo altered course, the orientation of the gyroscope would change, causing the rudders to shift and get the torpedo back on its proper path. Whitehead purchased the patent from Obry and thus ensured that his design would be able to outperform that of any of his competitors.

The explosive used in the torpedo's nose was standard gun cotton, nitro-cellulose, the same material used to coat early filmstrips. The substance was always flammable—film strips regularly caught fire, destroying the film and sometimes a movie theater as well—but when dry and compressed became highly explosive. Detonation was always by percussion on contact with, it was hoped, the hull of a ship. Whitehead's initial design was spindle-shaped, but this limited the amount of explosive in the nose. Eventually he discovered that a rounded, blunter nose not only increased the weapon's potency, but also its performance in the water. By the time Holland was ready to utilize them, torpedoes had attained much the shape that they remained for more than a century.

Testing for explosive power, however, presented a unique set of problems. Precision instruments are expensive and torpedoes cost between $2,000 and $5,000 each, prohibitive if the device was used only once, either because it had exploded or had been lost on the bottom. As a result, live charges were never used and torpedoes were always retrieved, generally by Holland employees, but sometimes, after one had gone off course and sunk, by a local fisherman. On those occasions, the fishermen were paid a reward to return the missile, which, by law of salvage, they had every right to keep. Most of the fishermen were happy for any remuneration—which was generally only fifty dollars—but after word got around as to how expensive the items were, there was no shortage of grumbling at what was seen as a pittance. The company never admitted to paying more, but it is likely that a clever fisherman could exact a much higher payment if he agreed to keep his mouth shut as to the amount.

In September, the *Holland* did launch live torpedoes, but they were not primed. Once again, they ran straight and true. With a boat capable of maintaining an even keel when submerged, a compass navigation system that held a steady course, and torpedoes that went where they were supposed to, the *Holland* seemed to have become the weapon the navy had contracted for. Its only shortcoming was the need to briefly run awash in order to sight its target, but if it could do so quickly and duck back under the water, even that objection might prove to be moot. The trade journals agreed. *Electrical World and Engineer* reported, "It would seem, indeed, that little remains but some actual test as would represent the conditions of naval warfare."[6]

Curiosity about this new undersea marvel was not limited to news reporters or military officers. The *Holland* even made the society pages, with items such as: "The following Sag Harbor and Brooklyn people were present at the recent test of the submarine Holland, at new Suffolk, by special invitation," followed by a list of notables.[7] As a result, as autumn set in, anticipation for the *Holland*'s official test was every bit as rife as Frost and Rice could have hoped. When the *Holland* was pulled from the water to be scrubbed and repainted (dark green) in early September, as many as five thousand people showed up in Greenport to examine it on the ways.

Occasionally, however, the reporters got a story that the boat's owners would have chosen to have ignored. On October 11, the *Holland* took another test run, which initially seemed to go remarkably well. Captain Cable reported, "The program provided for a surface run of several miles, a submerged run of two miles, a torpedo attack on an imaginary enemy, and a flight under the sea. The exhibition was intended to prove that if an unsuspecting vessel was anchored, she would have gone to the bottom as did the *Maine* in Havana Harbor. . . . The torpedo we used, the regulation Whitehead, was dispatched 600 yards away from the imaginary ship. Immediately after firing, we turned, still submerged, and disappeared. The torpedo made an accurate run and struck the imaginary ship squarely in the center."[8]

But that part of the story was not featured in the newspapers. Instead, "the boat was lying at the dock after having come in from a morning practice trip in the bay, when it was noticed by those of the dock that the crew remained down below with all the ports closed." As this was unusual, a boarding party was sent onto the *Holland* and "discovered the entire crew, six in number, apparently lifeless at their various posts in the interior of the vessel." The boarding party realized immediately that there must be a gas leak and "with no little difficulty" carried the men out.[9]

As Simon Lake had learned, if the exhaust system for the Otto motor was not perfectly sealed, carbon monoxide fumes, lethally colorless and odorless, would seep into the boat and overcome the crew. Anyone not removed promptly would die.

The gasoline engine on the *Holland* had no reverse but the electric motor did, so, as the boat neared port, the gasoline engine was shut off and the dynamo engaged, the same sequence as would be undertaken when the boat ran submerged. Cable was standing on the deck with two of the crewmen as the boat neared the dock and gave the order to reverse the electric motor, but the boat did not respond. The crewmen went through the hatch to investigate, but didn't reappear. Then Cable went down. The motor stopped but Cable didn't reappear either.

Two men from shore rushed aboard as soon as they could reach the boat, went below and pulled each crewman in turn from the interior. The men recovered and the incident might have passed as just one of the inevitable mishaps that come with testing any complex new invention, except that among the spectators for that run were a greater than usual number of reporters and two present or former United States Senators, William Stewart of Nevada and Matthew Butler of South Carolina, whose continued support would be crucial in persuading the navy to finally disburse the funds to build the boat.

Afterward, "those on board refused to talk about the matter," although as everyone present was aware, "had the incident happened when the boat was out in the bay, all the men would doubtless have been killed."[10]

Although Cable noted, "The talk went that this was the last of the submarine," the incident did not result in a setback. The gas leak was dismissed as a minor malfunction easily repaired. Just why the two senators were not more alarmed at the near death of the entire crew was a mystery, unless one considers the coincidental rumors that

Frost and Rice had agreed to hold blocks of Electric Boat stock in trust for certain key supporters both in the navy and in government. In fact, a former navy captain, William H. Jaques, once president of Holland Torpedo Boat, a post that had been entirely ceremonial, dissatisfied with the amount of stock he had received when Rice bought the company, had allegedly threatened to expose the stock-parking scheme, but Frost's Washington attorneys had succeeded in having any congressional investigation squelched.

Rice was apparently unconcerned because just one week later, he bought out the remaining interest in Electro-Dynamic and folded it into Electric Boat. The purchase included two factories, one in Newark, New Jersey, and the other in Philadelphia.

In addition to senators, reporters, American naval officers, and thousands of members of the public who came to watch trial runs of the *Holland* in Little Peconic Bay, there was occasionally another category of spectator. In early October, "before the submarine boat left her moorings Herr Wellenkamp and Baron Captain A. von Rebeur Paschwitz, naval attaché to the German embassy at Washington, escorted by Mr. John P. Holland, inventor of the boat, visited the vessel and spent nearly two hours inspecting the interior of the strange craft." Their interest went beyond dockside inspections. "Wellenkamp, constructor in the German navy, who is visiting the United States to inspect the larger shipbuilding plants and investigating the naval methods of this country, were on board the submarine boat. They were very favorably impressed with the mechanism of the vessel and pleased with her performances."[11] Wellenkamp was later quoted as saying, "In the hands of competent men, the boat would prove a formidable weapon."

On November 6, 1899, the *Holland* was finally ready for its official trial. The boat would run a straight course for one mile submerged, then quickly surface, fire a torpedo at a target, and then dive again. Under the water, it would reverse course and return to the starting point at full speed. Another torpedo would be loaded in the tube and fired, again at full speed, and a third torpedo would be fired while the vessel was on the surface. In addition, there would be a series of required maneuvers, including quick diving and surfacing, and rapid changes of course while submerged.

Before the launch, members of the Naval Board of Inspection and Survey, including a rear admiral, a captain, a builder, and two engineers, "went into the *Holland* as she lay at the dock and minutely examined the mechanism and workings, and satisfied themselves that the required conditions as to the boat itself existed."[12] Since none of them knew anything about submarine navigation, how insightful an inspection they were capable of is problematic. The one man who had been present for earlier trials and knew the *Holland*'s workings intimately, a highly experienced naval engineer, Captain John Lowe, remained aboard the lighthouse tender that would serve as another of the observation posts during the test.

After satisfying themselves that the Holland looked the part inside, the board members repaired to an accompanying tender, the *Cactus*, where they would observe the test and decide if the refurbished *Holland* demonstrated the fitness to attack and sink enemy surface vessels. John Holland remained the public face of the company, and it was Holland to whom the board members addressed their questions. They virtually ignored Frost; Charles Creecy, a Washington, DC, lawyer and old friend of E. B. Frost's father, who acted as the company's representative in the capital; and even Rice himself, all of whom were also aboard.

As the test was to begin, "the *Holland* was sighted gliding along at an eight knot rate . . . looking not unlike the back of a small whale as she bore down on the starting point. Suddenly, two short, sharp toots of the *Holland*'s whistle announced the beginning of the trials. Within a boat length of the first two flags which mark the course, the *Holland* dove quickly beneath the surface and sped along at a depth of five feet."[13] The boat descended to nine feet—the depth could be measured by the flags mounted on twelve foot poles fore and aft—completed its run, surfaced, fired a torpedo, dove quickly and returned to its starting point. That sequence, as well as subsequent aspects of the trial, were completed smoothly and without incident. Although the board members refused to comment, the consensus among other observers was that the boat had handled brilliantly, meeting or exceeding every standard, even those the navy had made more stringent the previous year. Buttressing that view was a strong subsequent performance by Electric Boat stock, attributable according to stockbrokers to "the success of the recent tests of the Holland submarine." Within two weeks, the stock would appreciate an additional 25 percent.

The test run was big news away from Wall Street as well. Across America, people once again read of the "Terror of the Seas," the "Engine of War," and the "Great Destroyer"—the mysterious wraith-like vessel that could sink any battleship. The *Holland* was described as having almost supernatural powers, in terms similar to death rays in the 1950s or neutron bombs in the 1980s.

On November 14, the board made its recommendations to the secretary of the navy in a report written by Captain Lowe. It was made public two days afterward. For once, the official reaction was a match for the breathless prose in the press. "The *Holland* is a successful and veritable submarine torpedo boat capable of making an attack upon an enemy unseen and undetectable and that therefore she is an engine of warfare of terrible potency which the government must necessarily adopt into its service." Lowe, who had been in the navy for four decades and had suffered through the ebbs and flows of modernizing the fleet, added some personal remarks. "Concerning the worse than worthlessness of the present above water torpedo system, its methods, theories, and appliances, the need for a deliverance from its absurdities and from the fool's paradise of its false security and instead the absolute need of a real torpedo system . . . a submarine service should at once be organized as a matter of necessity and security. The government should at once purchase the *Holland* and not let the secret of the invention get out of the United States."[14]

E. B. Frost then asked the navy to buy the boat for $165,000, a not unreasonable number since almost a quarter-million dollars had already been spent in developing it. He and Rice also decided that it was time to bring the *Holland* in from the provinces and allow government officials in Washington to see what they were buying. They had the boat sailed from New Suffolk to Bay Ridge in Brooklyn, and from there to Elizabethport, in preparation for bringing it to the capital.

The timing for the move seemed perfect. In the wake of the board's unqualified praise, rumors of a planned new submarine fleet abounded. On November 18, the *Washington Evening Times*, published an article whose headline read, "The Navy May Ask for Fifty Holland Boats," and that "The New York Tests of the Craft Promise a Revolution in Fighting at Sea—Could Easily Destroy the Largest Battleship—Highly Praised by the Board of Inspection." Newspapers discussed the purchase of the Holland submarine as if it had already been approved, or at least that approval was only a formality. The recent "very strong report" of Captain Lowe urging purchase "by the Government of the vessel and all patent rights connected therewith, has, it is thought, removed all doubt as to the practical character of the vessel as an engine of naval warfare."[15]

Certainty in the press, however, was not matched within the navy itself. The rear admiral in charge of construction claimed to "know nothing in an official way about the Holland boat." Still the admiral, as well as any number of other officials interviewed by the newspaper all agreed that, if the report was accurate, the Holland submarine would be a vital component of any modern navy, and that its existence would change naval battle tactics forever.

Movement within the navy and Congress remained desultory. If the American navy could not muster the will to commit to the (American) undersea miracle, the press reported, others were eager to. On November 23, an article was syndicated across America, with the headline, "Great Britain Wants the Holland."

Captain Charles T. Ottley R. N. naval attaché to her majesty's embassy to the United States came from Washington today for the purpose of inspecting the Holland boat on behalf of his government. He was taken to the boat, which is moored in the Atlantic Yacht club basin in Brooklyn, by John P. Holland who explained the workings of the vessel to the captain. For more than two hours Captain Ottley looked over the boat. He seemed very much impressed with what he saw and when asked his opinion, said, "It is my intention to recommend to the board of admiralty of the British government that they immediately consider the merits of the Holland with a view to adopting vessels of her type into the British navy. She is, to my mind, the most formidable type of submarine boat and has demonstrated that she is the only successful one. The vessel could not only be used in keeping the harbor and the coasts free from invading fleets but with vessels of the Holland type there would need be no fear of submarine mine or other obstructions to navigation as she could destroy them readily. It is my opinion that there is no question that the submarine boat has come to stay and that such boats can be reckoned on in future naval warfare."[16]

The following day, another syndicated article appeared, "France Wants the Holland." It began, "Lieutenant Gontran De Faramond De Lafajole, naval attaché of the French embassy, Washington, DC, and M. Louis Revier, naval engineer, representing the French government, have been in the city recently inspecting the Holland boat and it is announced that negotiations have been entered into between the representatives of the French government and the company controlling the submarine torpedo boat for the construction of several vessels of the Holland type and also for the exclusive use of the patents for the submarine boat for the French government."[17]

Although each report seemed authoritative enough, neither was followed by an actual sale nor by an announcement by Electric Boat that a sale was pending. The British and French representatives vanished from the newspapers as quickly as they had appeared. But the public was being fed a steady stream of positive publicity, which could not help but to increase the pressure on their elected representatives.

On December 2, the *Holland* left its old berth in New Jersey, accompanied by the tender *Josephine*. The original plan was for the boat to make its way down the Atlantic coast, but no insurer would cover an ocean route, so an inland course through New Jersey on the Raritan Canal was chosen instead. Frank Cable, now permanently installed as captain, reported that everywhere he cruised, large crowds lined the banks to cheer.

The *Holland* reached Washington on December 19, and was assigned a berth at the navy yard. Holland, who had traveled by rail with Frost, was there to meet his boat as it pulled into the dock with Frank Cable, in a new custom-made captain's uniform, striding across the deck. Senator Stewart had already introduced a bill authorizing the navy to purchase the boat but it was still pending. Accordingly, Frost arranged for a series of test voyages, similar to those carried out in Peconic Bay, to convince any remaining skeptics of the boat's worth.

The trial runs in Washington went every bit as well as had those in Peconic Bay. Finally, on March 14, 1900, the *Holland* was exhibited on a test run between Fort Washington and Mount Vernon before an elite group of naval officers, political leaders, and other men of influence. The most important of the guests was Admiral George Dewey, then a national icon, "the hero of Manila Bay," but also present were Rear Admiral Rodgers and Captain Emory of the advisory board, William Kimball, now a lieutenant commander, "who commanded the torpedo boat flotilla during the late war in Cuban waters," the navy's judge advocate general, two builders, five senators, an assistant attorney general, and the assistant secretary of the navy. Secretary John D. Long, who continued to resist issuing an official endorsement of the submarine project, was listed as "unable to attend." E. B. Frost, Charles Creecy, and John Holland joined these men aboard the yacht *Sylph* to observe the trial, while Isaac Rice remained on the *Josephine*. Lieutenant Harry Caldwell, Admiral Dewey's personal aide was assigned to sail with the *Holland* during the test run.

The exhibition, which included the firing of torpedoes, a series of quick, porpoise-like dives, and long runs under the surface, went spectacularly well. Subsequent demonstrations for other naval officers and members of foreign legations were equally impressive and momentum generated by the *Holland* at long last became inexorable. The following month, the House Committee on Naval Affairs held hearings to decide whether or not, finally, to purchase the boat. Admiral Dewey was the first to testify. In his opening remarks, he said, "The boat did everything that the owners proposed to do. And I said then, and I have said it since, that if they had had two of those things in Manila, I never could have held it with the squadron I had. The moral effect—to my mind it is infinitely superior to mines or torpedoes or anything of the kind. With those craft moving under water it would wear people out. With two of these in Galveston, all the navies of the world could not blockade that place. I think it would be money well spent. I think it would tend to keep peace. That is what we want a navy for. We want peace."[18]

Rear Admiral James Edward "Fighting Jim" Jouett, who had helped Admiral David Farragut blockade Mobile during the Civil War, added, "If I commanded a squadron that was blockading a port and the enemy had half a dozen of these Holland submarine boats, I would be compelled to abandon the blockade and put to sea to avoid the destruction of my ships from an invisible source and from which I could not defend myself."[19] Rear Admiral Philip Hichborn, head of the navy's Bureau of Construction and Repair was equally insistent that the navy add submarines to the fleet and that it train constructors to build them. William Kimball and Lewis Nixon also testified, as did Harry Caldwell and a series of other junior officers all engineers, all in favor of the navy acquiring the *Holland*.

The final witness was John Holland, the only representative of the Holland Torpedo Boat Company to be called. After recounting the difficulties he had experienced in getting the navy to first show any interest in his invention, and then to live up to the rules of its own competitions, Holland was asked by legislators if he would be willing to turn over all his patents, both domestic and foreign, to the United States government, if he was paid appropriately. He was also asked if he was a United States citizen. Holland assured the congressman that he would be pleased to do so and keep the submarine as the exclusive property of the United States. The committee members seemed unaware that the patents were no longer Holland's to sell.

When the hearings ended, as a result of unstinting praise from senior line officers, especially Admiral Dewey, opposition to the *Holland* evaporated, and in April 1900, the navy purchased its first ever submarine for $150,000. Two months later, Congress approved another appropriation for the purchase of five additional boats.

Thus, after years of delay, Isaac Rice within fifteen months had secured contracts for the Electric Boat Company for six new submarines of the "improved Holland type," each to cost no more than $170,000.* The navy also agreed to cancel the *Plunger* contract if Electric Boat would return the $85,000 it had paid out in construction fees, which the company happily agreed to do. To ease the pain,

---

*   About $4,250,000 each in today's dollars.

the navy ordered an additional boat. They also assigned a military crew to learn the submarine's operation. Lieutenant Caldwell had requested he be allowed to captain the vessel, and both Dewey and the navy agreed.

The *Holland* was sailed regularly in the ensuing months, Caldwell taking on more and more of the responsibilities of command, and at the end of September, off Newport, Rhode Island, it was deemed ready for an unprecedented test. For the first time in United States naval history, a submarine was to take an active role in a mock battle at sea.

The war game was an extensive, complex exercise involving almost twenty ships in which a large attacking force, including three battleships, would attempt to circumvent a blockade manned by a much smaller force, and then sink the single battleship behind the blockade line. One of the three attacking battleships was the *Kearsarge*, which led the flotilla. Guarding the defending battleship *Massachusetts* was one cruiser, a single gunboat, a tug . . . and the *Holland*. On the second day of the exercise, the *Holland*, under the command of Lieutenant Caldwell, sailed quietly from its mooring and headed for the opposing fleet more than seven miles away. In a letter to Congress, Caldwell described his voyage.

> The *Holland* left the Torpedo Station at sundown and was placed in a partially submerged condition with the turret and about six inches of the hull above water, ready to dive at short notice. Cruised in this condition to S and E of Brenton's Reef Lightship. Sighted two vessels of blockading fleet and fired torpedo signal at them, but was not answered, and they disappeared before I could ascertain their identity. About 9 P.M., about seven SS. from harbor entrance, sighted U.S.S. *Kearsarge* within range and fired torpedo signal. Followed her and getting within 100 yards without being discovered, showed light, hailed her and informed her commanding officer that she had been torpedoed. The *Holland* was not seen by any vessel of the blockading fleet or torpedo boat, although she was within range of three of the former and several of the latter. I consider that the attack was a success because the *Holland* could in all

probability have torpedoed three blockading vessels without being discovered.[20]

The letter was an accurate re-creation, except for what Caldwell yelled up to the battleship's watch. What he actually said made head-lines the following day. "Hello, *Kearsarge*! You're Blown to Atoms. This Is The Submarine Boat The *Holland*."[21] The *New York Sun* led with, "The Holland Gets Her Game: Theoretically Sinks the Great *Kearsarge* Off Newport Harbor: The Little Submarine Steals Out Through Blockading Squadron And 'Sinks' Hostile Flagship."[22] The reporter pointed out that a $150,000 submarine firing a $3,000 torpedo had sunk a $5,000,000 battleship, and, in an eerie prediction of Weddingen's feat in September 1914, could easily have sunk two others.

Although navy officials later retracted the kill credit—the *Kearsarge* had its running lights on and was thus deemed not an active target, for the public as well as for most observers, the submarine had without question proved its value as a weapon. The captain of the *Kearsarge*, William Folger observed, "It is clear that the Holland type will play a very serious part in future naval warfare. There is no doubt whatever that the vessel at Newport can approach a turret ship unseen, either by night or day."[23]

On October 12, 1900, the United States Navy officially commis-sioned its first submarine, the USS *Holland*. For Rice, Frost, and Creecy—and for John Holland—it must have seemed like the inter-minable battle for acceptance of the Holland submarine had ended.

It had not.

CHAPTER 19
BOTTOM FISHING

With every hallelujah for the Holland submarine, Simon Lake's conviction that he had been the victim of a miscarriage of justice grew. In late 1899, he wrote a letter to President McKinley as the "inventor of a type of submarine boat that is well adapted to the needs of the government . . . for either harbor or coast defense or for purposes of blockading or destroying fleets in foreign waters or for destroying mines or cutting cables." Having heard that Congress was considering purchasing submarines, he observed to the President, "It would be to the great advantage of the government if the merits of my vessel were investigated."[1] Lake went on to extol the virtues of the *Argonaut*, complain of the shabby treatment he had theretofore received, and ask McKinley's aid in negotiating the crosscurrents of government bureaucracy. He closed by noting, "I am also writing to the Secretary of the Navy and others, and believe if an investigation is made where I can submit plans and have a hearing, I can convince anyone of the great value of this type of vessel to our government."[2]

He received no reply, either from McKinley or the navy secretary. To Lake, the reasons were apparent. Isaac Rice and E. B. Frost had succeeded in seducing a series of debauched and venal Congressmen and naval officers. Lake could not contain his disgust.

"In 1900," he wrote later, "the methods of the lobby were neither subtle nor surreptitious and lobbyists were about as clandestine as bull elephants." The *Josephine*, anchored in the Potomac, was a particular den of iniquity. "If reports could be trusted *Josephine* was a pretty loose lady. From the shore one could see lovely creatures floating about the deck, being served by Negro servants in white uniforms; terrapin and champagne and Congressmen seemed to be on the daily bill-of-fare. The ladies who made a habit of visiting the *Josephine* lived at the best hotels in Washington and some were said to move in the highest social circles. Votes for the projects . . . were secured by a combination of seduction, good fellowship, open purchase, and blackmail. Wives of many a prairie Congressman cried their eyes out while their husbands whooped it up on the *Josephine*."[3]

Primed with righteous indignation, Lake had no intention of ceding the field to Rice and Frost, thieves and frauds who were foisting an inferior product on easily corruptible government officials using women, liquor, and payoffs. Although he had never designed or built an attack submarine, Lake was convinced that he could and would build a version far superior to Holland's. His motivation seemed to have little to do with business, but was rather almost entirely personal. In his autobiography, Lake made a strange admission.

"I had never been much taken by the military possibilities of the submarine. It would be a magnificent weapon some day. Anyone could see that. But I was not interested in drowning people and sinking ships. The thing I had always had in mind was the salvaging of cargoes from ships already sunk, and doing other commercial and scientific work. There must be enough jewels on the floor of the sea to hang a necklace on every good-looking neck in America. And there were plenty of heavy cargoes, too, that would be worth bringing to the surface."[4]

Local sea captains had told Lake that he would "make a fortune" if he could discover the location of wrecked cargo vessels. Lake assured them that he would do that very thing, and would thus fund his attack on his enemies with the riches that he had literally picked up from the ocean floor. "The rebuilt *Argonaut* was practically fitted to the sound new business on which I proposed to embark. It was big enough to hold a crew large enough to do the work. It wheeled over the bottom as though it were a bicycle on its wheels with their foot-wide tires. A 'cushioning' bowsprit was also fitted, with a heavy wire running from its tip down to the keel. With this arrangement I could run over boulders or small wrecks. When we went automobiling on the bottom of the sea it could rise over any obstacle the bowsprit could top, and travel safely up the sides of declivities with angles of as much as forty-five degrees. No surface automobile could do as well."

Lake was not the first to see the profit potential in undersea salvage. Treasure hunting had in fact become popular fodder for Sunday supplements as inventors devised new ways to scour the sea bottom. In 1899, for example, a syndicated article, "Treasures of the Sea," began, "The treasures hidden by the sea have from olden times formed a strong temptation for man's ingenuity and greed; and in ancient mythology treasure troves, entrusted to the waves play a disastrous part in individual and national fate. No sooner has, in our time, some inventor brought out a new submarine device or diving apparatus, when, to use Shakespeare's words, all the profound sea hides in unknown fathoms begins to glitter before man's eyes with its demoniac allurement."[5]

The article referred not to Simon Lake, but rather to an Italian engineer, Piatti del Pozzo, who had designed an ingenious spherical diving apparatus, ten feet in diameter, fitted with three screws that enabled it to shift its position at the bottom of the ocean. He had achieved stunning success in raising sunken ships from the Aegean.

"A hundred and thirty years ago next July a famous sea fight took place off Tsheshme, an Asiatic-Turkish seaport, between the Russians and Turks. Count Alexis Orlov, the Russian admiral, defeated the Turkish fleet there on July 15, 1770, with great losses on both sides. And now the sea gives up its treasures from the bottom of the Aegean. The divers report that the whole ground about the wrecks is covered with a gigantic carpet of silver coins. In view of the immense yield of treasure, the operation thus far has been confined to the

Russian flagship, which lies at a depth of a little over 130 feet. A very large amount of Venetian, Austrian and Russian gold pieces has been brought to light. Besides the coin, bars of gold, gold and silver crosses, medals, and religious Images, sliver and gold services, a Bible bound in silver and adorned with gems, etc., have been found."[6]

Still, even with del Pozzo's descending sphere, treasure hunting remained a hit-and-miss operation, relying a good deal more on luck than science. Even if a sunken craft was located, getting items of value to the surface was laborious and problematic, especially for anything heavier than jewelry or coins. Lake, who could patrol along the bottom, would bring rigor and the method to undersea salvage. "No one had ever tried to salvage cargoes in a really businesslike way. Divers had been sent down to break into the strong-rooms of vessels in an effort to recover treasure, but salvaging of that kind is disproportionately expensive and rather dangerous. It is miserably easy to foul a diver's lines, and the necessity of deflating the diver that is a heartless way to put it, perhaps, but that is precisely what happens when the air-pressure is lifted is a tedious one. If it is not managed properly the diver will be attacked by the painful 'bends' and perhaps die. I had realized that my enterprise would only succeed if we had new methods.[7]

Lake's submarine was not built to carry salvage material, especially if the cargo was industrial. This necessitated repeated trips to surface. A vessel dedicated to storage, however, would make the entire process far more efficient, and therefore far more profitable. "I built a submersible cargo-carrier which proved to be a complete success. It was shaped like the pressure-resisting portion of the *Argonaut*, cylindrical in form and airtight. In practice it was anchored near a wreck, and by means of air- and water-valves the air was permitted to escape and water to enter. When on the bottom the diver removed the hatch cover, the boat was loaded, the compressed air was turned on and the water forced out, and the boat rose to the surface. That operation was easy enough if the conditions were right."[8]

By mid-1900, Lake's improved *Argonaut II* was operating out of Bridgeport, Connecticut, prowling the bed of Long Island Sound with its cargo-carrier in tow. The results were spectacular. Able to cover twenty square miles per day, Lake claimed salvage rights on more than thirty sunken ships. One of his earliest and most lucrative finds was a load of copper ore and copper matte (a mixture of iron, sulfur, and copper, especially rich in the latter) that had been lost seven years before. Others had searched in vain for the cargo, worth tens of thousands, but it was assumed irretrievably lost. Lake located the wreck in two days. He quickly transported the goods to the surface, sold them back to their original owner and made a hefty profit for himself. His cargo-carrier—which newspapers called a "submarine wrecking car"—was built to accommodate even the heaviest material. "Some of the sunken boats were loaded with coal, which is an easy cargo to handle. We merely ran the muzzle of a big suction pump into the hold, drew the coal into the submersible freight boat, and then walked away with her."

Lake developed a second method for extracting material from sunken vessels, a long tube that stretched from the surface to the sea floor, "large enough for a man to descend comfortably on a ladder, and with a well-lighted observation chamber at the lower end from which he could walk into the water just as though he were stepping out of the water-lock on the *Argonaut*. This tube had one very great advantage over anything that had been tried before. A diver was not continually yanked and mauled by the currents of the sea."[9]

Within months, Simon Lake had become a wealthy man, with the promise of growing yet wealthier—"it seemed to me that the Lake family could hardly avoid having one millionaire in it," he wrote. With money came prestige. By fall 1900, Lake was widely touted as one of Bridgeport's leading citizens, and leading citizens are sought after, especially by politicians. No longer would Lake have to shuffle through the halls of Congress, helpless to prevent other leading citizens from destroying his dreams.

And so, having obtained the means to engage his enemy on equal footing, in early 1901, Lake began to plot out a design for a true warship. This time, little was initially leaked to the press. "Great secrecy has been observed by everyone connected with the designing of the boat . . . [but] it is believed that there are a great many features to recommend her to the Navy Department which are being withheld, and will not be divulged until the experimental trials are made."[10] Eventually, however, the basic details emerged. The vessel, which Lake would call the *Protector*, would be sixty feet in length and carry five Whitehead torpedoes. Like the *Holland*, it would run on an Otto-style gasoline engine on the surface and storage batteries while submerged, an arrangement that would require Lake to purchase Exide batteries, although where he obtained his supply was never made clear. The *Protector* was described as being "capable of being navigated on the surface, at any predetermined depth, or on the bottom," using the *Argonaut* design, but "with more power and finer lines, so as to get more speed."[11] Also like Lake's salvage boats, wheels would be fitted on the bottom, and a diving compartment built into the bow. One aspect of the design that would not change was the manner of going under the water—Lake insisted on maintaining his even-keel method of descent rather than adopt the Holland porpoise method.

With his warship almost completed, on June 10, 1901, Simon Lake incorporated the Lake Torpedo Boat Company in New Jersey, capitalized at $1,000,000, and officially joined the battle to produce the navy's undersea fleet. The corporate charter was described as "very wide," but Lake announced that the company's sole purpose was to design attack submarines that could compete successfully against the Holland design. Lake's principal partner was Lebbeus Miller, who had also been a major investor in the salvage company. Miller, by then almost seventy years old, was an expert in precision machine tooling and had made a small fortune introducing modern methods to the production of sewing machines for the Singer Manufacturing Company. He viewed Simon Lake as a mechanical genius and had become something of a mentor to the man three decades his junior.

Lake was by this time sufficiently experienced to recognize that mechanical genius was not enough. If he were to do battle with Electric Boat, he would need to do so in the newspapers and in Congress as well as with naval engineers. Newly appointed to the Lake Torpedo Boat board of directors was Foster Voorhees, a well-placed Washington, DC, attorney, who just months earlier had been governor of New Jersey. But Lake's most important agent in the capital was his local

Congressman, Ebenezer Hill. At Lake's behest, Hill, who had made a good deal of money in banking, lobbied tirelessly and volubly on his constituent's behalf, accusing Electric Boat of malfeasance, attempting to stifle competition, violating the terms of its contract with navy, and attempting to perpetrate a fraud on the United States of America. Hill's scandal-mongering resulted in the House agreeing to revise the terms under which naval appropriations were granted to allow competition between "*existing* government submarines and those of *any* American inventor," which Lake hoped—and Hill insisted—should be between the *Protector* and the ill-designed *Plunger*.[12] With the question raised of whether the *Holland* could be deemed an officially sanctioned design, Lake set out to aggressively promote his own boat. And, where he might have refused to adopt Electric Boat's means of submerging, Lake was all too happy to adopt the Electric Boat ploy of evoking the interest of foreign governments.

Just one week after the Lake Torpedo Boat Company was incorporated, Lake was able to extol both the boat's international appeal and his own patriotism. The *New York Tribune* reported that Lake's designers had been working on the new boat for six months and had just that week completed their work. Plans and specifications had been sent to construction companies and "Mr. Lake, the inventor of the new type of torpedo boat who is president of the company, expects to place the contract for the trial boat this week."

Demand would be vigorous but Lake wanted Congress and the public to know he intended to put his own nation first. "During the last few weeks, representatives of the British, Chilean, Russian and Japanese governments have been in Bridgeport investigating the *Argonaut* type, and efforts have been made to purchase outright from Mr. Lake the rights to manufacture the boats for these foreign governments. 'I have refused to consider the offers of foreign governments,' said Mr. Lake, 'until after my own, government has had an opportunity to decide if it cares for the *Argonaut* type of submarine torpedo boat. If the United States Navy does not want the boat, then it will be time enough to consider the offers of foreign governments.'"[13] As with Electric Boat, however, Lake's patriotism was thus not unconditional. If Congress and the navy insisted on moving forward with Holland

Torpedo Boat's ill-gotten contract, Lake made it clear that what he insisted was a superior machine would be sold to foreigners.

Lake was apparently unaware, however, that his threat might be rendered moot as he would no longer be competing with the *Holland*. As he had been blindsided when the *Holland* had been substituted for the *Plunger*, on June 14, 1901, only four days after the Lake Torpedo Boat Company was incorporated, the Holland Torpedo Boat launched a far more advanced vessel for its first test run.

CHAPTER 20

DISPLACEMENT

Despite its success against the *Kearsarge*, opposition to Holland submarines within the navy hierarchy remained intense. Admiral Charles O'Neil, who headed the Bureau of Ordnance, while recognizing that "several eminent naval officers," looked favorably on the Holland, "was at loss to understand them" as the boat "has never shown the ability to do anything more than run at slow speed on the surface and make submerged runs of short duration at a much slower speed, always in carefully selected localities and under most favorable conditions."[1] Admiral George Melville was equally skeptical. Melville headed the navy's Bureau of Steam Engineering, which had insisted *Plunger* use that manner of motive power. "From the time that the Senate and House naval committees look with favor on these boats, there will be a decreased construction of battleships . . . to be able to fire one torpedo from a submarine after hours and even days of preparation is far from promising work."[2]

How much of this was genuine and how much attributable to Simon Lake's machinations cannot be discerned. But with money, stock, and favors flying thick and fast, it is impossible to say how heartfelt was any condemnation or testimonial. Both O'Neill and Melville were, not surprisingly, Lake advocates.

In each camp, detractors were demonized and supporters deified. Melville was described by Lake as "a fine old seaman. He had long white hair and a kindly face and the most honest eyes I ever looked into, and he swore like the very devil. It was shocking to hear him, not because of his profanity but because he looked so much like a saint." Lake's recollection of their first meeting was consistent with that description. "'A lot of Goddamned treasury-robbers are trying to shove boats down the Navy's neck,' [Melville] bellowed. 'Our hands are tied. I cross the street when I see one of the Goddamned thieves coming my way.'" Melville then supposedly said, "We'll take a look at your damned boat anyhow. By God, they can't keep us from doing that."[3]

According to Lake, "[Maine Senator Eugene] Hale felt the same way and so did many other honest men in both Congress and the Navy Department, but there was not much that could be done about it. Congress did the buying and the insiders knew how to slick their little jobs through the congressional committees and how to set up interference against the outsiders."[4] By insiders, of course, he meant Frost and Rice, although by then Lake himself had become very much of an insider as well.

Regardless of their open partisanship and that both O'Neil's and Melville's critiques seemed extreme, even gratuitous, each man was of sufficient rank that payment by the navy for completed Holland boats might not be assured. Holland had proposed to build an enhanced version of the *Holland* the previous year, but had been rebuffed—Frost and Rice had refused to undertake yet another expensive project for which there was no guaranteed return. But with Lake in active competition, there seemed little choice. If for any reason the seven contracted-for submarines were rejected after construction, Electric Boat could be bankrupted. Frost and Rice, with Frank Cable in total agreement, decided they had better construct Holland's improved prototype. In late spring 1901, solely at company expense, they undertook to build the *Fulton*, which would serve as the model for the government boats, which were to be called *Adder, Moccasin, Porpoise, Shark, Grampus, Pike*, and, ironically, *Plunger*.

The new vessel was "larger, roomier, faster, and simplified and improved as to details." It was ten feet longer than the *Holland*, with a submerged displacement of 122 tons to the *Holland*'s 75. The Otto engine had been increased to 160 horsepower from 50, and the electric motor to 70 from 50. The upgrading of the engine was described as "a large step in advance over the original *Holland*, as it enables fair speed on the surface to be made while charging batteries." The *Fulton* could run at eight knots on the surface and seven either awash or submerged. In addition, the gasoline engine and electric motor were geared in such a way that either could be used to operate the air compressor and the pump. For simplicity, the steering and diving rudders were manually operated, rather than employing the automatic apparatus that had guided the *Holland*. The *Fulton*, as had its predecessor, featured a single bow-mounted torpedo tube, although it carried five torpedoes rather than three. To make room for the additional torpedoes, the pneumatic gun had been removed.[5]

Fulton

Lake was no more impressed with the *Fulton* than he had been with its predecessor, and continued to insist that Holland's premise of a diving boat was fatally flawed. John Holland, he insisted, was simply too stubborn to abandon his pet idea, not realizing that the same criticism could apply to him. But just as Lake was no longer competing against the *Holland*, nor was he competing against its designer. Appointed instead to draw up the *Fulton*'s final blueprints and then supervise its construction was E. B. Frost's handpicked choice to replace John Holland as chief engineer, naval lieutenant Lawrence York Spear.

Spear, only thirty years old, had been born in Warren, Ohio, son of a judge of the Ohio State Court, and attended the Naval Academy, from which he graduated second in his class in 1890. After brief tours on the *Pensacola*—one of the last United States naval vessels still made of wood—and two other ships, he was assigned to the Naval Construction Corps and sent to the prestigious University of Glasgow to study naval architecture and marine engineering. Two years later, Spear was back in the United States with a bachelor of science degree and was soon named "assistant superintendent of construction" of the "protected" cruiser *Olympia*—meaning its deck was armor-plated—which would become Admiral Dewey's flagship. Spear also assisted in the building of the battleship *Oregon*, and supervised the construction of a surface torpedo boat in Seattle. In each of these and other assignments, he received glowing reports from his superiors.[6] He was so well thought of that at twenty-seven he was put in charge of instruction of graduate-level naval architecture at Annapolis.

In addition to his teaching duties, Spear was assigned to conduct inspections of various shipyards where naval vessels were under construction. In 1899, he visited Lewis Nixon's Crescent Shipyard in Elizabethport, New Jersey, where he got his first look at the *Holland*.

While Spear was convinced the submarine's performance could be upgraded, he knew instantly that he had come upon a unique and invaluable craft that would be a significant feature of future of wars at sea. He contrived to make frequent visits to New Jersey and soon insinuated himself into the planning for both the new prototype and the seven contracted-for boats. Soon afterward, Frost offered him the post of chief engineer, which was, at least on paper, still John

Holland's title. As was the case with Holland's two-month trip across the Atlantic, there are two disparate versions of how and why Spear was able to insinuate himself so successfully into Electric Boat.

In one account, Spear struck up a friendship with Frank Cable, who shared both his vision and his enthusiasm. He did not grow particularly close to John Holland, who by then viewed every new face with suspicion. In this case, Holland's mistrust was justified. Cable informed E. B. Frost that he had come across a talented and willing architect and soon Spear was contributing ideas on improving Holland's design. After Frost and Rice decided that the *Fulton* should supplant the *Holland*, and it became clear that Spear's ideas would take precedence over his own, Holland grew to despise him. Frost then resolved the conflict by appointing Spear as chief engineer and shunting Holland permanently off to the side.

Typical of the acrimonious encounters between Spear and Holland, this story goes, was one in which Spear, abetted by Cable, overruled Holland on the mechanism by which the *Fulton* would be controlled by its captain. "To operate his submarines," one historian recounted, "[Holland] introduced many and varied automatic devices, his belief being that these were essential for the proper performance of all subsea craft. For instance, he contended that the operator should sit on a camp stool and manipulate the submarine by means of push buttons and switches. This is beautiful in theory, provided it always works; but it is a well-known fact that machinery is without conscience. Thus it became the conclusion of Spear and Cable that hand-operated gear was far safer and more dependable.

"After Spear and Cable had taken upon themselves the removal of Holland's contraptions from these first American boats, Holland chanced to look down from his office one day to discover his pet equipment lying dismantled on the dock. Demanding an explanation, Spear and Cable reasoned with him, but with little effect. In tears, Holland said, 'You might expect this from a young whippersnapper from the navy. He has ruined my life's work.'"[7]

But the account is without corroboration. Evidence that it is fanciful, simply an after-the-fact justification for removing Holland from a position of authority, was supplied by Cable himself. Cable viewed the new chief engineer not as a savior of a company sent floundering by a dreamy, dissociated John Holland, but rather, while "a brilliant technician," one who had "no practical experience in submarine construction." As a result, "theories prevailed," and "much of the mechanism designed to go into the boat was left out, and most of the mechanism left in was changed. This not only delayed completion, but entailed great expense."[8] In one case, "Our chief engineer [Spear] insisted that cast iron was suitable for the gears and clutches and my protests failed to change his view." At one point, after the chief machinist went into the boat to start the engines, "he reappeared with blood streaming down his face. A large chunk of cast iron he brought with him told the story. One of the gears had broken and a detached piece struck him in the face. Thereupon we determined to have no more cast iron gears or clutches. The change cost thousands of dollars and considerable delay."[9]

To Cable, then, "As in the case of the *Plunger*, she was not our own child in certain essential features." The *Fulton*, however, was constructed under far different circumstances than was the *Plunger*. The new boat was built for experiment and testing solely with company funds. Frost was under no obligation to allow Spear any input at all, let alone to assign him to supervise the boat's construction. John Holland had little question why Frost had done so but, at that juncture, no one rose in his defense.

Even before the *Fulton*'s initial sea tests, construction had begun, under Spear's authority, for four of the other seven boats using the *Fulton* design. These would come to be called "A-class" boats, for *Adder*, whose keel was first to be laid. Beginning the *Adder* and her sister ships was a risk—if the *Fulton* developed significant problems later, the expense of rebuilding all the boats whose construction had begun would be enormous. But, despite the delays and added expense, the *Fulton* performed extremely well, so the project moved ahead. By fall it had become clear that, whether or not John Holland received due credit, he had designed a remarkable submarine.

On November 23, 1901, Frank Cable proved it. The headline the following day was, "All Night Under the Sea: Crew of the Fulton After Test Say They Could Live Comfortably as Long as Food Would Last: Submarine Boat Surpasses Fondest Dreams." The *Fulton* had remained submerged for fifteen hours while a storm raged over eastern Long Island, far surpassing anything previously achieved, including by Lake's *Argonaut*.

The description of adventure left no doubt of its magnitude.

> With the wind blowing sixty miles an hour and an abnormally high tide washing over her, the submarine torpedo boat Fulton rested on the bottom of Peconic Bay on Saturday night. The six men who were in her emerged at 10 o'clock yesterday morning, and declared that they never spent a more comfortable night anywhere. They were, Rear Admiral John Lowe, U. S. N. (retired), Captain Frank T. Cable, Mate John Wilson. Engineer John Saunders, Electrician Harry H. Morrill, and Boatswain Charles Bergh. At 7 o'clock on Saturday night, Captain Cable closed the hatch of the Fulton's conning tower, and the boat sank out of sight in about fifteen feet of water. All night long she lay there, having absolutely no communication with the outside world, and utterly ignorant of the fact that the fiercest gale of forty years was sweeping over Peconic Bay. The test was made to demonstrate the truth of the contention that the air in the Holland submarine boats is sufficient in quantity and quality to enable their crews to remain under water for practically an indefinite period. Food to last all night and bedding enough to make all comfortable were placed in the boat, and the men took turns standing watch.*[10]

Cable told reporters fifteen hours submerged "far exceeded his expectations," and that "it showed the possibilities of the boat to be practically unlimited." He had stored four flasks of compressed air in the boat, assuming the crew would need to use a good deal of it, but he reported that the air supply was more than sufficient and the flasks were not opened at all. During the night, heat and light were supplied by the battery array, which held a charge for the entire fifteen hours.

A naval officer, Lieutenant Arthur MacArthur Jr., had been assigned to Cable's crew. MacArthur, son of a Union army general and Medal of

---

*   Lowe had retired a few months earlier and been promoted to rear admiral retroactively.

Honor recipient, had chosen the navy—and had been named to captain the *Adder* when the boat was commissioned—unlike his younger brother Douglas, who elected to follow in his father's army footsteps.

Admiral Lowe, who had lost none of his ardor for submarines, described the conditions during the test as "wonderful." He "regarded the demonstration as perfect, and thought that the length of time that the *Fulton* could remain under water was limited only by her capacity to carry food for her crew. He said yesterday that the air in the *Fulton* was perfectly normal all night. He slept several hours, and it was a perfectly natural sleep." While he slept, those on watch "played cards and read." Lowe noted that such a supply of clean breathable air, "upsets all the theories of physicians and scientists who tell us that what we did last night was impossible." He added that his unstinting praise had been well earned. "I was very critical all night and nothing escaped me," although this assertion must be viewed with some skepticism as Lowe had been awakened periodically, at his request, and, according to Cable, made liberal use of the bottle of scotch that the crew had included in the provisions.[11]

Fulton crew. Frank Cable *is standing, second from left, and Arthur MacArthur is standing at the right.*

Conditions on the surface were far different. In a storm that would deposit a foot of water on the streets of New Suffolk, the commander of the tender *Winslow*, anchored directly above the *Fulton* to provide emergency assistance, spent the entire night attempting to prevent the rolling and pitching vessel from swamping in the high winds. On the Electric Boat Company yacht, which spent the night at anchor, E. B. Frost and Lieutenant Spear "were in the party that saw the *Fulton* go down, and they were watching for her reappearance when she came to the surface. Both were highly elated over the demonstration." Absent from the test for the first time for a major demonstration of a Holland submarine was John Holland.

Even in triumph, Cable offered a suggestion to improve the safety of the crew. One of the primary dangers of running submerged, as he and his crew were all too aware, was a carbon monoxide leak. Cable advocated a simple yet effective solution. Like a parakeet in a mine, on any voyage where the hatch would be closed, the submarine would carry a mouse in a cage. If the mouse passed out, the boat would surface immediately and throw open the hatch. Although this could prove awkward in a combat situation, it would work quite nicely at all other times.

With the *Fulton*'s headline-grabbing feat and the construction of the other boats, Holland Torpedo Boat seemed to finally have made the transition from entrepreneurial startup to going concern. They had settled on a design, vanquished their chief competitor—or so it appeared—and had a lucrative contract with the United States government that did not preclude foreign sales, an opportunity they intended to exploit without delay. All that was needed was to solidify their management structure, which mostly involved replacing John Holland with someone more willing to adhere to the corporate philosophy.

On April 25, 1902, the following item appeared in Washington, DC, newspapers: "Naval Constructor Lawrence Spear has resigned, to take effect in a few weeks in order to engage in more profitable private business. . . . He became a naval constructor with the rank of lieutenant in November 1898, and has been superintending naval construction at the New York navy yard since October 1890. He is a valuable officer, and his resignation will be accepted with regret."[12]

A new post with Electric Boat was not the only big move up in Lawrence Spear's fortunes in 1902. On June 2, he wed Lillian Wing, to whom he would remain married for rest of his life, forty-eight years. Daughter of a successful businessman and Harvard graduate, marriage to Lillian got Spear into the *Social Register*. One month later, the following item appeared in society pages, "Mrs. E. B. Frost, a prominent society woman of Washington, has taken a Manhanset cottage for the season. Mrs. Frost is entertaining this week Mrs. Lawrence York Spear, of New York, who was Miss Lillian Wing, her marriage on June 2 having been a brilliant affair."[13]

CHAPTER 21
COUNTERSTRIKE

Although once again outflanked, in mid-March 1902, Simon Lake journeyed to Washington, DC, to press his case personally. He claimed that his trip to Washington was not at his initiation but rather was prompted by supporters in an attempt to right the injustice of the Holland submarine contract. "Melville called me to Washington to appear before the Naval Affairs Committee of the House. The Navy wanted Congress to give it power to buy the boats it wanted and Congress was stubbornly holding onto its authority. I had to hang around Washington for several weeks before I got a hearing, but they were not wasted weeks. [Speaker of the House] Uncle Joe Cannon and [Congressman] Oscar Underwood sat at my table at the hotel, and I almost forgot to eat in my interest in what they had to say."[1]

But a letter from the Lake Torpedo Boat Company dated February 27, 1902, belies Lake's assertion. The letter was aggressively circulated in Congress by Ebenezer Hill, who then presented it to the committee in a special hearing on March 28, describing his role in the affair with more than a little disingenuousness. "My knowledge of the situation is confined wholly to an acquaintance with the stockholders of this company, and I am here simply to say to you, gentlemen, that they are perfectly reliable financially and in every other way. What their respective interests are I do not know. . . . I will be glad to call attention to some of the stockholders whom Captain Lake informed me about I do not know who they are, except indirectly."[2]

The letter, however, was quite direct. In it, Lake stated, "The Lake Submarine Company has successfully mastered submarine navigation for commercial and wrecking uses and the Lake Torpedo Boat Company is now engaged in the construction of a submarine boat for naval warfare, and the same will be ready for inspection in a few months. The boat is being built by private interests unassisted by financial aid of the Government, with the hope that it will be purchased if deemed satisfactory and useful to the United States Navy."

Of course, appropriations for submarines had already been exhausted on the Holland boats. Congressman Hill had laid the groundwork to undercut the solidity of that appropriation the year before and Lake now attempted to take it one step further. He proposed incorporating into the naval appropriations bill a clause that authorized the secretary of the navy to purchase an additional three submarines for no more than $175,000 each.

Lake also suggested that the new appropriations should not simply follow along after older ones. He included a passage that stipulated that prior to any purchase, "any American inventor or owner of a submarine boat may give reasonable notice and have his, her, or its submarine boat tested before October 1, 1902, by comparison or competition, or both, with a Government submarine boat or any private competitor." The comparative results, with recommendations, would be forwarded to the Secretary of the Navy, "who may purchase or contract for submarine boats in a manner that will best advance the interests of the United States in submarine warfare." Lake insisted that his only goal was to ensure that "American inventors may have a fair and impartial opportunity to compete in the science of submarine warfare and thereby engender healthy competition, which will develop the highest type of submarine craft and reward American inventors."[3]

While the "free and fair" competition Lake proposed applied only to new orders—and there were none proposed in that year's naval appropriations—it could certainly be extended to existing contracts as well. If Lake won, the navy could simply then refuse to accept any Holland boats and award the existing seven boat contract to him as well.

That three free and fair competitions had already been completed, with Holland winning each one, seemed to Lake merely an inconvenience. Still, those competitions had been judged only on the basis of plans. Lake was now proposing that they be repeated using actual boats. Congressman Hill succeeded in securing a special session of the naval affairs committee on March 28 specifically to allow Lake to press his case. For his appearance, he brought along Foster Voorhees, acting as the company's attorney.

Before Lake testified, Voorhees reiterated Lake's plea for a government-sanctioned competition to break Electric Boat's monopoly. "Believing that this type of boat is coming into use, and that the Government ought to get the very best type possible, and anticipating that those behind the type already adopted will probably make application at this session for an increased appropriation for the purchase of new submarine boats made by them, we have thought it best that this committee should first be acquainted with the merits of the Lake submarine torpedo boat."

Voorhees also stressed that the "respectfully submitted" clause his client wanted the committee to approve was "perfectly fair on its face." With studied innocence, he observed, "It simply says that the Secretary of the Navy may, if he is satisfied after comparisons and tests have been made, order not more than three boats." Lake was asking Congress to pay for neither the construction nor the equipment, but was merely saying, "We have a boat here which we desire to have tested. If you think it is worth purchasing, buy it and, if not, ours is the loss." Then, undercutting Lake's later assertion that he had gone to Washington only at the behest of ardent supporters of his design, Voorhees noted that "Captain Lake" had "asked for this hearing."

Simon Lake's boats might not have contained torpedoes, but his testimony to Congress did. Lake's first line of attack was to lump Holland's boats in with all previous efforts—the *Hunley*, for example—recounting the many fatalities and failures of what he described as "diving type" boats. (When the committee members referred to submarines as the "Holland type," Lake asked them to say "diving type" instead.) Of course, Holland boats had never been responsible for a serious injury, let alone a fatality. The closest call had been the gas leak, a mishap that occurred on the *Argonaut* as well. The danger, Lake assured the congressmen, was that if a diving boat got out of trim, became heavy in the nose from even "one ounce" of extra ballast, it could easily plunge to the bottom. "The 'Tuck' boat *Peacemaker*, experimented with some years ago in New York Bay, ran head first into the mud, and the records show that many of this type of which I have spoken have done the same thing." Lake omitted mentioning that Holland's boats were positively buoyant and in case of a failure of the motor, would simply bob to the surface.

Even if they did not sink, Lake insisted, diving boats were longitudinally unstable, with a shifting center of gravity, another untruth since Holland had engineered his boats with a fixed center of gravity in order to dive and surface safely. Lake painted a far different picture. "You are like a vessel in a fog, going between the surface and the bottom. You have no guiding medium, and instead of having only two directions in which you can go, right and left, as a surface vessel has, you can go in all sorts of directions. Currents will deflect your course; every wave rolling above the vessel imparts an up-and-down motion to the particles of water beneath, so a vessel remaining stationary takes on, of course, that motion." For a Lake vessel, crawling along the sea bottom, he stressed, longitudinal stability ceased to be an issue. This was a repetition of Admiral O'Neil's assertion that Holland boats could operate only in calm waters, which ignored that many successful submerged voyages had occurred with storms raging overhead. Lake leveled a number of other criticisms at Holland boats, each either a distortion or an outright falsehood, for example, that Holland had not yet figured out how to maintain an accurate compass heading, or that it was impossible for a Holland boat to cruise submerged at a constant depth.

Lake was on firmer ground describing the virtues of his own boats, of which there were many. Nonetheless, his main thrust was an attempt to undermine faith in the Holland design. The hearing was held in the manner of a grand jury procedure, with only the prosecution present. Lake's indictments solidified the opposition of some of the committee members—who Lake and likely Ebenezer Hill were actively cultivating—and created doubt in the minds of some who had until then been supporters of Electric Boat.

But Isaac Rice, who Lake described as a "pushing, ruthless, hard-finished millionaire," was not about to absorb body punches without returning some of his own. Rice's first blow was robust. As Lake recounts the story, after he testified in Washington, "I got a wire: 'The Electric Boat Company has attached everything. They have men in possession at the dock and they have seized all our papers.'" Lake rushed home, "half sick with worry." When he arrived at his plant, "I found one deputy sheriff loafing on the unfinished boat and another asleep on a drawing board in the office. Up to this time I had not known what it was all about. Now I discovered that I had been sued for half a million dollars on a charge of libel, the Electric Boat Company being the complainant."[4]

Lake was stunned to find his business at risk, and he soon claimed to have found out what had precipitated the lawsuit. "Some days previously I had prepared a letter to send out to my stockholders. We needed more money for construction purposes and I was appealing to them to stand for another assessment. In my effort to assure them of ultimate success I used a phrase something like this: 'I have the authority of high officers of the Navy for the statement that the Lake boat is far superior to any other.' I did not state the names of the officers concerned, but any one familiar with the situation could have guessed at them. Mr. Lebbeus B. Miller was then treasurer of the Lake Torpedo Boat Company and he objected to the letter when I read it at a directors' meeting. 'I wouldn't send that letter out, Simon,' said he. 'It isn't wise.'"

According to Lake, he did not send the letter, "but some spy turned a copy of it over to the Electric Boat Company, and they sued us." Under Connecticut law, the very initiation of a lawsuit could trigger an attachment. "Samuel Fessenden was the attorney for the Electric Boat Company, and promptly tied our property up hard and fast. Judge Foster told me there was but one way in which I could get the company property released and go on building the boat. That was to put up a bond of $1,500,000, as required by law."

Facing disaster—he did not have sufficient cash—Lake was saved when Lebbeus Miller posted the bond from his personal assets, requiring nothing more from Lake than his word. The bond would not be released for ten years. "In all that time, we could not get into court for a trial. But we were not worried any more, for Mr. Miller's action gave us the semblance of financial stability we may have lacked before, and no one cared to attack us recklessly."[5]

If the events transpired as Lake said, however, the letter that prompted the lawsuit would have been an internal communication, limited to Lake Company executives, and therefore could not be the basis of a libel suit. That status would not have changed if the contents had been leaked to Electric Boat by a "spy." One cannot, in effect, steal the property of another and then sue based on illegally acquired evidence. Even if Electric Boat had become aware of the contents innocently, there were still no grounds for legal action unless the contents were more widely disseminated and by someone other than Electric Boat. One cannot libel oneself. In addition, Lake's assertion that the letter merely stated what was already publicly known—that Admirals O'Neil and Melville favored his design—could hardly be libelous. Libel or slander is defined as publishing defamatory material that the publisher knows to be false. Finally, the seizure of assets pending the posting of a bond was not mandatory—a judge would first have been required to decide that the action had sufficient merit to justify seizure. Without that discretionary power, Connecticut would have been buried under an avalanche of frivolous lawsuits.

That the seizure was approved meant that the contents of the letter were more than a restatement of publicly known facts and that they were made available to wide audience, in this case, those who would decide the disposition of naval appropriations allocated for submarine construction. Or, far more likely, the letter was not the precipitating agent at all, but rather it was Lake's testimony to Congress, in which he more or less described the Holland submarine as a deathtrap, and implied that Holland Torpedo Boat Company representatives lied to the naval affairs committee to obtain their initial appropriation and then intentionally misrepresented performance results of their product. Given that both Melville and O'Neil questioned the very same performance criteria—which by then had been established before any number of witnesses—would indicate this explanation was more likely.

Rice didn't stop with the libel suit. He also requested a hearing of his own before the naval affairs committee, this one both to examine Lake's accusations and to take testimony from a variety of witnesses, including naval officers, who had direct experience with the Holland boats. His request was granted and the hearing opened on May 20.

Where Lake had relied almost solely on his own testimony and the opposition of Admirals O'Neil and Melville to the Holland boats— although neither was questioned by the committee—Rice brought with him a potent roster, beginning with Richard Wainwright, superintendent of the Naval Academy. The *Holland* had been anchored at Annapolis for almost two years and been run in Chesapeake Bay almost daily. Wainwright, who had commanded a warship during the Spanish-American War and had himself been aboard the *Holland*, was thus sufficiently authoritative to evaluate the boat's performance.

As to the decision whether to include submarines in the American fleet, Wainwright was unequivocal. The *Holland* submarine could no longer be characterized as experimental, but was rather an important, fully formed instrument of naval warfare, that, had it been deployed properly by the Spanish, would have lengthened the war and made it more costly in American lives. When asked to detail the *Holland*'s imperfections, Wainwright replied that he didn't see any. "Every mechanical device can be improved," he added, "but I could not pick out any particular line of improvement which might occur."[6] He told the congressmen that not only could the *Holland* fire a torpedo as accurately as any other submarine, but also as accurately as any surface torpedo boat.

Wainwright was equally firm in emphasizing that this conclusion applied only to the Holland design. Although he had not seen the Lake boat—no one in the navy had—when asked if he had sufficient information from the plans and specifications to make a comparison,

Wainwright expressed no doubt. "I have, sir. [The Lake boat] is not suitable for a naval weapon, except to raise counter-mines."

Soon afterward, Congressman Alston Dayton of West Virginia broke in and directed a hostile line of questions to Captain Wainwright. Dayton would take this same quasi-prosecutorial approach to any witness who spoke favorably of the Holland design. He made no mention of the virtues of the Lake boats per se, but did all he could to gain an admission that the accusations leveled by Lake two months earlier were accurate, and that these witnesses were equivocating for reasons never stated but nonetheless quite clear. Others on the committee, including the chairman, George Foss of Illinois, also tried to elicit criticisms of the *Holland*. What was apparent from this first witness was that the committee was sharply, and perhaps rigidly, divided.

Wainwright, however, would not be rattled, and did not budge from his testimony. Dayton was then forced to resort to silly arguments, such as, since it did not take that long to build a submarine, why not wait until war is imminent before undertaking construction? Wainwright and other witnesses pointed out that for testing and training the crew, if for no other reason, new technology such as a submarine must be built in anticipation of future conflicts.

The most significant exchange came when Dayton tried to press Wainwright to support Lake's proposal that a competition be held. Dayton asked, "Do you not believe it would be wise policy on the part of Congress to experiment with all of these boats and encourage all improvement, all development, and if it is a patented article, eventually purchase the right to construct its own?" But Wainwright was ready for him. "I believe it would be a waste of money, Mr. Dayton, to experiment on a boat that was known to be of the wrong principle. As far as I am concerned, I am confident that those that you mention [the Lake boats] are on the wrong principle. The *Holland* is on the correct principle."

The next witness was Lawrence Spear. Although Spear opened by informing the committee that he had handed in his papers and was leaving the navy for a post with Electric Boat, he was questioned in his capacity as "superintendent of construction of all the vessels building at the Crescent shipyard." He was asked the same questions as had been Captain Wainwright and gave the same answers. The Holland design was no longer experimental; the porpoise method of diving and surfacing was necessary in a submarine warship; it could launch torpedoes quickly and accurately and then dive to avoid a counter-attack; an electric heater kept the crew comfortable; the *Fulton* carried sufficient provisions and had adequate sleeping space for an extended time at sea. Spear also dismissed Lake's assertion that the Holland boats could keep neither a straight course nor maintain longitudinal stability as "moonlight on the lake." It could in fact navigate perfectly under the water, and it ran with excellent stability with minimal intervention by the crew.

Most important, however, was Spear's explicit assertion that "the Holland boat is far superior for military purposes." The reason was simple. "The Holland boat is designed as a submarine torpedo-boat. The Lake boat, if we allow the inventor all he claims, becomes in effect a dirigible, self supporting diving vessel, which would be useless for a torpedo-boat."

Spear, while certainly not impartial, nonetheless presented the best explanation of why the Lake boats would be unsuited for combat.

Captain Lake's preferred method is to drop down to the bottom of the water and run on the bottom—a sort of submarine auto-mobile on wheels, as he expresses it. His preferred method is to lower the anchor-weight and then pull his boat down by those anchor-weights until he rests on the bottom, and then to run ahead. When he wants to come up again he releases the anchor-weight and blows out a little water-ballast, and rises to the surface. Now let us assume he is using his boat as a torpedo boat, and he wants to attack vessels blockading or bombarding. Whenever he wants to come to the surface—he cannot see where the enemy is; the enemy may be moving and he cannot see more than forty or fifty feet under water—he has to stop his boat. He has to absolutely change its movement, change the condition of the weight, and rise to the surface. He then takes a bearing on the enemy, and then puts his winding-gear in operation and pulls his boat down to the bottom, and then resumes operations and goes on. While he is doing that the Holland boat would come up to the surface without any loss of speed, under way, making her full speed. Her conning tower would be out of water not exceeding five seconds, and she would go down again and be on her way perhaps half a mile before the Lake boat resumed operations.

Although once again Congressman Dayton attempted to force an admission from Spear that the *Holland* had been oversold to the navy—so accusatory that he needed to be restrained by the chairman—Spear held his ground. The next two witnesses were Lieutenants Harry Caldwell and Arthur MacArthur. Each praised the *Holland* and each was subjected to a similar and unsuccessful cross-examination by Alston Dayton and other opponents of the boat.

The most persuasive witness, however, was the final naval officer to be called, a twenty-five-year-old ensign named Charles Preston Nelson. Nelson, four years out of the Naval Academy, and with only two as a commissioned officer, was acknowledged by all sides as completely impartial. He had come to submarines not through either of the competitors, but rather simply because he found the technology irresistible.

Nelson had recently returned from extended assignments in the Philippines, in China, and then Japan. When asked if he had any familiarity or knowledge as to the Holland torpedo-boat, Nelson replied, "Yes, sir. During my six weeks' leave at Annapolis I made it a special point on account of being very much interested in them, and took every run that the *Holland* made. I went down just for the special purpose of learning all I could about the boat." He added that he made "sometimes two and sometimes three runs a week." He had also been aboard the *Fulton*, when it sailed from New York headed for Norfolk.

His technical knowledge proved equal to Spear's, and superior to Wainwright's, Melville's, or O'Neil's. He was so effective that even when Alston Dayton tried to break him down, the tone of his questions lacked the hostility and sarcasm to which Dayton had subjected other witnesses.[7] When asked for specifics on the *Fulton*'s performance, the congressman learned that Nelson had kept a detailed record, which included scrupulous data on diving, surfacing, speed, course, torpedo launches, as well as fuel and air usage, even the agreeability of the food and accommodations available to the crew.

Nelson pronounced the boat's performance as "excellent" and also clarified another point that Lake had put at issue. When the chairman noted that the *Fulton* was "not the government's boat," which Lake had intimated was somehow conspiratorial, Nelson agreed that "she is the company's boat," but added, "she is the counterpart of the boats built for the government. While at New Suffolk, I took special care to go through these boats and to see that their arrangement is the same. She is an exact counterpart of the government boats."

Another point Lake had raised was that the *Fulton*'s gasoline tank, mounted inside the hull, was, due to the possibility of leaks or explosion, a danger to the crew. Lake's notion was to mount the tank externally, on the deck. Nelson gave short shrift to that idea. "I think it is more safe to have it in the boat . . . the gasoline tank corresponds to a magazine on a ship. It is the most explosive part of the whole boat. If it is put on deck, and that boat is hit, the only part of her that is visible is her superstructure. If a shot hits that superstructure it goes right into your gasoline tank. If that tank should blow up, the fact that the thing was on the outside of the boat would not save the boat at all, because the explosion would be violent enough to smash her all to pieces; whereas a shot will not penetrate the water to any depth, and by having the tank below the water line you make it safe from that source. The leakage of a gasoline tank is very improbable, because as it is intended to contain an inflammable material, it is about the strongest and most carefully constructed part of the whole boat."

In the end, while Ensign Nelson agreed that the government should only purchase "the best available boats," he insisted Holland's were "the only proven reality." Finally, when asked, "Is it then your deliberate, candid opinion that the Holland submarine boat in its present state of development is a practical weapon of war, and that its possession in sufficient numbers by this country would be a valuable and economical feature of defense?" Nelson replied, "I am very strongly of that opinion, sir."

With the naval officers done, the committee moved to Electric Boat personnel. They asked Frank Cable much the same questions they had asked of the officers, briefly questioned Charles Creecy about a competing patent claim that turned out to be frivolous—although Congressman Dayton did his best to make it sound legitimate—and then, finally, heard from Isaac Rice.

Unlike most of the other witnesses, Rice would have no defenders. The tone of the questioning varied from cold to antagonistic and focused only on money. Even members in favor of the boat seemed to dislike him. At the outset, some implied that, as the Holland Torpedo Boat Company did not actually build the submarines, it was merely a shell to funnel government funds into Rice's pockets.

It was the obvious opening, and Rice was prepared. He parried that line of questioning with a shot at one of Simon Lake's most vociferous supporters. "I see Admiral Melville, in an article in the *North American Review*, says anybody can build a submarine boat; that all you have got to do is to go around and buy some machinery and put it in a boat. I told a friend of mind that reminded me of a criticism of Columbus. It was said that Columbus really did not do anything; he just bought an ordinary boat; it was not even the best boat in the market at the time; he just sailed on an ordinary ocean, and that all he had to do was to sail west and find something."

He had also anticipated that Electric Boat would be accused of conspiring to prevent the Lake submarine from being evaluated against theirs. "We are not opposed in any shape or form to competition. The idea has grown up, somehow or other, that we are a monopoly and want to keep a monopoly. Not at all. What we do believe we are entitled to is what we have purchased under the Constitution of the United States in our patent rights. That is all we ask. We have to take our chances in business in any other respects. Everybody else ought to be allowed to compete with us. If a better submarine boat is built, we have to take our chances."

But when pressed as to whether he was willing to conduct the test, Rice became incredulous. "At our expense, of another boat? That is too much to ask." When one of the committee members countered, "You have seven million dollars, according to your own figures. Why should you not be willing to make tests?" Rice replied, "If Mr. Lake has his own boat, we cannot make tests for him."

But at that point, Simon Lake did not have a boat to test. "If Mr. Lake . . . should come in and say the Government must only have the best, you cannot tell whether you have the best or not until the boats are built. Let them first build all these boats, and then you can see which boat you want. If this were a plaything, that is all right; but the Government is in the business of defending the country. Suppose I was in need of machinery and the inventors came around to tell me they have a machine that is better than mine. I would keep on buying my machine. I need it for my business, until the next best invention was produced. Then I would drop the old machine. That is the point we make. We are a little afraid that a good deal of this cannot possibly be in good faith . . . but is merely designed for the purpose of saying: 'This may be better or that may be better,' and we get no appropriation, and nobody else gets an appropriation. That is what we object to."

When the committee tried to pin Rice down, have him agree on the record to an actual test, rather than simply acceding to the principle, Rice said, "You would not require our permission. You have got the Government boats, and could make the tests with them. We could not help that. We would give you every facility, everything we knew of, to make that test."

There didn't seem anywhere to go with that line of inquiry, so the committee switched to questioning why Electric Boat could possibly ask for appropriations for additional submarines when they had yet to deliver a single completed boat that had been contracted for. Rice was characteristically deft in his reply. After noting, "No company has ever treated the Government with the consideration that we have given," he said, "we could have finished these boats if we had gone simply on the specifications which were drawn by the Department. But in order to give the Government the very best possible results, we first built our own boat, the *Fulton*, at our own expense, because on that boat we are permitted to make such changes and experiments as we chose. We could not do it with a Government boat. There is too much red tape. So we built our own boat [which] cost us fully as much as the Government pays us for boats. As changes have proved themselves on [the *Fulton*], we tore things out and put other things in, and gave the Government the benefit without one cent of charge." And besides, he added, the *Adder* and other contracted for boats were either completed or virtually so and would be delivered as soon as they were tested, a matter of weeks.

The committee members next appealed to Rice's patriotism, or rather his lack of it. Electric Boat had concluded a deal with Vickers, Sons & Maxim in Great Britain to build five Holland submarines, which the Admiralty had agreed to purchase for £35,000, or $175,000, each. The first of these boats had been tested and accepted by the Royal Navy, the first Holland boat to actually be purchased. Terms of the agreement were vague—Rice first claimed he was paid a royalty, but when pressed, said it was instead a "consideration arrangement," a sharing of profits, although he declined to be more precise. In any case, it later became clear that when Vickers built subsequent models, they owed Electric Boat nothing. Rice dismissed the committee's concerns by indicating that accessing the British market simply gave the company another opportunity to improve the product for the American navy at no cost to the American taxpayer.

With every successful feint and dodge by their chess-master witness, the frustrated congressmen's questions grew more hostile. Even a cursory reading of the record reveals an antagonism to Isaac Rice that was absent with any preceding witness. In some ways, this should not be surprising. Rice was rich, urbane, condescending, and Jewish, all traits that the committee members, most from rural districts outside the northeast, might well have found at the least unappealing. That they were unable to squeeze from him the slightest concession or admission would hardly have softened their dislike.

They remained determined, however. When Rice claimed the company needed "encouragement" from Congress in the form of continued appropriations or Electric Boat would not be able to afford to keep its experts employed, Chairman Foss repeated the accusation, once again by O'Neil and Melville, that Holland boats cost only about $70,000 to build, less than half of the selling price to the navy.

Foss then asked, "If it be true, what Admiral Melville or Admiral O'Neil says, that you have made a profit of $100,000 on each of these boats, do you not think that is pretty good encouragement on the part of the Government?"

This allegation was absurd since, in the first place, neither O'Neil nor Melville would have had the vaguest firsthand knowledge of the costs of a Holland submarine—although Lake had almost certainly been whispering numbers in their ears—and in the second, Holland Torpedo Boat had yet to recoup a penny of the more than $250,000 they had spent in development. After besting the committee members on far more difficult issues, Rice should have been able to brush away this question with ease.

Instead, he blundered.

Whether he had become overconfident, distracted, or merely bored, instead of the adroit, ambiguous responses he had given previously, Rice instead replied, "In answer to that, I will say very frankly that if we made $20,000 on each of the boats, we would be perfectly satisfied."

Foss pounced. "Twenty thousand dollars? . . . Would you be willing then for the Government to build these boats to pay you a royalty of $20,000 on each one?"

Rice was caught. He tried to backpedal, citing the need to satisfy stockholders, "who were entitled to something," and that $20,000 allowed the company to "simply get along," but the committee would not budge from $20,000 as a fair profit.

The hearing was adjourned soon afterward. How much Rice's testimony harmed his case cannot be determined, but when the House passed its naval appropriations bill the following month, there was no provision for purchasing additional submarines. The Senate tried to restore the appropriation, but the House rejected it once more. Finally, Ernest W. Roberts of Massachusetts, a member of the naval affairs committee who was favorable to the Holland submarine—although the reasons for his advocacy would come under serious scrutiny—introduced a separate bill to provide funding for ten additional boats.

That bill set off months of bare-knuckle fighting, which culminated in a scandal that was splashed across front pages throughout the United States. And so, history's first submarine battle took place not on the high seas, but in a committee room of the United States House of Representatives.

CHAPTER 22
PROXY WAR

The unlikely centerpiece of the spectacle was an obscure, half-term congressman named Montague Lessler, who for one year only represented New York's Seventh District, which comprised parts of lower Manhattan—including Wall Street—and all of Staten Island. Lessler had won a scandal-scarred special election to fill out the term of Nicholas Muller, a Tammany Hall Democrat who had resigned in December 1901, because of what he said was "ill-health." The real reason, it was widely believed, was to allow August Belmont's son Perry to be elected in his place. Money was said to have changed hands to induce Muller to step aside. (Perry Belmont later admitted to giving a "valuable oil painting" as a gift to Muller's son.)

Cornelius Vanderbilt took umbrage at such a blatant abuse of the public trust by his fellow millionaire and threatened to contest the race as a Republican. Vanderbilt, like Belmont, did not live in the district, which was reliably Democratic and heavily favored to remain so, and thus his flirtation with public office quickly faded. Forced to put a name on the ballot, Republicans chose Lessler, a Staten Island lawyer who had never before held public office. In a brief but acrimonious campaign, the patrician Belmont committed the fatal error of refusing to pay due homage to Tammany Hall, who began a "down with the carpetbagger" whispering campaign. Amid charges by Belmont that operatives of his own party had sabotaged his coronation with bribery and vote rigging—a former Democratic alderman would be indicted and acquitted of both charges—Lessler won by only 394 votes on January 7, 1902.

Lessler, who seemed stunned that he had actually been elected, arrived in Washington to take his seat only days later, and was promptly assigned to the naval affairs committee, just in time to be present for Simon Lake's appearance in February and the hearings on Lake's charges in May.

Montague Lessler

During the hearings, Lessler looked favorably on Simon Lake and was mildly antagonistic to the witnesses supporting the Holland submarine, although not as blatantly as was Alston Dayton. He did, however, exhibit marked antipathy to Isaac Rice who was, even at that time, a business associate and close friend of August Belmont. Afterward, Lessler announced his opposition to further appropriations for Holland submarines and, although he had been a guest on a test voyage—which he described as "quite an experience"—he voted to cut off funding.

In November 1902, Lessler ran for a full term but, because of reapportionment, was in the Eighth District rather than the Seventh. There, despite a substantial overlap in the districts' territories, he had the misfortune to be matched against Big Tim Sullivan, a Tammany Hall leader so corrupt that the *New York Times* called his nomination "disgraceful and revolting."[1] Sullivan, as predicted, won easily, and as a result, the following March, when the new Congress was sworn in, Montague Lessler would be sent home.

The House convened for its lame-duck session in early January 1903. Two weeks later, on January 20, Lessler approached his colleagues on the naval affairs committee with stunning revelations that he later claimed he expected to remain private.

Just weeks after his defeat at the polls, he said, in either late November or early December 1902—he couldn't recall which—a Republican operative from his district named Philip Doblin paid a visit to his congressional office on Nassau Street in New York City. Doblin, who he described as a "young man" he knew only casually—although Doblin, at thirty-seven, was four years Lessler's senior—was a familiar figure on the fringes of New York politics, having served as a state convention delegate and a member of the board of elections. He was also familiar to Lessler, as he had worked full-time on Lessler's reelection campaign and continued to have permission to use the congressman's office and telephone whenever he needed to. Newspapers would later describe him as "known around City Hall as Lessler's man."[2] When Doblin was appointed as a receiver for bankruptcy court in mid-1902, he gave Lessler's office as his business address.

As Lessler recalled the encounter, Doblin "came in one morning and he asked me if the Holland submarine boat proposition was would come again before the House and I said that I supposed so. He said, 'Are you still opposed to it?' I said, 'Yes.' He then said that he had been sent for by [former New York congressman Lemuel] Quigg, and that

Quigg had said to him that there was $5,000 in it if I could be brought to the other side. My recollection is that I simply laughed at it and told him that I did not want to hear anything more about it. . . . He said that Quigg was a man of power and influence in New York, and that of course if subsequently I wanted to come back here [to Congress], in aiding him I would aid myself in such a proposition in doing him such a favor."[3]

According to Lessler, Doblin was summarily dismissed. Then, either the following day or as long as ten days afterward—Lessler was again uncertain—Quigg telephoned him from his office at 100 Broadway and asked to come by. That Lessler's timeline seemed indistinct struck some as odd since the incidents had occurred less than two months before and were such that they should have left a stronger impression. In any event, Lessler said that Quigg showed up at his office an hour after the telephone call, where the two "passed amenities," and, before Quigg could even mention the Holland submarine, Lessler "said at once that there should be no question of money in this business."

Quigg was then said to have fallen silent while Lessler "explained to him at quite some length" the source of his opposition "going into the history of the construction, and what they were, and describing the whole business—the technical—so far as I knew it." Quigg then "got up and said, 'I see that you are opposed to this proposition, and have evidently looked into it. I have no interest in it.'" Lessler also recalled Quigg expressing distaste for Isaac Rice, although he could not recall the reason. Finally, Quigg said "he had absolutely no interest in the boat or the company, but said that a man by the name of Hunter—my recollection is that he had done him some favors—had asked him to see me and look into it. That ended the conversation, and he went out."

In addition, Lessler confided to the committee members, Doblin's visit was not the first instance in which he had been approached. In June 1902, after the Senate had reinstated the submarine appropriations, but before the Roberts bill had been introduced in the House, John McCullagh, New York State superintendent of elections, paid Lessler a visit in his Washington office. "The conversation took place on the Monday night preceding the first meeting of the committee when we considered the Senate bill . . . and so he said, 'I have been sent by some men in New York who can reelect you or beat you, to ask you to vote for the Holland submarine boat.' I said to him, 'I will see you in hell first—I will see them in hell first.' He then said, 'Then do it for me,' but I said, 'No, Chief; I can not do it.'"

From there, Lessler recounted, the conversation became surprisingly civil. "I remember getting down the books that I had on the subject and explaining to him in detail, so far as I could, what I knew about the boat, and he left me about 10 o'clock in the evening. He said to me, 'Congressman, I am sorry that I came. I did not understand the situation.' That was the end of that whole conversation. I have never spoken to him since on the subject.'"

After hearing this tale, the committee met in executive session—where no public record would be made available—to investigate Lessler's accusations. Doblin, the key witness, was not subpoenaed but rather summoned by Lessler to come to Washington to speak to the committee members, Lessler assuring him that anything he said would remain private.

When Doblin arrived in the capital, he learned that his testimony would not be private at all, but rather be part of a public hearing to begin on Friday, January 23, 1903. For reasons that would later be in dispute, he agreed to testify without first hiring a lawyer.

When the hearings opened, soon-to-be-former Congressman Lessler was the first witness, and he repeated what he had told the committee privately. Lemuel Quigg's attorney pressed Lessler as to why he waited more than two weeks to inform other committee members of Doblin's bribery attempt. Lessler claimed it was simply a matter of conflicting schedules and the holiday rush. Lessler also repeated that his relationship with Doblin was casual at best, despite Doblin having access to his office and telephone. No one asked why he had failed to report the conversation with McCullagh at all.

But of Lessler's sympathies there could be no doubt. When asked if his motivation in bringing these charges was to "injure the Holland company," he responded, "It has been common knowledge in Washington, in the vague, rumory way that we call 'common knowledge,' that all sorts of pressure has been brought, and as you know has been mentioned in this committee, about this submarine proposition; and my intention was to tell the members of my committee just what had happened in the proposition, and I repeat again that I thought I was telling the members of my committee and no one else." Lessler repeatedly denied that he either desired or expected his remarks to his colleagues to spark an investigation, a statement either grossly naïve or one that reflected a culture of payoffs so pervasive that any new allegation would be considered unworthy of notice.

After Lessler was excused, the committee adjourned. The following day, January 24, in a rare Saturday session, Philip Doblin took the stand, without benefit of counsel. There, not requesting immunity from prosecution, he totally corroborated Lessler's version of the events—he admitted to offering Lessler a bribe, and added that Quigg had told him that there was $1,000 "in it for him" if Lessler accepted. Even more damning, he noted that he had met with E. B. Frost at the Waldorf Astoria late in December, although there did not seem to be anything untoward in their conversation.

When asked why he had requested neither counsel nor immunity, Doblin, who had been around lawyers and politicians his entire life, claimed that the committee's counsel threatened him, told him he must respond to any questions, and he merely complied. When he learned that the hearings would be public, Doblin added, he spoke with a lawyer friend of his, Leonard Obermier, but continued to believe that he needed to speak to the committee without official representation.

In testimony that lasted almost three hours, it was difficult for anyone to see Doblin as anything more than an amiable dupe, willing to transmit Quigg's offer to Lessler in the hopes of gaining a powerful man's favor, and perhaps a $1,000 bonus if he was successful. Incredibly, under questioning, Doblin did not even seem aware that offering money to a congressman in exchange for a vote was in violation of the law.

With Doblin disposed of, John McCullagh appeared and the contrast between the two witnesses could not have been sharper. McCullagh had spent almost three decades in the police department, rising through the ranks to become chief. He was famous for cleaning up the "Bloody Sixth" precinct, which included opium dens in Chinatown and the notorious "Five Points" district. After his retirement from the force, he had been handpicked by Theodore Roosevelt to head the newly created elections bureau, to combat the rampant fraud that accompanied many local elections. By all accounts, he had been zealous in the performance of his duties and elections were a lot cleaner as a result.

At the hearing, McCullagh came armed with an affidavit from Henry Herts, one of the architects working on Isaac Rice's Eighty-Ninth Street mansion. Herts, it seemed, had been talking to Rice, and in the course of conversation both the Holland submarine and Lessler's opposition to funding additional boats came up. Rice "stated his regret that he had encountered opposition from Mr. Lessler, who he thought was not fully informed as to the merits of the boat. In the course of the conversation, I suggested to Mr. Rice that it would be proper for some gentleman who knew Mr. Lessler to interview him on the subject. Thereafter I consulted my brother, Mr. A. H. Herts, a member of the [Wall Street] firm of Freedman Bros. & Co., in reference to the matter. He informed me that the only person he knew of who was acquainted with Mr. Lessler was Mr. John McCullagh, the State superintendent of elections, and that he would see Mr. McCullagh, who is a personal friend of his of many years' standing."

Herts stressed that he was a member of no political organization, not did he have any interest in either the Holland Torpedo Boat Company or Electric Boat. But he went with his brother to see McCullagh "and laid the facts of the matter before him, explaining to him my interest in the matter, which was entirely personal. I impressed upon Superintendent McCullagh the fact that I was a firm believer in the utility and value of the submarine boat from having witnessed demonstrations of its efficiency, and that I considered the submarine boat one of the most important adjuncts to the national defense that had ever been discovered."

McCullagh explained that he was only barely acquainted with Lessler, but agreed to speak to the congressman and pass along the message.

His recollection of the conversation bore little resemblance to the strong-arm threats to which Lessler had testified. "We sat down and talked for a little while about the interesting things that occurred during the special election . . . then said, 'Now, Mr. Lessler, I have come here to ask for a favor. A personal friend of mine has requested me to come. He has no interest whatever that I know of in the Holland submarine boat. Neither have I. It is purely personal. If you can see your way clear to vote for this' . . . we talked about the merits of the boat . . . 'I believe it has got some merits.'

"He abruptly said to me, 'I want to be frank with you, Mr. McCullagh. I won't vote for it. You don't understand this situation as I do.' Then he spoke something about the governor of the State, in a general way, sending down to my office and asking a subordinate in my office his opinion about how to run the office, and how ridiculous it would be. He said, 'I have made a thorough investigation of this thing, and I am perfectly familiar with the details. I want to say to you, Mr. McCullagh, that I am not a damn fool. I was not born yesterday, sir. I have got my suspicions about this thing. There is not a man on that committee with me that I would trust except one man.' He named the man [almost certainly George Foss or Alston Dayton] but I will not.

"What brought that about was that I said, 'Why, you are the only man, Mr. Lessler, that seems to be standing out on this thing. It seems to me ridiculous. You are a young man just elected to Congress. What is the object of it?' Then he repeated just what I have said. 'Furthermore, I have weighed the whole thing, and while I can't prove it I believe there is a lobby here and there is boodle. The position of the whole thing down there, from my standpoint, and what I have seen of it, is wine, terrapin, and women'—and the 'woman' was the most vulgar expression I have ever heard a man use. I said, 'Mr. Lessler, if that be true I am sorry I came here. I shall certainly go back and tell my friend in New York City.' His secretary was sitting there. I did not know the man was nominated for Congress, nor did I know that he was running for Congress, until he happened in my office [two months later]."

Perhaps it was coincidence but "wine, terrapin, and women" were exactly the terms Simon Lake used to describe the goings-on aboard the *Josephine*.

The committee members, especially Dayton tried to rattle him or catch him in an inconsistency, but McCullagh would not alter his testimony. Even when Dayton pressed him on why he would travel all the way to Washington to meet someone he didn't know and urge him to vote on an appropriation he could not have cared less about, McCullagh steadfastly maintained that he had seen Lessler strictly out of friendship with Herts, had paid his own way, and had no financial interest in the outcome. McCullagh flatly denied ever saying "I have been sent by some men in New York who can re-elect you or beat you, to ask you to vote for the Holland submarine boat." Lessler's secretary denied hearing that phrase as well. McCullagh also flatly denied saying, "Then do it for me," and that Lessler had ever said that he'd see anyone in hell first, an exchange than the secretary had also failed to mention in his testimony.

In the afternoon, Lemuel Quigg testified and expressed equal incredulity. Like McCullagh, he did not deny attempting to persuade Lessler to reexamine his opposition, but the genesis of the attempt was also based on friendship, not profit. According to Quigg, in early December, at the Waldorf Astoria, he happened on an old acquaintance, W. R. Kerr, a partner in the Batcheller Pneumatic Tube Company. Kerr asked Quigg if he knew Lessler, and Quigg said he did. Kerr than asked if, strictly as a favor, Quigg would speak with Lessler about the Holland torpedo boat, in which Kerr admitted he had an interest. When Quigg asked what the matter was with Lessler, Kerr replied, "He is not only opposing it, but he is opposing it in a very personal and bitter and vindictive way. The character of his opposition has been violent and noisy." When Quigg asked what he could do, Kerr asked only that Quigg attempt to "cool him off a little," a phrase Quigg specifically remembered.

Quigg agreed to speak to Lessler if he saw him, but warned that they didn't meet often. But Kerr pressed and asked Quigg to make a special effort. Quigg said, "I cannot make much of an argument for the Holland torpedo boat, because I do not know much about it."

"I do not expect you to do so," Kerr replied, "but if you would ask him not to be so violent and pestiferous in his opposition, that is all I want you to do."

Kerr continued to press, and ten days after their first meeting, Quigg finally tried to locate Lessler. The congressman's office did not know his whereabouts, but said he was with Phil Doblin, so Quigg sought

Doblin out. After speaking with Doblin, Quigg eventually went to Lessler's office to press his case. Lessler flatly refused.

As Quigg recalled, "He talked, I should say, ten or fifteen minutes to explain to me the merits or the demerits of the boat. Well, I said that was all right, and that was a good reason for being opposed to the boat; but what was the use of making so much fuss about it? 'Well,' he said, 'they are the worst lot down there. A set of rascals through and through. You have no idea of the abominable methods to which those people have resorted. They maintain the most unscrupulous lobby in Washington, and it is as much as anybody's reputation is worth to have anything to do with them.'"

Quigg claimed to have been dubious, and then asking Lessler if anybody had attempted to bribe him.

"No," Lessler replied, "nobody has attempted to bribe me; but they are down there and all around."

Quigg said he replied, "I would not pay much attention to that. It is very natural that they should be down there and all around, and it is very natural that they should come here to you to talk over the thing and very natural that they should send their friends to you, and there is no ground for offense about that." He added that as Lessler felt so strongly, he should do as he liked, but not to get "so excited and ill-tempered about it, and do not talk about this lobby business, because it seems to me very silly." Lessler said that "he would go on opposing it, and I said that was all right, and I got up and went on out."

When he was questioned, Quigg denied that Lessler had ever mentioned money, or even intimated that any offer had been made to him by Doblin or anyone else. Nor did he know either Isaac Rice or E. B. Frost, even though their offices were on the same floor in the same building in New York as his. He had no financial interest in Electric Boat nor any other company relating to the Holland submarine. He did admit to meeting with Doblin, known to be a close associate of Lessler's, and ask that Doblin speak with the congressman and make one last try to persuade him to soften his tone.

As with McCullagh, Quigg was attacked in cross-examination, but his testimony also held up. "I should like to make the most sweeping as well as the most particular denial that I ever said anything to Mr.

Doblin in Mr. Lessler's interest," he concluded, "or to Mr. Lessler in his own, or in Mr. Doblin's, or to either of them, in respect of any money or other advantage that would come to both or either from doing anything in connection with the matter. And when I saw Mr. Lessler, I concluded my conversation by saying to him that I had no request whatever to make of him, as I think he has stated, substantially."

The committee then adjourned for the day. McCullagh's and Quigg's denials notwithstanding, government bribery scandals were big news and this one was no exception. But however lurid were the following day's headlines, such as the *New York World*'s lead, "Briber Acted for Ex-Congressman," the headlines a few days later would be much more so—on January 26, the *World*'s headline would read, "Doblin Admits Perjury, But Is Not Arrested: Disgusts the House Committee on Naval Affairs by Swearing that His Testimony Against Quigg in the $5,000 Bribery Charge was False."[4]

It seemed that with Sunday to think over both his testimony and his legal position Philip Doblin had a change of heart. He walked into the committee room Monday morning—this time with a lawyer—and retracted his entire testimony from the previous session.

"The fact is that the statements I made regarding Mr. Quigg were not true. I was told by Lessler, 'You have got to stand for this story,' and I said, 'Oh, that can't be done.' 'Well,' he says, 'Then I am politically dead.' Then I said, 'Well, you will carry me with you.' He said, 'You will be all right. You just appear before this committee. I will go and see the Speaker and I will fix it up.' He goes out of the room and comes back and says he has seen the Speaker, and it will be all right. And he says, 'Now, all you have got to do is to go up before the committee and substantiate my story.'"

As Doblin would tell it that Monday, the bribe offer was phony, concocted by Lessler to ensure defeat of the Roberts bill. But Lessler had intended the tale to remain behind closed doors and never to be for public consumption. When asked later in his testimony where Lessler had come up with the $5,000 figure, Doblin said the congressman, when first speaking to his colleagues about the underhanded methods of Electric Boat, told Doblin he had "blurted it out." He had then been forced to embellish the story to include Quigg and McCullagh, both of whom had spoken with him of behalf of the Roberts bill. Once the bribery story was out, he became in need of a close associate to corroborate it, and for that delicate task, he had chosen his good friend, Phil Doblin. Lessler, aware of how fragile his position was, assured Doblin that the bribery charge would remain off the record—in that way, the Roberts bill would certainly fail without the necessity of putting anyone at risk of a perjury charge. Whether any other members of the committee knew the whole truth, Doblin could not tell, but those members against the Roberts bill were not about to question Lessler's story.

Doblin was fully aware that this second rendition would be greeted with a good deal more skepticism than the one that preceded it, so this time he had brought proof. After his initial statement, Doblin turned to Gustavus Rogers, the lawyer he had engaged in New York, and asked for a sheaf of telegrams. The first one, dated January 20, was from Lessler. Doblin told the committee it was how he had first been summoned to Washington. "Take midnight train and come to me. Want to see you. Keep this confidential." It was signed, "Monte."

From that moment, the tenor of the hearing changed—it seemed certain, at the least, that Montague Lessler—Monte—did not have the offhand, casual relationship with Doblin he had originally described. (It was later established that Lessler had recommended Doblin for jobs with the election commission and may have, on more than one occasion, loaned him money.)

When Doblin arrived in Washington, he said, he went directly to Lessler's hotel room. There, Lessler told him the bribery story that he must stick to. Doblin said he could not.

"You needn't have any fear," Lessler told him. "There is nothing going to happen to you. You appear before this [subcommittee empanelled to investigate the bribery allegation]. They are friends of mine. They will report to the whole committee and there won't be anything further to it."

Lessler then left the hotel room to speak with like-minded colleagues, and two hours later, Lessler's secretary returned to fetch Doblin. "Come along with me," he said, "and we will get into the

Capitol. Nobody will see you. You will be able to go up through a side elevator which is right close to the Naval Committee door, and you can get in, and I will see that nobody sees you."

After Doblin was snuck into the committee room, "I sat down, and after a little time Mr. Foss handed me a cigar. I took the cigar and smoked it. It made me feel, agreeably to the conversation I had with Lessler, that these were friends of his, and he was inclined to be a good fellow anyhow. He specially was to me from time to time, and I took it for granted that it was all right."

Then Doblin recounted an extraordinary exchange with some of the committee members, in literally a smoke-filled room. "One of the gentlemen said, 'Wasn't it Mr. Quigg said to you that there was $5,000 in it for Lessler and $1,000 for you?' And I said, 'No, sir; I didn't say that at that time.' There was a discussion in the room as to how I stood. I refused to answer at that time until the gentlemen seemed to all agree. 'There is nothing to it; you just go on and make your statement.' Feeling agreeably at home, I made my statement according to the way I read it in the paper, and [Ohio Congressman Robert] Tayler put in my mouth—I think it was Mr. Tayler—something about the money proposition which I didn't state before, until I realized that I was in the hands of my friends." From there, he decided, "I will back up Lessler. There won't be anything about it. All there would be to it is the [subcommittee] will report to the whole committee and Lessler will be vindicated and I will be vindicated and that will be all right."

Once again, Doblin had support for his assertion. When he returned to Lessler's hotel room to pick up his things before going to Union Station, a telegram was waiting for him. It read, "Statement all right. Have no fear." But Lessler's reassurance was premature. "I consequently go on about my business and think no more about it. I had done another fellow a turn, in my way of thinking. I got home pretty late that night, and I found this telegram: 'I am instructed by Naval Affairs Committee to request your appearance for bearing before it to-morrow [Friday] morning at ten thirty. Geo. Edmund Foss, Chairman.'"

Doblin was then stuck, but after Lessler's further assurances, decided to repeat the bribery story in the public hearing, which did not take place until Saturday. He showed the committee two telegrams Lessler had sent to his wife, the first on Saturday morning before his testimony and the second that afternoon, when he was done.

Washington, D. C, January 24, 1903.
To Mrs. Philip Doblin, 433 East Eighty second Street:
Phil arrived all right and will stay with me in Washington. You need have no fear about him at all. I shall try and see you if possible. He sends love to you and children.

Washington, D. C, January 24, 1903.
To Mrs. Philip DOBLIN, 433 East Eighty-second Street.
Phil examined. Substantiates story in every way. He is all right. Will stay here for a time.

Both were signed: Montague Lessler.

When Doblin completed his statement, Congressman Tayler, Chairman Foss, and the other opponents of the Roberts bill were livid. Those on the other side were furious as well. The hearing quickly descended into a free-for-all with members on both sounds assailing Doblin—and one another—with questions, accusations, requests for clarifications, and threats. But Doblin, as had the witnesses in the previous session, stuck to his tale. Lemuel Quigg had never at any time mentioned money. He had merely inquired as to whether Lessler might be persuaded to temper his opposition to the Holland boat. Doblin knew nothing of the McCullagh conversation at all. He thought he was helping a friend whose assurances he had believed. He had been persuaded to see a lawyer by his family after he returned to New York Saturday evening. And yes, he did believe in God. The only admission Tayler was able to wring from Doblin was that his assertion that Tayler "had put words in his mouth" was an overstatement—Tayler had merely asked him to repeat his story with specific reference to the $5,000 number.

The next day, at his request, Montague Lessler returned to the witness table. As expected, his rendition of the events was quite different.

Mr. Chairman, I desire to deny absolutely and unequivocally as false the statement made by the witness Doblin here yesterday as to any collusive scheme or any of the substantial details sworn to by him here, and I desire to reiterate that the facts as originally told by me are true. I desire to call attention to the following facts: That as to the telegram . . . 'Take midnight train and come to me. Want to see you. Keep this confidential,' the members of the subcommittee will remember that the statement I made to them was on Tuesday afternoon; that at that time everything before us was in camera, and that I said I would produce the witness Doblin in the morning, but I did not desire his name to appear in any way. The result was that that telegram was sent by me here from this committee room. Mr. Doblin came into my room a few minutes after 8 o'clock. I had left the door unlocked and he knocked at the door, waking me up. I asked, 'Who is there?' He said, 'Phil,' or 'Doblin,' I have forgotten which. I said, 'Come in.' He came into the room with his overcoat on, and I said, 'Phil, I have gotten you into trouble.' He said, 'How is that?' 'Well,' I said, 'I have told in committee the whole story of the submarine proposition.' He said, 'Oh, that is terrible; that is terrible.' 'Well, now,' I said, 'keep up your nerves, all you have to do is to tell the truth here, and nothing but the truth.'"

Lessler was also forced to repudiate the denials of McCullagh and Quigg. As did Doblin, he accounted for every seemingly damning piece of evidence with an explanation that, while logical, in some cases stretched credibility. He even called his uncle as a witness, to testify that Doblin, in the uncle's presence, openly discussed the bribery offer in the middle of a popular restaurant just after Christmas—which, if true, did not jibe with Lessler's original account and also once more raised the question of why Lessler waited three weeks to report a felony. In the end, there was no way to definitively determine which story was more accurate—it seemed certain that neither man was giving an unvarnished version of the events.

The questioning of Lessler was, if anything, more contentious than it had been of Doblin. While the Lake boat supporters, principally

Dayton, Tayler, and Chairman Foss were solicitous and leading, Holland advocates, Roberts—who Lessler had as much as suggested was in Isaac Rice's pocket—and some others, were aggressive and sarcastic. Tempers flared and voices were raised throughout the session, as Lessler was walked again and again through every detail of the alleged bribery offer.

One area left strangely unexplored was the source and intensity of Lessler's opposition to the Holland boat. He was not questioned, nor did he provide voluntarily, how he learned of the perfidy allegedly being perpetrated by Electric Boat, nor who told him about the supposed bacchanalia aboard the *Josephine*. But the only other person known to have cited the same evidence was Simon Lake. Lessler had also on many occasions claimed to have undertaken a thorough study of the Holland design, and was stunned to discover its profound flaws. But Lessler had no engineering training, nor had he ever been involved with either mechanical devices or boats.

With his own integrity impugned, Congressman Roberts demanded to make a statement, although, at least at first, he was not under oath. He claimed that on January 21, "I was coming through Statuary Hall, on my way to my committee room, and I met Mr. Lessler coming from the opposite direction. Mr. Lessler spoke to me, and said, 'Can we not stop this thing? My God, I cannot stand it. It is killing me.' The thing he referred to was the proposed investigation, which we had authorized to be made by the sub-committee. I said to him that the investigation was nothing of my seeking; that I had no benefit to gain from pressing it. But there were other parties besides myself in this matter. The statement had gone out to the country in the press that the Holland Submarine Boat Company had attempted to influence his action by an offer of money, and I did not know whether the Holland people would be willing to have the thing smothered; that that phase of the question would have to be considered. Mr. Lessler thereupon volunteered—the suggestion came from him—that he would make any statement regarding the matter that was thought to be fair and reasonable."

When Roberts told Lessler that, as the full committee had heard his charges and would be unwilling to terminate the investigation, Lessler replied, "I think that I can fix them, and I think I can arrange that all right." Roberts then prepared a statement for Lessler's signature.

When they next met, on the floor of the House, Lessler assured Roberts that the matter had indeed been fixed. Roberts then handed Lessler the statement he had written up:

January 21, 1903.
Holland Torpedo Boat Company,
Corcoran Building, Washington, D. C.

Dear Sirs: In reference to the statement made by me before the Naval Committee of the House on January 20, in which, by inference, your company was connected with a promise of money for my vote on the proposition of the submarine boat, I desire to say it was never my intention in any manner to create the inference that your company, or any of its officers or stock-holders, were connected in the remotest degree, either directly or indirectly, with that offer. That offer, I am now satisfied, was made without your knowledge by an irresponsible party. I sincerely trust that you will not be injured by the publicity given to my statement. Very truly yours.

"I handed the paper to him. He glanced at it, and did not read it, and said, 'That is directed to the Holland Torpedo Boat Company, and I will not sign it, or any other statement.'"

In questioning, however, Roberts admitted that the statement had been drawn up by E. B. Frost, and that Roberts had been a regular visitor to the Holland offices and spoke with Frost regularly. But Roberts denied any nefarious motives in suggesting that Frost draft a statement to his liking. "I had no interest in having a retraction from [Lessler]. It was a statement that should be made to the Holland Tor-pedo Boat Company. They were the party affected by his statement. I telephoned to Mr. Frost that I had met Lessler, and he had expressed a willingness to make a statement."

The questioning was conducted by Charles Wheeler, a Democrat from Kentucky, another ardent opponent of the Holland submarine.

Roberts and Wheeler were soon shouting at each other, Wheeler demanding that Roberts be sworn in, and Roberts at first refusing and then agreeing. Their confrontation devolved into mutual accusations of impropriety, which soon threatened to involve the entire committee.

As the acrimony reached its apex, it all suddenly ended. With Roberts and Wheeler doing everything but throwing punches, everyone tacitly seemed to agree that things had gone far enough. Adjournment soon followed. Many questions remained unasked, and many areas of potential wrongdoing were left unexplored.

On February 3, the committee issued its report, and it showed both a good bit of horse-trading, and more than a little absurdity. As many expected, Philip Doblin was made the scapegoat for the entire affair, the committee deciding that he approached Lessler "on his own initiative and responsibility, with the idea of making money for himself." But the committee also declared that there was no evidence implicating Lemuel Quigg in the scheme, nor was there any evidence that Electric Boat was involved. Left unanswered, then, was how, if Doblin had perpetrated this entire fraud on his own volition, he expected to make any money. Who had he intended to collect it from if not Quigg or Electric Boat?

The minority report, signed by Roberts and two others, made a good deal more sense. While agreeing on the final two points, that there was no evidence that Quigg or Electric Boat had committed any wrongdoing, they also concluded, "The charge that an attempt was made to corruptly influence a member of the Committee on Naval Affaire respecting proposed legislation pending before the committee and the House is not sustained."

<hr/>

Although the majority report had asked that it be forwarded to the attorney general, who should "take such action as the law and the facts warrant," Philip Doblin seems never to have been imprisoned, or even arrested and tried for perjury. In fact, he was listed as a receiver on several bankruptcies in the months following the hearings, so he doesn't seem even to have lost his job. In March 1903, Doblin was found "wandering in Central Park," subsequently examined by physicians, declared insane, and ordered confined in a sanatorium in Astoria, New York.[5] His confinement could not have been for too long, however, as one month later he journeyed to Albany to "urge an appropriation provided for him in the Supply bill for work he did for the State while in the Controller's office." Doblin walked onto the floor of the state senate and spotted a senator who had referred to him as "a contemptible scoundrel" a few days earlier. Doblin walked up to the man, who did not know who he was, shook his hand, thanked him, and said, "People would have forgotten I was alive if it had not been for you."[6]

Lemuel Quigg spent the remainder of his life in the shadow world of politics. He never held office but became known as an adept fixer, or "accelerator," in the parlance of the times. He grew close to the Whitney-Ryan cabal that attempted to gain a monopoly on surface transport in New York City, and then purchased the Selden automobile patent, which they used to bring infringement suits against scores of independent automobile manufacturers, including Henry Ford.[7] Quigg was linked to any number of shady goings-on, but was never convicted. He died in 1919, at age fifty-six.

John McCullagh fought to keep his post, but was not reappointed. Although he helped organize election bureaus in Cuba and the Panama Canal Zone, he soon drifted into retirement. He died in 1917, leaving no survivors.

Montague Lessler set up a practice with Leonard Obermier, and remained in practice until his death in 1938. He would never again hold public office.

The biggest casualty of the Lessler hearings, however, was the American submarine. Although there is no proof that Lessler was bought, or Roberts, or just how much undue influence Rice or Lake attempted to exert, the Roberts bill was withdrawn and, in its place, Congress, on March 3, 1903, "authorized the Secretary of the Navy, in his discretion, to contract for or purchase subsurface or submarine torpedo boats, not exceeding $500,000," and provided for certain tests. While the money would technically remain available until the close of the fiscal year in 1904, the scandal had made the purchase of additional submarines impossible. And so the American market, at least in the near term, appeared to be closed.

CHAPTER 23
SKEWED COMPETITION

The refusal to add submarines to the fleet was a particularly Pyrrhic victory for Simon Lake. Not only had he failed to persuade the navy to cancel the original Electric Boat contract—all seven were ultimately purchased—but he had closed off his most potentially lucrative market at a time when his company was again coming under extreme financial pressure.[1] Even worse, there were indications in the ensuing months that if the United States were to purchase new submarines, Lake might well have been the person they bought them from.

During the May 1902 hearings, Isaac Rice had predicted it would be several years before Simon Lake was ready with a boat that he could enter in a competition with a Holland model. Instead, it was only months. On November 1, 1902, Lake had launched his first true military submarine, the *Protector*, at Bridgeport, and rather than the error-prone prototype in need of major debugging that Rice had described, it was an exceptional, finely-rendered vessel.

Lake's Protector

The *Protector* was sixty-five feet long, eleven wide, and displaced 170 tons submerged. For surface running, it was powered by twin screws, each connected by direct drive to a 250-horsepower gasoline engine. A one-hundred-horsepower dynamo had been installed for running submerged. While Lake had clearly borrowed his powering array from Holland, the *Protector* compared favorably with the *Fulton*, whose single 160-horsepower gasoline engine would dissipate power because of indirect gearing. Lake's boat could make eleven knots on the surface, superior to the *Fulton*, and the same seven knots submerged. The *Protector* carried its 1,400 gallons of fuel in external tanks mounted on a flat deck-like superstructure, while the *Fulton* carried 850 gallons internally.

Although the *Protector* was built with wheels for bottom crawling—this time retractable—and a diver's compartment and air lock in the bow, Lake had made a significant design upgrade by installing hydroplanes amidships, two on each side, a means of depth control also borrowed from Holland. His boat would still submerge negatively buoyant on an even keel, but with the hydroplanes, the *Protector* could actually "dive," rather than merely drop straight down. Because Lake had once again installed anchors to aid in submerging, however, the *Protector* could not do so as quickly or nimbly as with the Holland design, but the boat held an additional enhancement, which would make even-keel diving more appropriate to initiating an attack on a surface vessel.

Lake called it an "omniscope," and it was undersea warfare's first working full-spectrum periscope. Mounted on a tube that could be raised or lowered, the omniscope had eight prisms, two trained ahead, two looking astern, and one for each quarter on the sides. An additional lens provided a simple straight ahead view forward. Unlike the camera lucida that Holland had tinkered with, the omniscope could afford an estimate of range, all while viewing the entire horizon. Because of the manner in which the images were transmitted to the eyepiece, the forward-looking prisms provided an upright view, the four side images were on edge, and the rear image inverted. While the omniscope tube could be partially rotated, the view degraded and the image would become quite dim.

With the omniscope and even-keel surfacing, the *Protector* could come to what would later be referred to as "periscope depth" without exposing any other portion of the ship to lookouts aboard surface vessels. Holland's boats could also change their angle of ascent so that only the conning tower protruded above the surface, but that operation required a delicate touch by captain and crew. Lake's boat, in addition, was less likely to cause a disturbance in the water as it neared the surface.

The *Protector* had three torpedo tubes to the *Fulton*'s one, two forward, above the diving compartment, and one aft, above the propellers. Torpedoes were carried within the tubes, with no extra missiles for reloading. Lake fitted the *Protector* with a five-ton detachable keel, which could be jettisoned from inside the boat—the two one ton anchors could be released as well—to provide an extra measure of positive buoyancy in an emergency.

The interior of the *Protector* was ingeniously laid out and, by the standard of the time, commodious. At the front of the craft, as always, was the diving chamber, from which a suited diver could pass outside "to cut mine connections and submarine cables." Immediately to the rear was an air lock, which could be pressurized to link the diving compartment to the rest of the boat. Astern of the air lock were living quarters, where eight men could sleep comfortably on padded berths, which folded back against the bulkheads when not in use. Next, separated by swinging double doors with glass upper panels, was a pantry, fitted with electric burners for cooking. A solid door separated the pantry from the engine room, which was in the sternmost section of the boat. The engine room was described in a journal as "a wonderful example of skillful installation. There is a wide, free passage between the engines, and space enough overhead for a six-foot man to stand upright."[2] The boat was also equipped with electric heaters, and an internal telephone hookup to allow communication between various sections of the boat. The compressed air reserve was sufficient to allow for sixty hours submerged.

Protector *interior. Lake's boats were always designed to provide comfortable accommodations for the crew.*

The conning tower, situated above the living quarters, was large enough to accommodate four men, and contained "all sorts of gauges, registers, indicators, means of communication, and facilities for control. The commanding officer, the steersman, and the man at the hydroplane wheel are in constant touch with one another, while automatic indicators advise the steersman and the gunner at the bow torpedo tubes of the proper bearing of the boat."

With the *Protector*, Lake had devised an innovative amalgam of his designs and Holland's. Whether the *Protector* maneuvered as well or as quickly as Holland boats was questionable—and would become more so—but that Lake had created a more *modern* boat was not. While again, it might have been coincidence, just after Simon Lake had begun to run test voyages on a submarine he was convinced had overcome any possible objections from the navy and Congress, Montague Lessler claims to have been approached with a bribe offer by Philip Doblin.

Through spring and summer 1903, with the future of the American submarine force very much in question, Lake's commitment was undiminished. Through allies in Washington, he continued to press for competitive trials of *Protector* and a Holland boat, convinced that once official Washington saw what his boat could do, appropriations would follow.

Faith in ultimate victory was buttressed by word that the Holland boats were performing unevenly with navy crews. There were breakdowns, engine failures, electrical mishaps, problems with the torpedoes, and a rash of other mishaps that, while not fatal, might certainly undermine Electric Boat's sway with naval officers and congressmen. The *Fulton* had experienced its share of malfunctions as well, including an onboard explosion from battery gas as the vessel was entering a harbor in Delaware. Five of the crew, including Arthur MacArthur, were sufficiently bruised to be sent to a local hospital, although all were discharged the next day, when the *Fulton* resumed its journey to Annapolis.

What Lake failed to appreciate, however, although he of all people should have, is that new technology will always come with imperfections. Prototypes like the *Protector*—or the *Fulton*—might minimize performance problems by keeping the design relatively simple, building only to the specifications required for acceptance by the buyer, and then operating the machine under carefully managed conditions. Once circumstances cease to be under the control of the builder, however, problems inevitably arise. The ease with which those problems can be solved, not whether or not they exist, is the determinant of the success of the device.

After months of only positive results, in June 1903, Lake wrote to Navy Secretary William H. Moody to say that the *Protector* was ready for official testing. While he waited for a reply, he did everything he could to promote his new design. When he heard that President Roosevelt was nearby, aboard the presidential yacht with his family, he offered them a tour of the *Protector*, an invitation the president accepted. Roosevelt was duly impressed. But Lake's more significant achievement had been to persuade the navy to send a young lieutenant, John Halligan, to observe the submarine's test runs. On July 1, Halligan was assigned as a full-time liaison in Bridgeport.

In August, Lake's perseverance had seemed to bear fruit. The March 1903 appropriation had given the Secretary of the Navy full discretion in the purchase of new submarines. With Halligan's enthusiastic endorsement, the navy expressed a willingness to hold competitive trials. The assistant secretary even forwarded a draft set of specifications, although the exact details would come later from the Bureau of Construction. There could be no guarantees of sales of course, but the mandatory first step seemed to be in reach.

Ebenezer Hill did everything he could to further Lake's cause. He requested that the Lake boat be allowed to conduct a mock attack on a surface ship during naval maneuvers in September at Newport, which the navy denied because the government refused to become responsible for those not in its employ or material it did not own. Hill, after noting that he had authority to speak on Lake's behalf, then offered to have Lake post a bond that would fully indemnify the government in case of accident or damage. This too was declined on the grounds that having "private parties participate in military maneuvers" would be "bad precedent." Hill then asked if Lake could simply sail *Protector* to the maneuvers and observe, a request that was granted. As it turned out, however, the maneuvers were rescheduled for Maine and Lake never got to show off his boat.

Electric Boat had also been informed of the decision to hold a competition and announced they would use the *Fulton* rather than one of submarines the navy had already purchased. Although the stated reason was that none of the other seven boats remained their property, far more likely is that Frost and Spear were unwilling to expose the vulnerabilities of vessels that had been in navy hands in a head-to-head duel.

The tests were scheduled for November 16 in Narragansett Bay, off Newport, Rhode Island, before a naval board of inspection. There would be speed trials, both submerged and awash, maneuverability, diving and surfacing, and torpedo firing. Weeks before, Lake got word that Electric Boat had informed the navy secretary that the *Fulton* was undergoing a major overhaul and would not be ready in time. Lake at first thought he would have an open field, but when he learned that the board of inspection intended to wait until the *Fulton* was ready, he dashed off an angry letter to Secretary Moody, demanding that Electric Boat participate in the November tests with one of the boats already in the navy's possession. He cited Isaac Rice's testimony in May, in which Rice insisted he would be happy for a competition.[3]

The head of the board of inspection, Captain Charles J. Train did not demand that a Holland boat be present for the November 16 trials, but rather that the test be conducted for "one competitor even in the absence of another." Left unanswered was whether or not a brilliant performance by the *Protector* would result in the cancelation of the pending test for the *Fulton* and a contract for Simon Lake.

Seizing the opportunity, Lake left Bridgeport three days in advance, sailing the *Protector* under its own power with a crew of six. On the night of November 16, however, the *Protector*, running on the surface in high winds, snapped the reverse clutch on one of the engines and the boat was crippled. Ordinarily, Lake would have ridden out a storm by remaining submerged and still until it passed, but that was not an option with the naval board waiting in Newport. With only one engine, Lake had no alternative but to postpone the trial. The new agreed date was January 12, 1904.

While repairing the clutch, Lake realized that, despite the engines' horsepower, his propellers would not generate the minimum speed required by the navy. He sent a letter to the Navy Department, in which he admitted, "The speed and endurance of the *Protector* will fall considerably below our original estimate."⁴ He requested a variance for the low speed, which he promised to rectify in an additional test. He had also sent a number of letters asking that testing criteria be changed to allow the *Protector* to demonstrate certain attributes he thought important, such as surface running using both motor and batteries. In each case, Captain Train replied that the navy was confident the criteria already established would provide ample input to allow for a fair judgment.

On January 10, the board members journeyed from Washington to a frigid Narragansett Bay beset by ice floes. They took one look at the icy water and decided no accurate surface speed test would be possible in such conditions. Lake assured them the ice would soon clear and asked that they remain in Newport. Train agreed but only if Lake would sign a letter affirming that the results of any test in which he participated would be final. Although he was informed that Electric Boat had signed a similar declaration, Lake refused. Over Lake's protests, the board then cancelled the trial and returned to Washington. Lake later claimed that a member of the board, a naval constructor named J. J. Woodward, was an Electric Boat agent, coming just short of accusing him of accepting payoffs. Ebenezer Hill was free with intimations as well. It is difficult, however, to fault the board for being unwilling to wait around Newport in the freezing cold for an indefinite period until the ice cleared to conduct tests that might well eventually have no meaning.

Lake, once again feeling he had been cheated out of a fair hearing, made another pivot. If he could not sell to the navy, there was always the army. Lake's associates petitioned Secretary of War William Howard Taft, and Taft dispatched a team of officers from Fort Totten to observe the *Protector* on a series of test runs. The army, responsible only for the coastline, had different needs than the navy. When the *Protector* navigated perfectly around and through the ice, on one occasion breaking the crust from underneath, and also demonstrated the ability to lay and cut cables for mines or telephone, the army board recommended the purchase of a series of Lake submarines at $250,000 each. For Lake, this would be a boon, since he was again nearly out of money.

An appropriation was quickly approved by the Senate, but perhaps because a bad taste remained from the Lessler scandal, the bill stalled in the House pending a review by senior officers of both services. In April 1904, the generals and admirals decided unanimously that the navy alone should administer the submarine program. That same month, on April 27, Congress again put the navy in the submarine business, at least in theory, when it authorized the secretary of the navy "to contract for or purchase subsurface or submarine torpedo boats, after they have been fully tested to his satisfaction and found to fulfill all reasonable requirements for submarine warfare."[5] To the $500,000 previously appropriated but unspent, an additional $350,000 was added. Once again, no specific criteria were attached to the appropriation, so the navy could choose whichever design it felt best suited its needs, and from whichever company. But after a barrage of demands, accusations of unfairness, delays, and then failures, Simon Lake had made few friends among the navy brass.

In mid-May, Electric Boat announced that the *Fulton* was ready for testing. On June 2, the board once more convened at Narragansett Bay, this time free of ice and howling winter winds. Lake and the *Protector* were expected as well as *Fulton*, but Lake never showed up, nor did he communicate with the Navy Department to explain his absence. There were rumors Lake had sold the boat, but no one would admit to buying it.

The *Fulton* was thus tested alone and the trials lasted a week. The conditions might have been less rigorous, but the standards were not. "The tests included running twice over the measured mile course at cruising condition and speed, and three times at full speed, both of these being surface runs. Then three submerged runs were made and three runs awash, with the boat ready to dive at a moment's notice. On these runs the *Fulton* made ten dives and a feature of the tests was the rapidity with which she could get under water. One of the observers said that she "dived to a depth of 20 feet in 12 seconds."[6]

The *Fulton* also performed various maneuvers during a week of trials and acquitted itself excellently. "The main feature," Frank Cable recounted, "was a difficult torpedo attack. We had a target fixed by means of two small boats anchored three hundred feet apart to represent the length of a small warship, and toward it we were to start at a distance of ten miles, running submerged the entire distance, and using only our periscope (the periscope had arrived at last) for observation.* The efficiency of the run was determined by the infrequency with which we exposed our periscope. The two boats lay about a mile eastward of Block Island . . . we had to take our course from the chart and ran the risk of error in direction due to an inaccurate compass. There was a considerable sea, which impeded our making swift observations through the periscope in the briefest possible time required."[7] Cable made his first observation five miles out, but the swells obscured the target. He made his second three miles later, but still could not see the two small boats. Finally, only two miles from the target, Cable saw where to aim. Running submerged, he passed between the two boats.

Other tests involved maneuverability, both on the surface and submerged, running with the periscope theoretically shot away, and remaining submerged for twelve hours. The *Fulton* passed them all. On June 11, the boat made a "triumphant return to New Suffolk," having covered the sixty miles from Newport in eight hours.[8]

The unmitigated success of the trials would be moot, however. In a meeting in Secretary Moody's office on June 24, the secretary voiced the opinion, backed by counsel, that Congress, in appropriating $850,000 for fiscal year 1905, intended that none of $500,000 for 1904 be spent, but rather be carried over to help fund the larger amount. Moody was due to leave office on July 1, and so intended to leave any decision on submarines to his successor.

The secretary also demanded of Fred Whitney, the Lake Company's attorney, that he produce evidence of corruption that Lake had all but insisted had impacted the selection process. Whitney, who earlier in his career had been clerk for the naval affairs committee, said he believed there had been "bias" shown for Holland submarines, but that "he knew of no officers who had received any money." When Moody

---

* The *Fulton* did not use an omniscope, on which Lake held a patent that he would not have licensed, but rather a less efficient, Italian version, whose range of vision was limited, but effective enough when moving straight ahead.

pressed as to whether this "bias" was based on anything but relative performance, Whitney was forced to admit that neither he nor Lake had any evidence of "anything that approaches or resembles corruption."[9] Ebenezer Hill then attempted to show how Captain Train had prevented the *Protector* from receiving a fair test, but Moody produced the correspondence from Lake admitting that his boat could not make more then 3.8 knots submerged, an immediate disqualification.

The meeting adjourned with Secretary Moody once more passing all questions of submarine acquisition to his successor, but he added, "I have one thing with which I must deal here today, and I want to repeat my question whether either of you gentlemen have any charges to make against this board," to which Hill immediately replied, "Leave me out. I have never made any charges." Whitney also replied, "I have not."

But still, no funds would be available for submarine construction in the United States for an indefinite period. Foreign governments, on the other hand, might prove to be a good deal more amenable.

CHAPTER 24
A WARSHIP IN SEARCH OF A WAR

Electric Boat had taken the lead in overseas marketing with its 1901 sale of five Adder-class boats to the British Admiralty, a transaction that had irritated members of the naval affairs committee. The British did not envision the submarine as an offensive weapon, but only as a part of their coastal defenses. Even so, purchasing submarines had proved unpopular among more conservative elements in the Royal Navy. In addition to the widespread view that submarines were a waste of money, as in Napoleon's time, the very idea of an undersea boat struck many senior officers as dishonorable and a violation of the gentlemanly rules of war. Royal Navy Controller Admiral A. K. Wilson, denounced submarines as "underhanded, unfair, and damned unEnglish," demanding that surface vessels should "treat all submarines as pirates in wartime . . . and hang all crews."[1]

But the Hollands had their supporters as well. When the boats were first sent out on fleet maneuvers, they succeeded in mock torpedo attacks on four warships. Admiral Baron J. A. Fisher, First Sea Lord, wrote, "It is astounding to me, perfectly astounding, how the very best amongst us fail to realize the vast impending revolution in Naval warfare and Naval strategy that the submarine will accomplish."[2]

But successes were mixed with all too frequent failures. Part of the problem was that, because construction had been licensed to Vickers, Holland's design was altered, often not for the better. A British expert who inspected both variations wrote, "One fault in the British 'Hollands' [is that] the interiors are filled with pieces of mechanism that might easily be dispensed with. What struck me especially on board the American boats (the author had an opportunity of inspecting several at Long Island in October, 1902) was the wonderful amount of space—or elbow room—they possessed, which must make a great difference to the comfort of those managing the boat during trials."[3]

While the boats generally performed well in sea trials—"A noteworthy feature of the test was her excellent diving propensities, which for three days were put to the severest trials"—there were any number of minor mishaps, most brought on by the testing of an alternative piece of equipment or new operating protocol, especially in the fourth and fifth boats.

How the Hollands fared, however, would soon be of little interest to Electric Boat. Because of the manner in which the licensing contract had been structured, the British could revise the design and build future boats without any obligation to the American company, which they almost immediately proceeded to do.

Rather than continue the licensing agreement, Great Britain commissioned from Vickers what became known as its "A-class" submarines. Thirteen of the one hundred foot-long bastardized Hollands were built between 1902 and 1905, but were beset by design and operating problems far more serious than had been experienced with the original boats.

On March 18, 1904, the first of the vessels, which had been designated HMS *A-1*, was attacking a surface ship during naval maneuvers, when it was struck by a commercial ship transporting mail. The collision ripped off the conning tower and *A-1* flooded and sank in a matter of moments. None of the crew could fight through the water pouring in the breach and all drowned. The other four boats, and all subsequent British submarines, were then fitted with a watertight hatch at the base of the conning tower. Others of the A-class were either lost in test voyages or decommissioned by the beginning of World War I. The few that remained were used only for harbor defense and never sent into the open ocean.

But Vickers was getting the hang of it. They soon moved to an improved model, the B-class, of which eleven were built, and then to the C-class, the last of the British Holland-style boats, which commissioned thirty-eight boats into the Royal Navy. Both B- and C-classes were used extensively in World War I, but almost always for either harbor defense or harbor blockade. Two more classes of submarines would be produced by Vickers during the war, each capable of patrolling in the open sea, although the Admiralty only very rarely employed the boats in attacking enemy surface vessels. Still, after the first five Holland boats were built, neither Lake nor Electric Boat would have again access to the British market.

Nor could either company look to France. For almost two decades, the French had been engaged in a robust submarine development program, the only viable one outside the United States. It had, in fact, been the progress of the French effort that had most spurred the British to build submarines of their own.

The first French boat, launched in 1886, commissioned by the marine ministry, was a primitive two-man craft designed by a prominent engineer, Claude Goubet. Like John Holland's early boats, the *Goubet I* was filled with clever innovations—it was powered exclusively by an electric motor driven by batteries, and, instead of rudders or dive planes, employed a "Goubet joint," a patented swivel mechanism that allowed the operator to change the orientation of the propeller to whatever horizontal or vertical axis he wished. The two men sat back to back in the tiny craft, peering through glass ports in a miniscule conning tower. Unlike Holland's early boats, however, Goubet's first effort did not work at all.

Despite an engineer's training, Goubet had never grasped the concept of longitudinal stability. He had fitted his boat with a weighted pendulum, to which he connected a pump, also battery-powered. The pendulum was supposed to regulate the flow of water ballast between ballast tanks fore and aft to keep the craft level. In practice, it was impossible to maintain either constant depth or a straight course. In addition, the motor could not produce sufficient power to propel the boat at more than two or three knots. Goubet had heavily promoted his idea to senior French government and military officials, but when he tried out his invention on the Seine and then at the harbor at Cherbourg, it was a total failure.

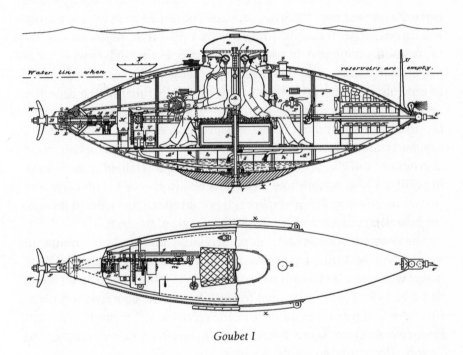

Goubet I

Three years later, still under commission from the marine ministry, he was back with an improved *Goubet II*. He had enlarged the craft, installed a more powerful motor and added tail fins to improve stability. He had not, however, overcome the fatal stability flaws of his first effort and the *Goubet II* did not fare substantially better in trials. The boat was rejected, the commission withdrawn, and Goubet ruined, his health "affected considerably."[4] He died five years later.

But the French had not given up on submarines. Prompted by Admiral Hyacinthe Laurent Théophile Aube, minister of the marine, a commission was granted to a marine engineer, Gustave Zédé, and Arthur Krebs, an automotive engineer who had pioneered the steering wheel, to complete an experimental submarine called the *Gymnote*. The vessel had originally been designed by Stanislas Dupuy de Lôme, but he had died in 1885, with work on the boat barely begun. Zédé and Krebs both proved expert in creating a practical prototype.

Although also powered solely by batteries, 564 cells to be exact, the *Gymnote* at sixty feet was four times larger than Goubet's machine, and carried a crew of five. Its motor, directly connected to the battery array, was capable of generating fifty horsepower, only sufficient to cruise at five or six knots submerged. In addition, the batteries themselves were not as powerful as Exides, and therefore a much larger number were required to generate equal energy. The boat was originally fitted with a primitive periscope (actually a "telescopic conning tower of tarred canvas fixed on steel") but it could not be made watertight, so it was removed and a standard conning tower installed instead.[5] Three sets of hydroplanes were also added, and the vessel, like Holland's always retained a small store of positive buoyancy. Although the boat was in theory to submerge and surface on an even keel, newspapers reported after a "downward plunge" the boat disappeared with a "shark-like wiggle of its stern."[6]

The *Gymnote* was, in fact, "uncontrollable" and could not maintain longitudinal stability, but it gave rise to a remarkable successor. Zédé began work on a 160-foot boat that he called *Sirène*. But, as had Dupuy de Lôme before him, Zédé died in 1891, before the boat was complete. Construction was turned over to Zédé's assistant, Gaston Romazzotti (who had married Zédé's niece), and the boat's name was changed to *Gustave Zédé* in honor of its designer.

The *Gymnote* had been unable to navigate a straight course because the metal hull played havoc with the compass. The *Gustave Zédé* was built with a nonmagnetic and noncorrosive alloy that Romazzotti called "Roma bronze." By 1893, Romazzotti was convinced that he had created the finest undersea vessel in history.

Testing for the boat, however, got off to a bumpy start, pointing out how new and uncertain a technology battery power was. "On account of defects in the accumulators, 18 months was lost. For in the battery of 720 elements with 29 plates each, an electrical power was collected such as had never before been experimented with, and it naturally required most expert operators to attend it. After a few days satisfactory work, however, short circuits were produced through the formation of pellicules of lead peroxide which fell into the tanks. It was then decided to isolate the plates (which were reduced to 27) with magnets, the positive plates being covered with a magnetised lining. When the new battery had been installed on board the charging current was put on with the result that the stern of the submarine was almost blown to pieces and destroyed, a violent fire breaking out showing the impossibility of using such batteries. The only remedy was to reduce the cells by one half, and at last after nearly two years of scientific muddling the *Gustave Zédé* was able to go on her first trials; but her fine designed speed of 15 knots was now only 8 knots. Another difficulty now cropped up. After being on the vessel a short time, her crew were all taken violently ill owing to the free discharge of large quantities of acid vapor throughout the hull. This matter was, however, speedily set right and with her wings clipped and reputation at zero the largest submarine boat the world had yet seen started to vindicate her character."[7]

The *Gustave Zédé*'s handling was not much better. "The moment she lost her buoyancy, the submarine became unmanageable and her course had so much in common with the switchback that her poor crew were unable to keep their feet and were hurled hither and thither. This improved a little when they became accustomed to the eccentricities of their craft, but even then the 'yaw' was between 14 and 18 metres, or 46 to 60 feet. These variations she accomplished in long swift swoops and all the endeavours in the world would not keep her on a straight course for more than a few minutes at a time. The uneven torpedo-like course of the *Gymnote* had been the cause of much comment and the much greater length of her big sister only accentuated the faults she had herself displayed. This 'yawing' although not dangerous where a sufficient depth of water existed would be absolutely fatal in a harbour or when wishing to pass under a ship which would of course be a frequent occurrence."[8]

The French marine ministry, however, displayed a greater commitment than its American counterpart, and the *Gustave Zédé* was tested and improved for six years. The original batteries were replaced with ones of higher capacity, although the original load was never restored; the wiring was simplified; the canvas conning tower was removed and replaced with metal; the operation of the pumps that regulated the water ballast was refined; a and a new system of six diving planes was installed, two forward, two in the center, and two in the stern. A single torpedo tube was placed in the bow, already loaded, with two extras, which could be loaded with a compressed air system that blew out the tube. Given the nature of the improvements, there seems little doubt that Romazzotti had studied Holland's designs.

Some of the *Gustave Zédé*'s features anticipated Lake's design. Although its field of vision was only twenty-seven degrees, not nearly as efficient as Lake's full-range omniscope, and the image obtained was distorted and indistinct, the *Gustave Zédé* was the first submarine to be fitted with a working periscope. A gyroscope was added to the compass to enable the vessel to better steer a straight course at constant depth.

By 1899, the boat was achieving twelve knots on the surface, although still only seven submerged, and it was longitudinally stable under the surface. Eventually, the boat would make more than two thousand dives, and travel underwater from Toulon to Marseilles. The *Gustave Zédé* was also the first submarine to make a successful attack on a surface warship, when it struck the cruiser *Magenta* with a mock torpedo during naval maneuvers in Toulon Harbor.

As large as it was, however, handling remained sluggish. In addition, as there was no means to recharge the batteries, its range was limited to the round trip distance *Gustave Zédé* could travel on a single charge.

Unlike the United States, which had to be shoved into technological innovation, France encouraged it. The French, who also had the most advanced automobile industry and would eventually also take the lead in aviation, had initiated an official competition in 1896 to find the most efficient submarine. In addition to the *Gustave Zédé*, French designers produced vessels like the *Narval*, a double-hulled, dual propulsion submarine that could run at high speeds both on the surface and submerged. Unfortunately, its surface motor ran on steam and so diving and surfacing involved extended delays, a fatal flaw for an attack boat. But whatever the merits or shortcomings of any particular design, France intended to restrict development to domestic designers and not open their competition to foreign builders.

Germany was also not a potential sales target. Led by Admiral Alfred von Tirpitz, the German high command largely disdained the submarine and refused to allocate funds even to study its feasibility as a weapon. As late as 1905, Tirpitz, the man who a decade later would oversee unrestricted submarine warfare in the Atlantic, thought the submarine little more than a toy.

The principal problem for both Lake and Electric Boat in trying to sell submarines in Europe was a lack of urgency among the buyers. In what was a rarity on the Continent, in those first years of the twentieth century, no one was fighting, and therefore no one felt an immediate need to invest in a new technology that might hold great potential but would also come at great cost. In the east, however, circumstances were different.

After years of growing animosity, in February 1904, Japan, an aspiring world power, had launched a naval attack on Russia's Port Arthur. Two Russian battleships were badly damaged and Japanese warships settled in just outside the harbor, instituting a blockade that bottled up the Russian Pacific fleet. Mines were laid extensively by both sides. Both to enforce a blockade and to break one were considered ideal uses for a submarine, which was an ideal sales situation for Lake and Electric Boat.

The Japanese in particular had been observing both companies' products for years and, at almost the same time Lake was due to compete against the *Fulton*, word leaked that it had made an offer for the *Protector*. But Russia seemed in the hunt as well. Reporters camped out at Bridgeport to await developments. In early June, as the *Fulton* was impressing the inspection board at Newport, their patience was rewarded—sort of—when one morning they noticed that the *Protector* was no longer at its usual mooring. The boat was gone, but no one knew where. One place it had not gone, reporters quickly determined, was Narragansett Bay.

That Lake had sold the *Protector* to one of the combatants seemed certain, and speculation ran rampant as to which one. On June 13, 1904, the *New York Tribune* gave the answer. "Japan Gets Protector," the front-page headline read. "The Mystery Cleared." The paper was justly proud of its sleuthing and described Lake's attempted subterfuge in vivid detail.

> The mystery which has surrounded the sudden disappearance of the Lake submarine torpedo boat Protector is at last cleared. The Protector is now the property of the Japanese government, and is on her way to her new owners. As soon as she arrives, she will be put in fighting trim and in charge of two of her original crew, C. M. Willson, chief engineer, and George H. Evans, diver. To avoid international entanglements, the Lake Company has been exceedingly careful about disclosing any of the plans of the Protector. Although the deal by which Japan became the owner of the submarine was consummated between two and three months ago, everything was done to throw off suspicion.
>
> On June 3rd, Protector left this harbor [Bridgeport] under her own power, but because of the fact that her storage batteries had been taken out and she was as a consequence able to run only on the surface, no one gave a serious thought to her contemplated long trip to Japan. The boat ran to New York, where on Sunday, she was taken aboard the Fortuna, a Norwegian steamship.
>
> When this fact became known, the question of what had become of the Protector's storage batteries arose. Then it became apparent why the storage batteries had been taken out. They are heavy, weighing nearly 80,000 pounds. In order to make the load of the Fortuna lighter, these batteries were shipped on ahead to Japan about a month and a half ago. When the submarine arrives at her destination these batteries will be replaced and she will be ready for war.

There was much to commend this story—all the facts were correct. Except one.

The *Protector* had been sold to Russia, not Japan, and the *Fortuna* was headed to Kronstadt, not Tokyo. But the *Tribune*'s reporter was not alone in misidentifying the *Protector*'s buyer. Japan thought it was getting the boat as well.

The machinations began in May 1904, when Lake was in Washington, trying to revive his fading hopes for favorable terms in the upcoming sea trials. He was being escorted through Congress by Ebenezer Hill when they happened on Senator Albert Beveridge, a highly respected progressive from Indiana and a future biographer of Chief Justice John Marshall and Abraham Lincoln. Hill asked Beveridge where his sympathies lay in the conflict between Japan and Russia. Beveridge said he favored Russia as it was "a white nation against a yellow one, a Christian nation against pagans, and an honest people against a lot of damned crooks."[9] Hill agreed.

Lake, however, claimed "no feeling of partisanship. When I had been asked by a man representing the Japanese Government if I would consider a sale to Japan, since my chances of selling to my own people seemed to have gone glimmering, I said that I would." The Japanese attaché said the order would be for two boats, and Lake asked $250,000 each, which was acceptable. Lake left with a provisional agreement, but nothing could be signed until the deal had been approved by the attaché's superiors.

"It was the next day after I had put a price on two boats to Japan that I got a telegram from Charles R. Flint of New York. Flint had been called the Father of Trusts by the newspapers, but he had been a diplomat, a banker, a promoter, and above all a dealer in munitions."[*][10] Flint asked Lake to join him at his New York town house for breakfast the following morning and, when Lake arrived, the Russian military attaché was waiting.

When Lake learned the identity of Flint's other guest, it "began to sound like money." Lake said later that his initial neutrality had been based in commerce, because he "had something to sell," but the talk between Hill and Beveridge had subconsciously influenced him. On the "inside," he decided, he was "pro-Russian, beyond a doubt." The

---

*   Flint would later represent the Wright brothers as their European agent.

three men talked about Lake's submarine through breakfast. "I told them what I could do with the *Protector* and why it was possible to do it and how I found out how to do it and about my series of trials-and-errors. I was not trying to sell anything, but I was having a bully good time, talking about the thing that was my life."

When the breakfast was done, Japan was out and Russia was in. The *Tribune* did get the price right, however. Lake had agreed to sell the boat for $250,000, and received a down payment, although the amount was never disclosed.

Getting the *Protector* to Russia, however, would require cloak-and-dagger furtiveness. The United States was officially neutral and any shipment of contraband might be blocked if word got out in advance. And word was certainly getting out. "Everyone knew that [I had failed to sell to the United States Government] yet suddenly I had money."

But Lake did not wait around for his government to cause him problems. He arranged to meet the *Fortuna* at midnight on a Saturday, because government offices were closed. When the freighter was late, Lake was convinced that his plan was blown. Eight hours later, however, *Fortuna* appeared out of the fog and the *Protector* was hoisted aboard and placed in a cradle designed to see it across thousands of miles of open ocean.[*]

Once his boat had been shipped, Lake shipped himself. After loitering in Bridgeport for two or three days "to avert suspicion," he sailed for Cherbourg and from there, made his way on to Russia where he was feted with the celebrity he felt he had been denied in his own country. He arrived in Kronstadt, a seaport near St. Petersburg, in time to greet his submarine when it arrived days later. Unfortunately, the batteries, which had been shipped separately, did not arrive until three months afterward. Once they did, the *Protector* made its sea tests

---

[*] That Lake had been a no-show at the sea trials, and had sold his boat to a combatant in violation of American neutrality, did not prevent him from writing a furious five-page letter of protest to the navy secretary when the inspection board issued a report stating that the *Fulton* was the only boat to meet the navy's criteria. Lake demanded that the report be withdrawn "unless it was first modified by striking out all references to the *Protector*." Lake's reasoning was that "since the *Protector* has never had the trial or comparison contemplated by law, it is not the subject of partial and misleading comparison with the *Fulton*, nor can the *Fulton* be compared to it." The report was not altered.

and the results were sufficient that the Russians ordered an additional five boats.

Lake remained in Russia for seven months, to oversee the start of construction. The five additional boats, however, were not completed before the war ended in a humiliating defeat for his hosts. The *Protector* was dispatched to the harbor at Vladivostok and although Lake claimed its presence helped deter a planned Japanese attack, it appeared to have had little impact.

Lake's stay in what Senator Beveridge had characterized as a "Christian nation" was an education. He had brought with him his wife and three children to "the most profligate society in recent history." He and his family were constantly exposed to excesses that would spark a revolution little more than a decade later. "Grand dukes did not hesitate to flaunt their mistresses before the public. So far as we could observe the public did not care. They appeared with their women at the theaters as nonchalantly as though they were wives. The public seemed to feel that four grand dukes plus four loose women in Worth gowns and Cartier tiaras made a box at the opera practically perfect. If there was a hint of criticism I never caught it."[11] Of course, the reason Lake did not see that hint of criticism was that he dealt almost exclusively with the aristocracy.

But the extent of profligacy at the Russian court was not Lake's only surprise. He was soon joined by an unexpected and almost certainly unwelcome guest. The Russians, it seemed, had acquired the *Fulton* as well.

Rumors had been circulating since April that Russia had put in orders for Holland submarines. That month, American newspapers had picked up the following item. "A naval correspondent writes to the *London Globe*: 'I learn that the Russian government has ordered twelve new submarine boats to be built with the utmost dispatch. All are to be of the improved Holland type. Six are being constructed by the Electric Boat Company in America and six are being built in Russian dock yards from designs and specifications supplied by the inventors and patentees. Special arrangements are being made to convey these new submarines overland to the Far East. They are intended to reinforce the Baltic squadron, which, it is expected, will leave in July for the theater of war. There can be no question that, provided the new vessels can be delivered in efficient condition at Russian naval ports in the Pacific, they must exercise a powerful influence on the naval situation.'"[12]

In the final stages of preparing the *Fulton* for sea trials, Electric Boat, while not issuing an outright denial that a deal had been made with the Russians, did note that it was plain to see that the company was not building an additional six boats at New Suffolk. Rumors from a conflict halfway around the world appeared and were disabused regularly, such as the assertion from an unnamed "retired naval officer," that Russian battleships had been sunk by Japanese submarines. That wild speculation persisted was fortunate for Electric Boat, because they had indeed already sold the *Fulton* to Russia, as well as six other submarines, which the company was building more or less in secret in California.

Publicly, Frank Cable busied himself preparing the *Fulton* for the inspection board. Out of sight of either reporters or government officials, however, he was formulating arrangements to immediately afterward ship the *Fulton* to Russia from New Suffolk. "Our first plan was to place her openly on the deck of a tramp steamer for transport direct to Kronstadt," but after the press reported that the *Protector* had been shipped to a belligerent, ostensibly Japan, "we decided not to take the risk."[13]

After the trials were done, newspapers had reported on *Fulton*'s impressive return voyage to New Suffolk. What they did not report was that Cable had rushed home not to impress the navy, but to rendezvous with the freighter that would ship the boat overseas. However, before Cable and his fellow conspirators could consider having *Fulton* towed out to sea, where their transport awaited them, there were formalities to be observed. "An initial difficulty to surmount was obtaining clearance papers. It was necessary to get them from the nearest point of departure (in this case Sag Harbor), and for our purpose, before the vessel was actually loaded." Any sight of the cargo on the deck might "arouse the custom's official's suspicions [and] our clearance papers refused." Cable had the freighter's captain ferried ashore, where the officials in Sag Harbor, perplexed at "probably the first vessel which had applied for clearance papers from that port in thirty years," scrambled about to find the proper forms. Eventually, the paperwork was completed and, while "no one in the town knew that anything unusual was afoot," the *Fulton* was towed out to Gardiners Bay in the dead of night.

Loading the submarine on the deck of the steamer took "hours of labor in the dark, only an occasional lantern, used when absolutely necessary, betraying our presence." Suddenly, "what seemed to be flame erupting from the funnels of a destroyer lit the darkness some miles distant, the craft evidently headed in our direction. We feared our lantern had exposed our nefarious operations, and instantly came visions of heavy fines and imprisonment." But the destroyer veered off and, at 3:30 A.M., the eighty-ton *Fulton* was loaded on board and the freighter "headed out to sea beyond the three mile limit, where safety lay." It was not until four days later that "the suspicion dawned on the customs officials at Sag Harbor that they had cleared a contraband cargo."

Like Lake, Cable had removed the battery array that powered the vessel underwater. In this case, though, both boat and batteries reached Kronstadt in roughly ten days time. When Cable arrived there to train the Russian crew, he noticed the *Protector* in a neighboring berth. Unlike Lake, Cable did not get to Moscow; in fact he rarely left the naval base where the training was taking place. He did, however, get to meet the Tsar when the Russian monarch came to inspect the *Fulton* (which had been renamed *Madam*) the day before Cable's departure.

Like the *Protector*, the *Fulton* had no difficulty satisfying Russian naval officers in sea tests, and, also as with the Lake boat, it was dispatched on Siberian Railway for Vladivostok, where it languished, never seeing action. Neither boat was ever heard from again. The five boats shipped by Electric Boat to Russia from California also arrived too late to be employed in what turned out to be only an eighteen-month-long war.

Frank Cable would nonetheless soon be training submarine crews of another nation in Asia. Demonstrating equality, if not neutrality, Electric Boat had sold submarines to the Japanese as well as to the Russians. But there would be competition in Tokyo as well. This time, however, it would not be from boats built by Simon Lake, but rather from boats built by John Holland himself.

CHAPTER 25
HOLLAND WITHOUT HOLLAND

olland, now sixty-three, had become a bystander. To ensure that he could not be a threat to the commercial colossus they wished to use his invention to create, Rice and Frost took every opportunity, be it in congressional testimony, public pronouncements, or private communications, to portray him as a doddering old fool whose memory and perhaps reason was failing him.

In 1904, Holland's five-year agreement with Electric Boat expired. On March 28, he sent Rice a terse note:

> Dear Mr. Rice,
>
> As my contract with company expires on the 31st, and as it is proper that I should then withdraw from my directorship, I beg to offer my resignation. The success of your company can never be as great as what I ardently desire for it.
>
> Yours, very sincerely,
> John P. Holland.

In fact, there was nothing at all sincere in Holland's good wishes. He had used the free time that Rice and Frost had forced on him to map out a larger, much faster, far more efficient submarine. Free from encumbrances—or so he thought—he drew up plans for the new design. Holland estimated his boat could make twenty-two knots on the surface and a stunning twenty-six submerged, which would make it faster than a battleship, whose top speed was sixteen knots.

Holland had willing allies in this new venture. Charles Creecy had left Electric Boat in 1903, also after disputes with Rice and Frost, and Lewis Nixon was prepared to offer his yard for construction if Holland could get funding. Creecy approached American naval officials, who authorized testing of a scale model of Holland's design in a tank at the Washington Navy Yard. The results were "encouraging," but Holland's request to meet with a special naval board was denied. The officers who had observed the test and examined the blueprints did not doubt Holland's numbers but were convinced that such speeds, especially underwater, would wreck the boat.[1] Nor were there any further tank tests authorized for the scale model. While there is no direct evidence that Electric Boat interests were working to quash any attempt to sell the navy the new design, it would be quite out of character if they were not.

Holland, as had Electric Boat, then looked overseas. He did not have to look far. Japan had been interested in Holland submarines since 1898, when a senior naval officer had discussed the military potential of the *Holland* with the inventor, and another naval officer had been a passenger during a trial run in the New York Narrows. They had closely followed Holland's progress from that point on and, in secret, had purchased the five Adder-class Hollands from Electric Boat. Also in secret, they purchased plans for Holland's new high-speed model through Takata and Company of New York.

As part of the deal, Takata agreed to fund the construction of two vessels at a Massachusetts shipyard. Both vessels were laid down in November 1904. Once completed, they were dismantled, sent across the United States by rail, and then shipped from California to Tokyo for reassembly. Two senior American engineers, former employees of the Holland Torpedo Boat Company, crossed the Pacific as well, to supervise construction and help train the Japanese.

The five submarines that Electric Boat had sold to Japan were also shipped in parts, although they had been fabricated in San Diego. As he had for the tsar's navy, Frank Cable was assigned to supervise construction and train crews to sail submarines for the emperor. He sailed from San Francisco in April 1905 on a "vessel laden with war munitions." Cable's appearance had caused the San Francisco newspapers to speculate on what seemed to be yet another violation of American neutrality. Leaving the freighter on which he and the engineers were passengers to continue on without them, "We abated suspicions by stopping at Honolulu, apparently as tourists in search of diversion." A few days later, they embarked on another vessel "also loaded with contraband," and, taking a circuitous route to avoid any sea lane where Russian warships might be encountered, eventually reached Yokohama on May 30, 1905. Cable was met by a group of Japanese officers eager to be the first to employ submarines in a genuine war situation.[2]

Just two days earlier, however, the main Russian fleet had been virtually annihilated in the Tsushima Strait. While Russia still retained a large number of warships, the battle ended any chance of a Russian victory. A humiliated Tsar Nicholas II sent emissaries to sympathetic nations, including the United States, hoping they might broker decent peace terms.

The Japanese, however, were in no hurry to end a conflict that they were so decisively winning, so submarine training proceeded. By the end of July, the Japanese crew Cable had trained was ready for official trials. "Unlike our experience with the Russian Navy Department, to say nothing of our own, there was no delay. In war, Japan's watchword was dispatch."[3] Within a week, the trials had been completed, the boat accepted, and a four-day maiden voyage undertaken by an all-Japanese crew. When the boat returned, it was fitted with torpedoes and readied for war. Before it could sail, however, an armistice was declared, brokered by Theodore Roosevelt, for which he was later awarded the Nobel Peace Prize.

He would have received a far different reception in Japan, however. For promoting terms that many in Japan saw as far too lenient to Russia—the tsar would pay no indemnities—America had become wildly unpopular. There were anti-American riots, American property was destroyed, and churches burned. Cable was forced to remain in his hotel for days, while the army was called out to quell the disturbances.

Afterward, Cable, now always under escort, began to train a crew for the second submarine. As before, he was impressed with the Japanese work ethic, their devotion to duty, and the speed with which they mastered complex processes. While engaged with the second crew, Cable heard that another boat was being prepared and another crew trained at the Kawasaki works in Kobe. This boat, it was rumored, was faster, more powerful, and more efficient than the Adder-class Hollands.

When he learned that his competition was also a Holland design, he requested permission to examine this new boat. Suddenly, the culture that he had praised for its eschewal of bureaucracy was awash in it. "I was anxious to see these boats, but, despite my acquaintance with Lieutenant Ide, the Japanese officer in charge of the work for his government, red tape barred me from the Kobe Yard." Cable did learn that "the boats were duly launched and put into commission," although not until after the war had officially ended on September 5, 1905.*

---

* Cable, *American Submarine*, 251. The Holland boats were designated "Type 6" submarines. Both saw extensive service and served as prototypes for Japan's extensive submarine program. The first of these, the "#6," came to as tragic an end as has ever appeared in submarine annals. Whether as a result of a construction error, or a mistake by a crew member, a valve was left open to the sea during a dive. Before the valve could be closed, the boat, commanded by Lieutenant Tsutomu Sakuma, with a crew of fourteen, had taken on water and sunk in Hiroshima Bay. When the boat was raised the following day, all were dead, suffocated by battery gas. Lieutenant Sakuma, it was discovered, had left a detailed, heartbreaking record of the crew's two-hour-forty-minute ordeal. It began, "Words of apology fail me for having sunk His Majesty's submarine #6. My subordinates are killed by my fault, but it is with pride that I inform you that the crew to a man have discharged their duties as sailors should, with the utmost coolness until their dying moments. We now sacrifice our lives for the sake of our country, but my fear is that the disaster will affect the future development of submarines. It is my hope that nothing will daunt your determination to study the submarine until it is a perfect machine, absolutely reliable. We can then die without regret." At one point, Lieutenant Sakuma wrote, "Surrounded by poisonous gas, the crew strove to pump out the water, and later, "The electric current has become useless, gas cannot be generated, and the hand pump is our only hope." He described the effort of his men, "wet and extremely cold," to pump out the water. When the effort became fruitless, Sakuma wrote, "A word to His Majesty the Emperor. It is my earnest hope that Your Majesty will supply the means of living to the poor families of the crew. This is my only desire and I am anxious to have it fulfilled." Finally, two and a half hours after the submarine sank, he wrote, "My breathing is so difficult and painful," and ten minutes after that, "I thought I could blow out the gasoline, but I am intoxicated with it." The log was published in newspapers and for their bravery and sacrifice, Lieutenant Sakuma and his crew were held up as heroes throughout Japan. They would remain so during the militarization that preceded the attack on Pearl Harbor, an attack in which five two-man "midget" submarines participated but did little or no damage.

The Japanese did not buy any more submarines from Holland, however, and Electric Boat was determined that no one else would either. In May 1905, Holland incorporated the John P. Holland Submarine Boat Company in Newark, New Jersey, capitalized at $1 million. The sale to Japan had not been made public, so Holland could not initially attract investment capital. That would change, he was convinced, when he sold his new high-speed boat in Europe. But Holland had no more luck selling in Europe than Lake or Rice, and his problems were exacerbated by uncertainty among European firms as to whether any feature of his new submarine infringed on Electric Boat Company patents.

Rice and Frost made certain that all doubt was resolved. Holland later asserted in a February 1906 letter to Chairman Foss of the naval affairs committee, that he was about "to start to work" on a prototype of his high-speed submarine for the American market, "when the Electric Boat Company filed a suit against me in the Court of Chancery of New Jersey, applying for an injunction, and claiming substantially that I had agreed to assign to them all my inventions and patents during the term of my natural life." An additional suit was filed "against me personally, alleging a verbal contract never to compete with the Electric Boat Company, was commenced in the New Jersey Court of Chancery."[4]

Not only would Holland be denied the use of his patents—it seemed he would not even have the use of his name. "Suit Over Holland's Name," the New York Times reported, which sought to "enjoin the recently incorporated John P. Holland Submarine Company from using the name of the inventor as a part of its corporate title. It will be instituted by the Holland Torpedo Boat Company of New York in the equity branch of United States Circuit Court. The complaining corporation alleges that it secured, on December 13, 1890, the exclusive right to use the name John. P. Holland."[5]

Holland denied ever entering into any verbal agreements with either Isaac Rice or E. B. Frost. "My contract with the Electric Boat Company to act as their engineer, and to give them my patents and inventions, was for the five years during which I acted as engineer, and no longer, and expired April 1, 1904." Holland added, "These suits have had the effect of frightening off the capital that I had enlisted, and I have not as yet been able to get the capital to build my new boat, by reason of these suits. The only object of these suits was to prevent me from building a boat and going into competition before the Navy Department with the submarine boats now being built by the Electric Boat Company under my old patents."[6]

He found it ludicrous that anyone could take the lawsuit seriously.

> The Electric Boat Company makes the allegation in their last bill of complaint that by threatening to discharge me from their employ and break their contract with me and stop my salary, that I agreed to a contract which prevents me from using my brains and inventive talent in building submarine boats for the balance of my life. This allegation is absolutely false. . . . This alleged agreement was not reduced to writing; the only evidence the Court has is the sworn statement of Mr. Rice; and when the fact is considered that Mr. Rice, formerly a professor of law at Columbia University, and having the assistance of Mr. Frost, also a lawyer, failed to have such an important agreement reduced to writing and signed by me, the whole proposition appears ridiculous and silly.

But whether the court agreed or not was beside the point. (The suits were eventually thrown out.) The aim, as Holland had correctly asserted, was to frighten away capital. The letter to Foss had closed with a plaintive appeal. "I am a poor man, while the Electric Boat Company has among its principal stockholders three or four millionaires, including August Belmont, Isaac L. Rice, and others. The capital stock of that company is ten million dollars. They have deprived me, by their flimsy lawsuit, from getting capital to build a boat under my new inventions and patents, and are now asking Congress to pass a law which will prevent the Navy Department from adopting my new plans and inventions, even should the entire department consider that they are far superior in every way to the plans now being used by that department."

Holland's plea to Congress was ignored. On December 4, 1906, the John P. Holland Submarine Boat Company was declared bankrupt. Although liabilities on that date were less than four hundred dollars, "there was no cash on hand to meet them."[7]

Holland's plans for a high-speed submarine were shelved, and John Holland's involvement with submarines was at an end.

CHAPTER 26

EXCESSIVE BALLAST

With Holland on the sidelines, Electric Boat's only remaining opponent was Simon Lake. Fortunately for Rice and Frost, Lake, unable to control either his temper or his judgment, made it easy for them.

The Lake Company wasted no time petitioning Paul Morton, William Moody's successor as navy secretary. Lake himself being out of the country, Fred Whitney delivered a letter on July 1, 1904, Morton's first day in office. "The Lake Torpedo Boat Company has the honor to give the 'reasonable notice,' and requests to have its submarine boat tested by both competition and comparison with Government submarine boats, or any private competitor, provided there be any such, prior to the purchase or contract for $850,000 worth of submarine boats as provided by the act of Congress taking effect July 1, 1904."[1] The problem, of course, was that the Lake Company no longer had a submarine to submit for the trial. Both Lake and the *Protector* were in Russia. He was building another attack boat, the *Simon Lake X*, at a

Newport News, Virginia, shipyard, but it would not be completed for months, and even then it would need testing and debugging. Morton, aware of the delay, and having been no doubt apprised of Lake's previous dealings with the board of inspection, tabled the request until September and then fired back a terse response. "When will your company be ready to make the test above referred to? An early reply will be appreciated. Yours, respectfully, Paul Morton, Secretary."

Whitney assured Morton that the Lake boat would be ready by the third Thursday of November and available for testing off the Virginia coast. The navy agreed on the date but asked that the test be in Narragansett Bay, "under precisely similar conditions to the recent test of a submarine boat in June, 1904, [*Fulton*] there being available in the vicinity of Newport excellent ranges and greater depth of water than is available in the vicinity of Newport News." That was acceptable to Whitney, and he reported to the navy in October that the *Simon Lake X* had been successfully launched.

But the trials never came off. In his autobiography, Simon Lake recounted the events, where once more he was the aggrieved innocent treated shabbily and perhaps illegally by a cabal that included corrupt naval officers, venal government bureaucrats, and disreputable capitalists.

It had seemed to me that my successes in Russia and Europe generally might have somewhat softened the heart of the Navy Department. After all, I had only been making and selling boats to Russia because I had not been able to sell them at home. I had a very real desire to put in the hands of our Navy a submarine which was better than the best anywhere else in the world, so I had instructed the Lake Torpedo Boat Company to proceed with the building of the *Simon Lake X* at the Newport News yards. There was an informal understanding that if Number Ten was all I said it would be, the Navy would buy it. When I was informed that Number Ten was about ready for its trial runs I came home, and brought some members of my operating staff along. My heart was light. I was a proud man. I should have known better. At the Newport News yards,

I was told that although the men had been working overtime, the Number Ten would not be ready on the date promised. I asked the United States Navy Department to grant me ten days' more time.

"No," was the curt reply.

The Navy Department absolutely refused to look at the Number Ten. Some unofficial runs were made by officers stationed at Newport News, along with officers representing England, Germany, and Brazil. One American officer went to Washington at his own expense to beg the officials of the Navy Department to conduct a test of the Number Ten. When he returned to Newport News he kept out of my way for several days. At last I met him by accident, and asked him what luck he had had.

"I feel like retiring from the Navy," he said bitterly. "I am ashamed, soiled."[2]

Lake was even stronger when speaking at the time. In January 1905, after he lost the contract for new submarines to Electric Boat, he spoke to reporters. "'I am up against stacked cards and have decided to throw up my hands and leave the country,' said Captain Simon Lake, inventor of the Lake submarine torpedo boat, today. Five of his craft have recently been bought by the Russian Government. Captain Lake made the above remark when shown a dispatch from Washington, saying that his company would file charges against Secretary Morton because the Lake Company had not been permitted to compete in the submarine boat tests. Captain Lake is indignant over the action of the Navy Department in giving additional contracts to the Holland Company without permitting him to demonstrate whether or not his invention is a more practical type of submarine boat. When asked whether or not charges would be brought, Captain Lake refused to talk."[3]

A damning assessment to be sure and, if true, charges most certainly should have been filed. But they were not—Lake's charges, as his correspondence with the Navy Department makes clear, were a total fabrication.

In the same letter of September 24 in which he required the test to be in Narragansett Bay, Secretary Morton noted that "in order that the proposed test may also conform to previous requirements of the Department"—to which Electric Boat had complied—"the Lake Torpedo Boat [sign] a formal statement that 'the boat which you submit to the Department for test is at that time finally completed and that you are prepared to accept as final, for the purpose of this act, the results which your boat is capable of developing on trial at the present time.'" Morton did not require the signed statement in advance but only "by the time of formally offering its vessel for trial In November."

Lake's justification for refusing to sign a similar statement the previous January was that the *Protector* had not yet fixed the design flaw that kept its speed below the acceptable minimum. Here, however, as he would have ample time to test the *Lake X* and ensure that all required minimums were met, there seemed little reason to refuse to conform to the navy's requirement.

Fred Whitney certainly thought so. He replied to the navy secretary that his company was "pleased to do everything possible you desire." But on November 15, just days before the testing date that Lake had requested, Whitney had to inform the navy that the boat was not yet ready.

"In conformity with your verbal request for a definite date for trials of the Lake submarine, I beg to state that the Newport News Shipbuilding and Drydock Company is doing everything possible, day and night, to rush the submarine *Simon Lake X* to completion for trials. If no untoward accidents occur it is estimated that she will be ready by the first of the month, and so I suggest that we settle on the fixed day of Monday or Tuesday, December 5 or 6, as may suit the convenience of the board, to begin the tests."

It was this request that Simon Lake later claimed received a "curt no" from the navy. The actual reply was, "The board of inspection and survey will hold itself in readiness to make an inspection and trial of the submarine boat of the Lake Torpedo Boat Company, the *Simon Lake X*, on December 5, 1904." On November 22, while continuing to accede to the delay, Secretary Morton forwarded "copies of the general programme under which competitive trials of submarine boats have been conducted by the board of inspection and survey," and also "pointed out that the formal statement requested by the secretary had not yet been received."

Morton received no reply, so on December 3, he asked whether the *Lake X* would be ready on the December 5 test day. Whitney replied that it would not. "Owing to unavoidable delays the owners of the craft will not be quite ready for test on date named, but will have their boat ready a few days thereafter. It will be ready for Government trial December 22, 1904." Whitney further added, "we respectfully suggest that the final decision of the matter of submarine boats, now under advisement by the Department, be postponed for a time until the utility of the Lake boat can be determined."

The navy once again acceded to the delay, but insisted on the declaration that once the *Lake X* was tested, the company agree that those results be accepted as final. To this, Simon Lake responded personally in a four-page, special-delivery letter to Paul Morton, the tone of which could not have been more insulting. Virtually assuring the secretary's enmity, Lake began by accusing Morton of not reading his own correspondence. "I take it for granted that you either dictated or signed this letter as a matter of routine and are absolutely unaware of the purpose or effect of the statement you demand." From there, Lake went on to say how he had spent $400,000 in development, how the Holland people had tried to frustrate him at every turn, and that even after Congress had passed the $500,000 appropriation "my requests for actual competition were ignored by the Department, and finally the board refused to proceed with trials, in January, 1904, and an attempt was made to have me sign the very statement you now demand." Then he noted how Holland influences prevented his contract with the army and "with bankruptcy impending from the Government's action toward me, I was forced to abandon my fondest hope, to protect the United States."

Then Lake made an extraordinary claim. "After refusing competition for months, the minute the *Protector* was out of the way the *Fulton* was tested by board, Secretary Moody having been assured in the Department that the *Protector* and the *Fulton* would be tested in competition together." After asserting the board's report had harmed his sales prospects overseas, Lake wrote, "The references to the Protector in the *Fulton* report were malicious defamation by a naval officer, but even under all this provocation my patriotism prevented me from discrediting the United States Navy abroad by revealing the true facts to the world when the embarrassing condition was created by practically one member of the board [J. J. Woodward] whose attitude and acts for and against the Holland and Lake submarines I will not now characterize." This from the man who just months earlier had been forced to admit that he had no evidence of wrongdoing by anyone in the navy.

From there Lake repeated his call for a "fair and open competition," and recited, at great length, the history of submarine procurement by the navy, during which Rice and Frost had consistently employed means at the very least unethical and probably even worse to strangle competition. And this despite almost universal agreement among naval officers that Lake had produced the objectively superior boat.

> An attempt is now made to have you unconsciously do what Congress positively refused to do—eliminate competition—by forcing me to sign in advance a statement that I will, in effect, accept as final a test of my submarine alone and not side by side under equal conditions with the Holland type. This is in effect a departmental amendment to an act of Congress. I refused to sign this statement once, and I now appeal to you to most carefully investigate affairs and reconsider your refusal to proceed with trials unless I waive what I regard as a lawful right, granted by Congress, in its folly or wisdom, but nevertheless clearly granted after an open debate and a decisive vote on the very question of competition. . . . An attempt has been made to studiously misinform and prejudice you against me, and I have taken our Mr. Whitney's advice and kept silent under the idea that direct competition would protect me from insidious influences. I am now denied a trial unless I sign a statement waiving lawful rights. I am forced to ask you to reconsider, as I feel this is doing us a great wrong.

Lake closed, at length, describing the pressure-filled conditions under which his constructors were laboring to complete the *Lake X*.

It is difficult to gauge Morton's reaction to this extraordinary document. But it could not have been positive as two days later, December 7, he replied with a scathing rebuke, in which he rebutted each of Lake's many distortions, half-truths, and outright misstatements.

He began by reminding Lake that he had responded to a solicitation from the Navy Department to compete for the 1903 $500,000 appropriation in a competition to be held October 15. When neither Lake nor Holland could be ready by then, the test was postponed until November 16, with the understanding that each boat might be tested at a different time. Lake not only offered no objection to the board of inspection seeing the *Protector* before the *Fulton*, "this recommendation [was] in direct response to a request of the Lake Torpedo Boat Company that the trial be not postponed beyond November 16, even though the competing boat be not ready for the trial. The Department approved this recommendation of the board of inspection and survey and so advised the Lake Torpedo Boat Company on October 20, 1903."

Morton then walked Lake through the chronology of delays initiated solely at Lake's request, followed by an admission that the *Protector* could not meet the minimum specifications required by the navy and agreed to by both parties in advance. He reminded Lake that he had insisted on an immediate test for a substandard boat, with the stipulation that he could ask for one or more retests until the *Protector* passed muster. The navy responded by declining to test any boat more than once but would wait until Lake was ready, as long as he agreed, as Electric Boat did, to make that one test final.

"Subsequent to January 12, 1904," Morton went on, "no communication has been received by the Department from the Lake Torpedo Boat Company stating that the defects in design and construction of their competing boat, *Protector*, had been remedied, or that they desired to fix a particular date for the trial of that vessel."

Then Morton penned a damning paragraph to the man who claimed to have been treated unfairly. "The Holland Torpedo Company accompanied their communication of May 13 with the formal certificate required by the Department, viz, that the Holland Torpedo Company were prepared to accept as final, etc., the results which the *Fulton* were capable of developing on trial on or after the date above noted. Under date of May 16, 1904, the trial board advised the Lake Torpedo Boat Company, of Bridgeport, Conn., of the prospective trial of the *Fulton*, and suggested that if their boat 'should be at the same time in all respects ready for this trial it would be of advantage for trial purposes that the two boats be tried at the same time,' to which communication the Lake Torpedo Boat Company apparently made no reply."

Morton then listed the delays requested by the Lake Company of the *Lake X*, each of which the navy agreed to, but requiring that Lake sign precisely the same release as had Electric Boat. "The Department," he noted, "has endeavored to afford the Lake Torpedo Boat Company every reasonable opportunity to submit a boat of their type for thorough trial under the terms of the acts making appropriations for submarine boats, and in doing so has possibly placed at a disadvantage a competing company, which, as reported by the trial board, submitted for test a boat which met the Department's conditions in all essential respects."

In view of the weight of evidence, Morton refused to promise delays beyond December 22 to test the *Lake X*. "Despite the liberal treatment accorded to the Lake Torpedo Boat Company by the Department, that company now questions the Department's understanding of its own correspondence in this matter, and disputes its legal right to impose conditions which have been long since accepted in good faith by the other competing company and which have hitherto been undisputed by the Lake Torpedo Boat Company itself." For emphasis, Morton included an advisory opinion from the judge advocate general that affirmed that the navy secretary had at all times acted within the law.

Even then, Morton tried to give Lake a chance to demonstrate his boat. On December 16, he wired Lake to ask if the boat would be ready. Lake, more contrite this time, replied that shipyard was working "day and night" to complete construction. He promised "a definite reply as soon as possible," to which Morton replied that Lake's response was "very indefinite." Lake then asked for "a few days more," beyond December 22.

On December 21, Morton offered to extend the deadline to exhibit the *Lake X* until May 5, 1905, but again only if Lake agreed to accept the results of the test as final. Lake did not reply.

At that point, Morton contacted Electric Boat and offered them a contract for two of the four boats to be built under the $850,000 appropriation. The remainder he held in abeyance, still unwilling to completely shut Lake out. On January 3, 1905, he again wrote to Lake, "Did you receive my letter of December 21? Formal acknowledgement requested." Lake did not reply. Morton sent a similar telegram the next day. Lake replied that he wanted to schedule a personal interview for January 5. Whether a face-to-face meeting ever took place is unclear, but Lake did not back off from his refusal to conform to the navy's requirements.

Only then, on January 6, did Morton write to Electric Boat. "Referring to your telegram requesting information as to whether 'the Lake Company has made the required stipulation, and if not if you have awarded the two additional submarines to us,' I beg to advise you that the Lake Company did not make the required stipulation, and that the Department is now prepared to enter into contract with the Electric Boat Company for the construction of two additional submarines, which will be the same in all respects as the smaller of the two submarines previously provided for. In this connection, the Department begs to advise you that it will not consider a price in excess of $185,000, for each additional boat."

Two days later, Simon Lake announced to the press that he was leaving the country because he was playing against "stacked cards." He returned to Russia to supervise construction of the five boats he had sold to the tsar.

But the drama had not quite ended. In early April, with Lake still out of the country, Lake's father sent an open letter to Theodore Roosevelt "calling on the President to order that certain contracts be cancelled for Holland submarine boats because said contracts were unlawfully made, and also to cause the statutory and criminal laws of the United States to be strictly enforced." The elder Lake "charges that the Navy Department has eliminated the competitive tests which were to be made between the Holland and Lake types of submarines, and this in the face of the fact that Congress refused to eliminate competition from the 1905 submarine law."

The language could not have been more inflammatory. "For certain officials to withhold from Simon Lake lawful competitive trials, drive him from America, steal his submarine features, seize his lawful property, and defy his lawful rights for competition, is a most censurable proceeding, and it demands your earnest and immediate attention and minute investigation." He did not stop there. "The complete clearing of the submarine affairs of the United States demands the enforcement of unquestioned criminal law as to perjury, and a telegraphic order for Philip Doblin's immediate arrest is necessary to prevent his escape from justice." He closed, "I call upon you as the only person powerful enough to call a halt on the manifest violation of plain law and common decency, and I hope you will use every means in your power to investigate this entire transaction and suspend Holland contracts during an investigation, if necessary, by special United States attorneys, and then give Simon Lake—an American inventor—'a square deal for competition,' nothing more, nothing less."[4]

Neither Roosevelt nor the Navy Department either acknowledged the letter or took any action on the charges. Lake himself made no comment from Russia.

But that did not mean he had given up.

CHAPTER 27
THE NEW CLASS

I n the summer of 1905, with American newspapers reporting the soon-to-be debunked tale of submarines' decisive role in the Battle of Tsushima Strait, Electric Boat's demeaning lawsuit against John Holland and Holland's bitter countersuit to get his patents back proceeding through the courts, and Simon Lake living in Europe, openly stewing over the perfidy of his own government, the American submarine program suddenly came of age during one memorable voyage.

In mid-August, the navy was planning to sea test a refitted *Plunger* from the Brooklyn Navy Yard.* Part of the work done on the boat in dry-dock was the addition of "shackles"—six steel eyebolts fastened to the deck so that the *Plunger* could be "hoisted out conveniently" if it was disabled in relatively shallow water. A French submarine, *Fafardet*, had sunk in mud off Algiers the previous month with many

---

* This was the Adder-class *Plunger*. The original, three-screw *Plunger* continued to sit unused, and would remain so until it was scrapped in 1917.

of the crew dying of asphyxiation, because chains could not be passed underneath the vessel to raise it.[1] A similar accident had befallen a British submarine a few months before that, and all hands were lost.

President Roosevelt was at his summer home at Sagamore Hill on the north shore of Long Island when he learned of the impending test. Instead of the navy yard, he ordered the *Plunger* to be put through its paces on Long Island Sound, just outside the entrance to Oyster Bay, so that he and his family could take in the spectacle. The boat was commanded by Lieutenant Charles P. Nelson, seen as one of the navy's foremost submarine experts since his testimony at the 1902 naval affairs committee hearings.

When Nelson and his superiors learned they would be undergoing a presidential inspection, precautions were extensive, both because they wanted the *Plunger* to perform perfectly and also because rumors had already circulated that the notoriously fearless and intrepid TR might not be content merely to *watch* a submarine voyage. Roosevelt had replied that such speculation was nonsense.

Before the *Plunger* could leave the navy yard, however, to Nelson's "disgust," an electrical flaw overheated the circuitry and the test had to be postponed. After working through the night, however, the apparatus was repaired and the *Plunger* was conveyed by tugboat to Long Island Sound on August 22, and there anchored just behind the presidential yacht, *Sylph*. "I do not know why we have been ordered to Oyster Bay," Nelson said coyly, "but I imagine the President wants to keep in touch with the improvements being made in this branch of the service."

The inspection was set for August 26, but two days before that, the president's wife and three of her children watched some preliminary maneuvers. The president remained at Sagamore Hill, and when questioned by reporters, he continued to deny that he would be any more than a spectator during the *Plunger*'s run two days later.

As almost anyone who knew him even vaguely would have been aware, Roosevelt was lying.

"President Takes Plunge in Submarine. Remains Below the Surface for Fifty-five Minutes. Once 40 Feet Under Water. He Manoeuvres the Vessel Himself and Is Greatly Pleased. Divers Were at Hand," read the banner headline in the *New York Times*. "President Roosevelt Under Water Three Hours in *Plunger*," wrote the *Evening World*. "President Goes to Bottom of Ocean in *Plunger*," blared the *San Francisco Call*. In fact, the president's venture under the surface was a page-one headline in virtually every newspaper in America, and many in Europe. And TR being TR, he milked every ounce of drama out of the event.

The New York Times story was typical. "Sheets of rain were falling when the President left Sagamore Hill in the afternoon in an automobile. . . . The President was the last person who was expected on the scene at that time. . . . When he arrived at the pier, a strong northwest wind was blowing and a heavy sea running in the Sound. Few were about at the time as, although a strict eye had been kept on the submarine boat, earlier in the day it had been said that the weather was too severe for any trip to be made. Nevertheless, he appeared all ready for the experiment, clad in khaki apparel . . . [when he arrived] the President donned a suit of oilskins as the seas were breaking over the pier in a way that made it impossible to pass along without being drenched to the skin."[2]

After being ferried out to the *Plunger*, Roosevelt soon disappeared into the conning tower. The boat submerged and remained stationary as Nelson briefed his insatiable commander in chief on every aspect of the submarine's machinery and operations. "After that, the Plunger descended to the bottom, a distance of forty feet below the surface . . . a school of porpoises went past the portholes . . . their appearance especially interested the President, who watched their movements for some time. Lieutenant Nelson caused some manoeuvres to be executed, sending the Plunger forward and backward, to the surface bow foremost, back again, and to the surface stern first. The Slyph's tender, Dart, caught glimpses of the submarine boat now and then flashing above the waves for a moment, then disappearing into the depths again."

Nelson then began to operate the boat at high speed, to which "the President expressed his delight." Then, in "one of the most thrilling experiments," Nelson doused the onboard lights while the *Plunger* was running at full speed, which in wartime would prevent the light coming through the portholes to be seen on the surface. Nelson executed a full set of maneuvers in darkness, after which Roosevelt exclaimed, "I have never seen anything quite so remarkable." At one point, to Roosevelt's glee, Nelson allowed him to take the controls.

When Theodore Roosevelt emerged from the conning tower into the pouring rain on Long Island Sound, submarines had become an integral part of the American fleet. "In well-informed quarters, there is an impression that the President's experience on board the *Plunger* will usher in a new era of this important branch of the navy, which up to this time is said to have received rather stepmotherly treatment at the hands of naval authorities."[3] The president also ordered that all officers and enlisted men who served aboard submarines, who to that time only received shore pay, get a raise to full sea duty.

One of the many headlines announcing Roosevelt's submarine adventure.

The swashbuckling American president was a worldwide celebrity and so Roosevelt's "stunt," as some phrased it, was also reported in newspapers around the world. Although there is no direct evidence, a number of nations—including Germany—which had previously thought submarines an affectation, began at about this time to initiate serious development programs.

Frank Cable returned from Japan in September to help with the planning and construction of the four new submarines contracted for by the navy under the 1905 appropriation. He also categorically refuted the story, reported as confirmed fact in the nation's newspapers, that submarines had sunk Russian battleships at Tsushima Strait. None had even been present. In the blush of President Roosevelt's undersea adventure, however, this story engendered little or no disenchantment with the new "terrors of the deep."

To build the four new vessels, Electric Boat cut the cord with Holland entirely. Rather than Lewis Nixon's Crescent Shipyard, the company chose Fore River Shipbuilding Works in Quincy, Massachusetts. The decision was a blow to Nixon, who had been professional, diligent, and creative in bringing the Adder-class boats to fruition. Fore River was a competent yard and had recently finished two cruisers for the navy, but none of its personnel had any experience building submarines.

Lawrence Spear by this time had a good deal of experience, and proved to be a talented second-generation designer. The four boats, to be called *Viper*, *Cuttlefish*, *Tarantula*, and *Octopus*, would not contain any great leaps over earlier principles—and would in fact be referred to as Holland-types—but would feature some outstanding innovations. In order to improve the design significantly, Spear decided to lay out the first three boats as extensions of the Adder-class, 85 feet long, but design *Octopus* as a larger, more experimental boat, 105 feet, which, if successful, would initiate a new generation of submarine design.

One of Spear's most significant improvements was the weapons system, which he installed in all four boats. Rather than the single, slow-loading torpedo tube of the early Hollands, Spear mounted two tubes side-by-side in the bow and perfected a much faster way to shoot and reload. Two of the four or five Whitehead torpedoes the boat carried would be in the tubes. Just aft of the tubes were "carriages," movable racks that were operated by compressed air and reloaded the tubes automatically. "The operation requires opening the cap at the mouth of the expulsion tube, discharging one torpedo, closing the cap, blowing out the water, opening the breach, automatically moving second torpedo into the tube, closing breach, re-opening cap, discharging second torpedo." The arrangement allowed two torpedoes to be fired in six minutes. "This device not only saves time and labour, but regulates the water-ballast in the compensating tanks, and thus prevents any change in the longitudinal trim of the boat."[4]

Interior of a Holland boat

While for surface running, *Viper*, *Cuttlefish*, and *Tarantula* were powered by single 250-horsepower four-cylinder gasoline motors, the *Octopus* was fitted with twin screws, each powered by a 250-horsepower motor, which increased its maximum speed from nine to twelve knots. A second 150-horsepower Electro-Dynamic motor was also added to increase the speed from six to nine knots submerged. In addition, "The propeller shafts of the *Octopus* are placed at a slight angle to the major-axis of the boat . . . with a view to producing a sufficient upward thrust to counteract the natural tendency of submarines to dive by the head." For all four boats, performance far exceeded the navy's standards. "In the course of their series of trials the four boats cruised at full speed on the surface 1,150 miles, 900 miles in the open sea and including three trips to Cape Cod in heavy weather. Eighty-five submerged runs were made, amounting to 800 miles and 36 torpedoes were fired, all of them successfully with the exception of three.[5] In another open-ocean endurance test, the *Viper* established a sailing radius of 1,000 miles without coming into port or communicating with any other vessel for four days.

Octopus

In diving tests, the boats "reached a depth of 20 feet in 4 minutes and 20 seconds. In the test of the automatic devices for blowing the ballast in order to allow the boat to come to the surface in case of accident, she rose from a depth of 40 feet in 43 seconds. In the twenty-four hours' submergence test in 30 feet of water, she carried down a crew of sixteen men, and came to the surface next day with the men in good condition. The 'Octopus' has been tested as to strength and watertightness by actual submergence to a depth of 200 feet."[6]

With French and British crewmen perishing in disabled boats, the *Octopus* was "built in five compartments, divided by water-tight bulkheads, and doors. Each of these compartments is fitted with a hatch, which can be opened from the inside in case of emergency." Each compartment contained safety jackets for the crew. "If an accident happened, in which the hull of the submarine was pierced, the damaged section would be shut off, and the crew would then have time to don their escape dress, fill the compartment with compressed air, emerge through the hatch, and float to the surface. This method is undoubtedly one of the best forms of safety appliances yet invented."[7] As an additional safety test, at one point, "*Cuttlefish* was submerged 200 feet. She was lowered by a derrick vessel and carried no crew. She developed no reefs or damage to her machinery, although at this depth the water pressure averages 15,000 tons on the whole boat."[8]

Simon Lake's boats continued to communicate with surface vessels or the shore by telephone, even when submerged, but Spear employed an equally effective wireless apparatus for *Octopus*. It consisted of "a pneumatic bell weighing 450 lbs, fitted in the stern and operated by compressed air from a special air reservoir. Two transmitters, or sound receiving tanks, have also been fitted inside the hull, one on the port, and the other on the starboard bow. These tanks may be termed the 'ears' of the submarine, for they catch, and magnify, the sound of submarine signals, coming from the shore, or from a super-marine vessel. The sound is then conveyed by telephone wires to the conning-tower, from which point the pneumatic bell is also operated." During the trials, "it was conclusively demonstrated that wireless messages could be exchanged at a distance of 30 miles."[9]

Even before the four boats were completed, Congress, with the president's wholehearted support, decided to appropriate even more money for submarines. On June 29, 1906, the secretary of the navy was authorized "to contract for or purchase subsurface or submarine torpedo boats to an amount not exceeding $1,000,000, of which sum $500,000 is appropriated."[10]

That sum of money was sufficient to goad Simon Lake to again attempt to break what he was still convinced was Electric Boat's illegally obtained monopoly. Moreover, despite his earlier conviction that Europeans would be more honorable and more clearheaded than their American counterparts, Lake was not having a great deal of success in selling his designs there. He claimed he was forced to forego a sale to the British because the tsar, angry that Britain had a naval treaty with Japan, threatened to cancel a $750,000 contract if Lake "so much as set foot in England." Lake also claimed to have been "gypped by the Germans," because they used his designs—for which he had neglected to obtain German patents—to build Lake boats without paying a royalty. "I am ashamed to look you in the eye," one German aristocrat supposedly said to him, a similar comment to the one he attributed to an American navy officer.[11] He also claimed to have been the one who changed Tirpitz's mind about submarines, an odd assertion since the German submarine program, about to go into high gear, would employed only the Holland porpoise-diving principle. The only successful contract Lake had concluded was for two boats to Austria-Hungary.

Mired in Europe, therefore, Lake found the 1906 appropriation irresistible. As he put it, "Prospects in the United States had again become promising, as they had had a habit of doing for years. Again the forward-looking officers of the United States Navy were trying, as one admiral said to me, 'to break the hold that high finance had on the Navy Department's throat.' The Lake Torpedo Boat Company had a very considerable surplus, and I had acquired quite a decent little fortune of my own through my European ventures. When I learned that there was a chance a sentiment had been aroused in Congress in favor of permitting the Navy's experts to have their own way in the buying of submarines, instead of allowing the congressional clique to continue in control, I determined to return home and try once more."[12]

The $1 million 1906 naval appropriations bill, as had its predecessors, contained a stipulation that the navy secretary could award contracts to the best of competing boats, and this time Lake was determined to have a vessel completed and fully running so that the dishonest officials he had been dealing with would have no excuse to deny a contract to his superior design. But Lake had sold the *Lake X* to Russia, as he had the four similar submarines fabricated at Newport News. Even before the appropriation had become official, while still in Europe, he ordered the shipyard to build another model, the *Simon*

Lake XV, which would become known simply as the *Lake*. At the end of July 1906, he returned to the United States to press for its approval.

When the *Lake* was completed, it sailed unescorted from Newport News to Bridgeport, four hundred miles, a journey Lake claimed was unprecedented although virtually the entire voyage was made on the surface. Still, newspapers across the nation featured a weekend supplement article lauding both the achievement and Lake himself for creating "the most successful submarine ever built."[13]

Lake XV

But for all the effort, Lake could not get the government to move. Charles Bonaparte had replaced Paul Morton as navy secretary after Morton had been tainted by a scandal involving kickbacks on railroad contracts, but Bonaparte was due to leave the post at the end of 1906 and chose to defer any new purchases of submarines until his successor was in place. Just after Christmas 1906, Lake sailed for Europe with his wife, three children, Fred Whitney, and Lake's new "confidential secretary," German-speaking William Scholz, "well known in music circles as an excellent violinist and an active worker in the cause of music," who was "prepared to do considerable playing for the Lake family, who are great patrons of music." He would also serve as a translator. In the party as well was newly hired Robert G. Skerrett, son of a well-placed navy officer.[14] Skerrett billed himself as an engineer although he had no formal training and had been employed by the navy only as a draftsman.*

The new navy secretary, Victor Metcalf, moved more quickly than anyone anticipated and scheduled competitive trials for Narragansett Bay in February. The trials were postponed, but not because the participants had asked for a delay. At the express recommendation of President Roosevelt, a new naval appropriation on March 2,1907, increased the amount for submarines to a staggering $3,000,000 and extended the test period to May 29. The terms were exactly what Simon Lake had repeatedly sought, in fact were almost precisely what Ebenezer Hill had drafted into his 1902 memo. "No part of this appropriation to be expended for any boat that does not in such test prove to be equal, in the judgment of the Secretary of the Navy, to the best boat now owned by the United States or under contract therefor, and no penalties under this limitation shall be imposed by reason of any delay in the delivery of said boat due to the submission or participation in the comparative trials aforesaid."[15]

If there were any remaining Americans whose ardor had not yet been stoked by submarines, a $3,000,000 prize was sufficient to do so. The impending contest between Lake and Electric Boat received as feverish coverage in the press as had the recent news that flying machines had finally been invented.** The *Washington Times*, for example, on Sunday, April 28, 1907, ran a full-page story, "Submerged Navies to Decide Supremacy of the Seas Hereafter. Sunken Silent Stilettos of the Deep to Deal Deadliest Blows in Future Warfare on the Sea." The *New York Times* ran a similar story on the same day, "Rival

---

* While in Europe, Lake announced he would attempt to salvage $6 million in gold bullion from a sunken French ship, the *Lutine*, but the effort never came off.

** The Wright brothers had yet to publicly demonstrate the airplane they flew at Kitty Hawk in December 1903, so the accolades had been reserved for Alberto Santos-Dumont, a Brazilian coffee heir living in Paris who had more or less bounced a large motorized box kite for a quarter mile in a Paris park. The Wrights would fly publicly in 1908 and induce awestruck gasps on both sides of the Atlantic.

Submarines to Race for High Stakes. The Peace of the World an Issue in Test to Take Place at Newport This Week. Conditions Arranged by Navy Department Under Authority of Act of Congress." In the body of the piece, the normally staid *Times* spared no hyperbole. "No sort of contest known to the civilized world, whether of yachts, horses, balloons, athletes, or even Presidential candidates, can equal the test that will be made this week at Newport of the two types of submarines for which Congress has hung up a prize of $3,000,000." The stakes of the race received equal treatment. "The result of the test will make for the peace of the whole world . . . it is hardly necessary to say that the contest, which has been twice made the subject of legislation by Congress and which has been under consideration for two years past, will be watched by the most expert military scientists of Europe and this continent, and the victor will be the hero of secret discussions in all the Chancelleries of Europe and the Orient."[16] The actual competition standards would be exhaustive, covering speed, maneuverability, stability, firing capability, and endurance, and last for four weeks.

In these trials, Simon Lake would finally be granted the head-to-head competition he had so desperately sought since he first submitted his plans in 1893. Whatever bluster, outrage, exaggerations, and even misstatements he had issued over the years, there is not a scintilla of doubt that he was absolutely positive he had built the better boat. And in May 1907, not unlike the prizefighter finally getting a shot at the title after being ducked repeatedly by the champion, he was going to have the chance to prove it.

Then Lake lost.

In a report dated May 30, 1907, the trial board, which consisted of one constructer and three line officers, "reported unanimously in favor of the Octopus type of boat," and on June 22 the report was accepted unanimously by the board on construction, staffed by four admirals, after which it was accepted by Admiral Dewey and Secretary Metcalf.

It was not that the *Lake* performed badly—the *Octopus* was simply better. It was distinctly faster both on the surface and submerged—where it traveled at a record eleven knots—dove more quickly and with better control, maneuvered more easily, had superior longitudinal stability, demonstrated endurance and ability to operate at significant depth, remained submerged for twenty-four hours, was efficient in operation, and, although there were a couple of false starts, could fire torpedoes quickly and accurately while submerged. The *Octopus* "broke all American diving records," at one point becoming completely submerged in twenty-three seconds and in another going at full throttle from the surface to even keel at twenty feet in less than four minutes.[17] With fog hanging over the bay, the *Octopus* dove to avoid a line of barges and passed under them, an unplanned demonstration of practicability.

Lake did set a depth record of 136 feet, remain submerged for twenty-four hours and successfully launched a torpedo, but was considered by the board members, none of whom were ever accused of being under the "influence" of Electric Boat, to be flawed and its even-keel submergence cumbersome. At one point, its tests had to be suspended because of a leak in a torpedo tube, and a few days after that *Lake* was dry-docked for one week to make modifications to the conning tower.

One section of the board's report read, "1. That the type of submarine boat as represented by the 'Lake' is, in the opinion of the board, inferior to the type as represented by the 'Octopus.' 2. The closed superstructure of the 'Lake,' with the large flat deck which is fitted to carry water ballast, and to contain fuel tanks and air flasks, which is an essential feature of the Lake boat presented to us for trial, is inferior to the arrangement on board the 'Octopus' for the same purposes, and also, in the opinion of the Board, is detrimental to the proper control of the boat. 3. The hydroplanes, also an essential feature of the Lake boat presented to us for trial were incapable of submerging the boat on an even keel. They are, therefore, regarded as an objectionable encumbrance."[18]

With the unequivocal decision by the board and with the endorsement of the admirals, Metcalf was prepared to grant contracts exclusively to Electric Boat to build eight *Octopus* class submarines for the navy. Before he could do so, however, he received a visit from John C. Lake, a vice president of the Lake Torpedo Boat Company, and Simon Lake's father.

The elder Lake had moved on from letter writing to running the company as his son's surrogate while Simon Lake tried to make sales in Europe. He was every bit as pugnacious and as aggrieved as his son and was at least as determined to break the monopoly on American submarines that both men had no doubt was achieved through dishonesty. The categorical defeat of his son's design in the Newport trials deterred him in this aim not one bit.

To press his case, John Lake had engaged John Mellen Thurston, who had served one term as a Republican senator from Nebraska but declined to run for reelection, choosing the far more lucrative occupation of Washington lawyer in its stead. To press the Lake Company's interests in Congress, Lake and Thurston had recruited George Lilley, a Connecticut congressman-at-large, to take the place of Ebenezer Hill, who both men considered ineffective.

Thurston got wind of the eight-vessel Electric Boat submarine award before it was publicly announced, prompting John Lake's emergency meeting with Victor Metcalf in mid-June. According to Lake, the secretary said. "Mr. Lake, I am very sorry to be compelled to say that I have to award the whole contract to the Electric Boat Company under the wording of the act and the decision of the board, and so forth." Lake added that Metcalf, "also said that he was very sorry, because he had hoped to get competition, to get another boat in, and hoped he could award a contract, but under the wording of the law as interpreted he could not. . . . He wanted competition in the Navy, and he wanted to get a competing boat in the Navy, and he hoped very much that he could award us a contract."[19]

Metcalf was also purported to say that many in the navy wanted the Lake Company to be awarded a contract, although, according to Lake, no names were mentioned. The secretary then added, "Mr. Lake, if you think that that law is susceptible of any other interpretation, I feel disposed to give you the advantage of it, and I have no objection to referring the matter to the Attorney-General for his decision in regard to this question in the law." Lake said that he replied, "We appreciated it very much if he would do that, and he consented to do it." At no time, Lake insisted, did he suggest that the matter be referred to the attorney general, that it was Metcalf's suggestion entirely.

Not surprisingly Metcalf's recollection of the exchange differed and included a more than vague suggestion by John Lake that his company would take legal action if the award was not split between the two companies. Whatever the correct rendition, Metcalf shuffled the question over to Charles Bonaparte, now attorney general. Bonaparte might well have been none too pleased to be drawn back into submarine politics, having gratefully washed his hands of them only six months earlier when he left the Navy Department. Although both sides submitted briefs, the solution was obvious. Bonaparte issued an opinion in August that the law indeed allowed for the award to be split, thus throwing the question back to Metcalf and excusing himself from further involvement, almost certainly in the hope that submarines would not pass his desk again.

Only one day after Bonaparte's decision was published, Congressman Lilley sent Metcalf an official letter. Although Lilley as a member of the naval affairs committee had voted for both the 1906 and 1907 appropriations, and had voiced no objection when the board of inspection pronounced the *Octopus* the clear winner in the sea trials, he now decided that the results should be at least partially ignored. In his letter, Lilley decried the evils of monopoly—an argument designed for appeal in the trust-busting Roosevelt administration—and added, "I sincerely hope that before awarding the contract you will examine not only the reports of sea-going tests, but also the plans and specifications submitted by the Lake Company, and that you will see your way clear to divide the business."[20]

Electric Boat of course contended that as the clear winner of the competition with a design that was almost universally judged superior, they should receive the entire award. The rules should not be changed after the game had ended. When Metcalf vacillated, Lilley followed with another letter in September in which he became more strident, all but accusing Representative Roberts and perhaps others of complicity, and implying Metcalf could potentially be swept with the same brush. "Among the well-meaning Members of Congress the Lake people have more friends because they have never employed the methods of the Holland type people. It is well known that the company Mr. Roberts appears to represent is doing more to-day in the employment of questionable methods to intimidate Members of Congress and the Naval Committee than all other corporations in the United States."

No one, including Metcalf, really wanted a Lake boat in the submarine fleet, but a protracted legal, publicity, and lobbying battle was even less appealing. But the navy secretary found the perfect solution. On September 24, 1907, one day after Lilley's letter was delivered, the *New York Times* reported, "Secretary Metcalf has concluded not to shoulder the responsibility of making the awards for the submarine boats authorized by Congress at the last session and will refer the matter to the President for decision."[21]

CHAPTER 28
SUICIDE SQUEEZE

B ut three weeks later, deciding which company should receive sub-marine contracts would be the last thing on Theodore Roosevelt's mind.

Although through much of 1907, rampant speculation had provided some support for stock prices, the economy had been steadily weakening. On October 15, it collapsed.

The precise underpinning of the crash has been debated for a century. The 1906 earthquake in San Francisco seems to have contributed by causing financial reserves to flow out of the New York banking centers to aid in reconstruction on the West Coast. The time of year also seemed to play a role, as each autumn, withdrawals to purchase agricultural harvests pressured banks' liquidity. When banks were forced to raise interest rates to replace lost capital, stock prices declined due to a corresponding decrease in equity investment. In 1907, with freight rates under the jurisdiction of the Interstate Commerce Commission, railroad stocks, the dot-coms of their day, were particularly hard hit.

Into this fragile environment entered two brothers, Otto and Augustus Heinze, owners of what they thought was the controlling interest in the United Copper Company, and the "Ice King," Charles W. Morse, among the most brazen and joyously dishonest financiers in American history. At Morse's instigation, the Heinze brothers intended to precipitate a short squeeze on the company's stock and then corner the copper market.*

Morse was an experienced manipulator—in 1900, he had cornered the ice market. Ice was then a vital product, acquired mostly from river water and stored underground. Once he had control, he proceeded to price-gouge families and businesses that had no other means of refrigeration. He doubled the price of ice sold to consumers and threatened further increases when the whether turned warmer. "This 100 per cent tax upon a commodity that is a necessity to all the people of this city has aroused the bitterest feeling in the community," wrote the *New York Times*.[1] Morse's ice-pricing scheme ultimately aborted amid scandalous revelations of bribery and political favors stretching all the way to City Hall, none of which diminished his position in polite society. In 1901, his box-mate at the opera was William Vanderbilt.

Morse continued to make provocative headlines—his marriage to an Atlanta socialite was annulled in 1904 when it was discovered she had not bothered to properly divorce her first husband. But he also continued to thrive. By 1906, among his other holdings, Morse served on the board of more than fifty banks, and was majority owner of eighty-one steamships.

One of the banks Morse chose to finance the Heinze brothers raid on the copper market was the Knickerbocker Trust Company, the third largest trust in New York. The president of the Knickerbocker was Charles T. Barney, who had achieved great success in finance with

---

* In a short squeeze, holders of a security will force the price up by hoarding a disproportionate percentage of a company's stock, strangling supply, thus obligating holders of short positions to buy back their appreciating shares at an ever-larger loss. Since most short positions are bought on margin or with borrowed money, the pressure to cut losses and buy back shares is intense. This forces the price still higher until, with the shorts out, the holders of the security can sell at an enormous profit. But the ploy only works if supply of the security has been greatly restricted.

the aid of his brother-in-law, former navy secretary William Collins Whitney. Morse had done business with Barney in the past and always found him a willing accomplice.

But the scheme backfired. The Heinze brothers had grossly underestimated the liquidity of United Copper stock. Instead of soaring, the price plunged, taking outstanding loans with their own bank, and eventually Knickerbocker Trust along with it. With no Federal Reserve Bank to control the ensuing panic, there were runs on banks everywhere and failures cascaded through the financial system.* The following month, on November 14, Charles Barney killed himself.

The Panic of 1907, as it was quickly dubbed, lasted only three weeks. The nation was saved when J. P. Morgan, with the support and acquiescence of President Roosevelt—although the two men loathed each other—stepped in and pumped liquidity into the system. But the aftereffects lasted for months. By mid-1908, there had been an 11 percent decline in gross national product, industrial production had dropped by 16 percent, and unemployment would eventually almost double.

Although the nation suffered greatly, the effects were not felt evenly. The impact was most acute on stockholders, at that time predominantly upper income individuals and families. And in a nation still largely agrarian, people who grew their own food, sewed their own clothes, and canned their own preserves were more equipped to

---

* One of the banks that failed was the National Bank of North America, in which Morse held controlling interest. Morse was arrested the following February as he stepped off the gangplank of a luxury ocean liner returning from Europe. He was charged with illegal manipulation, selling essentially worthless American Ice stock to the bank for hundreds of thousands of dollars, as well as obtaining overdrafts of more than $200,000 "at the height of the panic," immediately before he was forced to liquidate his interest. Morse was convicted, but got the last laugh. After exhausting his appeals, he finally went to prison in 1910, but two years later contracted a mysterious illness that a team of army doctors agreed would soon kill him. He was pardoned by President William Howard Taft and sailed to Germany for treatment. He recovered miraculously, and later revealed he had been drinking soapsuds and a chemical brew to precipitate his symptoms. Again a free man, Morse returned to New York and the shipping business, which he conducted no more scrupulously than before. He was ultimately indicted for mail fraud and war profiteering, among other charges, but never spent another day in prison. He died peacefully in 1933 at age seventy-seven, in Bath, Maine, the town in which was born.

weather the storm. Consequently, the market crisis was felt disproportionately by city dwellers and the wealthy.

Isaac Rice was one of them. The value of Rice's holdings plummeted,
so much so that in December 1907, he sold his beloved Villa Julia for
$500,000, less than half of what it had been worth six months before,
and moved his family to an apartment in the Ansonia Hotel. To the
press he said that, as he was spending a great deal of time in Europe,
he had no need for such a sprawling mansion, but to his fellow busi-
nessmen, many of whom despised him, it seemed at last that Rice
might be easy pickings. He was rumored to have been forced to sell a
good deal of his holdings at a severe loss.

The one holding Rice was determined not to liquidate or even dilute,
was Electric Boat. He was convinced that submarines would become
a necessity for any nation that wished to present itself as a serious sea
power. And while the profits he had garnered from his sales to the
American navy were nowhere near what his detractors had implied,
continued contracts to build submarines could provide a bridge until
he had reacquired the wherewithal to rebuild his fortune—unless of
course the Lake Company succeeded in supplanting Electric Boat as
the government's primary contractor.

That was precisely what Simon Lake, his father, and their associates,
sensing opportunity, were determined to do. They identified Victor
Metcalf as the weak link and concentrated their efforts on him.

With Roosevelt otherwise occupied, Metcalf was again responsible
for allocating the $3,000,000 appropriation. The Lake Company
wanted half, and they were convinced they could bully Metcalf into
acquiescence. In addition to continuing to bombard the navy secretary with entreaties and threats, they attempted to engage Congress
to support splitting the appropriation. This Thurston did by writing
a bill, which another Connecticut congressman, Nehemiah Sperry,
introduced, stipulating that the "appropriation for submarines be
expended in a way that would this year again admit the Lake Company to competition," and then writing a long letter to Chairman Foss
explaining why it was in the best interests of the nation to divide the
award evenly. Foss had been an ally in the past, although after the
Lessler affair, his support could no longer be taken for granted.[2]

The effort met with some success as, in early February 1908, likely just to avoid further contention, Metcalf approved a contract with the Lake Company for a single submarine, reducing the number to be purchased from Electric Boat from eight to seven. Metcalf did include a rankling condition—Lake would have to design and build the boat at solely his expense, and the navy would only buy it if it met certain standards in sea trials. If Secretary Metcalf thought that one-eighth of the pie—for which they might not even be paid—would satisfy the Lake forces, he was mistaken. With the monopoly broken, and Rice seemingly unable to protect his interests, the Lakes and Thurston decided that rather than half, they should have it all. To squeeze Rice out, they would move from veiled intimations that Electric Boat had obtained their contracts through bribery to open accusations. For their wedge, they would use the 1908 appropriations bill, still under consideration in Congress.

The 1907 annual report from the navy, the draft of which was drawn up before the October crash, had recommended the addition of four battleships to the fleet as well as four submarines. In January 1908, however, with the economy in a tailspin, the naval affairs committee seemed prepared to reduce the number of battleships to two, but to add appropriations for four additional submarines. Battleships were extremely expensive, almost $10 million each, and so, with the Treasury under stress, the decision, which would save $17 million, seemed to make sense. In addition, the president was said to favor eight submarines, although he was insistent on the four battleships as well. The proposed legislation did not mandate splitting the submarine appropriation, although once more, the navy secretary would have discretion over choosing the vendor or vendors.

On February 10, the committee approved the proposed changes, after a bill introduced by Nehemiah Sperry to award submarine contracts based only on low bids was defeated. In the next few days, newspaper articles began to appear implying that Electric Boat had used chicanery to halve the battleship appropriation and then in securing the exclusive right to contract for the four additional submarines.[3] Most of the articles did not specifically mention bribery, but an anonymous letter was also sent to the editor of the *Detroit Free Press* suggesting that a Michigan House and naval affairs committee member, George Loud, had been blackmailed by Electric Boat. "A Congressman does not want to get what happened to Lessler, but here is a big story tip for what it is worth. The submarine people brought out a candidate, a prominent lawyer, against Loud. He withdrew upon agreement of Loud to vote for submarines."[4]

The following day, the *New York Herald* and the *Washington Post* also received anonymous communications, these asserting that a panel of experts had unanimously agreed that $1,476,296.60 paid to Electric Boat for submarines was based on egregiously and fraudulently inflated cost estimates. Two days after that, the *Free Press* received a second communication. "Loud voted for this $1,476,296.60 graft in the Naval Committee. There is a story in circulation that the Holland people got a prominent attorney to become a candidate against Loud last time; that Loud finally agreed to vote for the submarines upon deal that the attorney withdraw. The attorney withdrew. Subscribe for the *New York Herald* and the *Washington Post*. Loud can be defeated on this proposition alone by you. Watch Congressional Record. Have your local papers play up proposition. Have them write Loud for explanation and whether the withdrawal story is true." A copy of the communication was also sent to Frank Edinborough, a Michigan state senator who had previously announced that he would contest Loud's seat in the next election.

Only days later, Lilley filed a resolution: "That a special committee of five Members of the House be appointed by the Speaker to investigate the conduct of the Electric Boat Company of New Jersey and their predecessors, the Holland Boat Company, respecting the methods employed by said companies in connection with past and proposed legislation before Congress." His reasons for requesting the investigation, which he stated for the record, were incendiary. "This Electric Boat Company has been a stench in the nostrils of the country for years, and, in my opinion, it has done more to corrupt legislation than all the other corporations on earth. I think the membership of this House is of the very highest quality, and that they are the best men, usually, from the districts from which they come; but with a flock of 383 here, it would be strange if there were not some sheep in it that had the foot-rot or scabies."

Geo.L.Lilley

George Lilley

Lilley was quite deft in avoiding specific charges against either Electric Boat or any specific member of Congress, including George Loud. But he made no secret that he expected to chair the investigative committee, from which he would wield full subpoena power, hire lawyers, and conduct interrogations as he saw fit. After he filed his resolution, he gave a series of interviews to the press. To the *New York Tribune*, he said, "I believe it is time for an investigation into their methods, so that the people of the United States may know and see for themselves how this company, maker of submarine boats, is enabled to usurp the power of the President, the Secretary of the Navy, and the Naval Board, and substitute a naval program of their own."

Lilley then laid out what those methods were, once more avoiding any explicit charges. "There are no new tricks in the way of lobby work and influencing members that the Electric Boat Company is not adept in. . . . Attorneys have been hired by these people, who have usually been influential politicians from the home districts of members of the committee, and candidates have been brought into the field to contest the nomination of members who have opposed their policies. They have gone so far as to find out what new members of the House had applied for positions on the Naval Affairs Committee and they have been assumed to have influence in securing the assignment to members of that committee. It has also been said that they have contributed to individual and party campaign funds."[5]

Other members of the naval affairs committee, even previously sympathetic ones, were none too pleased at Lilley's implication that they might have been either actively or tacitly bought. In other interviews, Lilley accused unnamed press reporters of taking bribes and noted that the *Detroit Free Press* had reported that George Loud had accepted a bribe. On February 25, the House rules committee summoned him and, although they did not place him under oath, demanded specifics. Lilley responded by reading a carefully worded prepared statement in which he retracted the charges against reporters, explaining they had been based on bits of gossip. But he maintained, again without details, that he had firsthand knowledge that Electric Boat was corrupt. Lilley was not a lawyer, so when he was asked who had prepared such a legal-sounding statement, he assured the committee that he had done so himself.

With Lilley's accusations receiving widespread coverage across the nation, the rules committee on March 6 appointed a five-man committee to determine whether Electric Boat "has been engaged in efforts to exert corrupting influence on certain members of Congress in their legislative capacities, and have in fact exerted such corrupting influence." The committee would of course have full subpoena powers, just as Lilley had requested.

The only problem for Congressman Lilley was that he would not be the one exercising those powers. He was not, as he assumed, appointed to chair the committee. In fact, he was not on the committee at all. Even worse for the congressman, the committee's first act was to demand that he turn over "every fact in his possession on which his accusations and suspicions were founded, especially as he had asserted before the Committee on Rules that he was 'not talking hearsay.'"[6]

The Lilley Committee

This was not how Lilley had envisioned the investigation being conducted. He responded by declining to testify, stating his intention to obtain counsel, and complaining that he was being "shadowed by detectives." He did give the committee a list of questions that, as committee chairman, he had intended to put to the witnesses he summoned. Lilley told his colleagues that he had prepared the questions personally, without aid of counsel.

A few days later, Lilley appeared before the committee once more, this time with two lawyers at his side. He refused to either supply materials or answer questions as to specifics, merely restating that he had made no charges against any member of the House. Committee members wondered how Electric Boat could have perpetrated the corrupt practices and gained favorable votes without the knowledge and acquiescence of sitting congressmen, but Lilley refused to elaborate on his charges. Lilley was also informed "that the men whom Mr. Lilley's suspicions had transformed into detectives hired to watch his office were raw recruits of the new police force of the office building, who were forced, while waiting for their uniforms, to patrol the corridors in plain clothes."[7]

On the same day that George Lilley arrived with his lawyers, Robert G. Skerrett, who had accompanied the Lake family to Europe, handed in an article to *Scientific American* and *Harper's Weekly*, echoing Lilley's charges and "extolling the merits of the Lake type of boat." Skerrett did not identify himself as an employee of the Lake Company, which he was, but did imply that he was an engineer with experience in submarine design, which he was not. *Scientific American* refused to publish the piece as an article but agreed to do so as a letter to the editor. They had to split it and run it in two parts, in succeeding weeks, beginning March 21. Before each segment, the editors made it a point to disclaim responsibility for the content. *Harper's* published the piece in full, but not until April 4.

Like Lilley, Skerrett presented no specifics but relied on innuendo. "The departure of the battleship fleet has left the Atlantic seaboard sorely crippled so far as the mobile defense of heavy fighting ships is concerned. Should circumstances develop threatening hostilities, the cities of the eastern coast could readily be laid under tribute or reduced to ashes by any one of the principal foreign powers. This fact has called forth earnest protest and has given occasion for a determined move to effect legislation providing for a large number of submarine boats in lieu of the regular departmental recommendation for four first-class battleships and only four submarine vessels."

But Skerrett was not really writing to save the battleship appropriation. "Setting aside the unwisdom of substituting submarines for battleships, the present effort to secure an increased provision for underwater craft could well be justified if the bill had not been drawn in a restrictive manner for the promotion of a single type of boat. This is not in keeping with technical advance, nor does it make for the nation's security viewed in the light of the state of the art in its widest developments."

His only motive, he noted, was patriotism. "The taxpayers of the country have a right to know if this substantial bounty of nearly five millions of dollars has brought a corresponding measure of national security against the day of possible need. The public has a right to know if all the sources of native skill have been drawn upon in this developmental work pursued by the government. And the people have a right to ask, 'Have we secured the best to be had for the prices paid?' It has been shown by competent authorities in their testimony before congressional committees that the prices paid for the submarines now in the United States navy were out of all reason *unless the cost of development had been borne by the builders*."[8]

From there, Skerrett presented a long and detailed history of submarine procurement filled with distortions, half-truths, and outright fabrications. Each of Simon Lake's discredited allegations was put forth as accepted fact. *Scientific American* was the preeminent journal of its kind in the United States, and the letter, for anyone not familiar with the actual history of submarine procurement, was bound to prompt outrage.

The committee hearings lasted more than six weeks. Dozens of witnesses were called to testify, virtually every person either directly or peripherally involved with either company, Congress, or in the press. The witnesses included George Lilley, Simon Lake, John C. Lake, Fred Whitney, George Loud, John Mellen Thurston, E. B. Frost, Lawrence Spear, Charles Creecy, and Isaac Rice. Robert G. Skerrett was questioned for two days as to the source of the material he published in his *Scientific American* piece. The committee apparently felt they were under scrutiny because the questioning of each witness, regardless of which side they favored, was scrupulous and aggressive. Every one of the sixteen charges that the committee had identified from George Lilley, be they in his resolution or public statements, was probed fastidiously. Each question that Lilley had submitted was put to the witnesses that he had identified as targets of his charges.

When the committee ceased proceedings at the end of April, the members and staff retired for almost two weeks to produce their report. It was submitted on May 12, 1908, and released publicly one week later. No one would accuse the members of being slipshod—the full record ran to almost two thousand pages. Everyone who had followed the hearings expected the committee's findings to be ruination of one company and the vindication of the other. The headlines made it clear which was which.

"Charges of Corruption Without Foundation," read the lead on page one of the *Washington Times*.[9]

Lake's plan had backfired. George Lilley and the Lake forces were caught in so many lies that the congressman was fortunate not to be expelled, and Thurston, Fred Whitney, and even the Lakes, father and son, not indicted. Of the twenty-three conclusions of the committee, in at least ten of them Lilley is said to have acted "in bad faith," "in contempt of the House," or had "violated his obligation as a member of the House." Another stated, "Mr. Lilley allowed himself to be used as an instrument of the Lake Torpedo Boat Company in its rivalry and attack upon a competing company," and yet another: "That Mr. Lilley had no information to justify the charges made before the Committee on Rules."[10]

In fact, the only evidence that the committee found of wrongful behavior was by George Lilley and Lake Company associates. Not only had Simon Lake met personally with George Lilley in a New Haven hotel room on February 14, six days before Lilley submitted his resolution—something both men had initially denied—but the resolution itself, Lilley's prepared response to the rules committee on February 25, and the list of questions that were to be asked to hostile witnesses were drawn up by John Thurston, and then transmitted verbatim by Congressman Lilley, who claimed the language was his own. Both the anonymous letters to the *Detroit Free Press* and the communication on cost overruns sent to the *New York Tribune* and the *Washington Post* had been written by Fred Whitney, and the $1,476,296.60 figure was totally fictitious, concocted by "an agent of the Lake Torpedo Boat Company."

The committee found not a scintilla of evidence to support any of Lilley's sixteen charges and concluded all were either total fabrications or distortions of behavior that was neither illegal nor unethical. The charge that Electric Boat had made campaign contributions to any of the naval affairs committee members who voted in their favor was false, as was the charge that reporters had been bribed. George Loud was totally exonerated. Robert Skerrett was found to have knowingly published material in his article that was fallacious, and no one in authority, save Admirals Melville and O'Neil, believed the Holland design inferior to Lake's. Quite the contrary.

The press coverage was eviscerating. *The New York Times* headline was "House Flays Lilley For Boat Scandal: [Congressman John Sharp]

Williams Denounces Representative as Guilty of Treason and Advocates His Expulsion." The piece began, "When the select committee appointed to investigate the submarine scandal got through with its report to-day nothing was left of Representative George L. Lilley of Connecticut, author of the charges, except his membership in the House."[11]

George Lilley was not expelled, however, although he became something of a pariah among his fellow House members. He did not seek reelection in November 1908, choosing instead to run for governor of Connecticut, the one place in America where the committee's report was considered an unfair attack on an honorable public servant. Lilley won. His triumph was brief, however, as on April 21, 1909, only three months after he had been sworn in, suffering from "nervous exhaustion," George Lilley died of "toxi-semia." He was forty-nine years old and was given a state funeral.

CHAPTER 29

GOING DEEP

The great irony for Simon Lake was that had he not once again overplayed his hand, he might well have succeeded in exposing at least borderline corruption. Electric Boat, while perhaps not violating the letter of the law, was pushing hard against its spirit, doing everything in its power to influence Congress. "Electric Boat's political aggressiveness and near-monopoly won the company more enemies than friends in the Navy. By pushing its product into congressional appropriations legislation, it essentially assumed the role of both market leader and naval policymaker. According to Naval Constructor and later Vice Admiral Emory S. Land, 'If you look up history, you'll find that the Navy Department frequently didn't ask for submarines, but they were put in the bill anyway, due to political pressure from [Electric Boat].'"[1]

As a result, even after public discreditation, Simon Lake was able to defy both odds and logic and survive. For another fifteen years, he would continue to alternate brilliant innovation, bluster, incredible perseverance, and self-defeating stubbornness, and thereby remain tantalizingly close to achieving his life's aim—to be the preeminent submarine designer in the world—but never quite get there.

Lake's maddeningly flawed amalgam of character traits was epitomized in his first navy submarine, the one built to fulfill the contract he signed just before he unleashed George Lilley. Called the *Seal*, it was 161 feet long, only 13 across, and built with wheels, detachable keel, air lock, and planes amidships. For surface running, Lake employed twin screws, each powered by two 300-horsepower gasoline engines placed in tandem on the driveshaft, and he used 375-horsepower electric motors for running submerged. In addition to bow torpedo tubes, Lake had mounted four external tubes in the superstructure, where they could be swiveled and aimed at a variety of angles, much as could a deck gun. The boat was sleek and fast, initially exceeding both the navy's surface and submerged speed specifications, and would set a depth record by diving 256 feet.

Simon Lake's Seal

Lake was not shy in extolling the boat's virtues. "The *Seal* did all that I claimed for it and more. . . . The day it was launched it was the best undersea boat that had ever been built or that had ever been proposed for our Navy."[2]

He omitted to note, however, that the *Seal* also was not delivered until October 1911, two and a half years late, was "a notoriously slow diver," and developed leaks in both the superstructure and torpedo tubes.[3] The tandem engines continued to cause breakdowns and so one of the motors on each shaft was eventually removed, which slowed the boat to where it could only attain minimal speed required for acceptance. Its endurance could never meet the navy's standard, and it only barely made it through sea trials. Even then, the lack of speed and quickness in submerging would limit the boat to harbor defense or coastal patrols. So uncertain was the navy of the *Seal*'s utility that Lake was not paid until in 1916.

Before the Lilley debacle was off the front page, when both he and his surrogates, both in and out of Congress were viewed as liars or worse, Lake again took up railing over the evils of monopoly and pressing the case for the Lake submarine in Washington. As a result, even with the delays in delivering the *Seal*, the navy ordered an additional submarine from the Lake Company in 1909 and one more in 1910. They would be called the *Tuna* and the *Turbot*, and be built from the same design as the *Seal*, except for the elimination of the wheels and the air lock. But Lake only made the changes to reduce costs, not because he had come to realize his design needed to be modified. The three boats would be called "G-class" submarines, and their reception by the admirals was inauspicious.

In 1915, "Yates Stirling Jr., senior aide on the staff of Commander, Submarine Flotilla, Atlantic Fleet, inspected the boat and concluded the G-class boats were crude and inefficient in comparison to current designs. Deeming 'their military value . . . negligible' he urged that a field of scientific or experimental use be found for them."[4] Each of the three boats would be decommissioned after only six years in service.

Lake was undaunted, ignoring the flaws and refusing to accept that some of his pet ideas, such as even-keel submergence, were impractical in a warship.[*] In fact, he would later insist that submarines built by for-eign navies, especially Germany, were based on his design principles.

---

[*] Others, of course, like the ability to send out a diver, would become standard as subma-rines increased in sophistication.

In 1916, when the trans-Atlantic cargo submarine *Deutschland* docked in Baltimore, he swore to prove it.

Lake had been advocating submarines for transporting cargo almost from the time he entered the field. In 1909, at a dinner in Berlin, he tried to convince Alfred Lohmann, the director of the North German Lloyd shipping line, to join in a venture to produce such a vessel. According to Lake, the conversation was quite detailed, but Lohmann declined. Soon after the war began, however, with German merchant shipping stifled by a British blockade, Lohmann approached the Krupp Company, which then built him such a vessel, 213 feet long, at its shipyard in Kiel. The *Deutschland*, as it was named, sailed to Baltimore with a cargo of precious stones and dyestuffs, intending to return with nickel, tin, and rubber. When it arrived in the United States, Simon Lake was waiting.

He informed the captain that the *Deutschland* had infringed a number of Lake patents and threatened to have the vessel seized. Lake later claimed that the captain talked him out of it by imploring Lake to allow the boat to return to Germany with its intended cargo of food, blankets, medicine, and other necessities needed by the German people. On humanitarian grounds, Lake agreed. Only afterward, he said, did he find out that the *Deutschland* was carrying war materials.

How successful Lake would have been if he had brought suit is questionable. While the *Deutschland* may well have infringed on some of his minor patents, in his conviction that German submarines had stolen his basic ideas, Simon Lake was again incorrect. The principles under which the *Deutschland* had been designed—as well as the *U-9* and every other U-boat—were John Holland's.*

But likely the actual reason Lake withdrew his claim on the *Deutschland* was that North German Lloyd promised to finance the construction of Lake cargo submarines in the United States. He certainly would have welcomed the influx of funds. By the time the *Deutschland* docked, the Lake Company had been in and out of bankruptcy. To build the *Turbot*, he had terminated his contract with Newport News

---

*   Thus the *U-9* had finally succeeded in achieving what Holland had set out to do almost fifty years earlier—sink British warships.

and opened his own shipyard in Bridgeport. But in November 1913, Lake, yet to receive any payment from the government, found himself overextended. With the *Turbot* still under construction, he was forced to declare his company insolvent. The boat was completed in New York. When the war began, he emerged from bankruptcy, but was still financially fragile. In any event, the *Deutschland* made one only more voyage to the United States, the last ever by a cargo submarine. The joint venture was never initiated.

War in Europe eventually brought prosperity to just about every arms manufacturer, however, even those in America whose products were of dubious worth in battle. Before hostilities actually began, Congress put through an aggressive naval program, which included an expansion of its submarine fleet. Lake was awarded contracts for three new boats—Electric Boat received more than a dozen—all for harbor defense, one of which he built at his shipyard, the other two subcontracted to a shipbuilder in California. All were completed and commissioned successfully by early 1918.

When the United States entered the war in 1917, submarine procurement became fervent. At one point in 1919, ninety-six boats were under construction. Although by that time, the navy had established its own construction facility at Portsmouth, New Hampshire, both Lake and Electric Boat were called on to shoulder an unprecedented burden of construction. When the war ended, though, the nation sharply cut back and Lake was hit particularly hard. Unlike Electric Boat, which had diversified sufficiently to survive a downturn in one product line, Lake's entire focus remained submarines, and the survival of his business depended on largesse from the government. That would prove difficult to come by.

"By April of 1920, it became evident that the Navy was more interested in developing the [Portsmouth Navy Yard] into a shipyard on par with [Electric Boat] than in supporting Lake. The latter had received only a handful of submarine contracts, and after the First World War, no others seemed forthcoming. On behalf of his Bridgeport constituents, Senator Frank Brandegee, Republican from Connecticut, appealed to the secretary of the navy. He questioned the wisdom and necessity of allowing the highly specialized workers at Lake's Bridgeport facility to lose their jobs as a result of . . . awarding the few available post-war submarine contracts to the Electric Boat Company and the Portsmouth Navy Yard. Unfortunately for Lake, its performance did not give the Navy enough reason to reconsider its reliance on Electric Boat. . . . Lake's boats exhibited poor diving qualities, and the company had great difficulty keeping submarine construction on schedule."[5]

Although Lake pleaded with the government to provide him the wherewithal to remain viable and some senior naval officials backed him because they found "the prospect of a monopoly in submarine work by the Electric Boat Company appalling," by 1924, Simon Lake was again forced to leave the attack submarine business, this time for good.

Lake, his mind always restless, turned to other pursuits. He designed and built prefabricated housing, and proposed a system of prefabricated concrete pipes. Both ideas showed promise but ultimately failed. In 1931, he refurbished a submarine he had built twenty years earlier, renamed it *Nautilus*, and set sail in an attempt to reach the North Pole. Although mechanical problems cut short the attempt, the *Nautilus* became the first submarine to sail under Arctic ice. Two years later, he borrowed money to mount a treasure-hunting expedition for a 1780 British gold shipment lost off New York Harbor. In 1936, reports that he had found the wreck turned out to be incorrect. All of these false starts sapped Lake's personal resources. At one point, he was forced to auction off personal possessions in order to have money to live on.

Simon Lake lived modestly for another decade, occasionally, after the start of World War II, sending letters to the navy on submarine strategy and coastal defense. He died of a heart attack on June 23, 1945, after the war in Europe had ended and just weeks before an atomic bomb would level Hiroshima. He left behind a legacy of creative invention, dogged determination, and failed promise. He also left behind a wealth of books and monographs that extolled the virtues of submarine technology, mostly his own, and what he saw as the tragic plight of the innovator. In 1935, he wrote:

All my life I have been an inventor. I have learned to accept the fact that a new idea which in any way departs from the routine of life will be repelled by the public. This is no doubt a phase of the protective machinery of society. The too ready acceptance of new things would make society even more light-minded and hair-brained [sic] than it now is. But a man with a new idea should not be regarded as a public enemy. He should be granted a hearing, and if his invention is worthwhile he should be protected in its possession and helped in its development. As matters stand today a greenhorn inventor may find himself working on some scheme that has been public property for half a century. If he has really struck into new territory he may fall into the hands of a shyster lawyer, who thinks only of the money he can wring out of the poor devil. If he escapes these early perils, a promoter may get hold of him and either waste his money or steal his invention. If he dodges the promoter and tries to interest possible backers on his own, he will be turned back by cigarette-yellowed office-boys and frozen by blonde transparencies.[6]

Isaac Rice, who would have rated a category all his own in Lake's denunciation, did indeed rebuild his fortune. In truth, despite the sale of Villa Julia, it is unclear if he ever lost it. He had either retained a substantially larger share of his holdings than rumors had indicated, or he quickly bought back when the market bottomed. In any case, his estate would include stock in many of the companies in which he had held shares before the Panic of 1907 hit and be of sufficient value for his wife Julia to donate, among many other endowments, $1,000,000 for the Isaac L. Rice Convalescent Hospital in Westchester County, New York, and an additional $1,000,000 to New York City to build an Isaac L. Rice athletic complex and stadium with seating for five thousand in Pelham Bay Park. Even during the years immediately after his supposed losses, Rice himself was frequently cited for generous contributions to educational institutions, chess societies, and civic betterment.

Nor did the Rices live frugally. They shuttled back and forth to Europe with first-class accommodations and were regularly featured in society columns. And, although the Rice apartments in the Ansonia might not have been up to Villa Julia standards, they were large enough to include a private ballroom in which the Rices entertained lavishly, hosting luminaries in the chess and social worlds.

This is not to say that Rice's net worth was unaffected by the plunge in the stock market in October 1907. Even Pierpont Morgan lost a great deal of money, at least on paper. But those who had the fortitude to resist selling at a deep discount were rewarded when the stock market rebounded significantly in the latter half of 1908. Rice, although he may have sold some shares, seems to have been among them.

One stock that remained depressed, however, was Electric Boat. With only a modest American submarine program and minimal foreign sales, shares in Rice's flagship company remained moored at $10 per share. But Rice was sufficiently convinced of the potential of the submarine that in 1911 he bought the New London Ship and Engine Company in Groton, Connecticut, to build diesel engines—which would soon supplant Ottos—and other components of submarine design. It seemed like a foolish decision. Even after war was declared in August 1914, most observers thought submarines would play at most an insignificant role in a war fought with giant armies on land and giant battleships at sea.

Then, on September 22, Otto Weddigen's *U-9* sank three British cruisers in less than ninety minutes.

Almost immediately "a twenty-million-dollar war order for submarine parts, periscopes and submarine 'detectors' was placed with the Electric Boat Company."[7] Frantic requests for boats or parts came in from more than a dozen different nations. Within weeks, Electric Boat had a two-year backlog of orders. The stock soared and Rice began to sell on the rise. Over the course of the following months, it is estimated that he sold twelve thousand shares at approximately $115, and in July 1915, he sold sixteen thousand shares at $150, netting him a total profit of more than $3,500,000. In addition, in May 1915, Julia Rice sold $3,200,000 worth of Electric Boat stock that had been "given to her by her husband," the previous October.

Four months later, Isaac Rice was dead. On November 2, 1915, in his Ansonia apartments, Rice, only sixty-four years old, suffered a massive heart attack. He died within moments with Julia at his side. Rice had become increasingly fatigued over the course of the previous year, but whether he knew he was gravely ill when he liquidated his Electric Boat shares is uncertain. In the wake of his passing, some commentators lamented Rice's judgment, since by October 1915 the price of Electric Boat stock had reached $550.[8] Had he held on, Rice would have made $16,000,000 rather than $3,500,000. But those critics assumed that Rice had sold off his entire holdings, which turned out not to be the case. A substantial position remained, as in 1922, Isaac L. Rice, Jr., a director in the Submarine Boat Company, as of 1915, Electric Boat's holding company, was reported to own in excess of twenty-five thousand shares.

After her husband's death, Julia Rice perpetuated both her husband's name and her own. In addition to the hospital and stadium, she endowed the Betsy Head Memorial Playground in the Brownsville section of Brooklyn, dedicated to Isaac, and donated his entire two-thousand-volume collection of French memoir to Bates College in Maine, which had earlier granted Rice an honorary degree. In addition to her philanthropies, which were extensive, Julia Rice continued to pursue her most passionate cause.

After the Rices moved into Villa Julia in 1903, they made a disconcerting discovery. Each night, tugboat captains on the Hudson River sounded their whistles to greet other captains, or even to signal friends on shore. The sound was piercing and impossible to sleep through. Villa Julia had a soundproof chess room, but the bedrooms were exposed. Julia Rice hired some Columbia University students to monitor the noise and they recorded between two thousand and three thousand whistles each night.

Julia did some research into health problems caused by sleep deprivation—one of the first studies of its kind. With her data, she secured endorsements from doctors, hospitals, and public health officials, as well as from luminaries such as Thomas Edison, William Dean Howells, and Mark Twain. Then she embarked on a furious lobbying campaign. Julia Rice went to police stations, health departments, regulators, and even Congress to press her demands for stringent restrictions of noise on the river. "There is no haggling about expenses," she told the *New York Tribune*, "because I pay them all myself." To press her case, in 1906 she established the Society for the Suppression of Unnecessary Noise, the first noise pollution movement in the nation.

The following year, New York and a number of other eastern cities enacted the noise restrictions Julia Rice had sought, and Villa Julia became a much easier place to get a good night's sleep. Of course, the Rice family did not get to appreciate their victory for very long, as within months, they would move to the Ansonia.

But Julia was not done. She campaigned against other sources of noise pollution, particularly in the vicinity of hospitals. She persuaded Mark Twain to help, particularly in convincing children to promise not to play noisily outside hospital windows. Julia Rice died of pneumonia on November 4, 1929, fourteen years and two days after her husband. Although many of the restrictions she secured were rendered moot when automobiles overran city streets, hospital quiet zones still survive and are Julia Rice's legacy.*

Elihu Frost's legacy was rather different. Although he remained a trustee of Electric Boat as late as 1919, in 1909 he sold most of his holdings and ceased active participation in the firm. When Frost died in August 1925, he left an estate of only $507,000, a substantial amount of money to be sure, but nowhere near what his holdings would have been had he not sold at the low. In addition, Frost had accrued some significant expenses over the years.

In December 1909, shortly after Frost left Electric Boat, his wife Marie obtained a divorce in Reno, Nevada, on the grounds of "extreme cruelty" and allegations of infidelity. Mrs. Frost "had for months endeavored, with the aid of detectives, to find evidence against her husband in New York. But believing that the New York courts would not

---

* The Rices' children also led extraordinary lives. One founded the Poetry Society of America. Another, Marion Rice Hart, was the first woman to graduate from the Massachusetts Institute of Technology with a degree in chemical engineering and obtained a master's in geology from Columbia University. While working as a sculptress in Avignon, France, at age forty-five, on a whim, she purchased a seventy-two-foot ketch and piloted it around the world. She served in World War II as a radio operator in the signal corps, often aboard a B-17, and became fascinated with airplanes. She learned to fly after the war, and eventually made seven solo trips across the Atlantic, the last when she was eighty-three years old. She continued to fly alone, often for thousands of miles, until she was eighty-seven. She had no children and her husband divorced her when she "refused to be like other women."

entertain the testimony of hired detectives, she induced a society friend to act as her detective, and one night learned enough of her husband's actions to make her realize that she could never live with him again."[9]

Frost luxuriated in the benefits of being a wealthy single man in New York until 1915, when, at fifty-five, he married twenty-two-year-old Rosalind Harrington. (Four years later, his ex-wife, Marie, married the extremely wealthy Baron de Cartier, the Belgian ambassador to the United States, and became a baroness.) But in only five years, in January 1920, Frost posted notices in New York newspapers stating that he would no longer be responsible for his wife's debts, and then two days after that filed for divorce. It seemed that Rosalind, long the subject of "lively gossip," had taken up, somewhat publicly, with a bartender at a local hotel. Frost evidently paid Rosalind a good bit of money not to contest the action or talk to the press.

For the remainder of his life, Frost plied his trade, often, ironically, as a divorce lawyer. In October 1925, two months after his death, the *New York Times* ran the following headline. "ELIHU FROST ESTATE LEFT TO A WOMAN."[10] The article reported that Frost, "inventor and pioneer builder of submarines . . . cuts off all blood relatives and his adopted daughter, and leaves virtually all of his estate to Mrs. Helen Evans, described in the will as 'a friend,' whom he is said to have met in the Fall of 1924 in Providence, R.I." A number of relatives sued, alleging that Frost's "friend" had used age-old means to improperly persuade a doddering old man—Frost was sixty-five—to ignore his loved ones in favor of a hussy. But fourteen months later, the courts awarded the bulk of the estate—$350,000—to Mrs. Evans. Frost's portfolio at the time of his death was said to contain "many worthless stocks."

With both Rice and Frost gone, Electric Boat was left in the hands of Lawrence Spear, described as "an undistinguished plodder . . . a born first mate, but an unpromising skipper."[11] Fortunately for the company, not only had war demand made it impervious to mediocre management but before he died, Isaac Rice had made a deal that ensured Electric Boat's continued prosperity.

Unlike Simon Lake, Rice had hedged his submarine bet with other product lines—Electric Launch (Elco) and Electro-Dynamic motors being the most prominent—so it could build surface craft and supply motors to other armament manufacturers as well. When Rice had switched from Lewis Nixon's shipyard to the Fore River yard, he found a kindred spirit in Fore River's owner, Charles Schwab, who also owned Bethlehem Steel and had guided it to unprecedented growth. Rice and Schwab joined forces, each essentially becoming the exclusive supplier or marketer for the other. Schwab secured for them an exclusive supply contract with the British Admiralty, understandably more desperate for submarines than almost anyone in the wake of the *U-9* disaster. Thus even after Rice was gone and the company had passed to less talented management, profits rolled in. During World War I, Electric Boat built 85 submarines for the navy, Elco built 722 submarine chasers, and the Submarine Boat Company built 118 cargo ships.

After the war, when demand for armaments, particularly submarines, essentially evaporated, Electric Boat survived when the Lake Company did not only because of their other businesses. At one point, the navy did not order an undersea vessel for eleven years. But when it did, Electric Boat was there, and has been the principal supplier of American submarines ever since, going from gasoline, to diesel, and finally to nuclear power. In 1952, the company, by then diversified into a full range of products, on air, land, and sea, most but not all for defense, changed its name to General Dynamics. It is now one of the largest defense contractors in the world.

John Holland, of course, shared in none of the company's success. For a time after his attempt to establish a rival to Electric Boat was litigated into dissolution, he sent letters to the navy secretary or other officials trying to interest them in his ideas. Eventually, he gave up. He settled into home and community life, teaching Sunday school, founding a local drama group, and becoming active in the American Irish Historical Society. He suffered from rheumatism, which got progressively worse, and his lungs grew weaker.

Frank Cable wrote, "Unknown to his neighbors as a man of any note . . . his small frame stooping, his gait awkward, his manner nervous due to his near-sightedness, which increased with the years, yet keen-brained, studious, and ambitious to the last, he spent much of his time at the rear of his home, where he had a workshop sealed with various locks. He did not marry until nearly fifty, and in his declining years was surrounded by a growing family of five."[12]

By late July 1914, he was bedridden and two weeks later, on August 12, John Holland, surrounded by his wife and children, died of pneumonia.

⁕

Submarines have progressed to the point that even the most imaginative science fiction writer of John Holland's time would have been incredulous. The most recent model produced by the Electric Boat division of General Dynamics—and an even more advanced model in the works—is the Virginia-class fast-attack submarine.

First launched in 2004, these boats are true marvels, 377 feet long, 34 wide, and with a displacement of 7,800 tons. They carry a crew of 15 officers and 117 enlisted men, their range is unlimited, and they can cruise almost indefinitely, limited only by food stores and maintenance requirements. They can dive to perhaps sixteen hundred feet. Nuclear powered on both the surface and submerged, Virginia-class submarines can make more than twenty-five knots in both attitudes. For weaponry, they are built with twelve vertical tubes to launch Tomahawk cruise missiles, and four torpedo tubes that fire intensely powerful Mark 48 torpedoes.

Although hardly designed with an open-floor plan, these boats bear almost no resemblance to the stifling, fetid, almost impossibly claustrophobic cylinders in which submariners were forced to live—and often die—through most of the twentieth century. There is decent air to breathe, decent food to eat, and ample room in which to move around.

The technology is stunning. Virginia-class submarines have no periscopes. Instead, two "photonics masts" hold a variety of digital cameras, both normal and infrared, mounted on telescoping arms. With no need for the captain to hang on to periscope arms—a standard scene in virtually every submarine film ever made—the control room has been moved down a deck to gain more space, with enough screens mounted on the walls to make it look more like Silicon Valley than the depths of the ocean.

For all these advances, however, Virginia-class submarines, like all modern submarines, are built around two basic principles—retaining a store of positive buoyancy while cruising submerged and maintaining a fixed center of gravity.

They all sail in the spirit of John Holland.

SELECTED BIBLIOGRAPHY

BOOKS AND ARTICLES

Archer, William. *The Pirate's Progress: A Short History of the U-boat*. New York: Harper & Brothers, 1918.

Barber, Francis M. *Lecture on Submarine Boats and Their Application to Torpedo Operations*. Newport, RI: United States Torpedo Station, 1875.

——— *Lecture on the Whitehead Torpedo*. Newport, RI: United States Torpedo Station, 1875.

Barnes, John Sanford. *Submarine Warfare, Offensive and Defensive, Including a Discussion of the Offensive Torpedo System, Its Effects upon Iron-clad Ship Systems, and Influence upon Future Naval Wars*. New York: Van Nostrand, 1869.

Barnes, Robert Hatfield. *United States Submarines*. New Haven, CT: H. F. Morse Associates, 1944.

Beresford, Charles William. *The Memoirs of Admiral Lord Charles Beresford*. Boston: Little, Brown, 1914.

Bishop, Farnham. *The Story of the Submarine*. New York: Century, 1916.

Bowers, Paul. *The Garrett Enigma and the Early Submarine Pioneers*. London: Airlife, 1999.

Bradford, Royal Bird. *Notes on the Spar Torpedo*. Newport, RI: United States Torpedo Station, 1882.

Burgoyne, Alan H. *Submarine Navigation Past and Present*. 2 Volumes. London: E. G. Richards, 1903.

Cable, Frank T. *The Birth and Development of the American Submarine*. New York: Harper & Brothers, 1924.

Clark, George R., et al. *A Short History of the United States Navy*. Philadelphia: J. B. Lippincott, 1911.

Compton-Hall, Richard. *The Submarine Pioneers: The Beginnings of Underwater Warfare*. Cornwall, UK: Periscope Publishing, 1983.

DeCanio, Stephen J. "The Future Through Yesterday: Long-Term Forecasting in the Novels of H. G. Wells and Jules Verne." *The Centennial Review* 38, no. 1 (Winter 1994): 75–93.

Dewey, George. *Autobiography of George Dewey: Admiral of the Navy*. New York: Scribner, 1913.

Doherty, William T. *The United States Navy, 1865–1907*. University of Wisconsin–Madison: Unpublished Thesis, 1920.

Domville-Fife, Charles W. *Submarines, Mines and Torpedoes in the War*. London: Hodder and Stoughton, 1914.

———*Submarines of the World's Navies*. Philadelphia: J. B. Lippincott, 1911.

Emery, Clark. "A Further Note on Drebbel's Submarine." *Modern Language Notes* vol 57, no. 1 (June 1942): pages i-xi.

Fay, Harold J. W. *History and Development of Submarine Signals*. A paper presented at the 29th Annual Convention of the American institute of Electrical Engineers, Boston, June 27, 1912.

Fennell, Philip and Marie King, ed. *John Devoy's* Catalpa *Expedition*. New York: NYU Press, 2006.

Field, Cyril. *The Story of the Submarine from the Earliest Ages to the Present Day*. Philadelphia: J. B. Lippincott, 1908.

Franklin, Roger. *The Defender: The Story of General Dynamics*. New York: Harper & Row, 1986.

Fyfe, Herbert C. *Submarine Warfare, Past and Present*. London: E. G. Richards, 1907.

Gray, Edwyn. *British Submarines at War: 1914–1918*. New York: Scribner, 1972.

Grudin, Robert. "Rudolf II of Prague and Cornelis Drebbel: Shakespearean Archetypes?" *Huntington Library Quarterly* 54, no. 3 (Summer 1991): 181–205.

Hansen, David M. "Zalinski's Dynamite Gun." *Technology and Culture* 25, no. 2 (April 1984): 264–79.

Hendrick, Burton J. "Great American Fortunes and Their Making." *McClure's Magazine*, November 1907, 33–48.

Johnson, Alfred S. et al. *The Cyclopedic Review of Current History, 1897*. Boston: New England Publishing Company, 1898.

Jolie, E. W. "A Brief History of U.S. Navy Torpedo Development." *NUSC Technical Document 543615*. Weapons Systems Department. September 1978.

Keidanz, Hermann. *Twenty Years of the Rice Gambit: In Memorium, Isaac Leopold Rice*. New York: American Chess Bulletin, 1916.

King, Charles Brady. *Personal Side Lights of America's First Automobile Race*. New York: Privately printed by Super-power printing company, 1945.

Lake, Simon. *Submarine: The Autobiography of Simon Lake*. New York: Appleton-Century, 1938.

—— *The Submarine in War and Peace: Its Development and Possibilities*. Philadelphia: J. B. Lippincott, 1918.

—— *Under-Water Torpedo-Boats: The Submarine Versus the Submersible, Their Merits and Their Menace*. Bridgeport, CT: Lake Torpedo Boat Company, 1906.

March, Francis A. et al. *History of the World War: An Authentic Narrative of the World's Greatest War*. New York: Leslie-Judge, 1919.

Martin, Thomas Commerford. *Electrical Boats and Navigation*. New York: C. C. Shelley, 1894.

Morris, Richard Knowles. *John P. Holland, 1841–1914: Inventor of the Modern Submarine*. Annapolis, MD: United States Naval Institute, 1966.

Niven, John, Courtlandt Canby, Vernon Welsh, ed. *Dynamic America: A History of General Dynamics Corporation and Its Predecessor Companies*. New York: Doubleday; General Dynamics Corporation, 1960.

Parsons, William Barclay. *Robert Fulton and the Submarine*. New York: Columbia University Press, 1922.

Poluhowich, John J. *Argonaut: The Submarine Legacy of Simon Lake*. College Station, TX: Texas A&M University Press, 1999.

Ragan, Mark K. *Submarine Warfare in the Civil War*. New York: Da Capo, 2003.

Rice, Isaac L. *What is Music?* New York: D. Appleton, 1875.

Rye, William Brenchley. *England As Seen by Foreigners in the Days of Elizabeth and James the First. Comprising translations of the journals of the two Dukes of Wirtemberg in 1592 and 1610; both illustrative of Shakespeare. With extracts from the travels of foreign princes and others, copious notes, an introduction, and etchings*. London: John Russell Smith, 1865.

Sleeman, Charles W. *Torpedoes and Torpedo Warfare: Containing a Complete and Concise Account of the Rise and Progress of Submarine Warfare. Also a detailed description of all matters appertaining thereto, including the latest movements*. Portsmouth, UK: Griffin and Company, 1889.

Speake, Jennifer. "The Wrong Kind of Wonder: Ben Jonson and Cornelis Drebbel." *Review of English Studies* 66, no. 273 (February 2015): 60.

Spear, Lawrence Y. "Submarine-Boats: Past, Present, and Future." *Transactions—The Society of Naval Architects and Marine Engineers*. New York: Society of Naval Architects and Marine Engineers, December 1902.

Sueter, Murray F. *The Evolution of the Submarine Boat, Mine and Torpedo, from the Sixteenth Century to the Present Time*. Portsmouth, England: J. Griffin, 1907.

Talbot, Frederick A. *Submarines: Their Mechanism and Operation.* London: W. Heinemann, 1915.

"Testing a Pneumatic Dynamite Gun." *Science* XIII, no. 312 (January 25, 1889): p. 56.

Tuchman, Barbara W. *The Proud Tower.* New York: Macmillan, 1962.

Weir, Gary. *Building American Submarines, 1914–40.* Washington, DC: Naval Historical Center, 1991.

Weiss, George. *America's Maritime Progress; A Review of the Redevelopment of the American Merchant Marine.* New York: New York Marine News, 1920.

Wheeler, Harold F. B. *War in the Underseas.* New York: Thomas Y. Crowell, 1919.

Whelehan, Niall. *The Dynamiters: Irish Nationalism and Political Violence in the Wider World, 1867–1900.* New York: Cambridge University Press, 2012.

MAGAZINES AND JOURNALS

American Chess Bulletin. New York: American Chess Bulletin.

American Engineer. Chicago: Smith & Cowles.

American Magazine. New York: Colver Publishing House.

Dive. Wilmington, California: Gaff Productions.

The Electrical Trade. Chicago: The Electrical Trade.

Electrical World and Engineer. New York: McGraw Publishing Company.

Engineering Magazine. New York: The Engineering Magazine Company.

Forum. New York: The Forum Publishing Company.

Marine Engineering. New York: Marine Publishing Company.

Marine Review. Cleveland: Penton Publishing Company.

North American Review. New York: Allen Thorndike Rice.

Science. New York: American Association for the Advancement of Science.

Scientific American. New York: Munn and Company.

Technology and Culture. Baltimore: The Johns Hopkins University Press.

Technical World. Chicago: Technical World.

GOVERNMENT AND OFFICIAL RECORDS

Annual Report of the Chief of the Bureau of Construction and Repair to the Secretary of the Navy. Washington, DC: Government Printing Office. 1896–1905.

Annual Report of the Chief of the Bureau of Steam-Engineering to the Secretary of the Navy. Washington, DC: Government Printing Office. 1898–1902.

Annual Report of the Secretary of the Navy. Washington, DC: Government Printing Office. 1883–1910.

Congressional Record, 47th Congress, 2nd Session. Washington, DC: Government Printing Office, 1883.

Transactions—The Society of Naval Architects and Marine Engineers Society of Naval Architects and Marine Engineers (US) New York: Society of Naval Architects and Marine Engineers, 1902–1906.

United States Congressional Serial Set 4033: 56th Congress, 2nd Session. Washington, DC: Government Printing Office, 1900–1901.

United States Congressional Serial Set 4039: 56th Congress, 2nd Session. Washington, DC: Government Printing Office, 1900–1901.

United States Congressional Serial Set 4414: 57th Congress, 2nd Session. Washington, DC: Government Printing Office, 1902–1903.

United States Congressional Serial Set 5227: 60th Congress, 1st Session. Washington, DC: Government Printing Office, 1907–1908.

United States Congressional Serial Set 5228: 60th Congress, 1st Session. Washington, DC: Government Printing Office, 1907–1908.

WEB SITES

http://www.bbc.co.uk/history/historic_figures/drebbel_cornelis.shtml

http://connecticuthistory.org/david-bushnell-and-his-revolutionary-submarine/

http://www.irishtimes.com/culture/heritage/o-dynamite-rossa-was-fenian-leader-the-first-terrorist-1.2303447

http://www.kcstudio.com/electrobat.html. Joseph Slade, "Bringing Invention to the Marketplace," *Invention & Technology Magazine* (Spring 1987).

http://militaryhonors.sid-hill.us/history/gwmjh_archive/Competition/Baker.html

http://www.public.navy.mil/subfor/underseawarfaremagazine/Issues/Archives/issue_16/simonlake.html

http://teachinghistory.org/history-content/ask-a-historian/19821

ENDNOTES

PROLOGUE: DEATH FROM BELOW

1   Francis A. March, Francis Andrew. *History of the World War; An Authentic Narrative of the World's Greatest War.* (New York: Leslie-Judge, 1863-1928. Published: (1919), 28.

2   Ibid., 30.

3   Frank T. Cable, *The Birth and Development of the American Submarine* (New York: Harper & Brothers, 1924), xv.

CHAPTER 1: BLURRED BEGINNINGS

1   Farnham Bishop, *The Story of the Submarine* (New York: Century, 1916), 4.

2   Murray F. Sueter, *The Evolution of the Submarine Boat, Mine and Torpedo, from the Sixteenth Century to the Present Time* (Portsmouth, England: J. Griffin, 1907), 9.

3   Speake, Jennifer. "The Wrong Kind of Wonder: Ben Jonson and Cornelis Drebbel." *Review of English Studies* 66, no. 273 (February 2015), 276.

4   Sueter, 10.

5   http://www.bbc.co.uk/history/historic_figures/drebbel_cornelis.shtml.

6   *Scientific American Supplement*, March 20, 1909, 185.

7   Sueter, 425.

ENDNOTES

CHAPTER 2: MADE IN AMERICA

1   Herbert C. Fyfe, *Submarine Warfare, Past and Present* (London: E. G. Richards, 1907), 166.
2   Bishop, 15.
3   http://connecticuthistory.org/david-bushnell-and-his-revolutionary-submarine/.
4   Bishop, 22.
5   Ibid., 25.

CHAPTER 3: AN AMERICAN IN PARIS

1   William Barclay Parsons, *Robert Fulton and the Submarine*, New York: Columbia University Press, 1922), 30.
2   Ibid., 35.
3   Ibid., 46.
4   Ibid., 52.
5   Ibid., 86.

CHAPTER 4: STARS AND BARS

1   Mark K. Ragan, *Submarine Warfare in the Civil War* (New York: Da Capo, 2003), 152.

CHAPTER 5: ENTR'ACTE; A FICTIONAL INTERLUDE

1   Sueter, 72.

CHAPTER 6: FOR AN INDEPENDENT IRELAND

1   http://teachinghistory.org/history-content/ask-a-historian/19821.
2   Philip Fennell and Marie King, ed. *John Devoy's* Catalpa *Expedition* (New York: NYU Press, 2006), 106.
3   Richard Knowles Morris, *John P. Holland, 1841–1914: Inventor of the Modern Submarine* (Annapolis, MD: Naval Institute Press, 1966), 25.
4   *Scientific American*, May 13, 1876, 303.
5   Francis M. Barber, *Lecture on the Whitehead Torpedo* (Newport, RI: United States Torpedo Station, 1875), 3.
6   Simon Lake, *The Submarine in War and Peace: Its Development and Possibilities* (Philadelphia: J. B. Lippincott, 1918), 93–94. Lake had conducted extensive interviews with many of those involved in the early Holland boats, including Holland's son, who had given him his father's detailed notes.
7   Ibid.

CHAPTER 7: THE *FENIAN RAM*

1   Ibid., p. 106.
2   Niall Whelehan, *The Dynamiters: Irish Nationalism and Political Violence in the Wider World, 1867–1900* (New York: Cambridge University Press, 2012), 141.
3   Morris, 40.

4   Ibid., 41.
5   Ibid., 44.
6   Ibid., 42.
7   *Lake, Submarine in War and Peace*, 108.

CHAPTER 8: COMPETITION FROM THE CLERGY

1   Paul Bowers, *The Garrett Enigma and the Early Submarine Pioneers* (London: Airlife, 1999, 92.
2   Ibid.
3   Papin's pressure cooker principle had, it seemed, finally found its way into a genuine submarine.
4   *Marine Engineer,* January 1, 1880, 192.
5   *American Engineer.* November 5, 1885, 187.
6   *Science.* July–December 1885, 394.
7   Lake, *Submarine in War and Peace,* 159.
8   Alan H. Burgoyne, *Submarine Navigation Past and Present*, volume 2 (London: E. G. Richards, 1903), 163.
9   *American Engineer.* November 5, 1885, 187.
10   An external tube that could fire a Whitehead torpedo had been installed between purchase and delivery.
11   Bowers, 136.
12   *Ibid.,* 143. The only payment record is a facsimile of a check for £2,000, although what percentage of the purchase price this represents is unknown.
13   Cyril Field. *The Story of the Submarine from the Earliest Ages to the Present Day* (Philadelphia: J. B. Lippincott, 1918), 126–30.
14   Fyfe, 229.
15   Bowers, 166.

CHAPTER 9: TREADING WATER

1   Cable, 314.
2   Ibid., 315–16.
3   Ibid., 317–18.
4   The weapon on the *Fenian Ram* is also generally called a "dynamite gun," but that is a misnomer since Ericsson's torpedo did not employ dynamite and the term did not come into being until after the *Fenian Ram* had been towed to New Haven.
5   David M. Hansen, "Zalinski's Dynamite Gun," *Technology and Culture* 25, no. 2 (April 1984): 264–65
6   In those days, the army did not view an officer engaged in private enterprise as having a conflict of interest.
7   Morris, 52.
8   *New York Times*, August 31, 1885, 1.

9   Ibid., September 4, 1885, 8.
10 Morris, 54.
11 *New York Times*, September 5, 1885, 8.
12 Lake, *Submarine in War and Peace*. 109.
13 Ibid.
14 *New York Times*, June 25, 1886, 3.
15 Ibid., February 6, 1887, 9.

CHAPTER 10: CHASING THE CARROT

1   *Annual Report of the Secretary of the Navy* (Washington, DC: Government Printing Office, 1883), 3.
2   George R. Clark, et al, *A Short History of the United States Navy* (Philadelphia: J. B. Lippincott, 1911), 408.
3   *Congressional Record, 47th Congress, 2nd Session* (Washington, DC: Government Printing Office, 1883). 1556.
4   George Dewey, *Autobiography of George Dewey: Admiral of the Navy* (New York: Scribner, 1913), 162.
5   *Chicago Tribune*. July 27, 1886. p. 6.
6   Burton J. Hendrick, "Great American Fortunes and Their Making," *McClure's Magazine*, November 1907, 38.
7   Cable, 320.
8   Morris, 60.
9   *New York Times*, September 9 1884, p. 8.
10 Ibid., November 21, 1886, p. 9.
11 Field, 139.

CHAPTER 11: CHALLENGERS

1   Morris, 65.
2   *New York Times*, June 26, 1892, p. 9.
3   *Scientific American*, July 30, 1892, p. 71.
4   Thomas Commerford Martin, *Electrical Boats and Navigation* (New York: C. C. Shelley, 1894), 73
5   Burgoyne, volume 2, 182
6   Morris, 69.
7   Lake, *Submarine in War and Peace*, 120
8   Ibid., 121.
9   *New York Tribune*, October 22, 1894, 4.
10 Lake, *Submarine in War and Peace*, 121.
11 *New York Times*, July 14, 1893. 9.
12 Morris, 68.
13 Ibid., 68–69.
14 *New York Times*, July 28, 1893, 4.

15 Morris, 69

16 Ibid.

17 *New York Times*, October 15, 1893, p. 20.

18 Morris, 70.

19 http://militaryhonors.sid-hill.us/history/gwmjh_archive/Competition/Baker.html.

20 *New York Times*, May 28, 1894, 12.

CHAPTER 12: UNEASY NEIGHBORS

1 Lake, *Submarine in War and Peace*, 128.

2 Ibid., 127.

3 Ibid., 128.

4 *New York Herald*, January 9, 1895, 1.

5 Lake, *Submarine in War and Peace*, 130.

6 Cable, 324.

7 Ibid., 325.

8 Ibid., 105.

9 Ibid., 326

10 Morris, 76.

11 *Washington Morning Times,* February 16, 1896, 1.

12 *Harper's Round Table*, January 1896, 236.

13 *The Electrical Trade*, May 1897, 49.

14 Barbara W. Tuchman, *A Proud Tower* (New York: Macmillan, 1962), chapter 3.

15 *United States Congressional Serial Set 4414: 57th Congress, 2nd Session* (Washington, DC: Government Printing Office, 1903), 199.

16 Ibid., p. 200

17 *Washington Morning Times*, May 3, 1896, 1.

CHAPTER 13: *ARGONAUT*

1 *Scientific American Supplement*, January 30, 1897, 175–85.

2 Lake, *Submarine in War and Peace,* 179.

3 Ibid., 179–80.

4 Ibid., 181.

5 John J. Poluhowich, *Argonaut: The Submarine Legacy of Simon Lake* (College Station, TX: Texas A&M University Press, 1999), 54.

6 Ibid.

7 *The Cyclopedic Review of Current History, 1897* (Boston: New England Publishing Company, 1898), 102.

8 *San Francisco Call*, December 17, 1897, 1.

9 *New York Times*, January 2, 1898, 37.

10 Ibid., January 6, 1898, 1.

11 *Washington Evening Times,* January 7, 1898, 5.

12 *Baltimore Herald,* February 18,1898, 4.

13 Simon Lake, *Submarine: The Autobiography of Simon Lake* (New York: Appleton-Century, 1935), 110.

14 Poluhowich. 57.

15 *New York Sun*, September 30, 1898, 3.

16 *New York Times*, September 29, 1898, 7.

17 Lake, *Autobiography*, 117.

CHAPTER 14: THE PLUNGE

1 Cable, 104. The identity of the investor or how the money had been obtained was never detailed.

2 *New York Tribune*, May 18, 1897, 4.

3 Thus, Lake, who had begun the *Argonaut* before Holland started his new boat, was technically the first to employ an Otto engine, but only by a matter of weeks.

4 Cable, 112.

5 Lake, *Submarine in War and Peace*, 164.

6 *Harper's Round Table* 17 (1896), 237.

7 *New York Tribune*, May 18, 1897, 4.

8 *New York Sun*, August 8, 1897, 1.

9 Lake, *Submarine in War and Peace*, 138.

CHAPTER 15: SHEDDING BALLAST

1 Morris, 82.

2 *New York Times*, March 20, 1898, 2.

3 See, for example, *San Francisco Call*, March 20, 1898, 1.

4 *New York Times*, March 22, 1898, 3.

5 *New York Times*, May 22, 1898, 3.

6 *Brooklyn Daily Eagle*, March 28, 1898, p. 5.

7 *New York Times*, March 27, 1898, 2.

8 Morris, 86.

9 Cable, 115.

10 Numerous sources, for example, Pulohowich, 73–74.

11 Morris, 86.

12 *San Francisco Call*, April 24, 1898, 17 (first page of Sunday Supplement).

13 Cable, 110.

14 Morris, 88.

15 *New York Sun*, May 27, 1898, 1.

16 For example, *Anaconda Standard*, August 7, 1898, 18; *Meriden Daily Republican*, August 6, 1898, 6; *The Morning Post* (Raleigh), August 12, 1898, 6.

17 *Brooklyn Daily Eagle*, October 12, 1898, 13.

18 *New York Sun*, December 1, 1898, 6.

19 Cable, 125.

20 Field, 232.

CHAPTER 16: KING'S GAMBIT ACCEPTED

1   *North American Review*, January 1883, 52.

2   *American Chess Bulletin*, December 1915, 264–65.

3   Joseph Slade, "Bringing Invention to the Marketplace," *Invention & Technology Magazine* (Spring 1987), http://www.kcstudio.com/electrobat.html.

4   *Economist*, December 30, 1893, 1565.

5   *New York Times*, September 6, 1893, 4.

6   Slade, http://www.kcstudio.com/electrobat.html.

7   *New York Times*, June 13, 1894, 1.

8   John Niven and Courtlandt Canby, ed., *Dynamic America: A History of General Dynamics Corporation and Its Predecessor Companies* (New York: Doubleday; General Dynamics Corporation, 1960), 27.

9   Charles Brady King, *Personal Side Lights of America's First Automobile Race* (New York: Privately printed by Super-power printing company, 1945), 19.

10 *Rock Island Argus*, November 29, 1895, 1.

11 Nivin, 27.

12 *New York Times*, March 7, 1897, 10.

13 The charging station was a marvel of logistics and engineering. For more details, see this author's *Drive! Henry Ford, George Selden, and the Race to Invent the Auto Age,* chapter 10.

14 The Whitney group proceeded to run the company into the ground and thereby doomed electric automobile technology for a century.

15 *New York Times*, August 5,1900, 22.

16 *Electrical World and Engineer*, December 2, 1899, pp. 870–71.

17 *Brooklyn Daily Eagle*, December 15, 1899, 1.

CHAPTER 17: A NEW SKIPPER

1   Roger Franklin, *The Defender: The Story of General Dynamics* (New York: Harper & Row, 1986), 22.

2   *New York Times*, March 16, 1899, 2.

3   Morris, 94.

4   *New York Times*, May 7, 1899, 6.

5   Franklin, 22.

6   Morris, 99.

7   *Brooklyn Daily Eagle*, June 26, 1899, 8.

8   Morris, 101.

CHAPTER 18: JOINING THE NAVY

1   *Brooklyn Daily Eagle*, July 28, 1899, 11.

2   *Annual Report of the Chief of the Bureau of Steam-Engineering to the Secretary of the Navy* (Washington, DC: Government Printing Office, 1900), 102

3   *New York Times* August 20, 1899, 3.

4   E. W. Jolie, "A Brief History of U.S. Navy Torpedo Development." *NUSC Technical Document 543615* (Weapons Systems Department, September 1978), 13.

5   *Engineering Magazine*, July 15, 1898, 90.

6   *Electrical World and Engineer,* November 4, 1899, 697–98.

7   *Brooklyn Daily Eagle*, July 31, 1899, 8.

8   Cable, 134.

9   *Brooklyn Daily Eagle,* October 11, 1899, 2.

10   *New York Times*, October 12, 1899, 2.

11   *Brooklyn Daily Eagle,* October 7, 1899, 7.

12   *New York Times*, November 7, 1899, 4.

13   *Brooklyn Daily Eagle,* November 6, 1899, 7.

14   *Washington Evening Times*, November 17, 1899, 1.

15   Ibid., November 18, 1899, 2.

16   For example, *Salt Lake Herald*, November 23, 1899, 6.

17   For example, *Kansas City Journal*, November 24, 1899, 1.

18   Burgoyne, volume 2, 64.

19   *United States Congressional Serial Set 4414,* 199.

20   Burgoyne, volume 2, 106.

21   Niven and Canby, 72.

22   *New York Sun*, September 26, 1900, 1.

23   Morris, 115.

CHAPTER 19: BOTTOM FISHING

1   Poluhowich, 69.

2   *Congressional Serial Set 5227, 60th Congress, 1st Session* (Washington, DC: Government Printing Office, 1908), 911.

3   Lake, *Autobiography*, 151.

4   Ibid., 128.

5   *Illinois True Republican*, September 27, 1899, 2.

6   *Los Angeles Herald*, October 18, 1899, 4.

7   Lake, *Autobiography*, 131.

8   Ibid.

9   Ibid., 134.

10   *New York Tribune*, June 18, 1901, 5.

11   Ibid.

12   Poluhowich, 83. Italics in the original.

13   *New York Tribune*, June 18, 1901, 5.

CHAPTER 20: DISPLACEMENT

1   Cable, 171.

2   Ibid., 171–72.

3   Lake, *Autobiography*, 150.

4   Ibid., 149–50.

5   *Transactions—The Society of Naval Architects and Marine Engineers Society of Naval Architects and Marine Engineers* (U.S.) (New York : Society of Naval Architects and Marine Engineers, 1902), 335–36.

6   Morris, 117.

7   Robert Hatfield Barnes, *United States Submarines* (New Haven, CT: H. F. Morse Associates, 1944), 25.

8   Cable, 174.

9   Ibid., 175.

10   *New York Tribune*, November 25, 1901, p. 1.

11   *New York Tribune*, November 25, 1901, 1.

12   *Washington Evening Star*, April 25, 1902, 2.

13   *New York Tribune*, July 13, 1902, 18.

CHAPTER 21: COUNTERSTRIKE

1   Lake, Autobiography, 156.

2   *Congressional Serial Set 5227*, 191.

3   Ibid., 190.

4   Lake, *Autobiography*, 159–60.

5   Ibid.

6   *United States Congressional Serial Set 4414*. All the uncited hearing notes that follow are from this set, pp. 1-217. Others are marked.

7   Nelson would later command three submarines, as well as two destroyers and a cruiser. He would remain in the navy until 1933, and retire as rear admiral. A destroyer, the USS *Nelson*, was named for him and fought in World War II.

CHAPTER 22: PROXY WAR

1   *New York Times*, October 4, 1902, 4.

2   *New York World*, January 22, 1903, 1.

3   *Congressional Set 5227*, 527.

4   *New York World*, January 25, 1903, p. 1; January 26, 1903, 1.

5   *Boston Evening Transcript*, March 10, 1903, 1.

6   *New York Times*, April 20, 1903, 1.

7   For a full account, see this author's *Drive: Henry Ford, George Selden, and the Race to Create the Auto Age.*"

CHAPTER 23: SKEWED COMPETITION

1   Salvage was a business with diminishing returns. There were only so many wrecks that could be located in the geographical radius accessible to Lake's

Connecticut base. In addition, his obsession with the navy caused a steady and significant drain on his resources.

2   *Technical World*, April 1907, 113.
3   *Congressional Serial Set 5227*, 907–08.
4   *Congressional Serial Set 5228*, 1141.
5   *Congressional Serial Set 5227*, 190.
6   *New York Sun*, June 2, 1904, 4.
7   Cable, 213–14.
8   *Washington Times*, June 11, 1904, 5.
9   *Congressional Serial Set 5227*, 956.

CHAPTER 24: A WARSHIP IN SEARCH OF A WAR

1   *Dive Magazine*, August 1964, 137.
2   Edwyn Gray, *British Submarines at War: 1914–1918* (New York: Scribner, 1972), 137.
3   Burgoyne, volume 1, 307.
4   Sueter, 77.
5   Ibid.
6   Richard Compton-Hall, *The Submarine Pioneers: The Beginnings of Underwater Warfare* (Cornwall, UK: Periscope Publishing, 1983), 88.
7   Burgoyne, volume 2, 286.
8   Ibid., 287.
9   Lake, *Autobiography*, 172.
10 Ibid.
11 Ibid., 192.
12 *St. Paul Globe*, April 8, 1904, 4.
13 Cable, 216.

CHAPTER 25: HOLLAND WITHOUT HOLLAND

1   Morris, 123–24.
2   Cable, 239-240.
3   Ibid., 247.
4   Lake, *Submarine in War and Peace*, 114.
5   *New York Times*, September 4, 1905, 1.
6   Lake, *Submarine in War and Peace*, 114-115.
7   *New York Tribune*, December 5, 1906, 4.

CHAPTER 26: EXCESSIVE BALLAST

1   *Congressional Serial Set 5227*, 959. All correspondence in this chapter is from this set.
2   Lake, *Autobiography*, 208–09.
3   *The St. Louis Republic*, January 20, 1905, 9.
4   *New York Tribune*, April 1, 1905, 6.

CHAPTER 27: THE NEW CLASS

1   *New York Tribune*, August 14, 1905, 6.

2   Ibid., August 26, 1905, 1.

3   Ibid., August 27, 1905, 5.

4   Charles W. Domville-Fife, *Submarines, Mines and Torpedoes in the War* (London: Hodder and Stoughton, 1914), 59.

5   *Marine Review*, August 29, 1907, 22.

6   *Scientific American*, December 7, 1907, p. 420.

7   Domville-Fife, 52.

8   *Technical World*, March 1908, pp. 329–30.

9   Domville-Fife, 56.

10 *Congressional Serial Set 5227*, 33.

11 Lake, *Autobiography*, 207, 211.

12 As he described it, the state of Lake's finances underwent some rather drastic swings, bouncing from near bankruptcy to prosperity and back again.

13 See, for example, *Deseret Evening News*, July 21, 1906, 10.

14 *Washington Times*, December 30, 1906, Woman's Magazine section, 5.

15 *Congressional Serial Set 5228*, 1800.

16 *New York Times*, April 28, 1907, 42.

17 Ibid., May 11, 1907, 4.

18 *Scientific American*. September 17, 1907, 167.

19 *Congressional Serial Set 5228*, 1224.

20 Ibid., 20.

21 *New York Times*, September 24, 1907, 5.

CHAPTER 28: SUICIDE SQUEEZE

1   Ibid., May 6, 1900, 18.

2   *Congressional Serial Set 5227*, p. 22. Unless otherwise noted, the chronology and committee's conclusions are all taken from this document, pages 18–79.

3   Ibid., 7.

4   *Congressional Serial Set 5228*, 1783.

5   *New York Tribune*, February 21, 1908, 4.

6   *Congressional Serial Set 5227*, 10.

7   Ibid., 12

8   *Scientific American Supplement,* March 21, 1908, p. 180. Italics in the original.

9   *Washington Times*, May 20, 1908, 1.

10 *Congressional Serial Set 5228*, 86.

11 *New York Times*, May 20, 1908, 3.

CHAPTER 29: GOING DEEP

1   Gary Weir, *Building American Submarines, 1914–40* (Washington, DC: Naval Historical Center, 1991), 12.

ENDNOTES

2   Lake, *Autobiography*, 228.
3   http://www.public.navy.mil/subfor/underseawarfaremagazine/Issues/Archives/issue_16/simonlake.html.
4   https://www.history.navy.mil/research/histories/ship-histories/danfs/g/g-1.html.
5   Weir, 53.
6   Lake, *Autobiography*, 277–78.
7   *American Magazine*, January 1916, 48.
8   Ibid., 49.
9   *New York Times*, December 20, 1909, 2.
10 Ibid., October 25, 1925, 28.
11 Franklin, 36.
12 Cable, 290.

ACKNOWLEDGMENTS

I'm not really a fan of acknowledgement sections that run to four and five pages and include everyone but the family dog. For this book, however, there are some people I simply must thank. The Pegasus team—Claiborne, Jessica, Sabrina, Maria, Katie, and Iris—has been wonderful, reminding me how much fun it can be to work with passionate people who are deeply invested in the books they publish. My agent, Michael Carlisle, was savvy enough to know that this was the right place for me.

I also must thank people in the submarine and engineering communities who were willing to take time and expend effort to help a stranger. There is no better feeling than when those expert in their fields show enthusiasm for your work, and, even more, say that they learned from it. So to Walter Gordon, David Paris, Bruce Elleman, Chris Rentfrow, Joel Holwitt, Leonard Zax, Justin L. C. Eldridge, Paul Varnadore, and Mark Obenhaus . . . thank you.

And since this is an acknowledgement section . . . my wife Nancy and daughter Lee are the best.

INDEX

ILLUSTRATION CREDITS

All illustrations are in the public domain, with these exceptions:

Pages 3, 316, 321, 329, 337. Library of Congress. Prints & Photographs Division.

Pages 228, 247, 310. Library of Congress. Chronicling America: Historic American Newspapers.

Pages 4, 42, 44, 69, 147, 196, 223, 312, 313. Naval History & Heritage Command.

Page 183. William M. Van Der Weyde, Museum of the City of New York.